The Coiled Needle – Yin Water

True Stories of a Demonologist: A Novel

Jonathan Schell, L.Ac.

Dao Press

Portland, Oregon

The Coiled Needle – Yin Water

True Stories of a Demonologist: A Novel

Jonathan Schell

Copyright © 2017 by 12 LLC

1017 SW Morrison #307A
Portland, OR 97205 USA

This is a work of fiction.

Cover Design and Photographs by Jonathan Schell L.Ac.
Library of Congress Cataloging-in-Publication Data:

Schell, Jonathan (Author)
The Coiled Needle – Yin Water: True Stories of a Demonologist: A Novel
Jonathan Schell. — First Edition.
pages cm
ISBN 978-0-9996473-0-1 (alk. paper)
1. Demonology. 2. Medicine, Chinese. 3. Religion. I. Schell, Jonathan.
II. Title: The Coiled Needle – Yin Water: True Stories of a Demonologist: A Novel.

All rights reserved. No part of this publication may be reproduced, stored in a retrieval system or transmitted in any form by any means, electronic, mechanical, photocopying, recording or otherwise, without prior written permission of the publisher.

International Standard Book Number (ISBN): 978-0-9996473-0-1
Printed in the United States of America

*To my family, friends, patients,
those who continue to seek,
and the story tellers who tell their stories without fear.*

Ascending lazily in a widening gyre,
  a raven soars, wind floating through his feathers,
  perceiving the existent earth, water, wood, and fire,
  Croaking out his call, truth-speaker regardless of many weathers.

His call echoes through the wood,
  a haunting melody, a sound from which form is rarely seen,
  I try to understand his words, portending what they could,
  wisdom from century to century, that which is, and what has been.

Oh, shadow of the forest, your light illuminates from within.

Meditations of Roland Pearce, Demonologist

Acknowledgments

I would like to thank the people who have graciously given me their time to listen to parts of this story as it was crafted. In no particular order, my thanks go out to: Sue Westermin, Scott Stuart, Jen Fuller, Lisa Salerno, Andrea Plichta, and Elizabeth Bourgeois.

Additionally, I would like to thank Philip Carr-Gomm and the International Fraternity of Sigma Chi for giving permission to use their respective quotes.

Special thanks to my copy editor Angie Jabine, who not only beat her estimate on how long her edit would take, but also put up with my "which vs. that" habits.

Lastly, I would like to thank all of my patients who have come to see me through the years.

Contents

Chapter 1		1
Chapter 2	The First Law of the Universe	6
Chapter 3	Continuation of the First Law	26
Chapter 4	Continuation of the First Law	47
Chapter 5	Continuation of the First Law	75
Chapter 6	Awareness One	159
Chapter 7	Awareness Two Dot One	169
Chapter 8	Awareness Two Dot Two	194
Chapter 9	Awareness Two Dot Three	217
Chapter 10	Awareness Three	264
Chapter 11	Awareness Four	285
Chapter 12	Continuation of the First Law	331
Post Script		351
Author's Note		371

Chapter 1

Rain. Coming down so hard that it feels like it is going to pierce the windshield of my SUV. They are saying that it is the wettest February on record, but that is what it is like in Portland, Oregon. There will always be another record to break for how much it rains. I smoke a cigarette – Nat Sherman MCD to be exact – and I drive to the office. It is another day in the routine, treating patients, and dealing with the seen and unseen. Who am I? My name is Roland Pearce, and odd as it might seem, I am an acupuncturist. Trust me, I have heard it a thousand time before …. Pearce, as in someone who pierces people with needles? Yes, yes, yes. No more odd than an orthodontist with the last name of Wrench, or a metal worker with the last name of Smith. So have your chuckle, and we can move on.

One month ago, Donald Trump took the office of President of the United States, and since then the dark side has been stirring. Dark side, you ask? As in the Sith? No, not that bad, but as in the opposite of the forces of light. The analogy to the Jedi might be pertinent if *Star Wars* were real, but let us just say that there has been a war bubbling under the surface of reality for millennia. This war is not earth-based only, but spans the entirety of this universe, and the dimensions that rise and fall from it. There has always been a light, and always been the dark, and many layers of gray in between. This is the plane that we live in: duality. Yin/yang, love/hate, black/white, Christian/Muslim, gay/straight, etc. The duality of division is the antithesis of unity, togetherness, and wholeness. These labels divide us. The anger, rage, depression, and despair, etc., these are all things the dark side feeds on. The expression of these emotions sends shockwaves through the terrasphere (the sphere of the earth) that can be felt both near and far. Like blood in the water, the emotional chaos draws the things that feed on it.

These things can be seen by someone who has been trained to see, or by someone with inherent gifts of sight, or simply by the average person who is willing to analyze the patterns. So I can tell that you are asking yourself:

"What is this guy talking about, demons?"

Yes, and much more than that: vampires, ghosts, black magic, possession, entities, supernatural beings, and were-beasts. I believe you would be surprised to know that these things are around us all of the time, both the good and the bad. We are naive to think that it could be otherwise, when all around the world tales have been spun about such creatures of different origins than us.

Now, I am not your typical acupuncturist; sure, I treat aches and pains like all of the rest, but I also treat things that are not so ordinary. You might say that I am a modern-day *Constantine*, but without all of the religious mumbo jumbo and the rather poorly conceived plot regarding angels. Mind candy for some, but not very real. For example: sit on the street or go to a party, and observe the people around you. Who is interesting? Who is not? Who makes the hair on the back of your neck stand on end? Who simply makes you uncomfortable? Who is someone you feel like you can talk to? Who is seductive? And, who makes your heart want to open? This is the beginning of the pattern analysis my master taught me many, many years ago. It is a skill we all have, and often do not pay much attention to. It is something I have spent my life honing. Take a few more steps down this path with more questions and more answers, and we arrive at the standard diagnoses or data analysis. More questions, more answers, more awareness, and more probing, and we start to reach the end of what people might call the physical senses, and start to enter the spiritual senses. This is where my world lies.

This is the realm where the extraordinary interacts with the ordinary. Our society, for the most part, does not believe rationally in any of this, as it often cannot be scientifically proven. In other times there were words for this: oracle, seer, magus, sorcerer, magician, wizard, priest, sage, hermit, monk, etc. All words which are still in our language, but little used. My master, who is hundreds of years old, would not call himself a master; he allows me to call him master as a way of respect, but he would say that compared to *his* master, my master was only a speck of cosmic dust. So too, I am not a master, only a man who comes from a long lineage of people that have spent their entire lives observing patterns.

I know that reading this, you want to know more. More about me, and more about my master, but all in good time, all in good time. Sit back, enjoy a glass of pinot noir and let me tell you about a few things before we get too far into this narrative. Think of this as your introduction to pattern analysis and your *Monster Manual* or your *Players Handbook*. Simply, that before I take you too far down the rabbit hole, you have to see the world a bit more as I do.

In the beginning, there was a bat who bit a man…. Or was it a boy who fell into a cave with a bunch of bats…. Just kidding, it was neither of these. In reality, in the beginning, there was nothing. Some call this the void, others call this potential. Whatever you want to call it, there was nothing. Then, at some point, there was something. This something became what we know as substance. I say substance here loosely, as it is merely the opposite of absence, and is not meant to describe things of substance or form as we know it. Substance, then divided in two again to create yin and yang (yin rhymes with gin, and yang rhymes with bong). Yin and yang created the duality as we know it today, where yin represents stillness among other things, while yang represents motion among other things. From here things get complicated, but simply stated, all things can trace their roots back to this point.

Think of life as a hierarchy of energy. The closer one is to this initial division, the more energetic its nature; the further away from this division, the more dense its nature. When one decreases vibration down below where humans vibrate at, one starts to see the appearance of what an astronomer would call a black hole. This is something so dense that it defies being able to be seen. The further one goes on this continuum, the closer one gets to what the Christians would refer to as hell.

```
▽――――――――――――――――――▽――――――――――――――――▽
The initial                The dimem-                    Hell
division                   sion we live in
```

One can also represent the emotions in this kind of continuum with fear representing one extreme, and love representing the other extreme.

Therefore, when one achieves mastery, one only increases one's vibration in an incremental way, so as my master would say: "Mastery is simply a perspective from where the observer sits." Since my master is so much farther along than I am, he appears to be a master to me, but from his own perspective he is simply a student on the path.

When it comes to things that are "dark," they follow this same idea: that a lesser evil is closer to our vibration, and a greater evil is farther away from our vibration. Therefore, a master of the dark arts is pursuing a path of decreasing their vibration in the direction of "hell," and a master of the light arts is pursuing a path of increasing their vibration towards "God."

As you can see, if there are a few that have reached a higher state of being, and a few that have reached a lower state of being, this creates a dichotomy where those that are higher want to bring others with them, and those that are lower also want to bring others with them. Both sides believe that they have found the truth, and the masses sit between the two extremes. Therefore, the war between the light and the dark, simply stated, is a war where the stakes are you and me. This war, the war of illumination and disillumination has been going on for millennia, really for as long as the universe could conceive of something and nothing.

So, I have been talking about the most extreme, as we say in the art, the macrocosm, but let us bring it back in a bit, to the microcosm, meaning how this plays out on earth. The living things of earth all have souls. Yes, you heard me right, the living things; not just humans. Plants, animals, humans, rocks, rivers, volcanoes, mountains, lakes, and the very earth itself. A soul is simply the part of us that records and reacts to the data of our lives, as in all of our lives. Reincarnation is a thing, just as your iPhone is a thing. If I asked you to tell me how your iPhone worked, the majority of people could not. They could show me what it did, the apps that were on it, how it turns on and off, how to take a picture, and play music, but none of this tells me how it is what it is. What makes a phone work are two things – its physical structure and the code that runs the software. Everything we, the average people use it for, is part of a GUI or *graphical user interface*. Basically, when we use a smart phone, we are allowing the GUI to do the heavy lifting of interacting with the code, and we press the screen and get the result we expect. It does not take faith to run a smart phone, it just is.

Reincarnation is similar. The life that we are living right now is the GUI of how we interact with our soul. Do one thing, and it causes a cascade of events, do another and it causes a separate cascade of events. For each life that we live, the events of that life are stored in the soul, and those memories of different lives are running in the background of your life, much like the app that you forgot to close on your phone. Just because you cannot see or remember the lives, does not mean that they are not there, and that they are not influencing your life. As with your iPhone, it does not take belief or faith to have past lives– they are there whether you acknowledge them or not.

All souls fall into this pattern, whether human, animal, vegetable, or elemental. Some people speak of the ongoing interaction of souls with each other as karma. You can call it what you like, but the simplest way to speak of souls is that everything is remembered, and that for every action, there is a reaction.

The ability to act is the ability to have choice. Each choice leads us down a different path, and each path has its own consequences. This is what is called free will: that you have the ability to make your own choices, and live by the results of your decisions. Now, as one becomes more elevated in vibration, or more base in vibration, one can argue that one's choices become more and more limited as each choice is made. But you see, this in itself

Chapter 1

was a choice. Generally, we make choices that paint us into a corner, and then we have limited choices until either the paint dries, or we learn to scale the walls around us.

Choices are all around us every day. We choose what to eat, when to sleep, who to sleep with, what vice to consume, what kind of exercise we like, how to spend our money, how to spend our time, etc. Each of these sets us down paths of attraction and repulsion, and conversely the absence of making choices also sends us down different paths. All of this, along with the behavior of countless other lives, again is stored in our souls.

So humor me with all of this. Have you ever experienced déjà vu? Or felt like you already knew someone when you had just met them? Why do you think that this feeling was there? Or have you ever veered off your normal route simply because you had a feeling that you should go a different route? Where do you think these ideas come from? Unless you have recently interacted with the "supernatural," the highest probability is that this feeling bubbled up from deep inside of you. This is how your soul communicates with you.

The importance of soul and choice cannot be overstated, as these are the foundation pieces to the shape of our lives. The shape of our life dictates what we interact with, our health, and where we fall in the unseen war that is happening all around us.

I pulled up to park on the street, paid my parking meter that is a not so hidden tax on all people who work downtown. I stuck my ticket to the driver's side window, and started my two-block amble to the office. The homeless people for the most part avoid me; the crows chattered at me as I walked by their perches in the small trees that line the Portland streets. As I walked by the burrito cart, the owner on his cell phone gave me a nod. Harvey, who runs the Indian food cart, greeted me with a big smile and a greeting of "Hey man! How are you today!?"

I walked by the old black man who works for the parking garage, and he gave me a nod while smoking his twentieth cigarette for the day. I walked by the computer repair place and the subterranean tattoo parlor and finally crossed the street to my office. On the street outside is the older couple, who are out there every day smoking their cigarettes. They are the eyes and ears of the neighborhood, and they know all the gossip about what is happening in the neighborhood. I said good morning as I walked by, then into my building, up the elevator, and to my office. I fumbled with my keys as normal, thinking that one of these days I had to put that colored ring on the office key. Finally, finding the right key, I put it in the lock, turned it, and opened the door. I walked in, put down my bag, took off my jacket, and flipped the sign from closed to open. It was time to work.

Chapter 2
The Wizards First Rule or really as Richard Rahl should have learned it: The First Law of the Universe: If I Can See It, It Can See Me.

Whether we want to believe it or not, there are laws to our universe, and these laws co-exist and surpass the laws of physics. I think we can agree that that which is deemed impossible is only so, because we have yet to discover that which makes the impossible possible. Fifty years ago, would we have believed we would be able to talk to an image of a person in real time on a hand-held device that fits in our pocket? Sure, Captain Kirk used a communicator to talk with Spock and the USS Enterprise, but even these devices were little better than walkie-talkies. Princess Leia had to use a recorded holograph of herself to send a one-way message to Ben Kenobi, but this was little more than a recorded video of herself. Or a hundred years ago, would we have believed that every person could have their own personal transport device that was not a horse? Needless to say, the impossible has become possible countless times over.

The spark of an idea that becomes a possibility comes from the imagination of a person who is either tired of doing things the same tired way, or who is curious about ways to approach a problem that are different from the way of the status quo. We give great accolades to founders of technology companies who come up with novel ways to solve problems, to chemists who cure diseases, and to mathematicians who, while discovering ground-breaking theories, accidentally learn how to create hydrogen bombs. Yet, we do not lavish our accolades on children with vivid imaginations, or the person who can tell a story from memory, or the person who invents a fictional world, or the artist who makes works of art from glass. It is apparent that the West's idea of imagination is contingent upon whether the creative nature of a person can be monetized or not. Yet, imagination is the seed of possibility. Not all seeds grow into plants, and not all seeds grow into the plants that we expect, but unless one commits to and plants them, they will never know what the seed will grow into.

We first learn to see in our imagination, as our mind tests whether we can handle what we are seeing. If we cannot, that is as far as it goes. Our minds and our souls act as our check on reality, in effect keeping us from having a break with reality. If our mind cannot handle seeing things in real life, then things will come to us via the sense that our mind can handle. So, these things might be sound, smell, thoughts, tastes, and dreams. If our mind does not crack with the occurrence of seeing the paranormal, then our vision will become more acute.

Now, let us for a moment be real. People always want what they don't have. People are also envious of this perceived difference between those who have, and those who have not. For example, if you are height-challenged, it does not mean that the person who is taller than you has an easier life. In fact, the person who is taller has other challenges that you don't consider when you are envious of their height. Such as: fitting in airplane seats or in doorways, or finding well-fitting clothes that are neither tailor-made nor look like they are from the 1990s. I feel for the tall women out there who want to wear three- or five-inch heels, but in doing so, tower over their boyfriend who is three inches shorter than they are. Or have you noticed that tall people often slouch in conversations? This is because smaller people have a habit of talking to the tall person's chest, not towards their ears. These are just a few things that those who are height-envious don't think of when they are saying to someone taller, I wish I was your height!

Well, the same can be said for the desire to see. There are some people who want to interact with spirit in a more direct way, so they do meditations that attempt to open their third eye, or take drugs to expand their mind, or chant mantras that open their abilities. While these things work to a degree, there is something that is not often thought about beforehand, which is the law of unintended consequences. What I mean by this is that once one is able to see, one cannot unsee. The world is not all sugar and spice and everything nice. In fact, there is a lot more darkness in the world at the moment than there is light. So, when one attains an ability to see, one does not see only angels and the realm of light, one also sees demons and the realm of the dark.

Therefore, the first law of the universe is: If I can see you, you can see me. Think of this simply as walking around with smudged glasses, and then cleaning them. In this example, the world goes from being obscured to unobscured. To be able to see is also to be able to take direct action, but also means that action can be taken directly against you. For the majority of people who have grown up without a master, in a traditional godfearing home, where the parents have no knowledge of the esoteric, seeing is a liability. This is simply because someone who has no training is little more than a fool to be taken advantage of by a being who does not live in the same time continuum as you and I do. Opening your mind to be able to see is not something I would prescribe lightly. Beings, both light and dark, who are not in a corporeal body, need not eat, sleep, work, do chores, drive, exercise, etc. – all of the mundane things you and I do on a daily basis. The more distracted you are by life, the more opportunity there is to take advantage of you. This is why many spiritual teachers advise one to be here now.

There is a knock on my door, interrupting my musings. Although the sign says open, he does not open the door. I go to the door and invite him in. In front of me stands a man, slight in frame, who looks to be in his sixties with sandy-gray colored hair which waves over his head and cascades down his neck. He is dressed in the simple clothes that is observed on many working-class people: brown Carhartts, work boots, and a flannel shirt worn over a white T-shirt. He is not wearing a jacket, even though as I mentioned, it is raining today. He steps into my office and looks at the raw herbs in bottles and bags stacked in shelves on the wall, the patent pill bottles on the shelf next to the raw herbs, the couch and the easy chairs I keep in the office for conducting patient interviews, and then back to me. He notices that I also am in Carhartts, outdoor shoes, and a Columbia fleece. His eyes are a piercing sky blue.

"Are you the acupuncturist?"

"I am," I said.

"I have back pain, and I was wondering if you can give me a treatment?"

Seeing as how I was simply sitting and musing my thoughts on the laws of the universe, I said: "Sure, I have time. I simply need you to fill out this stack of paperwork, and this other stack over here, and file this, and sign that. Oh, and I need you to sign away your right to sue me …." I chuckled, and he didn't even blink. "I am kidding, of course. I do need you to fill out a basic health history and arbitration form, but you don't need to file anything for me," I chuckled again, while he still stood there unfazed. I pointed him towards the couch, gathered together the paperwork with a clipboard and pen, and then went back to sitting in the La-Z-Boy while he scratched away at the paperwork.

Health histories are something we are all familiar with. Some are simple and some are in-depth. They are required by law, and if filled out with consideration, give the practitioner the necessary information they need, before asking a single question, to focus on the problem at hand, while taking into account any and all other patterns that might be happening simultaneously. In Asian medicine there are over thirty patterns at least, which we have to filter.[1] The simplest way to think of our diagnosis is to think of what

---

1. This is really being conservative, if I wanted to bore you to tears, I would talk about the hundreds of patterns.

we call the eight principles or interior/exterior, hot/cold, yin/yang, and deficiency/excess. All diagnoses eventually come back to some combination of these principles, and truthfully, it only becomes more complicated from here. Therefore, something that originates outside of the body is exterior (imagine a contagion here), while something that originates inside the body is interior (like a polyp in your intestine). Hot and cold are self-explanatory. Yin and yang are amorphous and can mean a number of things, but as noted before, think of motion equals yang, while stillness equals yin. Deficiency is not having enough, and excess is having too much. Therefore, a basic diagnosis can be something like yang deficient cold, or yin deficient heat, and other permutations and combination of these eight principles.

The sandy-haired man was looking at me expectantly, clipboard in his lap; all scratching of the pen had stopped. I blinked, came out of my mid-thought and said: "Obviously, from the sign on the door, my name is Roland."

I pushed myself out of the easy chair, and stepped in front of him reaching out my hand. As he put the clipboard in my hand, he said: "Josh. My name is Josh Sheppard."

I gathered up the clipboard and began flipping through the pages while making notes on his chart. He sat solidly, occasionally stretching out his legs, then bringing them back to a regular 90-degree position, feet on the floor, knees bent. There was something odd about this case history, but I couldn't put my finger on it. I looked up from the chart and asked, "It says here that you injured your back at age nine. I presume that you have had back pain since then?"

"On and off. It has gotten worse as I have become older."

"Does anything help it?" I asked.

"Heat, exercise, movement."

"Was the initial injury a break, a strain, or a tear?"

"I don't know," he said.

"Did you go to the hospital?"

"No," he said.

"How then, do you know that this has to do with what happened when you were nine?"

"I know," he said.

I was intrigued. This man was claiming an injury of unknown origin, which happened over fifty years ago, was the cause of his back pain. More importantly, he was certain of it.

"Have you ever had an x-ray of your back taken?"

"Yes .... My spine is fused from L_2 to L_5," he said.

This was turning out to be an odd conversation, and my "spidey senses" were tingling.

"Did you ever have surgery to fuse your spine?"

"No," he said.

"When did you have your x-ray taken?"

"When I was eighteen. I had been complaining of back pain, and my doctor wanted to take an x-ray, just to rule out any odd spinal problems. When he saw the x-ray, he started asking me the same questions you are asking me now," he said with the mild frustration of someone who has obviously had this conversation a few times.

Were they even doing spinal fusions forty years ago? I asked myself. Well, supposedly the first spinal instrumentation (wiring of a spinal fracture) was performed by Berthold Hadra in 1891, but modern spinal fusion as we know it really didn't start to develop until the 1980s, and this would have been long after Josh's x-ray.

The standard back pain has several causes in Chinese medicine, and these are: long-term exposure to cold, such as lying on a cold floor; maladjustment of the hips causing the low back to be sore as compensation; too much sex or over-expenditure of energy; and trauma. There are other less common reasons, such as aneurysms and such, but they are atypical and usually have other factors involved. While one could come to the conclusion that in this case the pain was from trauma, it would not be recent trauma, and would be sequela of an initial trauma. Then I would be looking at something which was more like arthritis, or if he had not already had a fused spine, then some sort of disc issue.

Josh did not seem forthcoming with any more information, so I said, "Well, let's get you up on the treatment table. Have you eaten today?"

"Yes," he replied.

"You can take your socks and shoes off, as well as your flannel shirt and t-shirt. Then lie face-down on the table. Have you had acupuncture before?"

"Yes," he said.

"OK, so would you say that your lumbar spine hurts in any place more than another?"

Josh moved the back of his hand to his lumbar vertebrae, about where L_3 and L_4 are located, and said, "In here, both above and below as well."

I started opening up packs of needles. These are single-use needles, packaged in a sterile environment, designed to be used once and then discarded.

"Josh, I am going to insert some needles around your spinous processes here, here, and here," as I touched the places I intended to needle. "Then I am going to put the electrostim on the needles and let you sit with that for thirty minutes. How does that sound?"

"Fine, as long as the pain goes away."

I palpated Josh's back looking for changes in skin temperature, deformities of the spine, misalignment of the bones, and tenseness of the muscles. Nothing unusual stood out, so I took out my pen, marked the spinous processes that I wanted to needle, then took the needle tube, and inserted a needle into it.

"OK, here we go," I said.

I began inserting needles into his back one by one. Josh neither flinched nor said anything. Occasionally, I would ask him, "How's that?" or "Can you feel that?" He would simply grunt in acknowledgment.

I hooked up the electrodes to the needles in his back, and said, "OK, I am going to turn this on, and you will feel a tapping like this …" I rhythmically tapped the back of his calf with my finger. "Then, it will be constant ..." and I held my finger on his calf for a few seconds. "Then it will tap again ..." and I tapped his calf again.

"OK," Josh said.

"I am going to turn it up until it is significant, but not painful. So, you just let me know when it is significant, but not painful."

"OK," he said.

I began to slowly turn the knob on the electrostim machine, "How's that?" I asked.

"I can take more."

"OK," I said, and slowly turned the dial up more. "How's that now? Significant?"

"Yeah, that's good."

"OK, now I am going to leave the needles in for thirty minutes. I will be right here sitting in my easy chair writing, if you need me to change anything."

"OK."

"Are you warm enough?" I said.

"I'm OK."

"Do you want to listen to music?"

"No, the street noises are fine," he said.

"OK." I picked up the clipboard, sat down in my easy chair and charted what points I had needled. I set the timer on my phone for thirty minutes, then reread his health history, and made a few more notes to myself about other things I could ask or follow up on for a later visit. I then took out my pad, and resumed my musing.

Thirty minutes later, the timer went off. I stood up, turned off the electrostim device, unhooked the wires, coiled them, and placed them in the bag I keep the electrostim machine in. I started to pluck out the needles, starting from the ones that were closer to his head, and working my way down toward his feet. I put the used needles in a red sharps container, which when full would be sent to a biohazard company to be incinerated.

"That's it," I said.

Josh lay there for a minute, then put the palms of his hands on the table and pushed himself up. When he had himself propped up, he swung his legs around, then sat upright on the edge of the table. He rubbed his palms over his eyes, then rubbed down his cheeks, and then the back of his neck.

"How do you feel?" I said.

"Good, I think. Hard to tell until I walk around a bit."

"No worries," I said.

"I would like to see you again in a week, and we can see how this treatment settles in. How does that sound?"

"Sure. I will be back in a week," he said.

We set up an appointment for February 28th the following week. He paid for his visit and left.

Generally, I have found with my treatments that either there is immediate benefit, or it takes three days or so for the treatment to settle in, and then the patient notices the effect. This seems to have to do with where the problem lies. If the problem is acute and just happened recently, then generally the patient experiences an immediate effect. However, if the problem happened a long time ago, it seems that the effects of the treatment take a while to manifest. The easiest way to think about this, I think, is from a neurological perspective. Let's say that you grew up in San Diego, and then you decide to move to Portland. In San Diego, you knew where everything was, and so when you drive somewhere, you know the quickest route to get there. If there is traffic, you know of a couple of alternate routes to avoid the traffic. But, when you move to Portland, you don't know where anything is. You are dependent on your phone or directions, and so you end up taking a number of different routes in the beginning to find your way to places. Your mind literally has to create a map for your new environment. When you are in your old environment, your mind has it all figured out, and so you drive basically by instinct, because the neuropathways have been wired to know that this is the best route. But, when you are in a new situation, your neuropathways are still building the map, so there is only a small amount of instinct, and a lot of learning as to what the best route is.

When we have a new injury, our body is still learning what and how we have to function to minimize our pain and symptoms. Therefore, the neuropathways are malleable and can change, because nothing has been set in stone. When a person receives treatment for a new injury, they are likely to experience change with that injury very quickly, because the brain is in a place where it is eager to change anyways. Conversely, when an injury is old, the brain has long ago figured out how to adapt to that injury, so we could say that the neuropathways are comfortable where they are; in fact, more than likely, the only way they will want to change is when there is some form of disruption to their status quo. Acupuncture and exercises can provide such a disruption, but it will generally take a number of visits, and in the end, the person will have to be willing to do whatever they need to do, to change their neuropathways. This then creates a trickle-down effect, because when the neuropathways are slowly convinced to change their behavior, and they shift, then the body shifts.

Because Josh's injury had happened so long ago, I suspected that he would experience moderate benefit from this treatment, but that the time that this benefit would last, would be short. It would be short because the neuropathways would be jarred for a moment, like riding over train tracks; then they would go back to their normal way of functioning. When the neuropathways reverted to their normal state, then the pain would come back. So, this case would require a number of treatments to disrupt his neuropathways and put them into a state where they became malleable again and would accept change.

February 28th came without mishap. Josh arrived promptly for his appointment, and knocked on my door. I opened it, greeted him, and welcomed him into the clinic.

"So, how did you feel after the last appointment?" I said.

"Better for a day or so, then the pain was back."

"I thought it might be like this. That just means that this won't be a quick fix, but something we will have to work on for a bit," I said.

"A day without pain was better than no days without pain. How many visits do you think it will take?"

"It is really hard to say, Josh. You have had this pain since you were nine, and you are in your early sixties now. That means you have had it for fifty years, the vertebrae as you say are fixed, and there is likely arthritis on top of this. In Chinese medicine there is a saying: The time a disease will take to heal is: if you take one month for every year that you have had the disease. In your case, under this theory, we would be looking at fifty months. But, I think that is really too long. How about we reevaluate in ten visits?"

"Man. Fifty months is a long time, but I am willing to commit to ten visits."

"For this kind of thing, the optimum treatment frequency would be twice a week, or twice a week one week, then once the next week, then twice the next week, etc. Do you think you could agree to that?"

"If that gives me more relief, I could make that work."

"The reason that I suggest two times per week is because your treatment only benefitted you for a day. This means we need to give you more stimulus, more often to keep the momentum going forward," I said.

"OK," Josh said.

Josh climbed up on the table, took off his shirt, socks, and shoes, and lay face down. As before, I marked some points, took out the needles, and inserted them. I added the clips of the electrostim machine to his needles, turned on the machine to his comfort level, and let him rest with the needles inserted for thirty minutes. I then turned off the estim machine, took out the needles, disposed of them, and told him that he was done. He got up, put on his clothes, paid, and arranged for an appointment in three days on March 3rd.

Three days later, Josh showed up on time.

The third appointment for me is crucial. Usually by this time the patient begins to build a rapport with the practitioner. The situation has gone from being new to being more routine. If a patient comes back for the third visit, this is when the truth begins to come out. This is not so strange. Most of us are not likely to share intimate secrets with someone whom we don't know. We have to build up a trust, and decide if the person we are meeting with can hear us. It is not very different from dating, where many people can tell in three to six dates whether they like a person or not. The big question is: are we in sync or are we out of sync? If we are out of sync, it is a sure thing that people will not tell their intimate stories about themselves. Josh had told me that his injury had happened when he was nine, and my curiosity was soon to be sated, as Josh had decided that he trusted me.

"Hi Josh, thanks for being on time. How did your second treatment feel?"

"I had relief for a day and a half. It gave me hope that this will improve," he said.

"That's great news! This tells me that maybe we are on the right track. Can you tell me anything more about how your injury occurred when you were nine?" I said.

"I generally don't talk about it, because most people don't believe me; I have never even told my family."

"It's OK, Josh, you are safe here," I said.

"Maybe because you are not part of the Western medical establishment, and you work with qi, perhaps you will believe me."

"I have heard some experiences in my time treating people, and you will find that with my own experiences as well, that I have quite an open mind," I said.

"When I was nine," he began, "I grew up near Stevenson, Washington. My family lived in the country in a small trailer community. I was a boy and I had the wilderness as my playground. I would take my Schwinn bicycle and bike all over the place, playing in the woods and in the streams. The only place I was not allowed to go was the swamp that was about a mile from my house. My parents would tell me that I was never to go there," Josh said.

"One morning I was bored, and I was riding my bike around. My parents were both at work, and it was just me. There was never any fear about leaving me at home, because we were in a very small community off the beaten path, and strangers really didn't come through our parts. I was riding around rather aimlessly as kids do, and pretty soon I noticed that I was about three-quarters of the way towards the swamp. I knew I wasn't supposed to go there, but when you tell a kid something is forbidden, it makes the curiosity even stronger. So, I thought to myself, what harm could be had from taking a look? After all, there was a big hill that overlooked the swamp, and I could sit there and gaze into the swamp without ever setting foot in it. There was a small cliff on the other side of the hill, but I told myself that I would be fine if I sat there, and looked at the swamp, then I could go home. No one would ever know," he said.

"I rode to the top of the hill, and there was a bit of a flat spot covered with pine needles sort of near the cliff, but still a safe distance away. The fir and spruce trees were thick around there, making this area secluded. I could have it all to myself, there wasn't even the sound of another person off in the distance.

"I had been sitting there for a bit gazing out on the swamp. I had learned that if I sat quietly, I could observe other things people didn't see. This was not anything anyone taught me, just something I had picked up from being in the woods so much. All of a sudden I heard a splash which sounded like a rock had fallen into the swamp, but I didn't see anything that could have made the splash. I crept up to the edge of the cliff to see if it was something beneath the cliff that I couldn't see. I still didn't see anything, and that was odd because it was a pretty big splash. I guessed that it could have been a fish, but it is the Pacific Northwest and the only really big fish we have are salmon and sturgeon, neither of which would be in a swamp. I sat there for a few minutes on my hands and knees gazing into the swamp, seeing if I could see what made the noise, or whether it would happen again.

"Then, the unthinkable happened. The ground underneath me gave way, and I was falling, or really tumbling down the side of the cliff. I hit the ground at the bottom, bounced, and landed in the swamp. When I landed in the swamp, I heard something snap in my back. I sank in the muck and mud up to my neck, then stopped sinking. Looking back now, I am glad that I didn't lose consciousness. I was pretty banged up and shaken. Here I was in the place where I wasn't supposed to go, and my bike was pretty well hidden in the place where I had been sitting. What was I going to do? Well, being a young boy familiar with playing in cold water, I thought that I would just work my way out of this, figure out how to climb back up the cliff, get on my bike, ride home, and not tell anyone. The first thing I should do is move my feet around to see if the ground under me was solid. I tried to move my feet, but they wouldn't move. So, I tried to reach down with my hands, but my arms wouldn't move either. In fact, I realized that I couldn't feel or move anything below my neck, and it hurt terribly to move that.

"Now I realized that I was trapped, I didn't know why I couldn't move or feel, but I knew it was bad. I was nine, and I was scared. I screamed for help, but my voice simply echoed in the trees. I cried and I yelled, and eventually I just started to whimper, knowing that no one would ever think to look for me in the swamp. The day slowly passed from mid-morning to mid-afternoon. Looking back, I don't know how I didn't get hypothermia. Mid-afternoon faded to dusk. As the last light was shining on the trees, I had an adult understanding that I was going to die here, and I didn't want to die! I wanted to live! I began to pray, pray to anyone and anything that would listen. I prayed to God, to Jesus, to Mother Mary. I asked the angels to save me. Finally, in despair, I said 'I will do anything to get out of this swamp, and be able to go home!'

"As the last golden light faded over the hill, there was a noise like a sucking from the swamp, as if something big was being pulled out of it. Suddenly, about twenty feet from me stood three hulking beings standing on the surface of the water.

"One of them said, 'We have been arguing amongst ourselves for the last 900 of your years, about what it is like to be human. Your back is broken. You will die here, but we can fix it, for a price. Do you accept?'"

"I will do anything to not die here," I said.

"The being who had spoken said, 'Offer accepted.'"

"Then the first one started running or moving quickly towards me, and when it was about three feet from me, it leaped at me. It hit me in the chest, and while there was no impact, it felt like I had been hit by a bolt of lightning. My second realization was that I was no longer alone in my body. The second being started to run, then it jumped into my chest at the same place, and I felt a second jolt of electricity. Then the third and last being started to run, jumped into my chest, and there was a third jolt of electricity. Instantaneously I could move. I crawled out of the swamp, somehow made it up the cliff, got on my bike, and rode home. Of course, I never told my parents," Josh said.

I blinked a couple of times at Josh, and I said to him, "That is fascinating. Were these beings comparatively slow of speech and in their movement?"

"Yes," he said.

"Not many people come across earth elementals in this reality, and I have never heard of three at once before. You are a lucky man," I said.

Chapter 2

"I am lucky to be alive," he said.

"Have you ever seen these beings again?" I said.

"No. They are still inside of me. Sometimes they talk to me, but most of the time, I feel like they are just watching the world through my eyes."

"Josh, your story makes me think that we should try another form of treatment. Have you ever had cupping before?"

"I haven't," Josh said.

"OK. Well, we are going to have you take your shirt off like with acupuncture. Then, I am going to put a bit of coconut oil on your back. Next, I will take some rubbing alcohol, apply it to a cotton ball, then light it on fire, and put the cup over the fire. The fire will burn up the oxygen in the cup, and cause suction to happen on your back. These cups are made of hardened glass, so they won't break from the brief time the fire is inside, like a regular glass would," I said.

"This will open up the pores of your skin and allow any residual pathogens out. When I speak of pathogens, I am not talking about viruses or bacteria, but pathogens as we would talk about them in Chinese medicine. These are things like cold, damp, heat, etc. Does that sound OK?" I said.

"If it helps with the pain, I am happy to try anything."

"OK. Well, if you disrobe, we can begin," I said.

Josh took off his shirt and lay face down on the table, while I took out the hemostat for holding the burning cotton ball, an ash tray, the rubbing alcohol, the cups, and my lighter, and laid them next to him.

For a while there has been great interest in the general public about fire cupping. Gwyneth Paltrow has shown up to gala events in backless dresses showing off her cupping marks, and most recently a number of swimmers on the US Olympic team in Brazil used it. I think it is important to say that, as with any other therapy, there is a time and a place for its use. First, it should not be used when the environment is cold, or when one has cupping, one should not go swimming in cold water, or otherwise expose the cupping marks to cold water. If one does not follow these prohibitions, then one can easily catch a cold, or worse, cause the area that has been cupped to hurt worse and feel more arthritic. The logic about these prohibitions is really very straightforward. Cupping increases the flow of blood, releases stuck energy, and works deeply to relax the muscles and sinews. Now, imagine going and having a nice relaxing massage, and at the end, the massage therapist does the ice bucket challenge on you. Do you think your muscles would still be feeling nice and warm, and relaxed? No, your muscles would be screaming profanities at you and the massage therapist, because all of the relaxed feeling disappeared in a mere heartbeat.

Therefore, whoever was doing the cupping on the US swimmers at the Olympics was potentially causing them harm. Lastly, cupping over highly vascular areas, on people with weak vascular systems, or people with poor wound healing – all of these situations should be avoided, as one can inadvertently cause a bleed by breaking the weak vessels, and thus cause a hematoma. A hematoma is simply a big bruise. Cupping often causes what appears to be bruises, but the discoloration that shows where the cups have rested is not a hematoma, but is merely the release of the pathogen within the body. These recommendations come from thousands of years of cultural experience within China, and should not be ignored.

I first rubbed coconut oil into Josh's lower back, then dabbed some alcohol onto two cotton balls that had already been pinched in the hemostats. Once the alcohol sufficiently soaked the cotton balls, I lit them on fire with my lighter, and held the hemostats in my right hand, while holding the cup in my left hand. The art of cupping is to be able to quickly insert the flame into the cup, then take the flame out so that it burns out all of the oxygen, but does not heat up the sides of the cup. Then one has to quickly set the cup on the target location before more oxygen fills the cup. It is a maneuver that takes a bit of practice.

I placed two cups on the lower back around L_3, tested them by gently lifting up on the cup to see if the suction broke, then said to Josh, "There. How does that feel?"

"A little bit like someone stuck the nozzle of a Hoover vacuum on my back."

"Good. That is exactly what it is supposed to feel like," I said. "I am going to leave those on there for a few minutes, and we will see what kind of pathogens, or as we say in Chinese medicine, *sha*, comes up."

I went and sat in my La-Z-Boy, set my timer for a few minutes, and took the time to write in Josh's chart. When the timer went off, I stood up, and took the few steps towards the table to inspect the cups. The right cup had some nice color that could be seen in the raised skin underneath the cup, but it was the left cup that drew my attention. It was full of white smoke, as if someone had burnt a piece of paper in the cup. There was no film on the cup, like one might expect if something had been lit within the cup, just white smoke. Frankly, in my years of cupping, I have never seen anything like it.

"How do you feel Josh?" I asked.

"I feel great. My back feels really loose!"

"I am going to take the cups off now. You will feel a bit of a pull, then they will pop off, OK?"

"OK," he said.

I pulled the left cup off, and the white smoke wafted up to the ceiling in a straight line, and then disappeared. No matter how much I think of it afterwards, it was one of the most unique experiences I have had when cupping up to that time.

Josh dismounted from the table, and I said, "OK. Let's see you again next week."

"Sounds good!" he said.

We made the appointment for March 10th the following week, Josh paid, and left. On March 10th, Josh arrived, and I said, "How has your back been since the last time I saw you?"

Josh replied, "I am not 100%, but the cupping treatment definitely seemed to hold more than the previous treatments."

"Then let's do it again," I said.

"Sounds good to me."

By this time, Josh had the routine down. He took off his shirt and lay face down on the table. I applied the cups to the same area as before, and gave them a few minutes while I sat in the La-Z-Boy. When the timer went off, I stood up, looked at the cups, and again in the left cup, there was smoke, but this time it was earth red. Perhaps, one could explain away the first cupping as simply a strange phenomenon, but to have it again, in exactly the same spot, but with a different color of smoke, well, this was bordering on the supernatural. I lifted the left cup off, and again the red smoke trailed to the ceiling in a straight line, then dissipated.

We concluded the appointment, and rescheduled for March 17th the following week. I did the cupping again in the same spot on the left side. After a few minutes of letting the cups sit, I checked them, and found that the left cup again had smoke in it, but this time it was black. I lifted the cup off, and the smoke streamed to the ceiling and disappeared.

"This has been pretty strange, Josh. In this one area, for the last three weeks, there has been smoke in the cup when I applied the cupping."

"I feel like something has left my body. Like something that has been there for a long time, is now gone. It is not quite like having a hole inside of me, but like something is gone, which I can't quite put my finger on," Josh said.

He got up and hopped off the table. He seemed to have more vigor. "How does your back feel?" I said.

Josh gave some twists to the left and right, bent down to touch his toes, and slowly straightened up. "Well, I haven't been able to touch my toes without significant pain in a long time. I still feel the pain, but it seems to be 60% better than it was when I first came in."

"What do you think about doing another round of cupping in a few days?" I asked.

"I am up for it."

We scheduled another appointment for March 22nd, Josh paid, and then left. In a few days he arrived at the appointed time.

"Good morning, Josh. How has it been these last few days?" I said.

"I think that I have finally held on to the gains. The pain stayed constant, and didn't seem to increase," he said.

Chapter 2

"That's great! Are you ready to give it another go?" I said.

"Let's do it!"

Josh got up on the table with his shirt off. As before, I placed the cups, sat in my easy chair and waited for a few minutes, then went and checked the cups. Not only was there no smoke, but there were no marks of any kind from the cups. When there are no *sha* marks or pathogens, this means that there are no more pathogens that can be removed by cupping.

"It looks like you are done with the cupping, my friend. There is no more *sha* to be removed. I will take these off, and then we can do some needles and the electrostim. How does that sound?" I said.

"Yep, sounds good."

I removed the cups, made some marks on his back with my pen, inserted the needles, attached the electrostim, turned it on to his comfort level, and settled into my easy chair to muse.

I have never seen this exact reaction to cupping before or since. Using cups for a few treatments, especially if there is back pain involved, is not unusual in itself. I don't use this modality often on patients, but will have it done fairly regularly on myself. I use it on myself typically for exposure to the elements, or for excessive exposure to electronics, and the reaction is usually a few red to purple circles of *sha*. These red to purple circles persist and slowly fade to yellow after a few days, as would a bruise; but smoke in a cup is unheard of.

As I see it, the truth is that it could only be one thing. These wisps of smoke in three different colors, which happened in three different instances – no more and no less – could only be the earth elementals from Josh's childhood leaving his body. Combining that with Josh's feeling that some indistinct "something" was missing, seemed to confirm this hypothesis. However, the interesting thing for me, was that beyond doing the manual procedure, I had not had to do anything remotely esoteric to have this happen. Nor did the elementals really interact with me in any way. They weren't malevolent, like some entities that one literally has to cast out from someone. Nor did they attack Josh once they left, as also might happen from something which has broken away from its host. Another way of saying this is: there seemed to be no negative feedback loop between

Josh and the elementals. In many ways, it is as if their "deal" with Josh was finished, and I was merely the facilitator to their release. I wondered whether they ever solved their dispute about what being human was like? Would they have left Josh's body earlier if he had sought treatment earlier? I supposed I would never know. The funniest part of the situation was that in the end, this could have happened to any acupuncturist who used cupping on Josh. Or, did it only happen in front of me, because somehow the elementals knew that it would not fragment my reality, nor cause undue stress on my mind? In this instance, was I simply the best door for this situation that Josh could find?

The timer went off, I got up, walked to the table, turned off the electrostim, and removed the needles. "OK. That's it," I said.

Josh sat back on his heels with his arms outstretched like a dog stretching his front feet or downward dog as it is called in yoga. He sat up, and said, "I feel good. Better than I have in years."

I shared my musings with him, "I'm glad that you are feeling better, man! So, I think what I saw in the cups, that is the smoke leaving, I think this was the elementals from your childhood. Does that make any sense?"

Josh looked at me, and did a long, slow internal look at the same time. "I think you are right. Over these last few weeks, I have felt like somehow I am more complete. I still see things that people around me don't see, but I feel like it is more me, and not much of the other. Does that make any sense? I mean, they never really interfered very much. I never felt like I was possessed or anything, but at times, especially in dangerous situations, I would seem to get guidance from somewhere."

"That makes sense," I said.

"You know, I haven't really talked about that day with anyone, because I didn't think they would believe me. I always felt different after that day, different like when it is cold outside and you are the only one not wearing a jacket, or you are in a room full of people and there is someone talking to you, but no one else can hear it. Do you know what I am saying? At times, I felt like I was crazy, and I asked at one time to be tested for mental illness, and all of my chemical markers and tests came back as clean. I wonder what life will hold for me now?"

"I can almost guarantee that you will have some back pain for the rest of your life, and I would suggest regular maintenance, whether it is from me or another acupuncturist. As to the rest, well from my experience, I would say that the gift of seeing is yours to keep. I suspect that you will never be the same as anyone else, in the same way that someone who suffers some trauma won't be the same way as they were before. But, 'not being the same' does not mean that you can't be healthy or happy. Going forward, in addition to regular acupuncture maintenance, I would recommend doing yoga or pilates to keep your back as supple as possible," I said.

"Thanks Doc!" Josh joked. I am not an M.D., but sometimes patients call me a doctor part in jest, and part as a way of conferring their respect, the same way I call my master "master."

"I am no doctor, Josh, but I do try my best. You're welcome!" I said with a smile.

Josh put his t-shirt and flannel shirt back on, put on his shoes and socks, and shrugged his jacket on. He paid for his visit, made an appointment for two weeks away, and told me he would find a yoga class.

As his hand reached for the door, I said to him, "You know, I never asked how you found me." My office is on the third floor of a downtown office building, with no street signage.

Opening the door, he looked at me with his eyes twinkling and a mischievous smile, and said, "They said it had to be you. I was actually on my way somewhere else, and all of a sudden, I heard them say to me: 'Turn here, up this flight of stairs. Down the hall, this office. This is the place where our deal ends. We have enjoyed your body, and we have much to think on, but for now, it is time to go home.' When I knocked on the door, you answered." Then, without waiting to hear my reply, Josh slipped out of the office.

Chapter 3
Continuation of The First Law

I gathered up my things, put on my jacket, turned the sign to closed and headed for the car. Josh had been my last patient of the day, and frankly, I was ready for a cigarette and some good food. I reached my car, shrugging off the big drops of rain that were coming down; sometimes I really wanted to give everything a big shake like a dog, but that doesn't work as well for humans. So, I brushed the drips off my jacket, got in the car, started it, turned on the heat, and opened my window halfway. I lit my cigarette, and watched as the coal turned to ash. I sat there in my car, watching the raindrops hit my windshield, sipping on my cigarette, and mused.

What we know of reality is impermanent at best. Josh was right, that speaking of earth elementals would get him the mental illness stamp by society, because that is not the reality most people live in. This brings up the first law of the universe again: If I can see it, it can see me. This invites the question, if I can't see it, does it not exist? There are so many examples in our agreed-upon reality that prove that this idea can't be true. Physicists talk about worm holes, string theory, and black holes – none of which can be seen by the naked eye. It is commonly agreed upon that everything is made of atoms, but most people I know can't see atoms on a regular basis. Further, most pharmaceutical drugs that people consume are made up of chemicals compounds, which at best can only be seen via microscope or through spectro analysis. At the most basic level, we cannot see air, and yet we know that without it, we will suffocate.

Another way of saying this, which I heard from a wise master: I will pay $500 to anyone in this room who can bring me red. Not something that is red, but red itself. You see, red is a concept, it is not a thing. We have put a vibration to it, a color to it, a spectrum to it, various hues to it, a number for coloring things in programming languages such as css and html, etc. However, these are all simply agreed-upon definitions for what most people see. It is a common agreement amongst people that this is red, but if you are color blind, or do not have the ability to see color, and instead see in black and white, or still further have no ability to see at all, then I ask you: What is red for these people? I heard the story of Neil Harbisson on the BBC World Service, in a piece titled *The Man Who Hears Color*.

This man was born with severe color blindness, and at one point had an antenna implanted into his brain. When he directs the antenna at something, it will give him a frequency, which he then turns into music. So, he has given a whole new meaning to the idea of color. This is an example of someone who has had to create his own rules, because the dominant culture's agreed-upon rules did not work for him.

So, reality, as we know it, is in many ways a social construct. The reality that most of us live in has been called the illusion by masters for millennia. Many movies have explored this idea, most famously in recent times with *The Matrix*, or "you can take the blue pill and go back to the life of ignorance, or take the red pill and be awakened from the illusion." This, is no more than a reference to Lewis Carroll's *Alice in Wonderland*. In both stories, the protagonists leave the comfort of the agreed-upon reality, to see the world as it is being shown to them. Truly, this is a collective myth and story that goes back to all of the tales of a mystical journey. Yet, even though these tales have survived in our oldest societal literature all over the world, the majority of us still live in the dominant construct. Why is this?

Maybe it is our education, our social conditioning, or that we don't want to seem to be like RT News or CNN, and be discerning consumers of "fake news," as the Donald would say. But, the fact is that for the last 6,000 years, dating back to Sumeria in written tradition, there have been tales of the other worlds, which would not have been considered fake news in their day. More important than whether something is deemed fake or not by the powers that be, one must first think about what the agenda is behind the idea.

All people who are invested in the illusion have an agenda. Or a nicer way to speak of an agenda is a narrative. Democrats, Republicans, Christians, Satanists, Anarchists, Conspiracists, Capitalists, Globalists, Nationalists, etc., all have a narrative from which they see the world. They constantly work to convert people to their narrative, because it furthers and solidifies their actions within the illusion. Democrats and Republicans or politicians want their party in power in order to enact their agenda. Christians want to bring people to Christ or to find Christ in order to help "save" people. Satanists want to bring people to the Devil. Anarchists want to live free of governance. Capitalists want to keep the money flowing. Globalists want the money to flow from portions of the world to other parts of the world. Nationalists want the money to stay in the nation state. These are simplistic descriptions, but the point I make is that these decisions rarely benefit the growth of people's spirit, or benefit and elevate people en masse. The very nature of an agenda is to facilitate and improve the narrative for those people who have the same beliefs as the person or group putting forth the agenda. These agendas have long-lasting consequences that keep people focused on the illusion either through chaos, debt, wealth, the appearance of power, adoration, etc.

Let's look at this from another perspective. If you had all the material possessions you could ever want, but were told you had to leave your house, could you? Would you? Could you renounce and let go of all things that had value to you, as far as stuff was concerned? Could you renounce your status and position? In effect, could you renounce that which makes you something in society? This is simply a thought experiment to illustrate how each of us is deeply enmeshed in the world that we believe to be reality.

But is it real or illusion? I think the simplest way a master would look at this question is: do you get to keep it when you die? This answer gives us a very clear answer concerning what is real and illusion. Simply stated, we keep four things when we die: relationships, personal growth, experiences, and memories. Since experiences and memories are often related to either relationships or personal growth, we can shorten this list to these two things. So, how much of our time in our lives do we actively work at building deep and meaningful relationships, and profound and intense personal growth? When I speak of personal growth, I am speaking of growing your spirit or soul – not your profession or outward trappings of life.

Compound this with the idea that the illusion as we know it exists in the third dimension, and that there are multiple dimensions stacked both on top and below this dimension, and reality really does become a tricky subject.

Let's go back to this idea of atoms for a second. In the third dimension, we have all learned that atoms vibrate, or if one wants to get technical, the protons and electrons orbit at incredible speed around a nucleus. When atoms cluster together they create stuff, and we call this matter. The more atoms vibrate, the more unstable they get; the more arrangement atoms have, the more solid the substance. Therefore, a gas vibrates at a high speed, while a solid vibrates but does not really move much and keeps its defined arrangement. We can see solids and most liquids with our naked eyes, but we have problems seeing gasses without either coloration or some movement upon matter. For example, clouds are composed of droplets or particles of either a liquid or solid so we can see them, but the wind that blows the clouds cannot generally be seen, except by how it affects the clouds.

What has a higher vibration than a gas? For the scientists out there, you can answer better than I, but again this is simply a thought experiment. We know that something we cannot see can affect the matter around us. Why could it not also be that the effects of other dimensions have an effect on us as well? And conversely, can we affect them?

My stomach rumbled, I put out my cigarette, and started the drive to New Seasons on 21st and Raleigh. The last few days the moussaka had been spot on, and I was craving a bit of lamb after my long day.

My phone started ringing playing the last verse from "Hotel California" by the Eagles. What? Who doesn't like the Eagles?

I answered the phone, "This is Roland Pearce. How may I help you?"

"Roland. It's Thomas. I need you to come out to the farm as soon as you can!"

"Heya Thomas. As soon as possible meaning tonight? Or will tomorrow be good enough?" I asked.

"Yeah, yeah. Tomorrow is fine. I don't think it will happen at night. It seems to be a day-light thing."

"OK. I will move some things around. Is any certain time better than another tomorrow?" I asked.

Thomas was an old patient. We went way, way back. In fact, I knew him when I was in high school. He is about twenty years older than me, and when I was in high school, he worked at a craft store that I used to go to. After I received my Masters in Chinese medicine, we ran into each other again, and he was one of my first patients. Thomas generally didn't need my services for esoteric purposes; mostly he simply suffered the aches and pains of being in his sixties. On-site visits cost more, and he knew that, but it wouldn't be the first time that I had visited his farm. Thomas is an herbalist by trade, and he grows a large number of Western herbs for wholesale markets on his farm in Corbett, Oregon.

Most of the reason I had been out in previous visits was to consult about why certain medicinals weren't growing correctly, or how certain medicinals needed to be prepared from a Chinese medicine perspective – for example, the difference between how the final medicinal constituents change when a medicinal is stir-fried, honey-fried, or alcohol-fried, versus what the chemical constituents of a medicinal are when it is in its normal state, after being harvested and dried. Since I read both Chinese and Japanese,

I give growers like him a different perspective than they get from the regular Western literature. It is good to have a few different skill sets, as it is not every day that someone needs a demonologist.

I have to say that the presidential race and the election of Donald Trump seem to have been really good for business. Not because Trump himself has made any policy changes that have directly affected my business, but more because his election has stirred up the collective angst in Portland. Outsiders see the riots in the streets on television, but what they don't see is the dark things that are feeding on the fear and chaos. And I haven't even looked or tried to see what monkeys are riding on the back of Trump and his people. Yet, wherever there is chaos, you can be assured that there is a dark being lurking somewhere behind it.

The next day, I went out Interstate 84 over the Sandy River and took the Lewis and Clark Park exit. There are faster ways to get to Corbett, but no way is nearly as pretty as this route. The road follows the curves and bends of the Sandy River, and then does a long slow crescent curve around an oxbow of the river. At this time of year, the maples and alders that line the river bed are barren of leaves, but it would not be too long before the new buds began to peek out from the skeletal branches to form leaves. The smell coming through my window is the rich tannins of decaying wet leaves, the slightly boggy smell of the river, and of the pines that live on the other side of the road. The rain spattered on my windshield as I hit the straightaway after the oxbow, and I passed the green steel bridge that takes one to the farthest extreme of Stark Street. Then I began to climb the slow grade that takes one past the small market in Springdale. I took a right on SE Hurlburt Road, followed that for a few miles, and then another right on to Gordon Creek Road. This dropped me back down on to the Sandy River directly across from Oxbow Park.

This very small stretch of road that goes the distance of Oxbow on the north side of the river has an odd tendency to be the dumping ground of bodies for people who have committed murder in the Sandy and Corbett area. Why different murderers would pick the same area as a dumping ground makes me wonder whether it has something to do with the land itself, or simply that the people who commit the murders simply all find it a convenient place to dump a body. I never have homed in and stopped in this area to see what the land had to say, as I usually am on my way somewhere when I cross through here, but maybe someday I will be so called.

Gordon Creek then switchbacks up a hill so steep that I know I wouldn't want to get caught on that set of switchbacks in one of the legendary Corbett ice storms. Then up the hill, and around a deep bend of the road that looks out on a massive pasture. Two does looked up from eating grass as I passed, and besides the rumble of my engine, the world was silent. The road soon Y'ed; to the left is Trout Creek Road and the Trout Creek Bible Camp, and to the right is Gordon Creek and the road I must follow.

A few more twists and turns and I came to a crossroads. To the left is Warriner Road, to the right is Bull Run Road, and straight in front is a driveway that is a long gravel trail. If one takes the left, up Warriner Road, one will quickly arrive at Camp Howard, an outdoor school for middle school kids in the Portland Public School system. Take a left at SE Camp Howard Road, go less than a mile, and you will run into the Bull Run Watershed, which until recently was the source of Portland's famously sweet water. The Bull Run Watershed is a 102-square-mile area of no-man's land, where man is not supposed to go. Established in 1892, ninety-six percent of it is owned by the federal government, and four percent of it is owned by the City of Portland. It seems that the federal government doesn't appreciate that this is "no-man's land," because they regularly sell portions of the Bull Run to be logged. Of course your average Portland resident thinks his water comes from a pristine area, but the locals of the area around Warriner road can tell you of the logging trucks that sometimes come down the road in steady streams.

I waited at the stop sign on Gordon Creek for one of said logging trucks to plunder by. It is heading from Warriner Road to Bull Run Road on its way to the town of Sandy and Highway 26. It is odd, but there are very few places left in Oregon that can boast that they have a pristine and protected area that is more than 50-square-miles, let alone 102-square-miles. Therefore, I have to say to the person who arranged the logging deal and sold the Bull Run Watershed land, perhaps if you would have left the Bull Run as a "no-man's land," Portland would not have to be treating the water supply for Cryptosporidium now. It is no secret that when there are more trees, and there is no cutting of trees, that there is less soil erosion. If there is concern that the Cryptosporidium is getting into the river because of heavy runoff from the soil, wouldn't one think that there is more runoff not from rainfall, but because more of the forest has been cut? I will leave it for the environmentalists to figure out, but it is always good to ask the question, "Why now?"

I crossed Warriner Road and go up the gravel road. It is a long three-quarter-of-a mile road, and at the end sits a metal barn and an A-frame-shaped house made of wood. Along the gravel road are a few apple trees, a big cherry tree, and a pear tree. The driveway circled around the house, but I turned left and pulled up right next to the house so that I am even with the covered porch on the front of the house. As I stepped out of the car, I looked across the gravel road. Last time I had been up here, the land on the other side of the gravel road had been filled with old-growth trees. They talked and rustled with the majesty of kings and queens, as some of them had easily been ten feet across. Now that land was filled with slash and stumps with massive scars where the beautiful trees had been dragged across the ground to the waiting trucks after they had been chopped down. Looking at that huge mess, my heart caught in my throat for what was lost when those trees were cut.

Thomas came out the front door, stood on the porch, and lit a cigarette, "You, too, eh? You can only imagine how I felt hearing them saw all day, and feeling the rattling in the house when those giants fell," he said.

I shook my head and lit my own cigarette, "There was nothing you could do?"

"I wasn't even notified. You know, one of the reasons I bought this house was because of those giant trees across the road, and the fact that I am just a mile from the Bull Run Watershed. The old man who had the land, well, he passed it on, and the kids wanted the money from the trees, so they hired someone to do the work. My first inkling was waking up to the sound of a falling tree," he said.

"I know I don't need to tell you, Roland," he continued, "what kind of shitshow it was as large portions of the land were cut, and the animals, dryads, nymphs, fairies, and who knows what else, were displaced. It was so messed up out there at night, that Helen here wouldn't leave the circle of light around the house," he said as he patted a big malamute that had walked up and leaned against his leg.

"Where did all of those creatures go?" I asked.

"I don't know about all of them, but I know that my property and the herbs were chaotic for a while. You know, there is a ley line that runs through this property east to west, so my guess is that the natural choice was to go upstream or downstream. Of course, I haven't talked to the neighbors on the other side of the clear-cut, because you are basically one of the few people I could talk about this stuff with," he said.

So much destruction, where once there was beauty. I took a couple of drags on my cigarette, and looked around me. Everything looked normal on Thomas's side; nothing was too chaotic now. From the way the slash was dried out, it looked like it had happened six months or so ago, maybe October or September. Obviously, that chaos had mostly subsided. Thomas stood there, also looking distantly at the forest that was no more. He patted Helen, who kept leaning in for more, as malamutes do.

Thomas was 5'8" or so, with reddish-gray hair, slightly stocky, but not fat. He wore a red and white Field and Stream flannel, and brown double-pleated Carrhartt dungarees. On his feet were an old worn pair of Danner lace-up boots with speckles of mud in the tread and on the sides. He looked good for a man in his mid-sixties. He didn't have dark circles under his eyes, and he didn't exude fear or anxiety. Helen, too, was mellow. So, whatever he had called me about didn't seem to be affecting his health.

"Coffee?" he said.

"Sure. Black, the darker the better," I said.

Thomas went inside and grabbed the drip pot off the warmer. I heard two cups clink together. The refrigerator door opened and closed, a box with some paper rustled. A plate was set down on tile. Helen, devoid of the human post she was leaning on, ambled over to me, and leaned in for the pets she knew would be coming.

"Hey, girl. Long time, eh?" I said as I started to give her the pet work-over. You know, all of the places they like it: between the eyebrows, ears, forehead, a little neck rub, between the shoulder blades, chest, and sacrum. I have a way with dogs and rarely have problems, even with the ones whose owners say that the dog doesn't like people. I generally don't have problems, and in fact often become the favorite uncle when I come over. By the time Thomas came back out onto the porch, Helen was on her back getting her belly rubbed, tongue lolling out.

"I see you didn't waste time seducing my pup, as usual," he said as he put two cups of coffee down on the small round patio table with a couple of dried-cherry scones. "From New Seasons, I know you like them. I was out yesterday grocery shopping, when you said you would come out," he said.

"All right lady, up to the porch with you," I said. I put my cigarette butt in the butt can on the rail of the deck, and sat down. The coffee was semi-dark, but a little tangy for me.

"Coava?" I said.

"Yep. You sure know your coffee."

"There are only a few places in town that truly dark-roast a bean. This is not my favorite, but as they say, beggars can't be choosers."

"Too dark and it upsets my stomach a bit, so this was a compromise," he chuckled.

"I can appreciate that. Well, you called, and I am here. Besides the clear-cut, the place looks balanced. Helen looks even-keel, and you look fine. So, what seems to be the problem?" I asked.

He looked at me and pointed with the scone he had just bit into. "That."

I looked where he was pointing, and there was a sort of squarish log sitting on the porch.

"That? The log?" I asked.

"Yep. Except that isn't a log. It is petrified wood."

"OK. So, how do I fit in here?" I asked.

"Look at it," he said.

I stood up and took a few steps over to it. It was layered in different colors like most petrified wood is, but around three sides of it one could actually see the bark, which had hardened into stone. The colors in the rock were also pretty stunning: a deep jade green with dark, brick-red veins running through the green, then a thin layer of white where the cambium layer would have been. The "bark" was a dark tan. The whole thing looked more like a piece of jasper than petrified wood. This piece was maybe fifteen inches long by four inches wide and four inches high. It appeared to be the perfect image of a limb which ran off the main trunk of a tree, complete with the knobs where the smaller branches would have branched from this branch. It was probably the most beautiful and best-preserved piece of petrified wood I had ever seen.

"It's a beaut Thomas. Where did you pick it up?"

Everyone who knew Thomas knew he was an avid collector of petrified wood. Most of the time he would venture to places like Eastern Oregon to find some, but he would also buy the odd beautiful piece.

Chapter 3

"Over there," he pointed just on the other side of my car.

"You dug it out there?" I asked.

"No, it was lying there on the grass."

"Did someone bring it to you and leave it?"

"That was what I thought, so I picked it up and put it here, thinking someone would call or email me to tell me they left it, but no one did," he said. "Then I found the next piece, a little further away. Then the third piece, the next day, even farther away. Then another piece."

"How long has this been going on Thomas?" I said.

"I found the twenty-ninth piece yesterday. Each piece is in a line to the NE, roughly close to the ley line," he said as he came over and picked up the piece of petrified wood. "But, this is why I called you. Follow me over here to the east side of the house." He stepped off the porch and ambled around the house, following the circle of the driveway. On the other side of the driveway was a half-acre of grass that had a small garden to the left, and a trail that led straight through the grass heading east. About ten feet out from the driveway in the grass lay twenty-eight pieces of petrified wood. They were in all shapes and sizes; some of them looked to be fifty to one hundred pounds. Stunningly, they fit perfectly together to form the top of the trunk and canopy of a tree in exquisite detail.

"I had to use the Bobcat to move a couple of these trunk pieces, but this piece fits here," he said as he placed the piece near the trunk of the tree. "Twenty-nine days since finding the first piece. At day four, I thought someone was pranking me. At day ten, I realized that the ends of some of the pieces matched, and I started to figure out that there might be a pattern to this puzzle. The piece I picked up yesterday showed that there was only one more hole to fill, and then there will be the entire canopy of a small tree here."

I looked and nodded. What else could I do? It was all laid out in front of me as you might say.

"It is all the same rock, you see? Green, red, white, and tan. These lines here, match and show the veins of the tree. This bark overlays on this piece," he said as he pointed to different pieces, showing how they connected. "Any way I try to arrange these, I keep coming back to this configuration. And, in this configuration, with the piece I just put in, there is only one piece missing."

"Have you gone out today yet?" I asked.

"No. That is why I asked you to come out. I am a little concerned about what might be out there."

"Do you want to go have a look?" I said.

"Sure. Let me put Helen in the house, just in case."

"OK," I said.

"Let's go, Helen!" he said. Thomas started walking back to the house, Helen taking her time sniffing this and that, but generally following Thomas. I looked at the petrified tree lying in the grass in front of me. It was almost the perfect icon of a tree, except for the missing piece.

Petrified wood is an interesting fossil formation. In order for it to be formed, the vegetable aspect or organic aspect has to be replaced with minerals that are high in silica such as quartz. This happens when the vegetation is covered by sediment or ash from a volcano. As water flows through the sediment or ash, it leaches out minerals from the ground and permeates them into the wood. The more minerals that inhabit the cells of the vegetation, the better chance of having something perfectly preserved. In this case, the quartz or silicate had trace minerals of chromium and copper, which formed the green color, and iron oxide, which formed the red and tan colors. The closest forest that would have been able to produce such a thing in our locale is the Agate Desert in the Upper Rogue River valley, which is near Medford, Oregon. This is roughly 290 miles away from Thomas's house.

Thomas walked up and said, "The last piece I found was over this way."

He strolled past the petrified canopy and headed toward a small natural arch of two spruce trees that formed the entrance of a trail on the east side of the small field.

"After the piece that I found by your car, there were a couple of pieces in the field, then there was a piece here in this archway. Then there was a piece about two hundred feet from the archway. The last piece I found was on the same line, but heading down to the creek."

The area we were walking through was young Doug fir, just on the edge of being harvestable. Thomas's property had a fair number of trees on it along with the medicinals that he grew. The part that we were walking through was what Thomas called his "tree farm," which was about eight acres of trees in a long swath. Through the trees ran a rocky trail which had been covered with hazelnut shells. As the trail gradually declined, if one looked due east, one would see the snow-capped peak of Mount Hood, that is, if it wasn't cloudy and rainy.

We walked along in silence with Thomas leading the way to where he found the last piece. The juncos chirped, a Steller's jay screamed out an alarm call, and the ravens croaked in the distance. Here and there I saw the tracks and scat of various animals, such as coyote, deer, and elk. It was peaceful, and apart from the current mystery, I was a little envious of Thomas's property, or at least the side past the house where you could not see the clear-cut any more.

"I don't intend to cut these trees. They allow me to get a timber deferral on my taxes, but more importantly, the animals need a place to be," Thomas said.

He was right. Oregon, long known for its commercial production of timber, has made a checkerboard of its lands, by clear-cutting twenty acres, then monocropping Doug fir on the next twenty acres, then clear-cutting the next twenty acres, etc. Oregonians who were born here before 1980 can tell you that the climate has changed. We have less rain and more sun. In the last ten years, Oregon has even suffered a drought to some degree. One might say this is simply climate change, but one might argue that this is a symptom of Oregon having very little native forest left. Why do I say this?

All one has to do is look at the water cycle to understand this. Water evaporates off the ocean and condenses to become clouds. The clouds then dump this water onto the land in the form of rain or snow. The snow is stored in the mountains, and the rain is used by the plants to grow. The rest of the water is stored in the underground aquifers, and becomes creeks, rivers, and streams. These then lead back to the ocean and recreate the cycle. However, the part that is not talked about much is the role of trees, which inject water back into the atmosphere. This process is called transpiration, and is a part of photosynthesis. The transpiration from trees is responsible for somewhere between ten and thirty-five percent of the rainfall. The lower number represents the extreme north, and the higher number represents the rainfall of the Amazon. As transpiration is part of photosynthesis, and photosynthesis happens to all plants, then one simply needs to ponder how plants are nearly everywhere. Then, it is easy to think about how much water is injected into the atmosphere by transpiration.

So, here is the chicken-versus-egg question: In areas with very little vegetation, does it not tend to be more hot and arid? Think of a desert. It's plants tend not to transpire much water, and instead tend to store the water within their flesh, like cacti for example. Therefore, one might ask: Did the desert come first? Or did deforestation come first? Another example: When the tropical rain forest of the Amazon is clear-cut for farms, how long do the nutrients stay in the soil? Does not the clear-cut area eventually become a kind of desert? And lastly, would California have fewer water issues if it planted more trees? More thought experiments I suppose, as I can't answer these questions. As to Thomas's statement, he is right – more trees equals more places for animals to live. The more there is a balance between nature and man, the more benefit there is for all creatures.

"I found the last piece here," Thomas said.

We were at the end of the Doug fir replant, and in front of us the trail continued on into native forest. The difference was striking. The replant or tree farm consisted of trees planted in relatively regular rows, all roughly a foot to a foot and a half in diameter. The planted trees had had their small branches removed up to the twelve-foot-high mark or so, to keep them from catching fire in the case of a ground fire. All in all, the tree farm felt like it was another crop (Thomas had not planted these trees), and it had the sense of man. In contrast, the native forest was dense, with a wide variety of large-diameter trees and small brush such as blue and red huckleberries, Oregon grape, salal, sword ferns, and moss. The trail was there, but it seemed like every few feet there was an obstruction in the form of a tree branch or a downed tree that needed to be crawled over.

Thomas again took the lead on the path, holding a branch here and there so it wouldn't snap back in my face. Ten to fifteen steps in, the forest became quiet. There were still bird calls, but they were muted. The hair rose on the back of my neck a little bit as we moved on the trail and passed from the seemingly normal into the sacred. There is a serenity or sense of implied wisdom to a deep forest that is hard to describe. I can compare the feeling to standing near large boulders, or old craggy cliffs; there is a sense of the enormousness and age of what one is witnessing. We walked further, and I could hear the rushing of a small stream.

Chapter 3

"The creek you hear is just over the rise. It is a trickle in summer, but tends to be quite full in the winter," Thomas said.

Cresting the small rise, we could see the creek, and there on our side of the bank was a piece of petrified wood. Thomas stopped and looked around, but on not seeing anything unusual, he approached the rock. I followed behind, generally keeping my awareness up, but as with Thomas, I detected nothing unusual. We stood there on the bank of this small creek, looking at this rock. It was no different than the other pieces, pretty in its own right, with the same deep greens and reds.

On the other side of the creek was a mammoth cedar tree with its limbs hanging low over the water. The blue-green of its leaves were reminiscent of the green in the petrified wood. The redness of its bark was similar to the red of the petrified wood. A Steller's jay called, the creek burbled, and then a voice said, "Greetings man-children."

Thomas looked back at me with that combined expression that said both, "Oh oh," and "I told you so."

From within the center of the cedar trunk stepped forth a hairy cloven hoof, then a hairy leg, a hairy waist, then a human abdomen that was brown, followed by human arms, and finally, a human head with curly hair and little horns. This happened in an instant. A second later another creature of the same type stepped forth from the tree.

"I see you have found the last piece of petrified wood," it said, although it was hard to tell which one had spoken, because neither of the creatures had opened its mouth – I simply heard the words. I looked at Thomas, and I heard him say, "Thank you," without opening his mouth.

"We led you here, because we wanted you to know that we are real."

The two creatures in front of me were called fauns. These beings were depicted in ancient Greek and Roman stories, and in more recent time C.S. Lewis's *Chronicles of Narnia*, and Lev Grossman's *The Magicians* series. But rather than being in a story, here I was speaking to two apparently flesh-and-blood beings.

"We have long lived in between worlds, and we are ancient. Your world is one of the places that we call home. What you call the natural world has a vast design that the man-children have yet to see. All is connected through the unseen web, and when in harmony, the areas outside the reach of man act as energetic storage places for those who live in higher planes. In the quest for short-term gain, man-children disrupt this balance. Thus, my brother and I have picked you to spread our message," it said.

If I hadn't known Thomas for a long time, I would have almost thought that he had spiked the scones or the coffee with some hallucinogenic drug, but he had the same slack-jawed look that I did.

"The cutting of the great native forests has repercussions that you cannot even begin to fathom. The light is love, and the dark is hate. Hate feeds on the chaos and anger of man-children, but have you ever considered how the light feeds itself? All things take energy to exist, and the light and dark are no different in this. However, we draw our energy from a renewable and clean place, which has nothing to do with the man-children. We derive our sustenance from the serenity of what you call old-growth forests, and as you cut and harvest our sustenance, we slowly starve. The light then wanes, and the dark waxes, for if we cannot sustain ourselves here, then neither can the light. When enough of the old places are gone, we will no longer come here, and the light will fade on your Earth, just as it did with the gods of light millennia ago."

"We have watched man-children fall prey to their own illusions of power, greed, and short-sightedness for more of what you call 'civilizations' than we can count. You rise to a point where you are almost awake, and then you fall each time. We cannot intervene on your behalf, because this is your lesson to learn. But when we and the light leave this planet, you will be left with only darkness. When this happens, you will have no more than six lifetimes, at best, on this planet, and at worse, three lifetimes. When you have destroyed all that lives around you, and yourselves, then this Earth will be barren for hundreds of thousands of your years. When there is no more hate, death, and chaos to eat, the darkness will then move on to another world. Then, when there has been stillness for a long while, we and the others like us will come back here and reseed this planet with light.

"We mourn for you, man-child. As before, your race's very inability to grasp the importance of yourselves within the entire system of this planet continues to be your downfall. All things on this planet are equal in the eyes of the light; nothing is more or less important. There is no dominant species, as all things must do their part. Let go of your egos, and truly see the destruction of the world that you have created, and how your quest to feel important is at the expense of all the creatures around you. Only the darkness is cruel enough to destroy all. When there is nothing left, the darkness will eat itself, and when the darkness inhabits the earth fully, so too will you eat yourselves.

Chapter 3

"Ever before, there have been a few that would hear our message, but a few points of light within the darkness cannot turn the tide. Only through the collective efforts of your entire race, beyond color, belief, or creed, can you right your direction. But, we fear that as with your other civilizations, your kind will hold on too tightly to what you have created, thinking of yourselves as manifesting greatness, when in reality you are caught in an illusion of your own making.

"This tree of petrified wood stood in front of a great palace at one time. Its denizens thought that they, too, were great. Then when those man-children upset the balance of nature, they first starved because of lack of food, dehydrated due to lack of clean water, then cannibalized their weak, old, and children in order that the strong could stay strong. Then nature created massive earth changes that destroyed those who survived. This stone tree witnessed all of this, as we did, until it was covered in ash from a volcanic eruption. Your cycle has repeated more times than you have history for, but the lesson remains the same in each civilization. Can you awaken from your own illusion, and right that which you have created, in order to take your place within the light? Can you change? And, can enough of you change in order to make a difference this time, before it is too late? Your time is nigh, man-child, and you have only have a small number of years before the time of decision will close, and we will leave you. The light will leave you, and all that will be left for you here is darkness, chaos, destruction, and war. We will mourn for you, as we have before. Hear our words, and spread this message which we have given you. Your race can be great, man-child, within the natural order of things, and this potential is limitless, but the path you are on is not the right path to order."

With that, the two fauns dematerialized in front of us. Thomas and I looked at each other, and I said, "Did you hear all of that about the light, dark, nature, man, and our place within the world?"

"I did," he said. Thomas sat down, drew his knees up, and held his head. "I think I am going to be sick."

I did not feel any malicious intent from the fauns, but their thought-words came with graphic images of the past, present, and future. It was a lot to process, as if they let us see a millennia of human civilization and its inevitable destruction through their eyes. Seeing this, it was hard to feel anything but despair for our world and our people. Yet, what I know about prophecy is that, while what is being prophesized has a high likelihood of coming true, a prophecy cannot take away the free choice of an individual. With great effort to prevent what has been prophesized, an individual or group can change the outcome. The fauns said the time of decision making was coming to a close, but did not say that this window had closed. There was some time left, and that gave me some measure of hope.

I debated whether to try to cross the creek to see if there were physical impressions where they had stood, and finally decided that if I didn't, it would be a lost opportunity. I took a few steps back, and took a running jump at crossing the creek. I almost made it – at least one foot made it – the other hit the very edge of the bank, then slid into the water. Luckily, I was wearing boots, not dress shoes, and my foot was only minimally wet. I took a few steps to where the fauns had stood in front of the cedar, and as I suspected, there was no sign or track where they had stood. It is not too hard to believe that anything that can literally materialize out of a tree could choose not to leave any trace of its presence. I gave myself a little bit more room to get a running start, and this time on jumping, I cleared the stream without getting my boots wet again.

"Let's get back to the house, and out of the rain, Thomas," I said. I nudged the petrified wood with my boot, "What do you want to do with this?"

Thomas put his right hand on the ground and pushed himself up while getting his feet under him. "I think I will leave it here for today. I need a cup of coffee and a smoke. To tell you the truth, I really could go for a double or triple Manhattan. Any interest in a drink?" he asked.

"If it wasn't 2 p.m., I might say yes, but I can't drink this early in the day. I might still have patients today."

"Suit yourself. Let's at least see if that coffee is still warm."

We headed back out the way that we came. As before, when we left the old growth, the activity of the forest seemed to increase.

"Did you hear their predictions?" Thomas said.

"I did."

"What do you think about all of that?" he said.

"Unfortunately, I think that they are right," I said.

"I knew you were going to say that. What is your take on it?"

"Well, the dark is definitely rising. The world has more chaos as a whole than it has for a long time. The people are less restful and more agitated. There is less security and more insecurity in general. The older generation is beginning to fade out of the work force, but the younger generations are not filling those positions for the same compensation packages. Healthcare is uncertain at best, and the plan to repeal the ACA really does not take care of the poor, old, weak, or young. The education system has failed, but it doesn't know that it is a dead man walking. The media are controlled by the few, and when people in power don't like the press they get, they call it fake news. The children and young people have mortgaged their future to have a future with student loans. Whole portions of the world either have war or famine. The places that don't have problems are using their natural resources at an alarming rate, or are using so many chemicals that they are poisoning the earth around them – whether that be through mining, fracking, or other pillage of the earth's inherent gifts. The climate is changing, the polar ice caps are melting, and the sea has risen enough that some Pacific Islanders no longer have land to live on. The Pacific Ocean is filled with trash and radiation from the tsunami in Japan and the Fukushima melt-down. There are deep sea creatures washing up in the Philippines, and there are massive species die-off all over the world. Isolated, each of these events is perhaps solvable, but together the odds against fixing what we have caused seems insurmountable. Worse, under some administrations, there is some talk, but often very little action, and in other administrations, there is no talk and no action," I said.

"I sometimes feel that the powers of government that have the greatest ability to create change are talking about how to put out a fire when they are standing in a room which is completely engulfed in flames. There is this idea that anyone could walk out of this room at any time, but all at the table know that the room is already surrounded. So, the only real discussion is: if one power does not participate, will the rest inadvertently save the ones who don't come to the table, or will every power just choose to perish rather than negotiate? What are the powers negotiating for? How much money and political clout they will burn, but, we just heard that these same egotistical drives have doomed man for many civilizations. Additionally, if one has been even paying a scant bit of attention in the world, one knows that the money or paper currency we all use actually has no real value. Money is a concept that is manipulated by banks and governments as a way to leverage real goods and services in exchange for a piece of paper whose value depends on the international consensus of what a dollar is worth.

"So, to answer your question, Thomas, I think that the fauns actually were overly generous with their projections and predictions. My very simple perception of what is going on in world politics is, by and large, that the people have lost hope that the established politicians can lead them and accomplish things for all people, not just the few or the one percent. The politicians have used up their collective good will that was presented to them by the people, and one day, in the nearish future, the people will rise up to take back that hope. Then the world will burn, and the cities will be in chaos. After that purge, perhaps the light will reestablish itself, but the more plausible thing is that we will be back in the dark ages."

By the time I was done ranting we had walked up to the porch, and Thomas let Helen out while he went inside to warm up the coffee. I heard three ice cubes drop in a shaker, quite a few glugs of bourbon going into a shaker with a drip of mix, and the sucking pop of a top coming off a maraschino cherry jar. There was a quick shake and Thomas came outside with his Manhattan in a large rocks glass.

"Coffee will be just a couple of minutes," he said. "Roland, if it is as bad as both you and the fauns make it sound, why even try? Why not just keep consuming, use those around us, and only take care of our own? Why treat people? Why help people we don't know? Why take care of the sick and poor, if the world is just going to crash around us? Why not just go ahead and let the darkness consume this world and us with it?"

"Because, Thomas, our choices have consequences. In the most selfish aspect, the choices we make are marked on the personal ledger of our soul, and in some incarnation, whether this one or another, that ledger has to be balanced. The more we do simply for personal gain at the expense of those who are suffering, whether they be human, animal, vegetable, or mineral, the more we, too, will have to suffer. Every action has a reaction. Nothing acts in isolation. Our choices have consequences, and by attempting to make the best choices, the hope is that our actions create a reaction in someone that causes them to also want to create a positive action, and similarly, a positive reaction in someone else. This is what is called doing good."

"Enough people doing good can change the world, but someone has to let go of their fear long enough to give the first hug, or pay the first compliment, or treat the first person well. Someone has to buck the dark trend and plant the seed in others, so that they, too, can buck the trend.

"Life is a series of relationships. We can aspire to simply change the lives of the people around us for the better without manipulation or other power-over strategy. When we can each be a beacon of light for those who choose to want to see the light for themselves, then the world will change. Truthfully, that is all we can do for others, besides making the best decisions that we can, and trying to mitigate the causing of as much pain, anger, hate, and suffering in the people who relate with us. We cannot let go of our hope and faith for something better.

"When we lose the ability to hope for something better, then a little piece of us dies, too, and that is the place where the darkness worms in. Every action has a reaction, and that reaction is often one of unintended consequences. Therefore, only through hope can we ever survive unscathed by the chaos around us. Only through bringing more light, love, and joy can we outshine and change these possibilities. In many ways we have to learn to live outside of the social construct, meaning that, because authority says something is true, does not mean that it is. At this time, we have to come to our own conclusions, and decide what feels right to us now. Listen to our small voices within our heart, and hear whether our heart agrees with what is going on around us. Then work on shining as much light as we can muster to be the beacon for others. Thomas, you do this by growing and crafting the best organic herbs that you can. Would you want to create a lower-grade product if you could make more money?"

"No," he said.

"Why is that?"

"Because my herbs help people, and sometimes do more for them than their Western prescriptions can," he said.

"Exactly, because the product that you create is done for the light, not for the money. The herbs live through you, and you live through the herbs. You literally grow things that store the light, and are selling them in their purest form, so that your customers can receive the light from the most direct and purest source as possible. This is why the fauns picked you, because you are turning the tide, one herb at a time. Would you want it to be any different than that?" I said.

"No."

"All that the rest of us can do is emulate you and dispense as much light as we can, in the places that society needs it most, without attempting to manipulate or control. This is the best that we all can do."

Thomas looked at me and said, "When you put it that way, I think I can see my way through," and then he smiled.

"I know you can, Thomas," I said smiling back at him.

"How much do I owe you?" Thomas said.

"Nothing," I said with a chuckle. "Seeing a faun in person was payment enough."

"I am glad you were by my side," Thomas said.

"Always, Thomas, always," I said.

"Cheers," he said.

I got back in my SUV and negotiated my way back the way I had come. The fir and pine trees whizzed by as I turned back to Interstate 84, and I thought about this rare experience. Seeing a faun, let alone two fauns, was the equivalent of hitting the fairy lottery. While the faun's message was ominous, it was also heartening to know that the other players for the light were out there and watching over us.

Chapter 4
Continuation of The First Law

As I drove back from Corbett, in my mind, I walked into the memory of my past. It was 1994, and I was attending the University of Puget Sound (UPS) in Tacoma, Washington. College life was fairly routine. On the week days I would get up at 4 a.m., put on sweats, a T-shirt, and a sweatshirt, and jog from where I lived on one side of Union Avenue, through the Thompson parking lot and the massive Doug fir trees that are the hallmark of the UPS campus. Down past the A-frames that held the security office and a few small dorm units, I would take a right at the massive field, where college kids would play pick-up Ultimate Frisbee. A quick few minutes later, I would arrive at the small Warriner athletic facility to meet my teammates.

I was on crew, you see, and the best time to row was in the early morning. In these two hours before dawn, the whole world is quiet, and if there is wind, it is a mild breeze. We would get into the cars and carpool down to American Lake on the Fort Lewis Army base. At the boathouse, we would take our Pocock shell off its rack, and as a team carry it down to the dock and put it in the water. This was not the mere launching of a paper boat, but a concerted effort of eight men, at their peak physical strength, slowly and carefully placing a thousand-pound boat in the water. We made it look easy, but nowadays, I would think it was anything but that.

Then we would carefully get in the boat, push off from the deck, and follow our number-one seat (the stroke) as he set the time for the rhythm of our strokes. We paddled out of the small lagoon where the boat house was located and began our practice. If you have rowed in the dawn hours, you will know my words. In unison, we would pull our oars, and in each measured stroke was the creak of the oars, the rolling of the seat of the slide, and the slight splash of the oar dipping into the water. The boat would surge forward as we pulled our oars; then there would be another small water sound as the oars slid out of the water at the end of the stroke. We "feathered" or flattened our oars, so as to not catch the water on the next stroke. This rhythm was the rhythm of my mornings, and was surrounded by the greater rhythm of a lake waking up with the gurgling croak of herons, the chattering cry of the kingfisher, and the occasional plop of a fish breaking the surface of the water. Best of all was the sun, which came up directly behind Mount Rainier and cast the mountain's shadow on the lake with the sun's glorious brilliance all around it. It is a sight that all people should witness once, and we were enriched with its sight most mornings, rowing in the shadow of a giant.

After practice came the team breakfast, which was always a raucous affair in the Rotunda, with many plates of food. Then I would head home for a shower, more comfy clothes, and my pack full of books. Ah, college, such a relaxed existence. Think what life would be like if all we did was exercise and learn. It would be very much like the way the nobility were purported to live in Rome. After class, I'd head back to Warriner gym for land workout, rowing on an erg, or down to Stadium High School to run bowls. A bowl was considered to be all of the steps in the stadium. "Multiple bowls" meant running all of the steps in the stadium multiple times. We also ran hills on North 30th Street. North 30th is a massive hill that climbs 250 feet in elevation in just half a mile. By the second or third hill in the workout, the sweat that streamed down my body felt like it was coming from a bubbling spring.

After land workout, sometimes there would be a pick-up Ultimate Frisbee game to play, then dinner, then back home to study. It was a life of little responsibility, lots of exercise, and a sense of fulfillment in completing of what was in front of me.

I was majoring in writing, and sometimes we were assigned to collaborative projects. On assignment of a project, we would have to pick our partner, and meet to do our combined work. For this particular assignment Franklin and I chose each other, as we happened to be sitting next to each other. Franklin was one of the few African American students on campus, and he was always cool, suave, and impeccably dressed, which was rare for the general college student. He also had a great sense of humor. I can't recall now what this assignment was about, but assuredly the professor thought that working together would give us more of a sense of what collaborating in the real world would be like. Perhaps that is what it did, but more often I found team projects to be grand affairs of swapping stories but little writing.

We picked a time, and met outside my house. We agreed to drive down to Café WA, which was down 6th Street a few blocks past the famous E-9 pub. Café WA had ceramic coffee cups and you could buy a refillable cup of coffee for a dollar, so it was a favorite with the UPS students. Franklin and I each ordered our dollar cup of joe, doctoring our coffee to our needs. I took mine with lots of cream, no sugar, and Franklin took his with two cubes of sugar, and a little bit of cream. We found a table, opened our books and notebooks, and began. It is hard now to remember a day when I didn't have a laptop computer at my side, but college was just such a time. Laptops had yet to be invented, while the internet and email were barely out of the womb. I had graduated from the Apple 2e, but the desktop Apple computer I owned really was not much better. I believe it had a hard drive with a mere 256K of ram, and basically was for word processing only. It was way too clunky to carry to a coffee shop, so pens and notebooks were what we used. There will come a day when kids won't even know how to write with a pen or pencil, it will seem that antiquated.

We sat there for hours, scribbling notes and really trying to put at least a half a heart (between us) into the project. More so, though, I learned about Franklin. How his parents owned an ice cream chain on the East Coast. How he also enjoyed photography, like I did, and how one of his favorite places to be was in the woods. We shared a love for Native American craft, we both believed in ghosts, and each of us had a few ghost stories to tell. As you might see, the night quickly devolved into getting terribly caffeinated and telling stories. In hindsight, perhaps this was the real object of the lesson, to get to know one of your peers better. And truthfully, the ability to get to know anyone is the skill that has served me most of my life, over any perceived skills I learned as an undergrad.

Sooner than later, 10 p.m. rolled around, and we both agreed we had to call it a night. Not because we were tired, but mainly because we hadn't achieved anything meaningful on the assignment, and neither of us could drink another glug of coffee (the bathroom breaks were actually getting a little ridiculous). We left and climbed into my big white K5 Blazer. It's odd to think that for more than half of my life, I have been a Chevy Blazer man, but who am I to argue when these SUVs keep finding their way into my life? The white K5 was a rough ride with manual steering and locking hubcaps for the four-wheel drive. Reminiscing about the good old days often seems to be a lot of thought about the days before technology made things better. Hopefully, dear reader, in your lifetime, you will not be reminiscing about the good old days when people were 100% human and not part cyborgs, like in *Ghost in the Machine*. The rate at which technology is growing is terrifying. In my grandmother's childhood, she rode in a horse-drawn carriage, and by the time she died, she had seen men go to the moon, cars reach 200 miles per hour, and ordinary people travel by airplane. What will it be like for the current generation of twenty-somethings by the time they are ready to die? Wherever technology is by then, it probably would blow the mind of someone like me.

So, the 1975 K5 Blazer, she kind of ambled down the road. She didn't go fast, even though she had a small block 400 as her engine. She didn't drive very straight, even though her alignment was perfect. She was old and stubborn, and this was her nature, take her or leave her. As we bumbled along, Franklin and I continued the conversation we were having as we left Café WA.

"Have you ever seen a ghost?" Franklin said.

"No. How about you?"

"I have seen a couple. They are relatively common on the East Coast," he said.

"Yeah?"

"Yeah. When I was a kid, I used to wake up to an old man at the foot of my bed," he said.

"What would he do?"

"He would stand there, with his hand on my footboard, and look at me. He never approached me, and never said anything to me," he said.

"Didn't that freak you out?"

"Yeah, the first time, but he came every night for a few years. After the first few times, I almost didn't even notice him. It was like he was my imaginary friend or something," he said.

"Could your parents see it?"

"No. In fact, the first time he appeared, I screamed, and my dad came in the room, and walked right through the old man. Neither seemed at all phased by this, but it was something to see," he said.

"Who do you think he was?"

"No idea. He did stop coming when I was seven though. He would just watch me fall asleep," he said.

"That is so odd."

"Have you ever felt like something was watching you, but you couldn't see it?" he said.

"I have," I said.

"Well, let's hear it."

Chapter 4

"It's just a weird story…. You know, I don't know whether it was real, or whether I imagined it," I said.

"And … ?" Franklin said.

"Well, when I was a kid, my parents decided to move neighborhoods. They found a nice house in a good neighborhood in Southeast Portland, and they made an offer on it. The woman selling the house had recently divorced her husband. She had caught him cheating on her with a neighbor down the street. She had received the house in the divorce, and it was her ticket to the financial end of her settlement. The woman had sold the house to my parents, but they had not finalized the sale, like it was in escrow or something like that, and then one day they received a call saying that she had committed suicide in a hotel by drinking alcohol and taking sleeping pills. The sale stalled. As she hadn't updated her will, the house fell back in the possession of her cheating husband. My parents ended up having to pay more to buy the house from him because he didn't agree to the sale that had been set up with his ex-wife. He was a general contractor, and he left parts of the house in various states of repair. I couldn't really say whether the house had been like that when the wife had it, or whether the ex-husband ripped up the house after she died. Needless to say, from the day we moved in, it never really felt like our house, it always felt like her house," I said.

"The house was a three-story Tudor, and my brother and I lived on the east and west sides of the south-side top floor of the house. My parents also had a bedroom on the south side of the house. At the right of the top-floor stairs was a door. This door led to the north side of the house on the top floor, and it was a huge unfinished master bedroom. This was where I felt like the ghost lived. I can't say why I thought she came back to the house after killing herself somewhere else, but I just felt like I could feel her there. Oddly, the whole time we lived in that house, almost fifteen years in total, my parents never finished that bedroom. It's almost like they knew there was a ghost that lived in that room. We didn't play in there, we didn't even open the door. The only person who went in there was my mother. Occasionally, I would hear odd sounds from that room, and I always felt like I was being watched."

"OK. I told you. That's odd, right?" I said.

"Not terribly. So you never saw anything?" he said.

"No."

"Boring," he said.

It was only a mile or so from Café WA to the UPS campus, and my story had exhausted that distance. I parked on Washington between 14th and 15th streets.

"Mind if I smoke?" Franklin asked.

"No. Go ahead."

He pulled out a pouch of tobacco and a paper, carefully rolled the tobacco in the paper, then licked it and lit the cigarette. We sat there in silence. Franklin smoked and I looked out the windshield. I was looking down your average street in your average residential neighborhood. The road was straight and flat, and there were houses going down both sides of the street. There was nothing special about this street, and it was part of a whole series of streets that really were nothing different than you would see in any other city. I had parked on the east side of Washington with the front of the car pointing north. The car was a little closer to the 15th than 14th Street. There there was a streetlight on the southwest corner. The streetlight cast a circle of light into the middle of the street, and either side of that circle was in shadow.

Franklin finished his cigarette, cranked down the window, and threw it out. Now, to be clear, from my vantage point in the driver's seat, I had a 180-degree view of everything in front of me. So, when I saw a little bit of movement step into the circle of light, when I had not seen anything walk into the shadow, I can tell you that I was surprised and attentive. What I saw materialize out of that shadow was probably the scariest thing I had ever seen up to that point in my life. Out of the darkness, a being slid into the light. It was completely black, as in the absence of color, but with red eyes. It had one arm in front of it, fist clenched, and the arm was bent at a 90-degree angle with the shoulder. The other arm, also clenching a fist, was at a 90-degree angle from the other shoulder. The front and back legs were also bent at 90-degree angles from the hips. Imagine taking a still photo of someone running down the street, and you will get the basic posture. This thing's arms and legs did not move, they simply stayed in this position, yet it slid out of the darkness in an upright position, slid across the light, and into the darkness. It appeared to be on its way somewhere, and it did not appear to be aware of us at the moment it crossed the street.

I think my jaw dropped open. It's one thing to swap stories, and a whole separate thing to create them. I looked at Franklin in disbelief, and said, "Did you see that?"

"Yeah," he said.

Fear gripped me. My heart was beating rapidly, and I had that shaky feeling that comes with adrenalin, which is actually amazing after the amount of coffee we had consumed. If I had been standing, my knees would have been weak. Franklin was also speechless; all casual banter simply evaporated in a split second. Then, in the rear view mirror, I saw the same black head and red eyes looking into the car from behind us.

"Oh, shit!" I said.

"What!?" Franklin said.

"It's behind us! And it is looking at us!"

"Shit!" he said.

I would look in the mirror, I would see it, human eyes meeting red supernatural eyes, and when our eyes would meet, it would duck down so I couldn't see it. When I would look away, it would pop its head back up to look in the window above the tailgate. Maybe this is why God invented tinted glass, so that you can't see anything darker than the tint, I thought with a mixture of terror and objectivity.

"What do we do?" I asked.

"I don't know."

"Stay? Go outside? If this thing is not physical, it doesn't seem like the car offers us much protection," I said.

"Shit," Franklin said again.

My spidey senses were tingling as we talked. I had the same sensation as what I had come to expect when I felt imminent danger. The sense was telling me that if we stayed something was going to happen, and it wasn't going to be good.

"I'm out, man! I think we should make a run for home, and be in the light with other people," I said.

"Yeah. Yeah. OK," he said.

"Count of three, and don't forget to lock the door, because I am not coming back out here," I said.

"OK," he said.

"One, two, three … !" I counted.

We both shoved open our doors and ran as fast as we could to our houses. I banged on the door of my house while I fumbled with my keys. Before I found the right key, someone opened the door, and I stumbled past them into the bright foyer of my house.

It's a funny thing about shared experiences. Franklin and I never talked about what we had seen that night, and for a year when I went out at night, I dreaded that I would see this thing again. I never did see another one, but the story doesn't end there.

During my junior year, my English professor Tim Hansen, who knew of my interest in Native American culture and practices, told me that he wanted to introduce me to someone. I trusted old man Hansen – he had a keen sense of observation, a bright intellect, a love for the outdoors, and a love of teaching young minds how to see through their own writing and other people's writing. He had been teaching at UPS since the sixties and had seen thousands of students come and go. If he had an insight about anyone he thought I should meet, then I was there.

Tim and I went to a Starbucks in South Tacoma to meet George Walker, the "Sandman". George was a Vietnam veteran and worked as a clinical psychologist at the American Lake veteran center. He worked with vets, helping them with the trauma and the post-traumatic stress disorder (PTSD) that they had experienced while fighting in the war. He was called Sandman, because his specialty was in working with dreams and using "sand play" to help his patients recreate and work out their dreams using action figures and figurines in a sand tray. By recreating a dream in this way, the patient can hold on to something tangible, and it helps them to make sense of the dream, and the hidden meaning of their unconscious.

In my opinion, the same concepts of sand play can be observed when watching children play with their toys. All one has to ask is, what are they doing with the toys, and how are they using them against each other, then asking, does this have deeper meaning? For instance, if my child beats every toy he plays with into submission, and breaks toys as soon as he gets them, could this not be reflect an inner tension between me and my partner? These are the kinds of ways sand play can be used in observing children. Usually adults are a bit more refined with their sand play, but it is food for thought. Now, the only "ologist" I am is a demonologist; however, my main element of study is to look for patterns. Children bear the silent wounds of their parents, silent wounds fester to become symptoms, and symptoms grow over years and years to become disease. At any point in this process, the wound the child suffers because of their parent's behavior can become an access point for an entity or demon. Because we suffer these silent wounds at such a young and impressionable age, we cannot remember the wound itself, or where it came from, and that makes healing from the symptom or disease process ever so much harder.

My meeting with George was the beginning of a long friendship and mentorship. I have been blessed to be taken under the wing of a number of older people, and given the gift of being able to listen to their accumulated wisdom. Our generation now thinks that the internet and Google know all things, but these cannot replace the human transmission from one generation of wisdom keepers to the next. Go befriend a person who is twenty years older than you, and you will be surprised what they know, I promise you.

George had been following the Red Road[2] for a number of years, he had a number of Native American contacts in the veteran community, and he also used his understandings of the Red Road to work with veterans. Tim Hansen knew about George's interest in Native studies, and this was the main reason why he introduced us, but what Tim didn't know was that George would show me the beginning of a number of paths, as if he had already cleared the brush from the trail and was showing me a way that was now traversable. I could not have asked for a better mentor. The rest of my junior year and all of my senior year of college, every two weeks I would meet with George to have dinner or coffee, or attend a sweat lodge. Sometimes medicine men would come and officiate at the sweat lodge, and sometimes it would be George and a few other vets doing the officiating. George would often invite me to powwows and lodges that he had been invited to. We became close, not just as mentor and student, but also as two people who had similar interests at that stage of life. I made a number of connections from knowing George, and I will share some of those stories, but later.

---

2. The Red Road is a general term for Native American spirituality. Each tribe has its own traditions, and this term is similar to referring to people who believe in Jesus Christ – as Christians, even though we know there are many denominations of Christianity. The basics tenets of the Red Road are that one should respect oneself, respect others, respect creation, and worship the Creator.

One weekend, George took me with him to a sweat lodge and ceremony on the Warm Springs Reservation in Oregon. There, one of the local medicine men, Jon Running Deer, was officiating a ceremony for veterans. It was a mellow affair, filled with talks by different speakers, meals in a common mess hall, camping, and participating in sweat lodge ceremonies. Jon Running Deer was old. His tribe had never reached a treaty agreement with the United States government, and he had lived around Tacoma for years, but on retiring he wanted to be in a place where he had real community. So he moved to Warm Springs, and for the most part, he seemed accepted as one of their own.

One night, we had sat in the sweat lodge for a couple of rounds, and at a break some of the older Native men were standing near a creek getting ready for a cold plunge. The Native guys were talking quietly and nonchalantly before they individually strode out into the creek. Comparatively, the Caucasian guys seemed to have to get a little more psyched up to jump in the cold water.

I walked over to Jon Running Deer, and he said, "Are you going to give the stream a try?"

"No. I don't like cold water much."

"It is good for the blood after sweating. I think it would be good for you," he said.

When a medicine man tells you something would be good for you, at that point do you really have a choice? I walked into the stream up to my knees and then as quickly as I could, I lay down and stood back up. After a minute, I got out of the water, toweled off, and stood there shivering a bit. Just upstream, Jon was lying face down in the water. Then he rolled over and lay on his back. I followed his eyes upward and could see the utter blackness of the sky with the brilliant stars peeking through. Jon lay there, looking at the stars in the cold running creek for a good five minutes. I was in my early twenties, he was in his eighties, and it was quite apparent who was tougher. Jon walked out of the creek, toweled off, and appeared to glow from somewhere deep inside of him.

When he was dry, I said, "May I ask you a question?"

He looked at me and nodded.

"About six months ago, I was in my car with another guy, and I saw this thing slide across the street from one pool of shadow, through a pool of light, and then back into darkness. It was all black, had red eyes, and seemed stuck in this position." I mimed the running man position. "Do you know what it is?" I said.

Chapter 4

Jon gave me a long, slow, steady, measuring gaze, looking directly into my eyes. It was not going to be the last time an elder Native man gave me that look, like he was weighing my soul. After a minute or so, he said, "We call it a nightstalker."

"What is it?" I asked.

"First, we don't talk about them, especially at night. It is their time, and just speaking of them can draw them to you," he said.

"OK."

"We believe that they are shades. Part wolf, part man, or something else. They are not natural, they don't belong here, and they are evil. They are not something that you want being aware of you," he said.

"If they have seen you, what do you do?"

"For you, youngster, I would say go to some place full of light and people," he said.

"OK."

"Our tradition says that thinking of them draws them. But they are also attracted to whistling in the forest, as this is how they communicate with each other. That is all I have to say now. Back into the lodge and we will give you a blessing, so that you don't see another one again soon."

"OK," I said.

We crawled back into the lodge and found our spots in the dark. The fire keepers put more rocks on the fire, and Jon placed some sage on the rocks, then some sweet grass, then a little tobacco. We sat there for the rest of the round, and after a bit, Jon lit his ceremonial pipe. He thanked everyone for coming and attending the ceremony, then took a few puffs of the pipe, and passed it.

"Please feel free to give thanks or offer prayers," he said.

The pipe passed from person to person. Some people prayed for friends and neighbors, some for themselves, some just puffed a couple of times and passed the pipe, praying silently. I was one of these. When the pipe reached Jon again, he said, "Creator, the earth is suffering. Mankind has not been good stewards for this planet. Please give us all the ability to be better, to act better, to think better, and understand better. It is through your wisdom and grace that we can help our mother the Earth. *Aho!*"

We sat there for a few more minutes drawing in the heat. Then the flap was opened and we crawled out of the lodge. The fire that had housed the rocks crackled in the stillness of the night, the stars twinkled, and the air smelled of Ponderosa pine, sagebrush, and smoke. We walked back to our respective sleeping areas in silence, and as I bedded down, I thought that not only had I learned something more than I had known before, but perhaps in some small way, I had gained a little of this old medicine man's trust. You can never have too many people holding you in their prayers.

Now, I wish this were the end of the *night stalker* story, but there is one more story to tell. A year after I graduated from college, I was trying to figure out what I wanted to do with my life. I had trained with a few noteworthy teachers, but none of them felt like my master. They were people who could possibly illuminate the light on the road for the next bend, but they didn't have or weren't sharing enough light to see that the road I was on, was my road. Even though we may have our own experiences while we are young, it seems like the twenties are about running with the herd. Most of us are not worldly enough or experienced enough to know yet what we want to do, or to differentiate ourselves except in polarity to our peers. Subtlety and nuance seem to come with experience of life. Our dreams sometimes have to implode a few times before we learn that life has many shades of color to it – that it isn't all black or white, or primary colors.

In many ways, I think that the teachers I studied with understood this idea. That as a young man, I was looking for hard facts and experiences, while as older people, they knew that there was more to life, and that clearly defined edges were the exception and not the norm. For our respective ages, we played our parts well. You see, had they given me more direction, I would have been inclined to follow their direction, and to some extent this would have been done at the cost of my free will. By having to learn lessons the hard way, I built character, resilience, and strength. None of these characteristics can be given to us, but have to be found. A good teacher or mentor simply shows you that there is a path, that the path can be illuminated, and that there are potholes in every decision and path, but that with care these can be avoided. A good spiritual teacher can neither choose your path nor as Kris Kringle in the animated Christmas special alluded to in *Santa Claus is Comin' to Town*: That to go anywhere you have to take the first step. After the first step you have to take another step. This is to say that only I can shuffle my own feet down that path.

Chapter 4

To sum up, I was experiencing some twenty-something-year-old angst. After I moved back to Portland, I tried to keep to the morning ritual of working out in the pre-dawn hours, but beyond being fit, there was no overarching purpose to it. When one is competing, there is a drive to push oneself to be stronger and faster, but without the motivation of a team or races, well, workouts became sporadic.

My brother Adam had been training to be a paramedic, and he needed to be in good shape for that work. So one day, he called me and said, "Hey man! Do you want to start running in the morning?"

In my younger years, my brother and I had never been particularly close, so I was happy to have him reach out to do an activity that could benefit us both.

"Sure. What time are you thinking?" I said.

"Like 5 a.m."

"How often?" I said, "Daily?"

"Nah, like twice a week?" he said.

"Sure, I could do that. When do you want to start?"

"How about Friday?" he said.

"OK. Meet at the track at Reed College, Friday at 5 a.m.?"

"Yep. Yep."

"Cool. See you there," I said.

I was no longer in prime crew shape, but I could still run a few miles without putting much effort into it. Obviously, I hadn't started smoking at this point in my life. Friday morning came and my alarm went off like in the old days. I rolled out of bed, put on sweats and a hoodie, and jogged the few blocks to the track at Reed College. My brother was not there, so I took a lap around the track, then sat down to stretch.

Of most of the exercise regimes one can do, I think stretching is by far one of the most important. As we age, our flexibility can save us from all sorts of problems. Being limber can save us from sprains and strains when we fall, keep us from damaging tendons when we misstep and roll our ankle, help prevent back problems, etc. It is something most people don't do enough of, yet it is something we can do all of our lives. I am a stretch-before-and-after-workout guy. Or, if not working out, then stretching on waking and before going to bed. In my life, I have met a lot of inflexible people, and I always think to myself, "This person could do with more stretching!"

I was about ten minutes into my stretching when my brother jogged up, panting.

"Hey," he said.

"Hey."

Now admittedly, he had come about five blocks further than I had, but if he was already panting, it was clear this workout was going to be more for him than it was going to be for me.

"Do you want to stretch?" I said.

"Nah, I'm warmed up."

"OK. How far do you want to go?" I asked.

"Let's do a few laps, then see."

"OK," I said.

We started out at a slowish pace. Watching tall people run is like watching a boulder carom down the face of a mountain. Their movements tend to be a bit herky-jerky without much grace, and they are always loud. We have big feet, and big bodies, and together these combine to sound a lot like the clack-clacking of a freight train rolling by. We found our stride together and did a couple of laps. After a while, Adam was ready to stop. We walked a couple of laps, and then I sat down to stretch. He looked at me and said, "Again?"

"Yep."

Chapter 4

"Fine."

I started with a simple stretch with legs wide, toes pointed towards the sky, torso vertical, then stretched my right arm towards my right leg, while leaning towards the right foot. Hold this for six breaths. Lean with the left arm stretched towards the left foot. Hold for six breaths. Adam followed my lead, and as we stretched, we chatted.

"Mom says that you can see things now?" he said.

"Well, I wouldn't actually call it seeing things, but yeah, I have seen a few things."

"Can you teach me?" he said.

Without changing position of the legs, both hands stretched towards the right foot, hold for six breaths. Both hands stretched towards the left foot, hold for six breaths. Feet and legs together directly in front of the torso, both hands stretched towards both feet, hold for six breaths.

"I don't know if it is teachable, per se, but I can explain what I do, I guess," I said.

Change position so that the right foot is behind the body at a 90-degree angle, knee and ankle flat to the ground, left leg straight in front of the torso, both arms stretched towards the left leg. Hold for six breaths. Left foot behind the body at a 90-degree angle, knee and ankle flat to the ground, right leg straight in front of the torso, both arms stretched towards the right leg. Hold for six breaths.

"Do you want to come over for breakfast?" he said as he held the stretch.

"Sure."

Change position so that both knees are out to the side, soles of the feet together, heels as close to the perineum as possible. The elbows of both arms apply downward pressure on the knees in an attempt to push the knees flat to touch the ground. Hold for six breaths. "We can walk through the gully on the way back to your house, by the outdoor pool, where the stream is. There, we can see if there is anything to see," I said.

"OK."

Change position so that the right leg is crossed over the left leg. The sole of the right foot is flat on the ground near the thigh, the kneecap points up towards the sky. The left leg is straight in front of the torso, and all parts of the posterior surface of the left leg touch the earth. Rotate right, using the left elbow against the right knee to provide additional torque to the twist. Hold for six breaths. Then reverse so that the right leg is straight in front of the torso, and all parts of the posterior surface of the right leg touch the earth. The left leg crosses over the right thigh, sole of the left foot on the ground. The right elbow presses against the left knee to create torque. Hold for six breaths.

"I have been down in the gully a couple of times recently. It is hit or miss. Sometimes there are things to see, sometimes not. Sometimes the energy down there is benign, sometimes it is downright creepy. We will see what today brings," I said.

"OK."

Change position, tuck the left leg under the right leg, so that the sole of the left foot points behind the torso and the right kneecap points to heaven; repeat the twist as described above. Hold for six breaths. Tuck the right leg under the left leg, so that the sole of the right foot points behind the torso, and the left kneecap points to heaven; repeat the twist as described above.

"I don't know how you are flexible enough to do half of this routine. It hurts me to put the soles of my feet together and try to pull them close to my perineum," Adam said.

"Practice and regular stretching before and after a workout. Anybody can be flexible, just like anyone can be strong, or good at anything. It just takes practice and initiative," I said.

"Well, I guess I am both out of practice, and hungry. Shall we head out?" Adam said.

"Certainly."

We stood up, Adam filled his water bottle in the primitive water fountain, and we walked north on the track towards the Art Theater. As we walked, I said, "Are you sure that you want me to explain this? The thing about seeing is that once you can see, I don't think you can unsee. In my experiences, few that they have been, I don't think that you get to choose. Meaning, that if you can see good, you can also see evil. This might open your mind to seeing things that are unpleasant, or downright terrifying."

"It's OK. I can handle it," he said.

"Your choice."

"I'm good," he said.

We took a right at the Art Theater and started walking on the road towards the swimming pool heading east.

"Do you remember those Tom Brown, Jr. books we used to read as kids?" I said.

"Yeah."

"Well his method is probably the easiest to begin with. He calls it 'wide-angle-vision.' The method is relatively simple," I said.

We had crested the small hill and were almost to the steps that led down the gully and the outdoor pool. At the foot of the steps, I held out my arms in a flat plane from my body. In this position, my body formed a cross, arms out to either side, feet planted on the ground.

"If I hold my hands out like this, I should try to get them to a place where, with the palms forward, as in in-line with my body, that I can look forward and just barely see my fingers wiggle," I said.

Adam copied my position.

"Can you see how, out of the corner of both eyes, when you wiggle your fingers, you can just see their movement?" I said.

"Yeah."

"This does something to your eyes and hence your brain. The trick is to hold a straight forward gaze, while being able to see your wiggling fingers," I said.

"OK."

"Now, put down your arms, and try to maintain that way of seeing. The thing about people is that our eyes are set forward. This is an anatomical trait of a carnivore. Herbivores in comparison, have eyes that are set to the side of their heads. This means that when we are intent on something, we look directly at it – focused. But the spirit world does not like to be seen per se. When we put our focus [our yang, as I was later to learn] on something that is intangible, then we cannot perceive it. However, when we look at it from a place where our vision is diffuse, and not focused, then we can see things. Does that make sense?" I said.

"Maybe?" Adam said.

"Let me put this a different way. If we think of our focus as street lamps on a street, we realize quickly that light inherently creates shadow, where our focus is the spotlight of the street lamp, but the street lamps are separated in regular interspaces; therefore, there is a lot of space between the street lights that is in shadow or darkness. We generally can't see into this darkness, so we don't pay too much attention to these areas. However, if we shine our focus on these areas, it simply moves the darkness to the areas around the place where we have focused. Make sense so far?"

"Yeah," he said.

"In these areas of darkness, which we register but don't apply our focus to, there are things that are happening here which we could say are 'out of focus.' Would you agree?"

"OK," he said.

"It is in these places that are out of focus where the real spiritual world is happening. Meaning the things that we cannot generally see, but that are inherent to this world with or without us. This is not too different to many quantum physics experiments, where it has been acknowledged that when the scientist focuses on the experiment with a certain expectation, it changes the results of the experiment," I said.

"OK," he said.

We trotted down the stairs, nature on the west side and a cinder block wall on the east side. It was no more than seventy regular shaped steps. At the bottom, we headed to a small bridge that crossed a small creek. The wooden bridge was no longer than five feet across, made of railroad ties, and covered with stray bits of gravel from the pathways that led to and from it. The stream was about four feet across here, with random round stones in its bed. Horsetail grew along its banks, and there was the general stink of moisture, damp earth, and sludge. Without the stream, this would have been a big pond, but the stream also came from an area of Reed College that was a natural swamp. The area had that same swamp smell of decay and stagnancy. Near the edge of the bridge, on the southwest side, was an area of grass that was slightly wet from the night's dew. I went there and sat, motioning Adam to join me.

"In this visual area, which is not what you are focusing on, is where you will see the movement of what is called the supernatural. This area that your brain registers, but does not focus on, is the area in which other things that live here, live. They are beyond perception for those who simply focus on one thing, then the next thing, then the next thing, then the next thing, etc. If you use 'wide-angle-vision' or a diffuse focus, where the purpose of seeing is not to home in on any one thing, then you will be able to see more than you normally see," I said.

"OK, I think I understand."

"Diffuse your vision. Look at the trees to the north there, and tell me what you see," I said.

"The trees glow. There is a white aura coming from them," he said.

"You suck," I said. "Do you know how long I had to practice this before I could see anything at all?"

"There are spheres in the trees that glow, but they are various shades of gray," he said.

Adam, it appeared, was a natural. I had to change the way my brain worked. He simply had to have it explained to him once. Sometimes the Creator makes me really annoyed, and this was one of those times.

"In my opinion, what you are seeing are the bird spirits and the spirits of other tree creatures. I see them too, but it took me awhile to get the hang of this," I said.

"Awesome!" he said. "What's next?"

"That's all I have to share at the moment, man. Keep practicing this, and you will see more and more, as you obviously are a natural," I said.

One can conjecture that those who see the world from the perspective of logic will likely have a harder time opening their mind to being able to see, while those who perceive the world from an artistic bent, be that visual or sensate, will likely be able to find the spiritual world easier to see. This really isn't rocket science, as those who see the world through logic will likely question that which they see, while those who are artistic already see the world through the lens of intuition. Therefore, artists are more likely to see the supernatural than those who use logic. This is not a question of belief, but merely a statement of how one has trained the mind. Adam had always been an artist, and I had always been a logistician. When I sat down and read a book from cover to cover in a relatively short time, this would irritate him to no end. The point I am making is that I really should not have been surprised to see him pick this up naturally.

We strolled up the gully towards the pool, then around the pool to the swamp. Here we made a left and headed up the gravel path towards Steele Street. In ten minutes, we were walking into his house. Adam took a pan down from a pot hanger, turned on the stove, and grabbed a dozen eggs out of the refrigerator.

"How hungry are you?" he said.

"I could do three. Do you have any toast?"

"Sure. Wheat or rye?" he said.

"Rye, please."

How do you like them cooked?" he said.

"Scrambled is fine."

Now some might wonder about the terseness of the conversation during the making of breakfast. The truth is that both Adam and I are men of few words. If there is something to say, we say it. If there is nothing to say, we are simply content around each other.

In our Western culture, I don't think there is enough thought put into the family bond. As our lives take their course, there are only a handful of people who get to see our metamorphosis through our lives, and those people are primarily our parents and our siblings. It is a given that we should have our parent's love, and while that doesn't always happen, we know that it should be this way. Our siblings, however, play a more dynamic role in our lives. We compete against them, fight with them, idolize them, support them, lie to them, cheat them, take care of them, and love them. They have the potential to be our greatest allies or our worst enemies. Often, all of these potentials are happening on an ongoing basis as we mature. In many ways, our siblings are the main people whom we polarize against in our early years, and because we define ourselves by being different from them, our siblings have the potential to be one of the defining parts of the personality that we become when we mature into adults. For most of us, our siblings will be there throughout the majority of our lives, and when no one else understands, our siblings will listen. For many sibling relationships, it seems that there is a continuum that starts in chaos and moves to greater stability as we age.

When comparing this sort of family dynamic to the family dynamic of other, more "tribal cultures," where family is paramount, what we see conversely to the Western or American family, is that individuals within the tribal structure tend to sacrifice their individuality to the needs of the greater family, such that what they want as individuals is less important than what the family wants for them or from them. In looking at these two dynamics, we see the dichotomy of the individual versus the collective. With this loss of individuality from a young age, while there isn't as much sibling antagonism, there is still a defining role that affects the personality that they carry as adults. That is, adults in "tribal cultures" then foster the role of the collective onto the next generation of children, just as adults in Western culture foster the role of the individual onto the next generation of children.

My brother passed me a plate of eggs and toast, and we sat in wooden chairs at the dining room table.

"What does seeing do for you, really?" he said.

"At this point in my progression, not much, actually."

"Does it help you with decision making?" he said.

"I think of it more as expanding my awareness. Sort of like when driving a car, being able to look left and right while you drive, rather than being fixed in a straight-forward position. In this way, it can help with decision making. This is just a small baby step into being part of a larger spiritual ecosystem, so I would expect that over time, being able to see will have other benefits," I said.

"OK."

"Do you want coffee?" he said.

"Sure. I will take a small cup."

Adam got up, put some water on the stove to boil, and took a bag of coffee beans out of the freezer. He measured out enough beans for two cups of coffee, then ground them in a small electric coffee grinder. He took out a glass French press, put the grounds in, and waited for the water to boil.

"How's your breakfast?" he asked.

"Good, as always," I said. My brother is quite an exceptional cook.

"Simple, but hits the spot, eh?"

"Yep. Good enough for me," I said.

"Why do you think that it took you until recently to be able to see? You would think that we would either have that ability or we wouldn't," he said.

"Good question, bro. I think that we are all born with the ability to see, and then it is essentially beaten out of us," I said.

"What do you mean by *beaten out of us*?"

"Well, Western society since all the way back into the ancient Greek times hasn't really been very appreciative of people who are different from the dominant group of society. We sort of behave as if we would like everyone to be the same with minor differences. The people who are different are, in a way, ostracized for their differences. We call these people all sorts of names: geeks, weird, strange, odd, etc. When people talk about their experiences with the mystical, society brands them as witches, warlocks, pagans, occultists, Satanists, etc. Most behave as if the mystical is outside of the natural order, rather than within it. The only place where it is reasonably OK to have mystical experiences is within the confines of religion, and even then it seems one's religious peers still regard and interact with the person who can see, as if they are odd."

Chapter 4

"After all, since the times when most myths and legends were composed, culture has essentially persecuted people who experienced life in a different way than the dominant paradigm. How many indigenous civilizations have been persecuted in the name of religion? We burned men and women at the stake in Europe, the British Isles, and then in the early United States because they heard voices, spoke to things that weren't visible, practiced herbalism, and practiced divination. One really must ask, how much of our true abilities and our ability to pass them on was lost by amputating part of human culture in the West?"

"If one thinks about it from this perspective, I think children learn from a very early age, that their parents would find it unacceptable if their child could perceive more of the natural world than the parents can. Have you ever noticed how infants always seem to be watching more than what is going on in the room? Or how two- or three-year-old kids, once they learn how to talk, will make odd comments like, "I remember when you weren't my mommy." Or, "When I was the mommy, I used to drink the red juice too." Where can these comments come from except memories of a life before this?" I continued.

"However, this kind of cognition, frankly, is at best uncomfortable for those parents who hear it, and at worst downright frightening. The parents become the main enforcers of denial. They tell the child that the child's perception certainly could not be so, just as many people told Galileo and Copernicus that the world must be flat. In other words, the dominant cultural paradigm of the day always believes that it is right, and the diverse or alternative ways of thinking are wrong. This idea of "rational order" allows those who don't experience life outside of the normal viewpoints to feel safe. Yet, simply teaching people that something does not exist neither proves a thing's nonexistence nor causes it not to exist."

"The reality is that if we take a hammer and hit a board enough times, eventually the board simply becomes fibers of wood. Keep hitting it and breaking it down, and eventually you can re-form it into paper or particle board. However, it will never be a board again, nor will it be a tree. This is what parents and schools do to children. In modern times, we call it turning people into 'productive members of society.' Now, don't get me wrong – there are good parents and education systems out there, and the truth is that we all have to work in order to eat and sleep these days, but you asked me about whether seeing was innate or not," I said.

Adam's eyes were glazing over a little bit.

"I know, bro, that was a bit more than you were looking for," I said.

The water was boiling, and he grabbed a hot pad and used it to hold the handle of the kettle while he poured hot water into the French press.

"OK, but you didn't answer why a person can initially see as a child, then lose the ability, but then see again. Why is that?" he said.

"This, I think, is both simple and complex. The simple answer is that we start to see again when we find ourselves again. The complex part is that rarely do we find ourselves again without seeking to find our self. People seem to do this by looking inward through meditation, martial arts, counseling, or any other form of study which makes us look at the strengths and weaknesses of our perceived ego, which we have created. This form of self-analysis does not always come because we set out to do so; sometimes it comes about because of our own suffering."

"Well, what about me, then? How come you can just explain it, and I can see it?" he said.

"Because you have an awesome teacher! No, just kidding. I think you can see so easily because for one reason or another your ability to see never fully shut off. I have met people who have always been able to see, who because of proper parenting, or pure stubbornness, or some other reason, refused to let their ability to see be shut off. For you, it could be because of your art, because you are visual, or because it has always been there providing you with information which your brain didn't process in a visual way. These are all guesses, really, and of course I can't scientifically prove any of this. I am only conjecturing based on the broad pattern of having talked to a number of people, and trying to make sense of their lives with the little amount of information they gave me," I said.

"So, what you are saying is that you don't know why some people see, and some people don't?" he said.

"No. I think what I have said is true, but there are always outliers and people who don't fit into the theory. This does not mean that I haven't found the basic premise that I just outlined to be generally true," I said.

Adam poured the coffee and handed me a mug. It was dark, earthy, and robust. It was good that we had the same taste in coffee.

Chapter 4

"Well, I have to start getting ready for work. If you want to hang out while I shower, I can give you a ride home," he said.

"Sure. I will drink my coffee and lounge in the living room," I said.

Adam took his mug of coffee and climbed the stairs to the bedroom. I could hear him walking back and forth as he got his work clothes together. Soon, I heard him turn on the shower.

I sipped my coffee for a bit, then set it down and reclined in one of his easy chairs. It was time for a little snooze. A few minutes later, Adam came down the stairs and said, "OK. Are you ready to go?"

"Yep," I said from mid-drowse.

We walked out the front door and hopped in his old Ford Bronco. Drove up the street past Trader Joe's on Schiller Street, and took a right on César E. Chávez Avenue (or as locals would say, 39th Avenue).

"What are you doing today?" he asked.

"I don't know yet. I might go to the woods or do some reading. It is hard to think too far ahead on the days I don't have to be at work until 11 p.m. I will probably just take it easy, then hit the coffee shop before I go in to work."

He drove down 39th to Woodstock Street and took a right at the light to head west down the hill towards Reed College. Then a left on SE 32nd Avenue, and a quick right onto SE Carlton Street. Then, straight west to the corner of 30th and Carlton, and I was home.

"Thanks man!" I said as I stepped out of the Bronco.

"Next Friday?" Adam said.

"Yep. It's a plan."

I shut the door and went in to the house. As I'd told my brother, I generally went to work and stopped by the coffee shop beforehand. There was always something to read in those days. Work was bartending at a large nightclub downtown, so my shift would always start late, just as the "party" was getting going. Then I would generally be off by 4 a.m. or sometimes 5 a.m. on a really busy night. Thus, coffee played an essential role at this time in my life.

Around noon the next day, my flip phone started to buzz. I had come home at 5 a.m., so I was still a little groggy.

"Hello?" I mumbled.

"Roland!" Adam said with panic and emphasis.

"Hey. What's up? Not me, yet," I said.

"Sorry to wake you up, but I saw something last night and it scared the hell out of me!"

"Like saw something, or *saw something* in diffuse vision?"

"No, I wasn't looking in diffuse vision or wide-angle vision, or any other kind of vision than I-was-simply-doing-the-dishes vision, and looking out the window while I was doing it," he said.

"And?" I asked.

"I saw this thing slide down the street from one place of shadow through the light, and into the next place of shadow. It was all black, had red eyes, and looked like a frozen running man while it slid by!"

"Did it seem interested in you?" I asked.

"No. Or, it didn't come towards the house or anything," he said.

"OK," I said. "Well, this is your first taste of seeing something evil. It is not pleasant at all, I know."

"Pleasant?! It was terrifying. I am not interested in cultivating this skill if I am going to see things like this," he said.

"Well, fear is their biggest weapon, but that is not to say that evil things can't or won't do harm, because they certainly will. Luckily for you, it wasn't there because it was interested in you. Although, it is an interesting parallel to that *bogeyman* which you saw looking in your window when we were kids. Dad went out there, but there was no trace of anything. Remember?" I said.

"Yeah. I haven't thought about that in years," he said.

"Me neither, but what if what you accidentally saw is essentially the thing that kids see when they see the *bogeyman*? Maybe this thing was hunting a kid?" I said.

After all, my brother was living in the same house I had grown up in. If the night stalker, which is what he had seen, really was looking in at kids while they slept, it very well could have been the same being that haunted my brother in that same neighborhood. It certainly would explain how my brother could still see with little effort as an adult.

"I have seen one of these too, but not here. I saw one in Tacoma. It is called a night stalker, and they are evil," I said.

"Well, if this is the kind of stuff you see, I don't want any part of it," he said.

"I told you that opening this door could have unintended consequences, and as I told you, I really don't advise opening the door of being able to see. That is, unless you are ready for the changes doing so will bring in your life. It is not for the unprepared," I said.

"I could have lived my whole life and been happy to not see that. The worst of this is I have had to confront not only how powerless it made me feel, but also how if it had tried to come inside, what would I or could I even have done? I don't even know what it was or why it was there, beyond your explanation. No, I don't need to dabble in this world, I barely know how to survive in the world that is what you would call physical reality. Spiritual reality will just have to wait in this life," he said.

"Those are some wise words, bro. I wish more people would think that way. One really has to pay attention to the world of unintended consequences sometimes," I said.

"Yeah. Well, thanks for showing me what you do, and I am glad that your mind has the wherewithal to handle it," he said.

"I don't think I am special by any means, man, but for some reason, I am able to move beyond what I see, even though there are things I've seen, like this being, which have truly terrified me. You are not alone in being scared of this kind of thing, and it is right that you should be. Spiritually speaking, this thing might as well be the *bogeyman*!" I said.

"Well, I wanted to hear what you had to say, and now I don't want to talk about this ever again," he said.

"I get it. No worries, bro. I don't think any less of you, and I love you," I said.

"I love you, too. Talk to you later."

"OK," and with that he hung up.

I have never encountered another night stalker, and like my brother, I am happy with it being that way.

As my memory of that event faded, I realized I was nearly home from Corbett. I turned off Highway 26 and took a few turns to pull into my driveway. I had barely noticed the trip back to Portland from Corbett, driving by rote instinct. I parked, and savored the last of my cigarette before going into the house. As I snuffed the butt out, my phone rang playing the last verse from *Hotel California* by the Eagles.

I answered, "This is Roland. How can I help you?"

"Roland, it's Zach. Do you have any appointments open for tomorrow? I really need a treatment."

"Sure, Zach. How about 10 a.m.?" I said.

"Great! I will see you tomorrow," he said.

Chapter 5
Continuation of The First Law

Mornings are special. Morning is the best time to meditate, in my opinion, and my favorite thing to do is roll out of bed and go right to my meditation cushion and sit. Many people try to make meditation so complicated, with gestures and regulation of breathing, chants, mudras, etc. I am not saying these things can't be helpful at times, but for the most part they are simply a distraction for minds that want to constantly be thinking.

No, meditation is as simple as emptying your mind. It is as if your mind is a placid pond in the wilderness, with no disturbance on the surface, and upon gazing into the depths, it is so clear that you can see the lake trout swimming at the bottom. The trick is in learning to let go of all of your control, and work at what it feels like to simply exist. Morning is a wonderful time to meditate, because the day's worries and concerns have yet to manifest. The mind and body are rested, so tranquility is easier to find.

I will sit on my cushion facing south with a blanket over my legs, and look at the wall, simply letting my eyes diffuse. I breathe normally with the breaths reaching all of the way down to my belly. My legs are crossed one over the other, with the left leg on the bottom and my right leg on top. My back is straight, and this forms a tripod with my legs and the pillow. My right hand is open resting in my left hand, and these sit on my hips level with my waistline. This is as natural as breathing for me, and once I begin, the time simply passes, where an hour may go by and feel like a few minutes. I can't remember a time when meditation didn't feel natural, but I am also like most people – I didn't grow up meditating. I had to learn how to do it, in the way that was best for me, and I had to spend a lot of time practicing the "skill" in order to make it a part of who I am. This meant many hours practicing over many years. Yet I, too, suffer initially if I stop and then start again.

I have taught a number of patients to meditate, and they all say, "It is so hard to sit for twenty minutes. How do you do it?"

"Practice every day at the same time. Set your alarm for twenty minutes, and sit there at the same time. After a month, your mind will not struggle with the constant desire to think. After two months, it will start to feel natural. After three months, you will wonder how you could have ever lived without it. When a thought comes to your mind, acknowledge it, and tell your mind that 'now is the time for meditation.' That you will give this thought some time, but not while you are meditating. In three months, you will begin to learn things that are unexplainable to your mind. I have seen it happen again and again, and if you do it, you, too, will succeed," I tell them.

The method itself is simple. The results, however, are profound. For example, if you were an athlete, how could you know what record you wanted to beat, unless you had a baseline or previous record for yourself to beat? In blood work, it is good to take a baseline Complete Blood Count (CBC) workup when you are healthy, so that you have something to compare against when you are sick. Well, meditation does the same thing for your spirit. If you know what you feel like when you are in spiritual harmony, and it is something that you check in with on a daily basis, it is quite easy to tell when something is wrong or out of balance spiritually. For patients, this helps them have a better understanding of their disease and where it comes from. For spiritual warriors, it helps one sense subtle disharmonies both within and without. This subtle sense can alert one to an incoming attack, or a problem that needs your awareness, or even something that is happening to someone you are close to.

We all have the innate gift, but it is a muscle that has to be worked, like all other muscles. Countless times over my life, I have heard people say, "You know, I thought about Johnny Keller today. I haven't thought about that guy in years."

Then, when I ask, "Well, did you reach out to him?"

The answer is usually something like, "I was going to, but I had to pick the kids up," or "Nah. What would I say to him?"

What doesn't occur to people is that this thought came specifically to them for a reason. This was not a random thought, but something that their mind intuited. The mind gave the insight, but rarely does the ego or intellect want to follow through, because it seems so odd to the ego. If one does follow through and reach out to the person "who is on our mind," then the unconscious sees that we are listening, and consequently will provide more information. If we do not listen, and instead ignore this unconscious thought, then it shows our unconscious mind that we are not listening, and it will speak less often. Nothing likes the idea that it is talking, but no one is listening.

My generation grew up on *Star Wars*, but how many have given real thought to what is called the "force," that this is really just a word for the unconscious, spirit, or as the Native Americans say, "the spirit that moves through all things." I encourage people to be a bit more like Obi-Wan Kenobi, when he says, "*I feel a great disturbance in the force,*" than someone who ignores "the force." As Master Yoda said, "*Don't try. Do!*" Regardless of where these ideas come from, these are wise words.

At some point, my meditation was over; it was done with me for the day, rather than me being done with it. Our minds, while vast, really can only handle the slightest bending of reality at any one time, whether that be in personal growth, physical growth, or spiritual growth. It is the rare person who heals from disease overnight, or wakes up with abs of steel, or becomes enlightened in one day. It happens, don't get me wrong, but for those to whom it happens, their entire being has been primed and is ready for this change. The rest of us have to get there by using small pebbles to build skyscrapers.

I generally follow the prohibitions against bathing or eating for thirty minutes before and after meditation. So I checked my email, and on not finding anything pressing, took the leisurely drive down to the Raleigh Hills Starbucks on the west side of the Fred Meyer parking lot. Fifteen minutes later, I was waiting in line when the Starbucks employee named Jake said, "Hey, Roland! Do you want your usual? Sixteen-ounce Sumatra pour over, right?"

"Yep. Thanks, Jake." I said.

Of the Starbucks that I frequent regularly, I would say the service at the Sylvan and the Raleigh Hills locations is tied – both have hands-down good service all the time, and they always greet me with my name and know what I drink. A close second to these two, is the Starbuck on Northwest 23rd and Overton. My least favorite is the Starbucks at Northwest 23rd and Burnside next to the Zupan's, but the employees are realizing that friendliness is part of being in a business which serves the public. My disappointment with any Starbucks location is simply that if I want a pour over coffee, regardless of what bean I want, I want to hear the employee say, "No problem," and not "Umm, we can only do the roast that is being advertised." Everyone knows that all Starbucks will make whatever you want, it is their company policy. Telling me that you can't make me what I want, when every other Starbucks in town will make me what I want, well, frankly, it tarnishes the brand a bit. If you haven't tried the pour over, and have opinions about the way Starbucks roasts their coffee, their pour overs will make you a believer in the brand once more. Do not take my recommendation lightly, as Portland is a coffee and tea town, and we have a nose for such things.

While I waited for my pour over, I thought about what I had learned in meditation, what the satyrs had said yesterday, the final conclusion with the earth elementals the day before, and finally my reminiscence of the night stalkers. It was turning into a busy week spiritually, almost like I was receiving a crash-course education. I wondered if the microcosm I was seeing was a reflection of a greater chaos in the world. It really wouldn't be too far-fetched to think so, but more than likely this simply was connected to the chaos of Portland. Soon the rain will go away for a bit, and allow a little much-needed sunshine. Then, hopefully, people will let more of their good natures out and not be attracted to the darkness as much. Chaos and upheaval are good for my business, but sometimes I would prefer business to be bad, and that people would instead be safe and happy.

"Here you go, Roland," Jake said, setting my coffee down.

"Thanks, Jake," I said.

I went to my car, lit a cigarette, and meandered home while leisurely smoking. Coffee and cigarettes go together better than coffee and donuts, but maybe not as well as coffee and chocolate. I began to think about breakfast. It is always important to be aware of your environment and the weather when considering what to eat. Today, it was rainy and still chilly. This meant that breakfast should be warm, as in cooked, but without any dairy products. I had the 10 a.m. appointment with Zach, so that ruled out cooking a steak or a pork chop. Based on what I knew was in the refrigerator, it would likely be two eggs and a piece of rye toast.

I pulled up to my house and smoked the last of my cigarette while listening to NPR. Trump is trying to ram through a new healthcare bill by bossing around the GOP: well, that probably won't work. The Senate is working towards removing net neutrality: this will be a disaster for regular folk. Lastly, Trump is going to go ahead and push the Keystone pipeline through: so much for the sovereign rights of Native people and the treaties that they signed with the US government.

The first thing one has to do when listening to the news is to ascertain what the agenda is with the news. I am not talking about propaganda or "fake news," but something much more visceral, which is: how does what one hears on the news stir you? Stir, meaning: does it feel like a call to action, something that makes you angry, or something that is simply information? One also has to think about how much the news or series of news items is ramming home a particular agenda. For example, with September 11th or Waco, or situations where whole groups of people are affected, or where riots are happening, there is first the agenda of distributing the news of that event, but often the secondary agenda is to stir the people who are hearing that news. In the case of September 11th, that agenda was to create fear in Americans, as an excuse to set up voluntary relinquishing of constitutional rights in order to feel "safer." Or to create entities like the TSA and Homeland Security, which were established in order to make people safer. I can't affirm whether these entities have made people safer, but I do know that they have helped cement the attitude of fear within the masses.

A while ago, I mentioned that there is a war between the dark and light. To be clear, this war is not an overt war, but a covert war. It happens behind people, events, and policies. I am not going to propel us down the path of conspiracy, but simply am saying that when an action or policy creates a wide amount of fear and uncertainty, then this has been a move that supports the dark side, which feeds on fear, uncertainty, and chaos. When an action or policy brings about community solidity, certainty, and order, this is a move that feeds the light side. This war is really that simple and moves the barometer or scale of darkness and light either in one direction or the other. Now, don't misunderstand me, this war is playing out on the scale of the world, nations, states, provinces, cities, communities, businesses, families, all the way down to individuals and their emotions. This war plays out on all of these scales; that is, when given the choice, do we interact with the people around us from a place of love, or a place of anger and hate?

In modern civilization, we say that you can vote your support of something with the dollars that you spend. You want more organic produce? Then you buy more organic food. You don't want GMOs in your grocery store? Then you don't buy GMOs. You want more electronic cars and clean energy? Then you buy these products. You don't want to support the Keystone oil pipeline? Then find out all the places where that oil goes, and boycott all of those places. Well, in the same way that you can vote with your dollar, you can vote with love or anger. Someone irritates you at work? You can respond with irritation or compassion. Someone has wronged you from your perception? You can react with vengeance or forgiveness. On a daily basis, we can tally how much we are voting for chaos and darkness or light and love simply by measuring our own actions. The further from center that we are, the closer to pure light or pure dark that we are in our daily actions, the more powerful we become, and the closer to God or Satan that we are. The more powerful we become, the more that our actions have ripples which affect those around us. The more that our actions and thoughts influence others, the more chance that the tide of this covert war will change. This is why it is important to understand the agenda of the news, because the more that you are afraid and uncertain, the less power that you have, and the easier it is to control you. The analogy is that people in the middle who react to life with equal parts love and hate are the sheep. Those who interact with life closer to pure hate and anger are the people that slaughter the sheep. Those who interact with life closer to pure love are the shepherds for the sheep. We all have the ability to choose what we want to be, and what we consume through information, news, food, relationships, business decisions, etc., all influence who we untimately are.

I will tell you though, that true and eternal power comes from within, and not from without. Meaning that the power that comes from domination, subjugation, control over others, manipulation, contractual relationships, etc. – none of this is true power. You may feel powerful for a few moments, but another situation will come by and strip your gain away, because it was never yours. True power comes from within, and this can never be taken away by an outside source. Think on this for a moment. Each time we manipulate someone for our own gain, it shows our weakness, not our strength of intellect or ability to play the game. Manipulation is a parasitic activity, because if that person were alone there would be no one to manipulate, and thus no power achieved. The only way to manipulate is to have someone who is willing to play the part of the submissive or victim, while the manipulator plays the role of the dominant or aggressor. Yet, without each other neither has any power; the aggressor cannot control and the victim cannot be dominated. People who play these games generally find each other like magnets. If this is your paradigm, read the above statement again, and think about what you gain out of it. It is an important lesson. I will talk more about this later, but think of this as a seed, and when it starts to sprout we will come back to it.

My master often has said to me, "The drama of mankind has always been adverse to the way of seeking mastery. For thousands of years the monarchs of China tried to draw the monastic class into its drama. At times, monks and priests would oblige and help guide the monarch to bring order to their reign, but the end was always more drama. You cannot fix what does not want to be fixed. When using wheeled carts on the road, the road will inevitably have pot holes. For humankind does not know how to live without drama, as much as the land under the road does not want to acquiesce to being dominated by the road. Seek out those who want to understand their nature, by rising above the drama. It is these people who can hear our words."

If one understands that what we consume as information affects our harmony and balance in regards to our spiritual discipline, then so, too one must understand how what we consume as food affects our spiritual life. I will try to give a brief understanding of how this works.

Chapter 5

The philosophy of Chinese medicine is both simple and complex. At its core is the idea of the five phases, the five natures, and yin and yang. There are other ideas, of course, but after enlightening you on this, then we can talk about what I am having for breakfast. Think of a pentagram – yes, the symbol of witchcraft and the occult. This is a very easy image to conjure in your mind, a five-pointed star with a circle around it.

We think of the leftmost point of the star (where nine o'clock would be on a clock) as the element of wood. The wood element has both yin and yang components. The yin of wood represents the liver, and the yang wood represents the gallbladder. The yin wood emotion is anger, and the yang wood emotion is resentment and passive aggression. The flavor of wood is sour. Wood affects the sinews. The season of wood is spring, and its color is green.

The next point of the star is the top of the star (where twelve o'clock would be on a clock) is the element of fire. The yin of fire is represented by the heart, and the yang of fire is represented by the small intestine. The emotion of yin fire is joy, while the emotion of yang fire is assimilation. The flavor of fire is scorched or bitter. Fire affects the spirit, the blood, and the cardiovascular system. The season of fire is summer, and its color is red.

The next point of the star (where three o'clock would be on a clock) is the element of earth. The yin of earth is the spleen, and the yang of earth is the stomach. The emotion of yin earth is pensiveness, while the emotion of yang earth is the ability to digest and understand one's own emotions. The flavor of earth is sweet. Earth affects the muscles. The season of earth is late summer, and its color is yellow.

The next point of the star (where five o'clock would be on a clock) is the element of metal. The yin of metal is the lung, and the yang of metal is the large intestine. The emotion of yin metal is grief, while the emotion of yang metal is letting go (or holding on, when unbalanced). The flavor of metal is acrid, as in spicy. Metal affects the lungs, breath, qi, and skin. The season of metal is fall, and its color is white.

The next point of the star (where seven o'clock would be on a clock) is the element of water. The yin of water is the kidney, and the yang of water is the urinary bladder. The emotion of yin water is depression, while the emotion of yang water is fear. The flavor of water is salty. Water affects the bones and marrow. The season of water is winter, and its color is black.

So the saying goes: When wood burns it creates fire. As fire burns it creates earth. Metal is mined from earth. When metal is left outside in the cold, water condenses on metal. In order for wood to flourish, it must be able to drink water. Therefore, there is a continuum that goes around the circle clockwise. We call this the generation cycle.

Yet, if the cycle goes counterclockwise, so that fire consumes all of the wood. Wood drinks all of the water. Water soaks the metal to create rust. The metal in the ground is so plentiful that there is no earth. Or the earth is so excessive that it puts out the fire. This is called the destruction cycle.

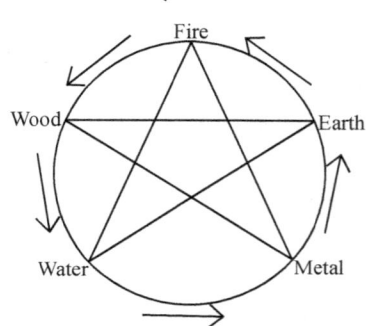

Two other cycles that are important to consider
are the control cycle, where wood controls earth (think of a root-bound plant), earth controls water (such as with a dam), water puts out fire, fire melts metal, and metal cuts wood. Conversely, in the insulting cycle: earth insults wood (where the seed is too deep in the ground to grow), wood insults metal (the wood is too strong and the metal can't cut it), metal insults fire (the metal is too hard and the fire can't melt it), fire insults water (steam is good in a sauna, but terrible within your body), and water insults earth (flooding of your foundation leads to a houseboat).

So to redraw the original diagram, these two diagrams would look something like this:

Controlling cycle:

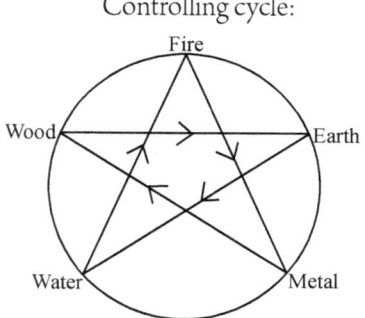

Insulting cycle:

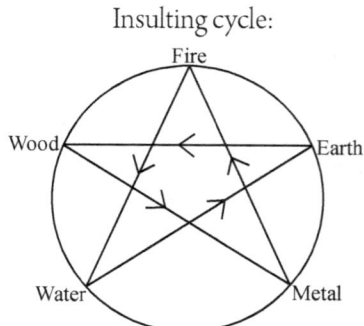

I also mentioned the five natures: these are hot, warm, neutral, cool, and cold. All foods have both a nature and a flavor. In truth, food usually has a dominant nature, a dominant flavor, and several sub-flavors. Take, for example, salt-and-vinegar kettle chips. These are made from potato. The nature of potato is neutral and the flavor is sweet. Potato influences the spleen and stomach. Then the flavorings of vinegar (nature: warm; flavor: sour and bitter; influences the stomach and liver), and salt (flavor of water; influences the kidneys) are added to the potato. So, in this particular chip, the neutral flavor of the potato becomes warm with the added flavorings, and the food influences the stomach, spleen, liver, and kidneys.

If we go back to our diagram, we can think about the insulting cycle, which shows the consequences of any one organ being too strong in comparison to the other organs. So, if I build up too much earth, it insults the liver wood. Liver wood is also known as that which gives us initiative. We think of the wood personality as the general, or the person who leads and gets things done. Now, to remind you, sweet is the flavor of earth. Who hasn't binged on sugar and then felt completely lethargic once the sugar high goes away? This is an example of this pattern. You eat all of the Halloween candy, then the next day you feel lethargic and don't want to do anything, but you also feel nauseous. This is because the spleen and stomach have been made so thoroughly resolute that it is like they are hard, and can't move or transport the nutrients.

Another example: If I smoke cigarettes, the tobacco when smoked has a scorched and bitter flavor. In small amounts this strengthens the fire organs of the body, but in large amounts this causes the fire to burn brightly. When this happens, the fire burns and melts the metal. The lungs are the yin organ of metal, and many people who smoke a lot have lung issues, whether that is shortness of breath, decreased respiratory capacity, or a chronic smoker's cough. These are all signs that the metal element is being harassed by the presence of too much fire.

Still another example of how this could work: Say a person likes spicy food. The flavor of spicy goes to the lungs. If they eat too much spicy food, the lungs and metal will become too strong and the metal will cut down the yin wood, which is the liver. Then the person might be susceptible to rash actions of anger, sinew and ligament tightness, feeling like they don't detoxify or cool down as fast as they should, as well as passive aggressiveness, etc.

The idea of the five phases or five elements is pervasive throughout Chinese medicine. It is used to understand the emotions, the spiritual components of the body, the food we eat, the herbs we dispense, and how disease both presents and manifests itself through the body. The five elements are one of the cornerstones of Chinese medicine.

Therefore, when one considers what one eats, one needs to consider these elements both in their microcosm (as in what is happening inside my body) and the macrocosm (as in what is happening outside my body). What is the state that I am in, and how do I want to move it to become more balanced? What is the season and the weather, and how do I eat to minimize the damage of the external environment with what I know to be true about my internal environment?

So, first one has to identify whether one primarily runs warm or cold in temperature. Do I feel hot or cold today? Do I want warm beverages or cold beverages? Do I dislike being in hot or cold weather? These kinds of questions help me to understand how my body is functioning on a day to day basis. Then we contrast this against what the weather is doing. Is it unseasonably warm or cold outside? Is it summer, but still feels like winter? Or is it fall, but summer has not departed yet? Lastly, where do I live? Am I in a cold climate or a tropical climate? All of these things also affect food choices. Do I live in the mountains closer to the sun, or do I live at sea level, or even below sea level? Once I understand these things, I can start to think about what foods are best for me, and what foods harm me.

Why is all of this important, you might ask. Because, it is easiest to follow the *Dao* (or the Way) when one's mind, heart, body, and spirit are in balance. When one falls out of balance in any of these things, then there is the opportunity to be manipulated by beings, people, or disease. If I know where I am balanced and feel at my best, then it is very easy to spot not only when I am out of balance, but also what the likely culprit was. If one rides through life as if one were riding the bumper cars, it will be hard to know which bumper car dented your car. But, if you drive carefully and are hit infrequently, it is easy to track how that event or person has affected you, and then you have the power and ability to change it.

Here is a real-world example of how all of this works:

Bob is a contractor working on road construction. He is in his fifties and is married to Lila. On this day, it is a hundred degrees, and he is hot because there is no shade. After his shift, a few of the other workers say that they are going to go have some beers and chicken wings at Fire on the Hill, a restaurant known for its spicy hot wings. The crew asks if he would like to join them. Although he is supposed to go have dinner with Lila, he's decided that he is hot and he deserves a few drinks, but he won't eat, so that he has room for dinner. He drives to Fire on the Hill and meets the construction crew there. They are drinking the Total Domination IPA brewed by Ninkasi.

Joe, one of the crew has ordered wings and says, "Bob, you have to try these wings, they are awesome!"

"What kind did you order?" Bob says.

"These," Joe points, "are the extra-hot, and these over here are the raspberry habanero."

Bob gingerly picks up a wing and takes a bite. "These are really good! Maybe the best wings I've had in town!"

Licking his fingers, Joe says, "Yep!"

Ordering his third pint of Total Domination, Bob has let his dinner with Lila slip his mind, and he is on his third plate of wings. His face is red, and he is sweating. The alcohol hit him a little while ago. After draining his third beer, he is tipsy and realizes he is now an hour later for dinner.

"Another round, Bob?" Joe asks.

"No, I have to go."

"Are you OK to drive?" Joe responds.

"I'll be fine." Bob says. He isn't slurring his words, he isn't too uncoordinated, and home is only a few blocks away. He pays his tab, leaves the restaurant, and drives home on the back streets.

Now, Bob and Lila generally have a loving relationship, but today when he arrives home, she is irritated, bordering on angry.

"You were supposed to be home at 6:30 p.m., and it is 7:45 p.m. What have you been doing? Didn't you remember that dinner was at 6:30 p.m.?!" Lila said in the cold and irritated voice she used when her anger had been simmering for a bit.

"Honey, it was hot on the job today, so I went to grab a drink with the crew. I'm still hungry, though." Bob told a half truth.

"What do you mean you're still hungry? Did you eat with the crew too?" she said, raising her voice.

"Just a couple of bites really, Lila. It's OK – we can eat."

"You left me here for an hour after I cooked dinner for you. No text, no phone call, and now I am supposed to have dinner ready for you?! Sorry, Bob, I love you, but when you do things like this, don't expect me to understand and just wait around for you. I ate, and the food is in the fridge. I also called Martha, and I am leaving to go have a glass of wine with her. Have a good dinner by yourself!" Lila grabs her purse, slams the door on the way out, and speeds off in their car.

Bob is angry at himself. He has made a bad choice and he knows it. The anger at himself builds until he wants to break something, so he goes to the garage, takes a hammer and begins beating a 2x4. His anger feels like a white hot flame, and as he hits the wood each time, he berates himself for making such a poor choice. Eventually, the anger washes away, and he feels drained. By 11 p.m. Lila has not yet returned home. Bob is getting anxious, as Lila generally doesn't stay out late. Bob has texted a couple of times, but Lila doesn't answer. He wonders if she is simply angry at him, or whether something has happened to her. By 2 a.m. Lila still hasn't responded, and her friend hasn't responded to Bob's voice mail either. Bob is so anxious that he can't sleep. So, he packs his bowl and smokes some marijuana. When he is done with the first bowl, he packs it again, and smokes another one. He is now so high, he finally feels less anxious, but now he is hungry. He warms up the spaghetti and marinara Lila had cooked and ladles it out. He is so high, that he can't keep his hands steady, and marinara splatters on the stove and Pergo floor. The food is good; Lila is a good cook. Why had he gone out with the crew?

After eating, Bob sits in the La-Z-Boy in the living room watching Netflix. He is there, snoring slightly when Lila comes home intoxicated at 4 a.m. She takes one look in the kitchen, swears, and goes to bed without waking Bob up. At 8 a.m. Bob wakes up in the La-Z-Boy, grabs a glass of water, guzzles it down, and goes to the bedroom. There, he sees Lila asleep, and he crawls into bed snuggling up next to her, but she rolls away. Rejected, Bob falls asleep. At 10 a.m. Lila and Bob wake up. They are still not talking. Lila puts on her bathrobe and goes to the kitchen, where she looks at the mess Bob created. Bob wanders in a few seconds later.

Chapter 5

"So, are you going to clean this up?" Lila says, pointing to the plate of mostly eaten spaghetti on the table with drips of marinara sauce covering the stove and leading to the table.

"Yeah," says Bob, "Do you want breakfast?"

"No. I am going to spend the day with Charlotte."

"Are you still mad at me?" Bob says.

"Yes, I am."

"Can I make it up to you?" he asks.

"No, you can't."

After a week, the event is gone, but not forgotten. Neither side is willing to budge. Bob smokes more pot, drinks more, and both partners find fewer reasons to be at home. Bob falls into a depression and Lila continues to be terse and harder on Bob. Neither wants to end their marriage, but neither do they want to reconcile. Bob starts to find he has problems with his sex drive, and Lila just doesn't have "the energy" for sex. As time goes by, they feel more lonely together than when they are apart.

The purpose of this example is not just to highlight how singular choices can have compounding effects. It is also to look at how this situation has come to pass using the five phases. In this story, we don't know what Bob and Lila's relationship was like before – we are only getting a snapshot in a period of time. This is very much like seeing a patient, because the patient comes with a problem. Sometimes they give you a backstory, and often they don't. So, one has to look for the pattern, and the pattern can often be broken down to the five phases, regardless of what the words of the story are.

So, let's decode:

Bob worked on a hot day in no shade. This made his body hot. He craved something cool to cool his body. The nature of hot is countered by the nature of cold if used in the appropriate amounts. Bob consumed 48 ounces of Ninkasi Total Domination which has a 6.7% alcohol by volume and an IBU (international bittering units) of 81, with the flavor of citrus and hops. Comparatively, Budweiser has an IBU of 7, while Bridgeport

Brewing's Hop Czar has an IBU of 87 out of 100. The math of beer is that the higher alcohol by volume rating it has, the sweeter it is, and the higher IBU scale the beer has, the more bitter it is. Therefore, a Total Domination has both a strong sweet and bitter flavor. The nature of beer is cold. Comparatively, cask-conditioned ale served at room temperature is cool, meaning it is warmer than cold, but cooler than neutral.

Bob innately tried to cool his hot body with a cold beer. Remember that the sweet flavor goes to the spleen, while the bitter flavor goes to the heart. However, because this is the bitter of hops, and not the bitter of the scorched flavor, than this bitter also tends to cool and drain heat. The spleen is averse to cold and likes heat. The heart likes an even-tempered fire; it neither likes to be blazing nor does it like to be embers. One pint of beer might have been just what Bob needed, but he probably overdid it with three. Complicating this are the spicy hot wings the he had. The spicy or pungent flavors go to the lungs. In moderation spicy can be highly beneficial, but in this case, the wings probably helped whet his thirst for more cold beer. If we again look at our diagram:

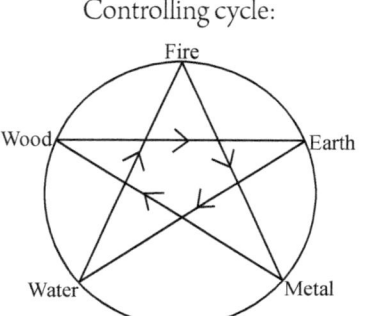
Controlling cycle:

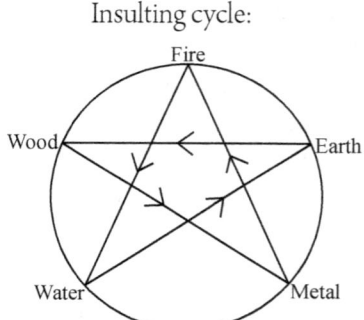
Insulting cycle:

We can see that Bob had engaged three organs with his choices: The heart/bitter/fire, the spleen/sweet/earth, and the lung/spicy/metal. Now, if one beer would have been enough, but three were consumed, then Bob has added more energy to earth and fire to some degree. The spicy food has added more energy to metal. Using the insulting cycle, we know that a strong earth damages wood, and using the controlling cycle, we know that a strong metal cuts wood. Therefore, by consuming these two things (hot wings and Total Domination) together, he has done damage to his yin wood.

When Bob goes home and Lila confronts him, rather than being externally angry, Bob is angry at himself. His wood has been shifted out of balance by what he consumed, so he has no "General" when it comes to his emotions, and while he does not lose control at Lila, he does lose control in his anger at himself. The energy of wood is to generate, and when one is angry it generates energy. But without the proper fuel, when the anger is extinguished, so is the energy. Now, Bob has an unbalanced yin wood that has been further depleted because of his anger. Wood fuels fire. So, when Lila doesn't come home, rather than being balanced and grounded, the fire burns up the remaining wood, and as the fuel is depleted, the fire starts to sputter, and this manifests as anxiety. The less fuel there is, the more severe the anxiety is.

Now to soothe the anxiety, Bob smokes marijuana, which gives the fire the scorched flavor that it wants, but at the expense of again damaging the wood, because he has now added more fire to his body. By increasing the fire, his body then craves more earth – thus eating simple carbs sates the earth. Yet, Bob smokes more than he needs to, so again this damages the wood. Remember that the sinews are connected to the liver, so as he becomes more intoxicated, he has less control of his limbs. By eating the pasta, he has now made his earth too strong again (in comparison to the imbalanced liver) and he starts to think while he is watching TV. However, the TV sedates him and he falls asleep. Upon waking he is thirsty, because he has excess fire from the marijuana. As he is rejected by Lila, he has grief and regret over his actions, thus depressing the metal. When the metal is depleted for long enough, then when the water quits being nourished there is depression, and consequently the sex drive goes away. As the water continues to be weak, the wood cannot recover because there is not enough nourishment for it, and so Bob becomes sullen and passive-aggressive, like a smoldering fire that smokes, but can't burn. As the wood is not fed, so too is there a depletion of fire, and the joy leaves their lives.

Now, this is a simple example of one incident with consequences, but, it illustrates how eating the wrong kind of food can throw off the emotions, and make it so that the normal and balanced emotion, which would normally shine through, is not then able to manifest when it is needed, and this sets off a cascade of tragic events. The moral of the story: is pick your meals carefully. Don't be Bob.

The way our energetic structure is ordered is from the most subtle to the most dense. The most subtle is our karma, then our spirit, then our intellect, then emotions, then protective qi, then the skin, then the fascia, then the flesh, then the sinews and vessels, then the blood, then the bones, and lastly the marrow. This is the continuum of subtle to dense. When we eat food, the energy expands outward through our subtle layers and inward to our deeper layers, as the organs are somewhere between the flesh and the sinews. Conversely, when we breathe, the energy first moves inward (on inhalation) and then outward (on exhalation). The energy that food provides is a denser, more compacted energy. The food we eat provides energy for about three days' worth of action. This is why when we fast, and stop eating, it takes about four days for our body to change from the process of catabolizing[3] glucose through the Krebs cycle[4] to gluconeogenesis[5] and beta oxidation.[6] In other words it takes four days for our body to switch from burning food to burning fat. If the idea is to attain balance, then being mindful of what we consume, how we consume it, and when we consume it, is the only logical choice.

As I mentioned, my breakfast was going to be two eggs and a piece of rye toast. Warm food for a cold day. The nature of an egg is balanced for the yolk and cool for the egg white. The flavor of an egg is sweet, therefore it enters the spleen and stomach organs. The properties of an egg are that it nourishes the blood and brightens the eyes. Rye is neutral in nature and sweet in flavor, and it is used to strengthen the stomach and alleviate fatigue. Both of these, served warm, add the warm nature to the meal. The advantage of eating property neutral foods is that they don't move your energetic system too much in one way or another. This is why so many monastic traditions essentially advocate a bland diet. By consuming a relatively bland and neutral diet, one can then add a little bit of one flavor or another to move the energetic structure in the desired direction. This is the equivalent of eating consciously. Compare this to someone who has three very rich meals in a day. How will they know which of the complex dishes and the flavors therein moved them in the appropriate direction? Or, if moved in an inappropriate direction, how will they know which flavor that they are trying to counter? This is not to say that I don't indulge myself occasionally; it is simply saying I know that, when I indulge myself, there will be a consequence to this indulgence. Also, that if I know I am going to go somewhere where the food will be wide and varied such as brunch, then I should think ahead and bring herbs that speed up my digestive system and help neutralize any strong flavors.

When delving into Chinese medicine, one quickly learns that it is not simply a medicine, but a way of life. Most of the Chinese medicine practitioners who I know live the medicine, and these same ideas go through their minds on a conscious or semi-conscious level. First, assess the body, mind, and spirit; then remedy the subtle layers with

---

3. A reaction that involves the breakdown of organic material (such as food) into compounds such as glucose, in order to provide chemically available energy (such as ATP).
4. A series of oxidation-reduction reactions and decarboxylation reactions that release the chemical energy from food.
5. The process by which new glucose is formed from non-carbohydrate sources such as lactic acid, and the glycerol portion of triglycerides.
6. The first stage in the catabolism of fatty acids, which eventually leads to the formation of ketone bodies.

simple things such as food, action, thought, and meditation. If this does not work, then apply medicinals, and if this doesn't work, then apply acupuncture and moxibustion.[7] The simplest things that we do on a daily basis often have the power to move us greatly in one way or another. However, this all begins with the ability to accurately assess oneself and know where one's point of balance is. This ability to assess is not complicated; it simply requires one to be aware of oneself. This means that when we become too mental, too emotional, too physical, or too spiritual, that we have the ability to rein this in and not continue down a path that eventually will lead to failure of one system or another.

I ate my breakfast, put on a hat, a coat, and a scarf, and got back in my car to make my short commute to the office. As I drove, I thought about Zach, my 10 a.m. patient. Zach had been a regular patient, coming in nearly weekly for three years. He has been consistent and focused in his desire to become a better version of himself. Zach, like many people, has had his share of trauma, and he at times has lived a life of debauchery, but most of that was in his younger years. This would include drug and alcohol use, sexual vice, poor food choices, and lack of control over his mind and emotions. He was in his fifties, and frankly for most people this kind of behavior in their past is not uncommon. What I have noticed is that when a person is born, they are born with light and vitality. Then, if they suffer trauma or abuse, especially at the hands of a loved one or someone that they trust, then the light is dimmed. As they reach their teenage and young adult years, it is easy to get to a point where they can no longer see their inner light. It is at this point, that most of people fall into what would be considered more risky behavior. If a person cannot see the light in themselves, then they can't see the light in others. This person then will seek out others who are like they are, and this leads to a further decline of their own light, as the people they choose to be around or to "hang out with" tend to have less and less light. Then there are those whose light is completely absent, and in its place is darkness. As they decline down this slope, their choices become more and more "risky." At some point, people either catch themselves and try to start climbing back up the steep slippery slope towards the light, or they despair, let themselves go and slide full-tilt towards the darkness.

Zach was one of those who had caught himself, who didn't want to see his daughter Terra ensnared in the life that he had lived. He wanted to be better and change for her. Some might call this being responsible, but really, it is an act of love and compassion. Zach actively sought for the light within himself, so that he could bequeath to Terra a life

---

7. Moxibustion is a heating therapy used to treat a number of conditions within Chinese medicine. Mugwort, also known as *Artemisia vulgaris*, is the most common substance used in moxibustion.

of light, not darkness. I enjoy working with patients who are on this path, and I have the ability to help guide them out of the darkness. I can't lift them out, as their choices are their own, but I can show them that there is a way, and that there is hope. It really doesn't matter if they relapse or "fall off the wagon," because if their desire is sincere, they will find the way.

Comparatively, it is much harder to work with patients who do not have a sincere desire to change, or who want to be the same person they were at twenty, or who want me to fix them while they do none of the work. These patients often lack personal responsibility and have a hard time seeing how their choices have caused their current state of being. If a patient cannot see that their choices have consequences, then how can they see that their choices can be powerful, and that they can enact the choice to be better? Working with Zach had always been a joy, because he had already learned that his choices had brought him to his current place, and he wanted to make better choices to be a better person. This, however, is not the path of mastery, it is simply the path to health. The path to mastery is the path of self-mastery, and means that one must see one's own light, and then making choices that lead to fostering more of one's own light. This process can begin once one surmounts the slope that one has slid down, and then begins the long descent towards the light one was born with as a child.

I parked my car and walked the short two blocks to the office. I said hello to Billy and Marla, the older couple smoking in front of my office. Walked in and took the elevator up. It was 9:45 a.m., right on time. Now, generally I would not say that I am the most punctual practitioner, as I am often five minutes early or late to an appointment, but compared to the service I have received at Western medical clinics, this small wait is nothing. When my patients arrive, they are immediately interviewed, assessed, and treated. The whole process generally takes forty-five minutes. Compare this to some Western medical clinics I have gone to, where I arrive on time or even a little early, check in, and then are made to wait for thirty minutes, simply to have a nurse practitioner come get you to check your vitals. Yep, I am alive. Then they stick you in a room to wait for a doctor to come assess you, which is often another thirty-minute wait. I once had an appointment at a doctor's office in Northwest Portland where they checked my vitals, put me in a room to be seen by a doctor, then promptly forgot about me. I sat in the room for an hour and a half (I am generally a patient fellow), before I walked out to the receptionist to see if they had forgotten about me. Sure enough, they had and, worse, the receptionist acted like it was my fault. I guess this is one of the reasons why this (purposely unnamed) clinic has only 1 ½ stars on Yelp. This has never happened to one of my patients, and never will. How can a provider provide healthcare if, at the minimum, there is not at least mutual respect between the provider and the patient? So, as I said, sometimes I am five minutes late. Compared to the Western model, not bad at all.

I walked up to my door, and one of my mentees was standing there.

"Hey Jessica. What's up?" I said.

"I was wondering if I could observe a few sessions with you?"

"Sure. If the patient agrees, I am fine with it."

Jessica was what I call a baby acupuncturist. Fresh out of school, she had started her practice a few months back, and was not yet busy. I take on mentees as they find me, and mentor them using my own experiences to guide them through running their business, billing insurance, creating business plans, and understanding bookkeeping. Most of all, I provide a willing ear for them to be able to talk about their patients and ask the questions they have regarding Chinese medicine post-education. In Western medicine this is an opportunity many schools provide with their residency programs, but Chinese medicine schools don't offer this opportunity. One might say that once Chinese medicine schools have taken all the financial aid a student can get from student loans, and the school has basically sold their students into a lifetime of indentured servitude due to the exorbitant cost of the education, they then throw these students to the wolves. The budding practitioners are then sent out to practice in a very competitive market with minimal business training, and these budding practitioners have the expectation that the education they received will be enough for them to get a successful practice going. I have watched this cycle for fifteen years now, and I can tell you that what the schools provide is often not enough. Some schools are better than others in regards to the competency of their students, but no school that I know of teaches a student enough business skills for the student to be successful based on that teaching alone. Worse, there are only three options for work once one has graduated in this career: own your own practice, work in someone else's practice, or teach in one of the schools. The standard practice in alternative medicine is what I call "the old eat the young." In this situation, an older, more experienced practitioner will rent a room to a baby practitioner. They say that they will refer patients to the baby practitioner, but the cost is that fifty percent or more of what the baby practitioner makes is paid to the older practitioner as "rent." It is, in my mind, quite a detestable practice, but it will probably continue until alternative medicine becomes institutionalized. Hence, the failure rate for acupuncturists after five years of practice is roughly seventy percent;[8,9] that is, seventy percent of people who graduate have failed in their practice after five years. When the challenge is too great, and the chick's feathers have not grown out, it will simply fall from the nest, and die. Push an adolescent eagle out of the nest once it has had time to grow its feathers, and it will fly. Therefore, I do what I can to help the "kids" who find their way to me, as Jessica had done.

I unlocked the door to the clinic, put my stuff down, and went to wash my hands. When I came back, Jessica was sitting in one of the La-Z-Boys, thumbing through one of the books in my library and writing notes in her notebook.

"Find something interesting to read?" I said.

"Yeah. I had been wondering about the treatment protocols in the *Great Compendium of Acupuncture and Moxibustion* the other day, and how they compared to some of my acupuncture notes from school. Do you mind if I look this until the patient comes?"

"Be my guest. It is always good to wonder, and then try to answer your own questions first. I will also sit and compose myself for when Zach comes," I said.

As was usual when I sat in my La-Z-Boy, and waited for the patient to arrive, I mused.

One has to know, in order to ask questions. If one does not know, how can one ask anything other than very basic questions? One has to have a basic understanding of the theoretical components of Chinese medicine in order to know how to ask questions that deepen one's understanding. One way to do this is to observe another practitioner work, after one has achieved an education, taken one's boards, and received one's license. In this situation, both practitioners are competent, but one of them has more practical experience than the other. To have a novice practitioner in the room can be educational for both practitioners, if there is mutual respect. The new acupuncturist will often ask questions such as:

"Why did you do that?"

---

8. Stumpf, Steven & R. Carr, Clifford & McCuaig, Shauna & J. Shapiro, Simon. (2012). "The U.S. Acupuncture Workforce: The Economics of Practice," *American Acupuncturist*. v56. 30-34, 40.
9. Stumpf, Steven & Ward-Cook, Kory & R. Carr, Clifford. (2017). "Comparing outcomes from the two most recognized acupuncturist workforce surveys," *Journal of Integrative Medicine*. 15. 37-43.

"How did you know to ask that?"
"What did you feel in the pulse, and what did the tongue look like to you?"
"Why did you choose those points or that medicinal?"

This kind of conversation happens after the patient has left, of course. By asking respectful questions, the baby acupuncturist can often help the more experienced practitioner put assessment decisions, which are often instinctual by this point in their practice, into words. This then helps both the inexperienced and the more experienced practitioners think about the medicine in a deeper way.

Jessica though, has another gift, which I often appreciated outside of her ability to ask insightful questions. She is able to see energy and she is energetically clean. This means that she can corroborate what I see in patients during a treatment, and we can mutually validate what we've seen. This is a valuable asset for a practitioner, as when two or more people see the same thing, it lends authenticity to what is being seen. It is not that one should ever doubt oneself, but another person who sees what you see can give additional confirmation that what is occurring is true, especially if the confirmation comes after the treatment has ended. Being energetically clean means that Jessica knows how to be present in the room in such a way that her own energy or issues neither cloud her judgment nor get in the way of treating a patient.

"Is the *Great Compendium* the best book on acupuncture and moxibustion of the classical texts? Meaning, should I focus on this book solely, or are there other books I should read, too?" Jessica asked.

"The *Great Compendium* is simply the most recent of the classical texts on acupuncture and moxibustion. It was written in the Ming dynasty, and therefore it is a collection of what has come before, with a lot of commentary on this collection by the author. One must understand, though, that one book will not answer all your questions. Read as many classics as you can get your hands on. They all have pearls in them that are directly applicable to treating patients, and they have material in them which you won't be able to find in modern books. I have a number of acupuncture-related books here which have been translated from the classics, and they all have taught me to see differently than I was taught in school."

"OK. I will see if I can compare and contrast some of what is in each book," she said.

"That is a good way to learn, as the understanding has changed over time. For example, some of the books that were the original source material for the *Great Compendium* actually present other uses for particular points that are not in the *Great Compendium*."

"Hmmm. OK, I will keep reading. Thanks!"

"No problem," I said, and went back to my contemplation.

Young doctors often have what I call "white coat syndrome," meaning that they have graduated from school, and they think that they know what is best: the best treatment, what is best for the patient, and how best to treat. It is an absence of humility, and an excess of ego. Baby practitioners have yet to learn that they are going to encounter situations that are either unexplainable or difficult beyond belief. Only through experience do the "white coats" learn that how they were trained does not answer all of the questions, and that they will have to see thousands of patients in order to understand that the root of disease is often far more complex than what the patient tells you. For example, many, many diseases started decades before the patient actually seeks treatment. It started because the patient made choices, which led to habits, which led to ways in which they formed their ego, and this ego construction led to a way of being that fosters a certain kind of disease.

Here is one example of this:

One day, a woman named Barbara called me, and told me that she would like to make an appointment in order to facilitate her getting pregnant. When she walked into my clinic on the specified date, I saw a highly manicured woman in high heels and business attire, with a slim build. She told me she was obsessed with her appearance, and it was very important for her to look a certain way, both with her attire and her body. She had a lot of muscular definition; she was sinewy, wiry, and what one might call a "hard body." She talked about her desire to be pregnant, but also talked about the pressures of her job, and how she had clawed her way to the top in a man's world. Any woman I know would be proud of her success at breaking the glass ceiling.

Barbara said she was an executive at a major company and had high levels of stress. Throughout her thirties, she felt like she had to be on the top of her game. Now, she had attained her goals, was financially stable, had a nice house, a nice car, and all the material things in the world that she could want. However, she had not been able to get pregnant. Her dream as a child was to be a mother of three, but she had neither found the right partner nor felt like she had the financial freedom to bring a new life into this world. Now, in her early forties, she had found Harrison, the man of her dreams, and wanted to create a family with him. They had been trying to get pregnant for two years, she had been tracking her menstrual period, and they were having sex on schedule when she was ovulating. Every morning she checked her basal body temperature to determine the best time to have sex is. Harrison also had been checked, and his sperm count was normal and healthy. When she was ovulating, they had copious amounts of sex, but she hadn't been able to conceive. She hadn't stopped menstruating yet, and a gynecologist told her that she wass fertile and still had eggs. Everything was "right," but for some reason she couldn't get pregnant. Barbara was frustrated and scared that her dreams of children and family might slip away from her. She had told Harrison she would do anything to have a baby, and that it was all she wanted in the world.

Harrison encouraged her to see an acupuncturist, because he had heard that acupuncturists can help a woman become pregnant. Barbara didn't understand how an acupuncturist could work this miracle for her, but as she told Harrison, she was willing to do anything.

At the end of her story, she asked me, "So Roland, how can acupuncture help me achieve my goal of having children?"

"It can't," I said.

"What?" she said.

"Acupuncture can't fix why you are not able to get pregnant," I said.

"I thought acupuncture can help women get pregnant!?" she said.

"It can," I said.

"You are not making any sense," she said.

"Acupuncture can't fix the reason why **you** are not able to get pregnant," I said.

'What do you mean?"

"Your inability to get pregnant has to do with yin and yang. To achieve what you have achieved, **you** at some point let go of your yin, or the nurturing aspect of your feminine nature. Your body is hard, your mind is hard, your will is hard. These are all characteristics of yang. You can't become pregnant until you embrace the yin side of yourself, and that is, in a sense, a polar opposite of everything that you have made yourself be in this modern world. There is nothing wrong with your decisions, but fostering the yang within yourself as you have done, to be more competitive in your male-dominated work environment, is in opposition to fostering your yin, nurturing nature. You have inadvertently created a situation where you act like a man, but are in a woman's body. Until you can let go of your need to be stronger, more competitive, more cutthroat, more calculating, and a stronger fighter, or, in other words, more masculine than the men you work with, you won't be able to conceive, because men can't get pregnant."

She looked at me, dumbfounded. "You are saying that my success has made me unable to conceive?"

"I am," I said.

"But, if I am not successful, then what is the point of all my struggle?"

"I can't answer that for you. You asked me to help you with conception, and I am giving you an honest answer. Have you ever wondered why a woman is the most fertile when she is in her twenties? Not only is her body functioning at the optimum place for pregnancy, but she has often chosen to pursue the path of being a mother. Being a mother is a different mental track than being an executive. It is not to say that a woman can't be both, but there is a softness to a woman in her twenties, that tends to lessen as she gets older. As we age, our hormones such as estrogen and testosterone tend to decrease, but our experiences tend to make us more jaded and "rational" about life. In other words, we lose our naiveté. From a simply physiological perspective, we can see this in our skin and how it begins to dry out, in our sexual organs and how they tend not to function as well, in our muscles and organs and how they tend to not work as well, and in our sinews and how we tend not to be as flexible. We see this in our emotions and how we tend to be less compassionate, less giving, less flexible, more judgmental, more irritable, more self-involved, more driven, and more goal- and task-oriented."

"I am not saying this is bad or good, only that it is. I understand that this goes against all that you have worked for in life, but if you want to get pregnant, you are going to have to find that twenty-something-year-old woman within yourself, and make peace with her.

Chapter 5

The woman who you were in your twenties, who relished pampering, who spoiled herself not with material objects, but who took long naps, and indulged herself in the nurturing aspects of being a woman. In other words, if you want to get pregnant, you have to foster your yin, and increase the softness within you. The baby that you want needs to have a soft and comfortable place within your womb. If there is no place within you that is soft, because you drive yourself to exhaustion every day at work, then there is no place for the baby to call home. If the baby has no place to call home, then there is no way that your womb will be able to hold a pregnancy," I said.

"This is not an uncommon problem, and is in part a product of our society, which teaches us that we can be anything we want and have anything we want, as long as we are willing to work for it. I am not even saying that you made the wrong choices in life, nor am I judging your choices, as I do believe that we should seek out that which we want in life. I am simply saying that when we make certain decisions for a certain direction in life, we do so at the expense of other directions or paths. Your choices led you down a certain path, and if you want to become pregnant, you have to make other choices that will take you down another path. If you are having a hard time conceiving, when all of the other factors of becoming pregnant, as you have mentioned, are positive, then you simply have to consider that this is less of a problem with your hormones, and more of a problem with the choices you have made in life," I said.

"But what if I don't want to give up everything I have worked so hard for?"

"Then you may have to reconcile with yourself that you may not be able to get pregnant, or have a family. This decision, in the end, is only yours to make. I can tell you that with acupuncture and medicinals we can help change your body from a yang state to a yin state by nourishing your yin, but if you don't make any other changes in your life, I don't think that this alone will solve your problem. This is solely my opinion. Of course, you should get other opinions as well, and I would recommend that you do so. After you do this, if you are willing to change, and want me to help you with this, I can, and will. But, you have to make the decision to change first," I said.

The problem with being honest is that sometimes it costs you patients. Most people think that after they have made a whole series of decisions, they can simply go to a medical practitioner to be "fixed," without either thinking about the decisions they have made, or making changes to their life. This is, in part, a notion that has been fostered by the allopathic, or Western, medicine model. This model suggests that the body is simply a product of many chemical processes, and that, if a disharmony is medicated or cut out, this will fix the rest of the body. It is clear to me from working with a number of patients, however, that this is a fallacy.

Every chemical we put into our bodies has unintended consequences. The stronger the chemical, the worse the unintended consequences. In medicine we call an unintended consequence a "side effect." A standard model in Western medicine is to give a drug for a problem, and then several other drugs to deal with the side effects of the primary drug. However, the secondary drugs also have side effects. This is when I begin seeing patients, primarily older people, who come into the office and are taking eight or nine drugs because they have a heart problem or high blood pressure. How can the liver and the kidneys (or main organs of detoxification) process eight or nine potent chemicals every day with outstanding accuracy? The reality is that they can't, and these patients will find that, over time, their kidney and liver functions will decrease, as the organs become "tired" from the amount of extraneous work which they are having to do on a daily basis.

Barbara's main problem was that she suffered from an "internal possession" to succeed in the material world. An "internal possession" is something within us which drives us to do things because of our fear. It is not a demonic entity, or something external that takes possession of our body. No, it is a behavior we have learned, or a primal or fundamental emotion that we have experienced through trauma or loss, and this acts as a prime mover or fundamental undercurrent in our unconscious and is a catalyst for our actions. Sometimes we can develop an internal possession because of the way we were raised, for example, when our families valued money rather than love. Such as: "If you don't make 'x' amount of money, then you have no value to me." Or the idea that in life the only thing that matters is financial success. Or your nuclear family has shamed you, demeaned you, told you that you were not good enough, pretty enough, smart enough, or that you were simply bad, ugly, or stupid. When we are treated in such a way at whatever time in our life, it creates a rebellion within us to prove such and such person wrong, or we make decisions for our life to make someone proud of us, so that we can attain their love.

This internal rebellion to prove that we have more value than how we were abused emotionally, physically, or sexually, then either breaks us, or becomes a foundational way from which we live our lives, and hence becomes an "internal possession." The converse of this act of internal rebellion is that when bad things happen to us, we take the time to process our emotions around such an issue, and make decisions that further our lives; however, we do this for ourselves versus doing this to please someone else. In other words, rather than rebelling against what happened to us, we accept the event that happened, and grow from it. To be clear, rebellion is a war-like act that actively fights against that which tries to dominate it, whereas acceptance is an act of peace, forgiveness, and harmony.

When we have an "internal possession," our egos tend to bend to the will of the possession. The only way to break this kind of possession within oneself is to come to a situation which challenges our fundamental view of self, and therefore challenges us to change. To step away from that which possesses us, in order to make a fundamental change, is seen by our ego in much the same way as a person would think about cutting off an arm or leg. The ego finds it difficult to understand how life could go on without this driving force of "internal possession," just as a person who loses a limb struggles to come to terms with this loss. Yet, without letting go of this "internal possession," it will be hard to find growth, understanding, and peace within oneself. As long as our actions are dictated by situations and people who are either dead or long ago in our past, how can we know who we are and what we really want in life?

Therefore, one can see how an "internal possession" drives our ego to want to be right. Being right fulfills our need to see ourselves as valuable, and hence one can understand how the idea of "white coat syndrome" comes into being. The idea that my way must be the right way is driven by all of these inadequacies that lie underneath the surface of who we are, and the idea that "I am right" gives a sense of power to one who has an "internal possession." However, when a "white coat" has the need to be "right," they often do so at the expense of the person whom they are treating. Therefore, when I say that Jessica is energetically clean, it means that even if she had "internal possessions," she understood that they had no place in the treatment room, and that her best way of being when a patient was in the room was to be a blank slate: to listen to a patient's problems without preconception, and to make treatment decisions based on the information she was provided, rather than from a need to be right. It is a way of being able to treat and listen from a place of humility, and a place where each patient who walks into the room brings with them an opportunity for all in the room to learn from one another. The value of this skill cannot be emphasized enough.

Barbara left our treatment, and I didn't see her again for a long while. Six months later, she called to make an appointment. She told me she had sought other opinions, and she had heard a number of "theories" as to why she was not able to conceive. She had worked with these other practitioners and taken their supplements, followed their advice, changed her diet, and so forth. Yet, she still was not pregnant. She felt that time was running out, and that while she had an innate desire to rebel against my opinion, she said there was a part of her that knew she had a fierce drive for success, and that she had been thinking about my observations for the past six months. She said that her parents only valued success, and as a child if she was not being perfect, they didn't praise her. She had crafted all of her life to get this praise from them, and even after they died she continued to seek praise for being perfect, at her job, at home, with her friends, and in public. She said she could see how she had driven herself to exhaustion in this quest for perfection, and that while she didn't really love my frankness, what I had said had made her think about things that she had not thought about in a long time. She told me that while she was continuing to work, she had cut her time and responsibilities at the office down to four eight-hour days, she was getting regular massages, and she was working at pampering herself more. She asked if I would be willing to see her and help her conceive. Of course I agreed. While we worked together, Barbara continued to try to understand how her possession and therefore her ego drove her. She continued to nourish herself, to be kind to her body, and to give her body as much rest as it needed. Three months later she told me that she had conceived. I advised her to keep nourishing her yin before and, especially, after she gave birth. I noted that pregnancy could be hard on an older body, and she would need even more rest time after the pregnancy and birth. Several months later she gave birth to a daughter, and she has continued to see me through the years as she has felt her drive trying to reassert itself. Barbara is proving to be an apt student of life, and her journey to conception continues to offer her many life lessons, as it should be.

There was a knock at the door to the clinic.

"Come in," I said.

The door opened, and Zach stood there, hand on the door knob.

"Hey Zach. Come on in. Do you remember Jessica? She was wondering if it would be OK with you if she observed your treatment," I said.

"Heya, Roland. Hi, Jessica. Sure, no problem."

Zach stepped in to the room and took a seat on the brown couch.

"So, what's up?" I said.

I have found that taking a casual style of conversation with my patients helps them to feel more comfortable, although it doesn't work for all of my patients. My master is fond of saying: "If you love your patients like they are your family, then they will get better." Aren't we all brothers and sisters in the end? I took out a chart, dated it, added Zach's name to it, and signed it, pen then hovering over the chief complaint line to write what Zach was ailing from.

"I was in a car accident yesterday and you have always said to come in right away if that happens."

"OK. Were you hurt?" I said.

"No obvious damage, but my neck and lower back hurt now."

"Are you going to file a Personal Injury Protection claim?" I asked.

"Yeah. I have talked to the insurance. I already have a PIP claim number."

"OK. What time did the accident happen?"

"1:10 p.m."

"Where did it happen?" I asked.

"At the stoplight of SE Stark and Grand."

"Was it your fault?" I asked.

"No, I was stopped at the light, and the other driver rear-ended me."

"Were they going fast?" I asked.

"No, maybe like 20 or 25 miles per hour."

"Well, that's not a gentle bump. Is your car damaged?" I asked.

"The back of the car is a mess of tangled metal, and the hatch won't open, but the car drives."

"Did you call the police?" I asked.

"Yeah, they came and took a report."

"Good," I said. "I recommend that you also get assessed by a nurse practitioner and your chiropractor. Have you been to either of those yet?"

"I went to the nurse practitioner at 8 a.m., and they wrote me a prescription for acupuncture and massage."

"Great," I said. "Did they write you a prescription for pain medicine? Or would you like me to prescribe herbs for you after I make my assessment?"

"They wrote a prescription for Oxycontin, but I didn't fill it. I would rather have herbs, as they are not addictive," Zach said.

"OK. Easy enough."

If there is one thing that Western medicine and the general public agree on about Chinese medicine, it is that Chinese medicine excels at the treatment of pain. This, is really only a tiny blip on the radar of things we excel at, but it is important that our ability to effectively treat pain has such widespread acceptance. I think Chinese medicine excels at pain treatment for several reasons. First, we see the body as a whole, and do not isolate treatment to a part of the body. By comparison, Western medicine breaks medicine down to specialties, where each specialty has in-depth knowledge only of the part that they work on. This means that it is difficult to understand the cascade effect in the whole body that happens on the path of disease, rather than once a disease manifests. In other words, Chinese medicine excels at finding disharmonies in the body before the disharmony concretizes to become one disease or another.

Also, because Chinese medicine sees trauma as a disruption in the flow of qi or energy, which then leads to obstruction of the meridians, then it is relatively easy to move the qi, break the blockage, and get the body functioning normally again. In effect, we don't try to numb the problem with some drug that affects the body's pain receptors, we treat the cause of the pain itself. Trauma from a car accident is a very acute problem, so we are able to get quick and effective results with the pain – when someone comes to us promptly. This does not mean that after a car accident, one should only go to their acupuncturist; that is not what I am suggesting at all. But the patients should have an acupuncturist on their team of providers as they are working to recover from their injuries.

Chapter 5

"The way a PIP claim works," I told Zach, "is that you have to show regular treatment, and we will have to grade your progress by asking you questions that quantify your pain and your range of motion (ROM). I am going to ask you a series of questions, and I would like you to do the motion I ask you to do, then tell me how much it hurts based on a scale of 1 to 10, with 10 being the worst. With these numbers, we will be able to have an idea of how well you are recovering on a week-to-week basis. OK?" I said.

"OK," Zach said.

"Additionally, you will need to see the other practitioners on your medical team at the frequency which they suggest. For example, I would suggest that for the first two weeks, you receive acupuncture twice per week, receive a massage at least once in the same week, and get at least one chiropractic visit during the week. This means a number of visits to your medical team each week for a while. None of these visits will cost you, as long as your PIP claim is valid. OK?"

"Got it," Zach said.

"OK. I would like to begin by having you sit straight up and look towards the ceiling, so that your entire face points to the ceiling. Do you have any pain with that?"

"Yeah, at the base of my neck,'" Zach said.

"On a scale of 1 to 10, if you would?" I said.

"Oh yeah. Maybe a 5?"

"OK. Now, I want you to look down at the ground with your chin touching your chest. Do you have pain?"

"Yeah, not as much, like a 3."

"Now, I would like you to put your head back up, so that you are looking straight in front of you, then rotate your head to the right. In this position, you will now be looking over your right shoulder," I said.

Zach rotated his head to the right and stopped at about 45 degrees. "That's as far as I can get. The pain is a 6 or a 7."

"Good. Now look over your left shoulder."

Zach rotated to look over the left shoulder, and stopped at 60 degrees. "That's it. Pain is an 8."

"OK, Zach, you are doing a good job with this. Just a couple more questions. Bring your head back to looking forward, and then try to touch your right ear to your right shoulder, without raising your shoulder."

Zach bent his head to his right shoulder and stopped at 45 degrees. "I don't have much pain, maybe a 1, but it is really stiff."

"Now, the same with the opposite side?"

Zach repeated the test on the opposite side. "Same. No pain, just stiff."

"Great. Now, please stand up."

Zach stood up.

"Extend your arms straight out from your body, as if you are a cross, palms down. Any pain?"

"No."

"Good. Now, extend both arms straight in front of the body, palms down. Any pain?"

"This one, I can feel behind my shoulders and into my scapula on both sides. A 4 maybe?"

"Now, put both arms at your sides. Bring your left arm back behind your waist and try to touch the middle of your back with the back of your hand."

"Ahh. This one hurts, like a 7." Zach's left hand rested just a bit higher than the beltline on his low back, but he could not reach his mid back.

"OK, now, do the same thing with the opposite arm."

"It feels the same," Zach said as he positioned his right hand behind his back.

"Great, Zach. That will do. We are looking at pain in your cervical spine from C_5 down to C_7, and in your thoracic spine from T_1 to about T_5. Do you have any questions, Jessica?" I said.

"Actually, I do," she said. "When you are figuring out the range of motion, how do you figure out the degrees?"

"Good question," I said. "Think of it like this: If you are facing forward, for example, facing east, the way your nose is pointing forms a line from east to west, and the line of your shoulders forms another line from north to south. So, when you are looking forward, without turning your head, your nose and your shoulders create an "L." This would be 90 degrees. As you rotate your head towards your shoulder, the angle becomes smaller. Then, this same kind of idea is applied to rotating the ears to the shoulders, or moving the arms one way or another."

"Thanks," she said.

"Let's get you on the table, Zach. You know the drill," I said.

"Yep."

Zach took off his shoes and socks, then his shirt. He climbed up and lay face down on the table.

"Zach, I am going to wash my hands, then I will be right back," I said.

I left the room, went down the hall to wash and scrub my hands, then walked back to the treatment room. Infection from acupuncture is rare. I have never seen it in my own office, but have heard about it in rare cases. In the first place, the filiform needle, which most acupuncturists use, is a tiny, solid needle, made out of stainless steel. When most people think of needles, they think of a hypodermic needle, such as is used with injections. These needles are far more painful than acupuncture needles for several reasons. First, hypodermic needles are a much-bigger-gauge needle, and they are like this because they are designed to inject something, usually a fluid, into the body. Secondly, because they are used to inject, the insertion of the hypodermic needle acts very much like the coring of an apple with an apple core tool. As the hypodermic is inserted, it "cores" the skin and flesh that are on the inside of the needle, as it is inserted. Then, when the fluid is injected, it pushes out this "core" of skin and flesh with the fluid. Lastly, the pain of a hypodermic needle has to do with where the shot is placed, and how deeply it needs to be inserted. For example, when we give blood, the needle has to penetrate our veins, which, while they might lie close to the surface of the skin, are still comparatively deep. Compare this to a filiform needle, which is so small in gauge that five or six filiform needles can fit in the needle tube of a hypodermic needle, and the filiform would have a difficult time penetrating a vein or a nerve. Additionally, acupuncturists have no reason to try to penetrate arteries, veins, tendons, or nerves, because we do not believe that the qi resides in those places.

Therefore, when a solid filiform needle is inserted into the skin, it simply pushes the cells to the sides. The hole is so small that it often doesn't bleed, and at most the insertion location will have only a single drop of blood. When single-use, sterilized needles are used, along with the tiny entry point, these factors make the chance of infection very slight indeed.

The caveat to this is: If someone is immune-compromised, such as being diabetic, or if they are taking blood thinners, then even the smallest wound may not heal quickly or may have complications. Or if someone was working in a coal mine and then received acupuncture right afterwards without taking a shower first, there is always a possibility of infection if the body is dirty. In modern, industrialized society, though, most people bathe regularly, as no one wants to be the worst-smelling person in the room. So, as I said, while I have never seen an infection from a single-use filiform needle, I also would not like to see one, so hand-washing is part of my regular routine.

I walked back over to Zach and said, "OK, Zach, I am going to palpate your neck and back."

"OK."

I laid my hands on Zach's neck and back, feeling the spinous processes of the spine, counting from the cervical vertebrae down towards the lumbar vertebrae. While counting, I marked a line on his skin with my pen in the space under each vertebra I was interested in treating. I was also looking for subluxations and rotations of each vertebra. Now, I don't manipulate bones chiropractically, but it is always something I note when feeling a back. When a vertebra is changed from its normal straight position, it is a clue that something is going on at that point and in that area, and there is almost always pain around this area. When vertebrae are rotated or sunken in (subluxated) or pushed out, there will commonly be a muscular tension in that area, a rib that is out of place, or, worst-case scenario, a pinched nerve. Inserting needles around a vertebrae that is misaligned can relax the muscles, and sometimes can allow the spinous process to go back into its natural position due to a change in contracture of the muscle.

"It looks like your C_5 and C_6 are subluxated; this is common when someone has experienced whiplash. Your T_1 is rotated to the left, as is your T_2. Your T_4 and T_5 are rotated to the right. The space between L_2, L_3, and L_4 seems compressed. You will want to see your chiropractor and have him assess your neck and back," I said.

"OK."

"I also have a massage therapist whom I like to refer my motor-vehicle-accident patients to, if you want her card."

"OK."

"All right, I am going to begin putting needles into the places I have marked on your back."

"OK."

I took a pack of needle off the shelf, opened it, removed a few blister packs of needles, and started opening the individually wrapped needles.

"OK, here we go," I said.

I began deftly inserting needles around the vertebrae I had marked. I inserted needles above and below the vertebrae that were subluxated on both sides of the spine. On the vertebra that was rotated to the left, I needled above and below the vertebra on the left side of the spine, and on the vertebrae that were rotated to the right, I needled above and below on the right side of the spine. For the compressed vertebrae, I needled above and below the vertebrae bilaterally. I then needled a spot near the crease that is formed on the side of the palm proximal to the fifth finger when making a fist with the hand. Then I needled the corresponding point to this on the outside of the ankle underneath the lateral malleolus. Lastly, I inserted a needle in a spot almost in the middle of the popliteal fossa (the back of the knee).

"All right, Zach, I am going to hook up the electrostim. You have had this before, so you know what it is like."

"OK."

I attached the clips from C_5 to the needle that had been inserted into the popliteal fossa on both sides.

"I am going to turn it on. Tell me when it is significant, but not painful. Right side first."

"OK."

I turned on the machine, and slowly began turning the knob up.

"That is good," Zach said.

"OK. Now, left side."

I then turned that knob up slowly.

"There," said Zach.

"OK. Now, it will be about thirty minutes on the needles. Are you warm enough?"

"Yeah, I am good."

"Do you have any questions, Jessica?" I said.

"I do. Why did you only put needles on one side for the spinous processes that are rotated?" she said.

"Well, there are actually a few ways to do this. You could needle one side of the spine, and use moxibustion on the other side. You could needle both sides. Or you could do it as I have done. The theory I am using here is that because the vertebrae are rotated, then they are being pulled out of place by muscle tension on the same side. By needling the afflicted side, one hopes that this tension will release, and thus allow the bone to shift back into its normal place of alignment. I say 'hopes' because this doesn't work one hundred percent of the time. For example, if the vertebra is rotated because a rib is out, this strategy might not be effective. But, if the rotation is simply because of tension by the erector spinae muscles (the muscles that extend from the neck to the low back), then this method will often relieve that tension, and allow the spinous process to assume its natural position. Additionally, because I take the approach of motor vehicle accidents being a team project, this way of treatment will make it easier for the chiropractor to make the adjustment, because the muscle will be more relaxed."

"OK. That makes sense. Also, why only use the electrostim from the cervical vertebrae needles to the needles in the popliteal fossa?" she asked.

"I do this because the electrostim then flows through the whole erector spinae, from top to bottom. We anchor it in the popliteal fossa, because this is one of the main governing points for the back."

"Got it. Thanks," she said.

"No problem."

"Do you still have that Gypsy Kings CD?" Zach asked.

"I do."

"Can I listen to that while I am lying here on the table?"

"Sure. No problem."

I picked up the CD Zach wanted to listen to, plugged it in to the CD player, and pushed the play button. Then, I sat down in the La-Z-Boy to chart. Some practitioners like to chart at the end of the day, but I have always found it best for me to chart right after I insert the needles.

"I am going to go get a cup of coffee. I will be back in twenty-five minutes," Jessica said.

"Great. See you then," I said.

Jessica knew that I preferred to have minimal disturbance in the room while a patient was "cooking"; it always yielded a better treatment. I learned this in my early days as a student at Five Branches University in Santa Cruz. Occasionally, in the teaching clinics, they would have multiple students under the observance of one supervisor assessing one patient. This is not an uncommon practice in any medical school, Chinese medicine or otherwise, but the resulting energetic soup caused the energy of the treatment room to spiral around like a vortex. It was anything but peaceful for me, and I doubt that the patient received much benefit.

Regarding energetic soup, in Chinese medicine, practitioners understand that when multiple people touch a patient, it will change the rhythm or the feeling of the pulse. When there is a group of students who take the pulse of a patient, the patient's pulse will make subtle changes that reflect the addition or subtraction of energy from the students who are taking the patient's pulse. One can liken this to being around a friend or peer who is in a terrible mood. They are angry, cursing, depressed, lamenting their problems, or whatever. In these situations, one has to work harder to keep one's own mood positive. Often, when we find ourselves in these situations, we self-limit our time with these people, saying that we have something else to do, or otherwise cutting our time with them short. Everyone has known a situation like this, where the darkness of another person's emotions seem to suck the light from everyone that they are around. This is why, in these situations, the supervisor or teacher feels the pulse first, and then the students feel the pulse afterwards. The longer that the student or practitioner touches the patient, the more energy that flows from one to another, thereby changing the pulse. I call this the "energy gradient."

The energy gradient is a natural energetic law. Namely, that which is full tends to flow towards that which is empty. Think of this like water running downhill. Water never runs uphill; it drains from higher in the hills towards lower in the valleys. Let's say that I meditate daily, do qi gong or martial arts, regulate my diet and emotions, and keep my having sex to a minimum. Then generally I am going to have more qi than someone who does not do these things. If my patient does not follow the above regimen, then whenever I touch them, my qi is going to flow into them, just as water flows downhill. The longer I touch them, the more qi they will receive from me. The more of my qi that flows in their body, the more likely it is that the beat of their heart will change, and this then affects the pulse. Conversely, if my patient has more qi than I do, then the qi flows the other way, from the patient's body to my body, and I will end up with more qi. Compound these ideas with the idea of seven or eight students who all have varying lifestyles (not everyone who practices acupuncture is full of qi), and you can see how this could get chaotic very quickly. There are ways to change this gradient situation, but all of the practitioners in the room have to be on top of their game and know how to tune, like the musicians in an orchestra tune their instruments before they act as a symphony. One instrument that is out of tune can wreck a whole symphonic movement. For practitioners such as surgeons, or other medical teams, this tuning becomes second nature. They act as a team, because they have learned, in an unspoken way, to intuit the needs of the team. These people would be considered professionals. In group situations, most students are still bumbling and fumbling with the medicine, and as their teams are changed every semester, the students rarely learn how to quiet themselves and be in tune with their peers. This is not a slight on Chinese medicine schools, but more of an observation that teamwork is advanced medicine, and if there is teamwork amongst practitioners, this can create profound healing. If there is not, it can create profound disruption. Teamwork is rarely taught in Chinese medicine schools, in part because Chinese medicine practitioners in the West often work for themselves, and do not often work with their peers in a regular treatment situation. However, I would advocate that team-building skills could be added to the Chinese medicine curriculum prior to a student entering clinic. These skills could help students when they are put into team situations in clinic. In the long run, harmony within the treatment room is one of the building blocks of a successful treatment.

Jessica knows my opinions about such things, and that when I treat, my goal for the patient, while the needles are in, is harmony and peace. This is yet another reason she is one of my mentees: she knows how to quiet herself so that she can truly listen, ask questions when appropriate, and take intuitive cues when needed.

While I am musing on this: Westerners rarely think about what the prohibitions for receiving acupuncture are. These prohibitions are pretty straightforward in my opinion. Let's list them as commandments; then I will discuss them.

1. **Thou shalt not receive acupuncture in a lightning storm.**
2. **Thou shalt not receive acupuncture while in a rage.**
3. **Thou shalt not receive acupuncture right after sex.**
4. **Thou shalt not receive acupuncture after strenuous exercise or with an elevated heartbeat.**
5. **Thou shalt not receive acupuncture when drunk or intoxicated on substances.**
6. **Thou shalt not receive acupuncture on an empty stomach.**
7. **Thou shalt tell your acupuncturist if you are prone to seizures.**
8. **Thou shalt not receive acupuncture in a room that is too cold, too damp, or too hot.**
9. **And my own commandment: Thou shalt trust your acupuncturist.**

These are pretty straightforward, right? **Commandment One:** Have you ever lost a computer or a fuse to a lightning storm? It is a total bummer. Well, your heart has an electrical rhythm to it as well, and getting a nasty shock while receiving acupuncture would not be fun at all.

Commandment Two: When you are angry or are in a rage, all of the qi goes to the top of your head. We call it liver yang rising. In this state your eyes turn red, you might end up with a headache at the top or vertex of your head, and, in the worst-case scenario, your eyes will roll back in your head and you will go berserk. If you have never seen someone berserk, count yourself lucky. Berserk, meaning bear warrior, was one of the honored forms of being a warrior in the Viking and Nordic traditions. Berserkers could fight with the strength of ten men, and they seemed impervious to even the most damaging wounds. The modern drug PCP (or angel dust) often puts people in this state, and police who deal with this kind of thing will say that they fired round after round into the person, but they still kept coming. Well, most people of Nordic descent don't berserk in war anymore; they use it in their home against their families. Putting needles into anyone who is in a rage or berserking is futile, won't help the patient, and won't help the acupuncturist, because people who are in a rage cannot be reasoned with at all. To the ragers and berserkers out there; learn how to take ten to twenty deep breaths. It will make your lives easier, before you do something which you will never be able to take back, or ever apologize for.

Commandment Three: No acupuncture after sex.

For men, you just gave up all of your energy; there is literally nothing for acupuncture to work with. Come back in a few days, when your sexual potency comes back. Oh, and take a nap – you know you want to.

Women, you just had a shot of espresso; how do you want to spend it? Realistically though, once you have had sex, then unlike the depletion in men your energy is surplus, but not in a way that is good for treatment, because in order to be assessed your energy needs to be in a place of balance for your body. I know that I have really opened the can of worms now. It is very hard to talk about the sexual taboos without talking about sex. Can I wave my hands, give you a cookie, and tell you *everything will be right as rain when you leave* .... No? I thought not. Well if we stray too far from the nine commandments, let me just remind you that this is not my fault. Or, maybe it is, a little.

Chapter 5

Sex. The act we love to love, love to hate, and love to spend way too much time thinking of, as a culture. You know that innocent thing little kids say: "Boys have a penis, and girls have a vagina …." Why is it that most of our culture has not moved past this? After all, it is something four-year-olds say to each other, yet all over the country men and women still essentially look at each other in the same way. I will try to discuss things for my gay and lesbian friends as well, but let's just say that you are not as stuck in this area of thought as much as heterosexual partners, and you know the sexual parts that you work with quite well. The point that I want to make with this brief musing on sex, is that, whatever our choice of sexual partner is, we tend to come at sex in a rather primitive way. It is an "animal instinct" after all.

Let's go back to the beginning of each person for a moment. Our parents had sex. Hopefully it was good, with a lot of grunts and groans, and mutual orgasming. What Mom and Dad ate, drank, smoked, or took in the previous three days, all plays a part in the health of the little semen swimmers trying to reach the fortress of the egg. You see, it is not just the RNA and DNA that cross over to combine, it is the very essence and qi itself. The sperm and the egg combine, mixing the genetics, qi, and essence of each parent, and life is created. There is that myth that only God creates life, but a male and a female in species all over the world, have the power to create life together. We will circle back to this.

Now hopefully, the parents-to-be are happy that they are pregnant, and no one has misgivings, or ends up dropping out from this team experience, essentially enslaving the other parent to a hard life of child-rearing alone before the birth has even happened. But let's just say all is on the up-and-up and Mom and Dad are ecstatic, which leads to more happy sex, because once pregnant you might as well enjoy it as much as possible, at least until the morning sickness arrives (although this is treatable).

Whether Mom and Dad are in France or not, determines how much stress Mom will have while pregnant. You see, France is the only country I know of that actually pays the respect to a mother that a mother is due. If you get pregnant and are a resident of France, whether a citizen or not, you get not only a year's paid leave from your job, but also a state-paid doula to help with cooking food, doing laundry, and such things, thus reducing the stress on mothers. All other countries pale in comparison, to my knowledge. This is important, because the more stressed Mom is, the more likely the child will have

ADHD or warrior mentality.[10,11,12,13,14] The research shows that the less the mother is stressed, the more likely it is that she will have a child who is a planner, capable of deep and profound thought; a scholar, if you will. The more stressed-out Mom is, the more likely she is to have a child who is hyperactive and quick to react to things. Here's looking at you, Donald; or a warrior, if you will. This has nothing to do with genes, but with the training a child receives while it is in the womb. Interestingly, if the stress diminishes after the baby is born, and the mother and father are both highly nurturing, it can ameliorate the stress that was learned in the womb. These are important concepts, because they dictate whether we are going to give birth to a generation of warriors or diplomats, and whether we want the cataclysm of world war or the harmony of world peace. I hereby name France the home of scholars and lovers. Now, if the French weren't so rude to those who don't speak French, it would be the perfect country.

I digress. So, we are born as either scholars or warriors. Presuming Mom and Dad keep it together until we grow up, and there aren't any other global or family catastrophes, then one day we will reach sexual maturity ourselves. One day we wake up and find ourselves sexually aroused. "Hmmm, what is this?" we ask ourselves. All of a sudden, touching ourselves is pleasurable. We are on the way to getting kicked out of Eden.... The opposite sex, or the same sex, no longer strikes us as a comrade, but suddenly invokes strange and desirous feelings within us. The parents decide to have the dreaded birds-and-the-bees conversation, but this is often inadequate at best. Mom and Dad seem to be stuck back at that conversation piece of a four-year-old, where "boys have a penis and girls have a vagina." I know, Mom and Dad, I have been stealing your *Playboy/ Playgirl* for a year now.

No, the conversation that lacks in Western household is actually the most important one. Men have semen and women have eggs, and each are finite, meaning you only have

---

10. "How Parents' Stress Can Hurt A Child, From the Inside Out," by Alice G. Walton, *Forbes*, July 25, 2012.
11. "Antenatal Maternal Stress and Long-term Effects on Child Neurodevelopment: How and Why?" by Talge NM, Neal C, Glover, *Journal of Child Psychology Psychiatry*. 2007 Mar-Apr.
12. "Prenatal Stress and Neurodevelopment of the Child: Focus On the HPA Axis and Role of the Placenta," by O'Donnell K, O'Connor TG, Glover V. *Developmental Neuroscience*, June 17, 2009.
13. "The Brain: The Switches that Can Turn Mental Illness On and Off," by Carl Zimmer, *Discover Magazine*, June 2010.
14. "Prenatal Stress and Risk for Autism," by Dennis K. Kinney, Ph.D., Kerim M. Munir, M.D., M.P.H., D.Sc., David J. Crowley, and Andrea M. Miller, *Neuroscience Biobehaviors*, 2008 Oct.

so many for your entire lifetime. When you run out, you are out; you can't get more naturally. Semen, and to some extent eggs, are the source of spiritual power. The less you have, the less bright your spiritual light will be. The faster you deplete your essence, as we call this, the faster you will age, and the quicker you will fall into the path of disease. This is general philosophy I am speaking of here; there are always special cases, such as children who get sick, and people who die young, but that is a conversation for another time. Additionally, I said "to some extent for women," because a women's essence is more complicated, and is tied up with something that is called "jade fluid," which is the fluid excreted from the vagina when the woman is either sexually aroused or orgasming. So, the more one orgasms (either man or woman) the more one loses essence.

Essence, in a nutshell, defines the strength of the body, and in some sense the ability to be able to conceive. The weaker our essence, the harder time we have conceiving. This is why it is easier to conceive children at twenty than it is at forty. I am not saying this is what one should do – live your own life. I am simply saying that there tend to be fewer complications in one's twenties.

Western culture has no belief in any of the above. We tell people that if you want to wait until you are forty to conceive, then science is there for you, but this is not the nature of the human body. Western culture also buys into the culture of sex. We strive to be the hottest things on the planet, regardless of our age. Fat is bad, thin is good; big breasts, big butt, big penis, firm abs, well-muscled pecs, whatever: it is all around us, and is used successfully to market anything from peanut butter to swim suits, such as the mankini. Yet, think of this: an anorexic female cannot safely carry a baby to term, nor does a heavily muscled man often have a high-enough sperm count to conceive. If one follows the line of reasoning that sex is all around us, therefore sex and conception must be the highest and loftiest goals we can achieve, but they are not. Our true highest and loftiest goals are to interact with the planet which we have been placed on, from a place of enlightenment, or as one holy book said: "As the caretakers of the earth."

To fulfill these goals, we have to approach sex as something that is fun and loving, but not something we do all of the time. *The Wolf on Wall Street* said something like "Brokers masturbate eight or nine time a day." No wonder the financial markets are crazy – they have no spiritual light. Along with this idea is that the more women are sexualized, the more men feel like they need to meet this standard as well. We could call it sexual inflation or a sexual arms race. At some point we have to see those around us as other spiritual lights in different bodies, and find the connection when there is a connection to be had. Nothing else will give us true happiness in the end. All bodies get sick, get old, have financial woes, lose their jobs, etc. If you like fast cars, it is better to buy one yourself than to marry someone because they have one. Eventually, your fast car will no longer be fast, and if you don't enjoy the journey that it takes you on, you'll simply have a slow car that you don't like so much.

I broke the taboo against talking about how sex is used in Western culture. I think the phrase is: "Sorry. Not sorry." I am a demonologist with roots to ancient traditions, and my main tool is to look for patterns of behavior. I assure you, that sex will come up later in these pages, but for now I need to get this musing back on track.

The Fourth Commandment: Thou shalt not receive acupuncture after strenuous exercise or with an elevated heart rate. This one is simple. If your heart rate is elevated, your pulse cannot be used as objective data. This means the practitioner will have to diagnose with one hand tied behind their back.

Do we really need to go over **Commandment Five**? "No acupuncture while high on anything" seems self-evident. **Commandment Six**, no receiving acupuncture on an empty stomach. This is because food acts as a ground, similar to an electrical ground. When your electricity is not grounded, there is a chance that you may get a shock. When you don't have food in your belly, there is a chance that you can go into shock. Shock sucks, to use a colloquial term. The symptoms of shock during acupuncture are: lightheadedness, fainting, thirst, sweaty palms and feet, nausea, and the two I enjoy the least – arrest of the heart, and seizure. If you experience any of the above while getting acupuncture, and hopefully before you experience the last two, ask that your needles be removed promptly, otherwise you might have the last two, or vomit. I can tell you, everyone is happier if you eat beforehand.

The Seventh Commandment: If you have a tendency to seize, tell your practitioner so they can be prepared for the worst-case scenario. There is nothing worse for all parties than watching someone start to seize and being taken completely by surprise.

The Eighth Commandment: The temperature of the room should be pleasant. Too hot, cold, damp, etc. puts you, the patient, at risk of your body temperature cooling down or heating up to the ambient temperature of the room. It is important not to be too hot or too cold while being treated.

The Ninth Commandment: Trust and communication can solve most problems. The more there are, the faster problems are resolved. This is because trusting means sharing, sharing leads to better understanding of the problem, and better understanding of the problem leads to a better diagnosis. "Treatment is only as good as the diagnosis," I say. Those are the nine commandments. One could probably add lesser orders of writ, but following these will mostly keep you from getting hit by a random meteor, bus, or other act of God.

Jessica, prompt as usual, gently opened the door and stuck her head in. She glanced at the clock on the wall and sat down in the couch, coffee in hand. The timer I had set went off a minute later. I stood up from the La-Z-Boy, walked over to Zach, and turned off the stim.

"All right, Zach, that's it."

I took the clips off the needles, and then plucked them out, moving from the head to the feet.

"That's all of them," I said.

Zach got up from the table, took his shirt off the couch, and put it on. Jessica slid over to one side of the couch so Zach could sit and put his shoes on. As he did so, I discussed what our treatment plan would be.

"Make appointments with the rest of your team, gather up their assessments, then I would like to see you in a week. Would you like to make an appointment now?"

"I don't know what my work schedule is for next week yet. Can I text you later with dates that work for me?"

"Sure, Zach. Would you mind if Jessica continued to sit in on your appointments?"

"That is fine. I have nothing confidential to discuss that you don't already know."

"OK. I will keep her in the loop. I will look for a text from you regarding next week. In that text you can provide me your PIP number and your car insurance policyholder's information. Also, here are some herbal pills to take for the pain. I want you to take eight, three times per day."

"OK."

As I mentioned, Zach was a regular, and waiting for his information was not a big deal, because we had history together. He trusted me to do the work, and I knew that he would get the payment information together. Shoes on, Zach again said he would text me, and then left.

"Do you have any other questions, Jessica?" I said.

"I noticed that you didn't take the pulse or inspect the tongue on this patient before treatment," she said.

"With MVAs, I don't often find it necessary. This is what we call a straightforward diagnosis. Sure, Zach has plenty of other things we could work on, but in this visit, he was coming to us for pain. The other observations we made at the beginning of the visit, along with the palpation of the back, provide the objective data in this case. We can take the pulse and inspect the tongue next time if you want, but I generally find that it takes a few days for the tongue to change, and the pulse can be variable because of the trauma. Or to speak more clearly, the pulse would simply tell us that he was in pain, so it doesn't add anything to our assessment at this time. Now, in a few weeks, when the pain diminishes, the pulse and tongue will play larger roles as Zach's baseline or root conditions begin to engage again. Does that make sense?"

"Yeah. Is this your strategy with MVAs in general, or just with patients whom you have seen for a long time?"

"It is my general strategy. But, with a new patient, one I'd never seen before, they would have to fill out the initial health history form. From there, we would make sure that they didn't have any cybernetic components such as a pacemaker or insulin pump that could be affected by our electrostim machine. If they did, then we wouldn't use stim in that region of the body. We would also look to make sure that there haven't been any brain changes, by asking cognitive questions, checking the eyes, etc. But, because I have a treatment relationship with Zach, I could tell that his brain was operating normally. Additionally, he didn't claim to have numbness, tingling, or anything that would correspond to the dermatome map. So, all in all, it is pretty straightforward."

"I agree. Will you send me a text when he schedules? I would like to observe this one to conclusion."

"Sure, Jessica, I will send it when I know."

"Great. Do you have any more today?"

"Yeah, a few, but they tend to be more private than Zach is."

"Got it. Then I am going to take off."

"OK. I will see you later."

Jessica left, and I went about my day. A week passed. I had still not received any message from Zach. Then on Wednesday, April 5th, Zach called me and asked to set up an appointment for Friday, April 7th. He sounded frantic.

I texted Jessica, "MVA patient will be back in on April 7th at 11 a.m."

She texted back, "OK. Will be there."

After work, I thought I would go over to Chai Societea on Alberta to do some work. I generally prefer the Chai Societea on Division Street, but I hadn't been to the Alberta location in a while. As tea goes, Chai Societea is not the highest quality in town – that would be the Tao of Tea. But the Tao of Tea on Belmont is set up for having small intimate gatherings while drinking tea, whereas Chai Societea is set up for hanging out in. Chai Societea has wifi, the Tao does not, so if one wants to be productive, Chai Societea is a better choice. Chai Societea also offers its kombucha on tap, which is a much better deal than buying it retail. The Division Street Chai Societea has better access to power outlets, but I learned long ago to follow a hit or idea even when it is outside of my normal habits, and my hit was that I should go to the Alberta Chai Societea.

I left the office, got into my car, and drove down Alder Street, forgetting that the Morrison Bridge was closed, and then remembered why I had been avoiding certain parts of Portland's east side lately, because it seemed like every other bridge is always closed. Inconvenient, but not a show stopper. I took a left on Park Avenue and another left on Washington Street to head back to 10th Avenue heading north. I took a right on 10th, and caught the red light at the intersection of 10th and Burnside across from Powell's Books and next to Sizzle Pie. The light changed to green, and I cruised relatively stoplight-free down to Lovejoy, so that I could cross the Broadway Bridge. At least this bridge wasn't closed.

The Broadway Bridge, however, is hit or miss. During rush hour it can be a good way to bypass the snarl on the I-405 bridge, but if there is a Blazers game or a concert, it is probably better to park your car and walk. Today, I was lucky and there was not an event. I meandered my way east on Weidler Street and took a left onto NE Grand Avenue to head north. NE Grand Avenue then becomes NE Martin Luther King Jr. Blvd in a block and a half. From here it would be a relatively painless cruise to Alberta Street. I had just rolled past Russell Street BBQ on Russell Street and Martin Luther King Jr. Blvd, when out of the corner of my left eye, a store sign grabbed my attention. It said, "Witchcraft and Witchcraft Supplies."

Ballsy. There are a fair number of people who practice magic in Portland, but I have never seen anyone be so bold about it. Well, this was worth a look. I hooked a u-turn, navigated my way back to the storefront, and walked up to the store.

This seems like a good place to insert a few ideas. I am not terribly supportive of witchcraft in general. It is not that I am averse, or antagonistic, but I generally see the practice as more problematic than helpful. First, one must discern whether a witch is practicing satanic magic or earth magic. Then, is it low magic or high magic? Then, within all of this, is there true capability to cause harm or benefit? I am not going to wax on about magic here, but simply put, agents of the dark need to be called out, and witches who practice earth magic are generally benign.

Originally, witches were the female component of the Druid order. I would postulate that our modern idea of a witch and a warlock came from this idea of druids and witches: he worships the sun, and she worships the moon. Philip Carr-Gomm in the foreword to the *Book of Druidry* by Ross Nichols says:

> "Druidry and Wicca are distinct and separate manifestations of the Western Path, and the best way to consider them, is as brothers and sisters – within the same family, and therefore sharing family characteristics, but also separate, with characteristics peculiar to themselves."

In the 500s or 600s, however, when Christianity invaded the English Isles, many Druids figured out that they could survive the purges by joining the clergy of the Christians. But this option was not available for women, and Christianity, like many religions, has long seen women as a threat. So, witchcraft went underground over time, rather than face the looming cruelty of the Christians. Of course, we know as a part of American and European history, that a mere thousand years later, witches were hunted, burned, drowned, and otherwise murdered by Christians and other religions. I believe it is accurately surmised that the Western path of herbal knowledge, gynecological knowledge, and healing knowledge was mostly burned on the stake with multiple generations of witches. The book that was often used to prove whether someone was a witch or not was the *Malleus Maleficarum*, which can be translated as the *Hammer of Witches*. This book, written by the Catholic Heinrich Kramer in 1487, advocated the extermination of witches, and the method of obtaining confession was through torture, with the promise of death if one confessed. We know that these brutal methods are about as accurate as George Bush saying that water-boarding was an effective practice of interrogation. In the 200 years after it was published, the sales of the *Malleus Maleficarum* were only bested by sales of the *Bible* itself, meaning that it was the West's second bestseller after the *Bible* itself. Looking back on history, one can probably guess that Herr Kramer was simply a man who had been rejected by a woman and then tried to take his revenge on the whole sex. The witches who were obliterated might well have wished that the printing press had been invented thirty years after the publication of the *Malleus Maleficarum*, rather than thirty years before it. The printing press gave the common people access to this book, fanning the fear of witchcraft, and regardless of whether the inquisitors thought the material worthy or not, the courts certainly justified its use for all burnings and drownings.

Now, this is a casual summary and not an exhaustive deposition, with the purpose of leading us to the point where organized religion obviously became thoroughly nasty, burning or drowning anyone who so much as hinted at deviating even slightly from the norm. Or, as was discussed in the *Malleus*, a woman who had any sexual desire of her own, and who was also different from the norm. When you think about it, Western culture seems to enjoy shooting itself in the foot – over and over again. These massive purges destroyed so much of the inherited knowledge in a number of different cultures, that it is surprising that any information on herbalism, astronomy and the seasons, mythical history, and occult or spiritual knowledge outside of organized religion survived in the West at all. The important thing to remember here is that these purges didn't just last a lifetime, but a period of over 300 years, or roughly six generations.

In a sense, if it weren't for the Arthur myth, would the general populace even remember what the Druids and witches were? Perhaps, perhaps not. The point I make with all of this is that modern witchcraft is a conglomeration of the remaining techniques that were not exterminated, or techniques that have been "rediscovered" after the witch purges of the past. Many of the old ways simply did not survive the purges. It is similar for the Druids as for the witches, and the Druids are pretty forthright that they have had to piece their traditions back together bit by bit. Therefore, it is uncommon to meet a witch who has true power. This is not to say that there are not any, but simply that of those who call themselves witches, the ones who are truly powerful are much less common. This is why I say that most witches who practice earth magic are benign. However, saying this, I wouldn't let someone who practices magic do any kind of energy work or spiritual work on me at this point. There are reasons for this that would take too long to explain here, but simply consider deeply before letting anyone mess with your spiritual body. There is a fallacy that most people fall into, which is that if you can't feel your spiritual light, and someone else can see it or feel it, then they must know what is best for you. As with all other guidance, this does not always prove true, and it can often be detrimental to your growth.

I walked into the store, noting herbs on the wall in jars, bundles of dried herbs hanging from hooks, and a display shelf with lip balm and lotion on it. The space was small, with a main front counter and a couple of small treatment rooms in the back.

"Is the owner here?" I asked the smallish young woman behind the counter.

"I'm the owner," she said.

"Great! My name is Roland Pearce, I'm an acupuncturist, and I am wondering what style of witchcraft you practice. Like, lotions and potions? That kind of thing?"

"I'm a witch from the south, so yeah, herbs, house clearing, feng shui, ceremonies, clearing ghosts, and I am good with removing possessions," she said with an inquisitive look.

"Ah, possessions – that is serious stuff. How did you get into that?" I said.

"I went to acupuncture school at Tai Sophia, and I discovered that I had these gifts while I was there."

"Did you graduate and take the boards?" I said.

"No. I decided that I wasn't as interested in acupuncture as I was in herbology and the mystical traditions which I grew up with."

She looked at me, I looked at her, and we sized each other up. The space didn't have a malevolent resonance, and she seemed on the up and up, or at least not threatening or obfuscatory, so I said, "Well, if you don't mind, I will take a few business cards, as I occasionally have people in need of your services." I picked up three or four cards and looked at them. "Are you Mary Jane?"

"I am."

"Nice to meet you."

"You also."

Then I walked back to my car, tucking the cards in my back pocket. Well, that was unexpected, I thought. I guessed I was expecting something a bit more nefarious. It is always nice to have another tool in the tool bag, and frankly if someone enjoys kicking bad spirits out of people's bodies, I can live with that. I may even send her a few patients.

I rolled down to the office at 10:30 a.m. on April 7th, offering my usual greetings to the street vendors on my walk in. Jessica arrived at 10:45 a.m. and said, "You're early."

"I wasn't sure how bad traffic would be. Highway 26 has been nasty lately. You know, if they would simply build a tunnel for all of the people going to the Ross Island Bridge somewhere after the PGE Park exit, a lot of the congestion would be dispersed."

"Yeah, the city would rather spend the money on more parking meters. You know that they are doing it just to piss you off," she said with a smile.

"Don't get me started about that. I grew up in this city, and I do take it as a personal affront. But I am not going to rant today," I said.

At 11 a.m. Zach walked in. He was pale as a sheet and dripping large globules of sweat.

"Hey, Zach. How are you doing?" I said.

"I feel terrible."

"Is this in regards to the car accident? I didn't get a text from you last week."

"No. Something else is going on. For the past week, I haven't been able to sleep. It feels like there is a hole in my heart. To get to sleep, I have to do energy work on my heart."

"Did anything unusual happen this week? High stress, someone dying, a breakup?" I asked.

"No. Nothing like that. About a week ago I woke up and while I was getting breakfast together, I heard a voice that told me to take three tablespoons of coconut oil. Then, right after that, I heard a voice tell me to put a gun in my mouth and pull the trigger."

"Was this a one-off experience?" I asked.

"No. I hear the same voice every few hours."

"Is it the same voice saying both things?" I asked.

"No, two separate voices. I started taking the coconut oil, but the voices are still there. Am I going crazy?"

"I don't think so. Let's treat you in the La-Z-Boy today," I said.

Zach sat down in the La-Z-Boy. I picked up a pack of needles and opened a few of the blister packs. As I approached Zach to assess him, clear as a bell I heard a voice next to my ear say, "Don't treat this guy."

I was dumbfounded. I am not generally clairaudient, that is, the ability to psychically hear people or spirits. I looked at Jessica, whose expression was changing from one of confidence to fear. It didn't appear that she had heard what I did, but she was having her own experience.

I said to myself, "Really? I know this guy!"

Again, clear as a bell, the words rang out, "Don't treat this guy."

"Bollocks! Can I treat his physical body?" I asked myself.

"No," said the voice.

"His emotional body?"

"No."

Chapter 5

"His spiritual body?"

"No."

I admit, I am sometimes a stubborn student, and even when having interactions with the other world, I sometimes want to simply do it my own way.

"Well, this sucks. I am going to stick a few needles in anyway," I said to myself.

Silence. In hindsight, I should have listened to the voice.

"Hey, Zach, I am going to put a needle here, in the crook of your arm, on the lateral side, near the crease of the joint. We will start there," I said.

"OK."

I took a needle, loaded it into the tube, and put my left hand on the crease of Zach's elbow while using my thumb and forefinger to stretch the skin – the opposite of a pinch. I took the loaded tube with my right hand, and placed it on top of his skin without inserting it. The second before I inserted the needle with my index finger by pressing down on the needle in the tube, Zach violently wrenched his arm up and away towards his chest with his hand ending up near his ear, the elbow cradled on his chest, with the opposite hand covering his elbow.

He looked at me with wide, scared eyes. "I didn't just do that, Roland!" he whimpered, "I didn't just do that! How did my arm just move without me doing it?!"

I sat down on my black rolling medical stool and rolled back from him.

"Well, this is a new experience," I thought to myself. People may often flinch when getting a needle inserted into them, but to have a full-blown violent jerk, prior to even inserting the needle – well, this was unprecedented. I looked at Jessica, and she was trembling. Not a good sign. Without any warning, darkness shot out from Zach's body right at me. A being as black as black can be. Black eyes, black lips, black arms, black torso, and a black cord coming out of its chest that was connected to the anatomical location of Zach's heart. I did not think, I simply reacted, and began dumping qi to erect an energetic wall between this being and myself. It stopped at the wall, and started pushing at it with its hands, silently howling at us. It was conscious, aware, and predatory, like a hunter trying to reach its prey. I erected my wall to surround Jessica and me, floor to ceiling, then in all four directions covering heaven and earth. We sat in a sphere of white light. It walked around the sphere poking at it with its hands, testing for cracks or holes.

I glanced at Jessica to say with my eyes, "Are you seeing this?" Her eyes were fixed exactly where the creature was, and her eyes followed it as it moved. I could see a soft glow emanating from her heart and filling the space between her and the creature, as she put her own wards into place.

These are the moments that make or break you. All my choices about diet, sexual regulation, minimal substance use, quality sleep, meditation and qi gong practice: all of these choices were paying their dividends right now. Come into a situation like this, without these factors in place, and I would have been lunch by now.

With a final silent howl and malevolent glare at me from just outside my wall, this dark being retreated and sank back into Zach's body. All of this had occurred in fifteen seconds or less.

I looked Zach in the eyes, and I simply said, "What did you get out of it?"

"What?!" he said. "What are you talking about?"

"What was the ritual you did? Or what was it you asked for? Or what kind of pact did you make? I don't know of any other way you would get a full-on, real and true demon to come reside in you," I said.

"A what? A demon? Surely you are kidding?!"

"You are hearing voices, right?" I said.

"Yeah."

"You feel like there is a hole in your heart?" I said.

"Yeah."

"Has anything else changed? Are you seeing shadows? Having affinity towards dark places? Having cravings for raw meat or other odd flavors? Having erratic mood swings, particularly rage or a desire to berserk? Desire to use substances or hard drugs?" I said.

Chapter 5

Zach's eyes were getting wider and wider as he recognized some patterns within himself as I listed things off. "Maybe I am schizophrenic?" he said hopefully.

"I have treated you for three years with no sign of mental illness, so my guess is, that is out. What is more important to me is: Did you see the thing that came out of your body and tried to attack us a few seconds ago?" I said while Jessica vigorously nodded her head.

"No. I didn't see anything," Zach said.

"What did you see, Jessica?" I asked.

"Something I never, ever, want to see again. Black, all black, the utter absence of color, black eyes, even black fingernails. It was stalking around the room howling, and it hated us," she said.

"I saw the same thing," I agreed. "So . . . . Zach, you don't know where you picked this up?"

"No."

"OK. Has your routine changed this week?" I said.

"Well, I have had a few shifts during the day at a ballroom, serving food and drinks," Zach said.

"A ballroom during the day? What kind of event is going on there?" I said.

Zach broke eye contact and looked away, appearing to be ashamed. "They are shooting a porn movie there."

"And you chose to work these shifts?"

"Yeah. The money is really, really good. $300 per shift, plus tips. I am not in the shoot, I am just delivering things from the bar and kitchen."

I closed my eyes, and I said to myself, "Well, since the psychic channel seems open today, show me what I am dealing with."

Images started to roll through my mind. A round banquet table, set with a white tablecloth. There were twelve place settings, but only one person sat at the table. He was Caucasian, with blond hair cut in a bowl shape.

"Who's the guy with the blond hair and the bowl haircut?" I said.

Zach looked at me with a puzzled expression on his face.

"He is sitting at a round banquet table, white tablecloth, and settings for twelve," I said.

"That's ….. that's my boss and the job. There are five tables. Each table has twelve settings," Zach stammered.

"OK," I said to myself, "bigger picture. What's going on here?" I stood above the room looking down. On casual observation, the five tables were scattered about the room. I climb up toward the ceiling, still looking down.

"Are the tables arranged in any order?" I said to Zach.

"They are kind of spaced out from each other. I guess it forms a circle of some sort," he said.

In my mind, I climb down from the upper space of the room and pass through one of the tables, so that I am underneath it, partly into the floor. There on the floor underneath the table, in this imperceptible lines, is drawn a pentagram with a piece of coal in the pentagram's fire position. I walk to the next table. Under this table is a pentagram with a small cup of water in the water position. I walk to the third table, and here is another pentagram with a bit of dirt in the earth position. The fourth table has a clear glass bottle full of air in the air position. The fifth table's pentagram has a little pool of blood in the spirit position.

In a standard pentagram the star appears as what we would normally consider a five-pointed star with equidistant points. This star could be seen as having one of its points facing up, and two of its points facing down. In these pentagrams, however, the single point of the star, which should be up, is facing down, and the two points of the star that should face down are facing up. In other words, this star was a reverse of the standard five-pointed star.

Chapter 5

I climb back up through the table and again stand at the top of the room. In the center of the circle of tables is a round, curtained area where the movie cameras and shooting set are. I now see the faint lines tracing between the tables to again form an upside-down pentagram from the placement of the tables. Outside the circle of tables is a bar with a bartender, and next to this is door which I presume leads to the kitchen. To deliver food and drink, Zach would have had to cross the lines of the larger upside-down pentagram multiple times.

"Did you go to the center of the room where the movie shoot was?" I asked Zach.

"No. We weren't allowed to. It was one man and multiple women, as well as the film crew, and they were the only people allowed into the curtained circle," he said.

"Did you eat or drink at any of the tables?" I asked.

"Yeah. We received a shift drink and a shift meal. We would sit at one of the tables and eat," he said.

In my mind, I climbed out of the room to the outside of the building. Hanging on the side of the building, as if it were King Kong, was the largest demon I have ever seen. When I say big, I mean sixty or seventy feet in height. If you think of the Balrog from *Lord of the Rings*, you are getting close to what I was seeing. Its skin was made up of writhing dark beings like the one I had seen in Zach. Two horns arose out of its skull on either side, almost like a bull's horns. It had large leathery bat wings and a long narrow tail that ended in a spade. The tail was like that of a possum, but the tail wasn't pink, and possum tails don't have spades on them. Its snout was also bull-like. The whole thing was like a minotaur with wings, a tail, and red eyes, which burned intensely. It was looking into the building at exactly the floor, which I had just left. As I stood there in the air, it turned its head to look at me, and I mentally and physically shivered as one who had just been seen by a nightmare.

I started off my stool.

"Zach, I need to confer with Jessica outside. Before I go, though, I am going to stick your feet in salt. Can you remove your shoes and socks?"

Zach removed his footwear, and I dragged over a tote of salt over that I keep in the room. I opened the container, and had Zach put both feet into the salt.

"Dig your feet in like you are at the beach," I said, while scooping handfuls of salt to fully cover his feet up to the ankles. Once he was settled in, Jessica and I stepped outside the office and walked down the hall a bit.

"Jess, this is a big problem. Not only do I think that I am not going to be able to treat this guy, but I think there will be repercussions. I think you should bail before it gets even more messy," I said.

"What the hell was that thing!?" she said.

"That … is a soldier demon. The lowest and least sentient of the beings who live in hell," I said.

"Shit. Shit, shit, shit. Why do you think it is going to get even more messy?" she said.

"Because that thing is corded to Zach's heart, but in turn, the soldier demon is tethered to one of the lords or princes of hell. Think of that thing as a fleck of skin on something that is much bigger, badder, and meaner," I said.

"How does a prince of hell get interested in Portland?!" she said.

"Because they called it in, or summoned it. They are using the porn shoot as the offering. Zach was simply in the wrong place at the wrong time," I said.

Interesting turn of phrase, but actually something Zach and I have talked about on more than one occasion. For years, I have counseled Zach to change careers, but the money was always better than other jobs he could obtain with his skills. Why would I counsel someone to change their career? It is complicated, but I will try to explain. Thoth, also known as Hermes Trismegistus, wrote in the *Emerald Tablets*, "*As above, so below.*" The Chinese say something like, "*As in heaven, so too on earth.*" This saying has survived in a number of cultures in alchemical and magical texts. This even survived in the Christian *Bible* in a number of passages, such as Matthew 6:10, "*On earth as it is in heaven*" and Matthew 18:18, "*Whatever you bind on earth will be bound in heaven, and whatever you loose on earth will be loosed in heaven.*"

"*As above, so below*," has many meanings, and many applications, but the one I want to focus on is the idea of hierarchy. The beings of heaven are organized by level of rank, order, and chain of command. God sits at the top of this hierarchy, and the offices, which include angels, descend in rank from God. According to Dionysius the Areopagite, the order is three sets of three. The lowest order is the Angels, and these are the messengers or heralds of God. The next most powerful beings are the Archangels, who govern unity. At the top of the lowest hierarchy are the Principalities, who govern authority. At the bottom of the second hierarchy of three are the Powers, who govern order and harmony. Next are the Virtues, who govern courage and virility. Lastly, at the top of the second hierarchy are the Dominions, who govern justice. At the bottom of the first hierarchy are the Thrones, who govern the seat of exaltation. In the middle of the first hierarchy are the Cherubim, who govern fullness of knowledge or wisdom. Lastly, at the top of the first hierarchy, closest to God, are the Seraphim, who govern fire, light, and life.

The order then is:
1) God
2) Seraphim
3) Cherubim
4) Thrones
5) Dominions
6) Virtues
7) Powers
8) Principalities
9) Archangels
10) Angels

As above, so below. Demons, as fallen angels, have a similar hierarchy. Their order is:
1) Satan
2) Thrones
3) Dominions
4) Principalities
5) Powers
6) Minions

Thrones are rulers or the princes of hell. Dominions act as bureaucratic entities similar to politicians and appointed officers in the demonic realm. Principalities are demons who have sway over a certain portion of the world. Some say that the world is divided into twelve regions. Each principality then has subdivisions; think of these as zip codes. In each zip code there is a different commander who controls that zip code, and reports to a higher demon in charge of the county. The demon in charge of the county reports to a demon in charge of the state, etc. Principalities work at influencing governments, politics, and bureaucracy. In other words, when a demon influences policy at a government level, it can make life a living hell for those people affected by that policy. As an example, the 2014 Flint, Michigan water crisis comes to mind. Powers are demons who tempt. These demons tempt us with our desires, that is, the desires that feed our egos. Minions are soldiers. Needless to say, there is a fair amount of speculation regarding the demonic hierarchy after Satan, the Thrones, and the Principalities. The Powers and the Minions have names, but there is less agreement here. It seems that the people who converse with demons do not keep the same quality or quantity of notes as those who communicate with angels, and the demonic hierarchy might even be suspect to some degree.

This brings us to man. We have societal hierarchies that have existed as long as humans have governed themselves. This hierarchy traditionally (with some name and office variation from culture to culture) is:
1) King and Queen
2) Prince
3) Duke and Duchess
4) Marquis and Marchioness
5) Earl and Countess
6) Viscount and Viscountess
7) Baron and Baroness
8) Knights
9) Soldiers

When one minor kingdom overthrew another minor kingdom, generally the royalty were held for ransom or imprisoned, the knights were imprisoned or disbanded, the soldiers were disbanded and disarmed, but most importantly the servants and those in the captured kingdom who worked directly with the royalty were, generally speaking, executed. The reason? Fear of retribution from a servant for the overthrow of their liege. This potential for being executed if your liege fell gave great incentive for the servants to be loyal, and whether they agreed with the king and queen or not, they followed his or her commands. In modern terms, we would say that the servants were contractually bound, if not owned by the royalty of their time. These servants had no free will as we know it today. They had the ability to make choices, but their choices could at any time be usurped by anyone who was of a higher station than they were.

In my opinion, workers in today's service industry fall into the same category as servants in the old ways. In the hierarchal structure, servants were below the lowest soldiers, and herein lies the problem. Think of when one goes to a nice restaurant. One wants the waiter to be attentive, but unobtrusive. One wants them to be perfect at taking one's order, perfect at anticipating one's needs, but otherwise invisible. This was the role of a servant in the old ways. No one likes going to a nice restaurant and making the experience all about the waiter or waitress, because most people would agree that in fine dining, the experience is about the food and the conversation, and not about the person who brings the food. This logic can then be projected onto many other parts of society. If a person's job position falls basically under the role of "keep your opinions to yourself and do your job," then one can readily tell whether the job in question is one of dominion or one of being a minion. The service workers or, one might say, the low-level workers at corporations are the worker bees who feed the queen, and the actions of their leader or boss have consequences for the workers – physically, emotionally, and spiritually. This is how Zach became infected by this demon.

As these thoughts ran through my mind, I gave Jessica direction: "I need to make a few phone calls. You head home." Hierarchy was present here as well. Jessica shouldn't have to take the hit for this demon with me.

"Are you sure?" she said.

"Yeah. I have already been seen, but you have not. I will tell Zach you weren't feeling well," I said.

"OK."

I dug the business card of the witch Mary Jane out of my vest pocket, took out my phone, and dialed her number.

"Witchcraft and Witchcraft Supplies," said the voice on the phone.

"Is this Mary Jane?"

"It is," she said.

"Hi, Mary Jane. This is Roland Pearce, acupuncturist. I was in your shop the other day and introduced myself?"

"Yes, I remember."

"I have a possession for you, if you are interested."

"What kind of possession?" she asked.

"A demon," I said.

"Oh, fun," she said ironically.

"I know," I also said ironically.

"I can take a look, but I can't promise anything."

"OK. Are you open tomorrow?" I asked.

"Yes."

"How about a noon appointment. Would that work for you?" I asked.

"Sure."

"I will book it for him. His name is Zach, and he will tell you that I sent him."

"OK."

"Please call me when you have seen what you can do," I said.

"OK," she said, and then we hung up.

I next called a friend of mine, Kathleen, or Kat as she called herself. Kat had been clairvoyant all her life. The phone rang a few times; she was in a different time zone, so I was a little worried that she might be out and about.

"Hello," Kat answered the phone.

"Hi, Kat. It's Roland. I have a situation and need some of your brilliant consultation."

Kat, always prescient, said, "You didn't listen to their advice, did you?" Kat knew me very, very well.

"No," I said.

"Were you seen?" she said.

"Yes," I said.

"By the small one or the big one?" she said.

"Both."

"You can't interfere with this one. Anymore interference, and you will bring even more suffering to yourself. You were warned before you began," she said.

"I know."

"Get him out of your office, clear your space, then prepare for what will come. Even I can't help you with this. The demon prince you saw will immediately know if you send his soldier back to the pit. He is already aware of you, and you don't want a full-on war on your hands," she said.

"So, there is nothing I can do for the patient?"

"No."

"Since I couldn't work with him directly, I called a witch who says she does dispossession and referred him to her," I said.

Kat started laughing, a full-on belly laugh. "Did you tell the witch what was coming?"

"I told her it was a demon," I said.

"Yes, but did you tell her it is attached to one of the rulers of hell?" she asked.

"No."

More laughter. "Poor witch is going to lose her lunch. You know, Roland, that wasn't very nice, even if you wanted to see what she could do."

"I know, but I don't know her very well, and she said she did dispossessions. When we spoke, she didn't seem wary or threatened by a demon … ." I said.

"Not nice, Roland," Kat said.

I admit, it was kind of uncool of me, but if Mary Jane could do it, she would be an awesome resource to have for situations like this. This was the first time I had ever been forbidden to do the work, so not only was it a new experience, but left me reaching to some extent for resources that were outside of my normal panacea.

"It will come back at night; you need to be ready. Good luck," Kat said, and hung up.

I had really taken the stick to the hornet's nest this time. Ten minutes after leaving Zach, I walked back into the office. Zach was nodding off with his feet still in the salt. I pumped more qi into my sphere of light, then said, "Hey, Zach, I have good news and bad news."

He looked at me and said, "Bad news first. It seems like that kind of day."

"I can't treat you. Even if this demon wasn't attached to something bigger, I literally don't have permission, as in I am forbidden from treating you," I said.

"What if I verbally give you my permission?" he said.

"I'm afraid it doesn't work like that anymore, because it is not just you in there. The other thing, the demon, wants nothing to do with me."

"Damn, Roland. What am I going to do? You're my guy. No one else would even believe me," he said mournfully.

"Well, that's where the good news come in. I have made an appointment for you with a witch who does dispossessions. It's at noon tomorrow. Can you make it?"

"I don't think I have much choice," he said.

"OK. Here is her card. Tell her that I sent you."

"OK," Zach said shaking his head. "This is sheer madness."

"I know, man. There are some things I can tell you," I said while taking Zach's feet out of the salt and brushing them off. "They may not help much, but these things also cannot hurt. What you are experiencing now is like an active infection or a spiritual cancer. The demon is melding with you, becoming part of who you are. If the progression is not stopped soon, you will lose the conscious idea of who you were before the possession and only be able to see yourself as the mix of the two. Your spirit, or the demon, whichever is stronger, will have the control of your consciousness. The demon is already in charge of your unconscious actions. This is why your arm jerked when I went to put a needle in you," I said.

"You will have to purify yourself. This means no sex, no drugs or alcohol, no meat, no sugar, no coffee. Water and vegetables are about all you should have. You need to meditate and pray to God. Ask for help. If you pray with fervor, you might have some kind of divine intervention. If Christianity is a faith you believe in, you can also read the *Bible* aloud to yourself," I said.

"But this witch can help me, right?" he said.

"I don't know, but I was led there two days before you came in today, so there might be hope there."

"If none of that works, then what?" he said.

"I don't know. I have been told it can't be me, and not simply from one source, but several sources. I am sorry."

"Of all the trauma I have suffered in my life, who would have thought that I would be possessed by a demon?" he said, shaking his head in disbelief.

"Our choices have consequences, Zach. This is the lesson you can walk away with today. Choose to be better. Choose a different career. Choose to seek out the good in yourself and in others. Choose to do all you can about this situation. Don't just accept it. All things can be solved, but now you need a different specialist than me. Seek out masters and gurus. Find someone who can help you purify yourself."

"Damn, Roland, I thought that would be you," he said.

"Even I can only buck the system so much, and I have done what I could. I will pay a price for helping you even this little bit. I wish I were allowed to do more for you."

"So, that's it?" he said.

"Unfortunately."

"What do I owe you?" he said.

"Today, Zach, pay what you want, or pay nothing. I didn't do much for you today."

"OK," he stood up, took a pen from the cup of pens, and started writing a check. "You know what's weird? In the last week, my handwriting is completely different. I almost can't read it."

Handwriting, of course, tells a lot about one's personality, but I didn't share this with Zach.

"Here you go," he said holding the check out. I took it, folded it, and put it in my pocket without looking at it.

"Can I come in next week?" he said.

"I hate to have to say this, because I don't want to say it, but I can't treat you again until this thing is gone. I can refer you to another acupuncturist or clinic, if you want names."

"Really!?" Zach said in disbelief.

"Zach, this isn't the common cold or a virus. You have a demon inside of you. I was told, clear as a bell, not to treat you, and I proceeded anyway. Then the demon came out of your body to defend itself and your body from me. I don't know what else I can do for you. If the demon won't let me put needles in you, and goes on defense when I approach with the intention of removing it, I don't know how I can treat you."

"I guess that makes sense," he said.

"I still want to hear how it goes tomorrow, so call me when you are finished. OK?"

Chapter 5

"OK."

Zach left the office. I took out the check he gave me, then went to the window and opened it. I scooped some salt into a ceramic container, and lit the check on fire, holding it between two fingers while it burned to ash, then snuffed the ash with the salt. This one was going to be "on me." I lit some incense, turned the sign to close, locked the door, and sat down to meditate. I was tired.

After an hour of meditation, I knew that I needed to pursue the rest of my day. It was 2 p.m. and I needed to eat lunch. Sunset would arrive at 7:47 p.m. and by that time I needed to be back in the office to face what would come. I walked down the street to the food carts and waited in the short line at the Whole Bowl. Not exactly demon-resisting food, but vegetarian at least. Beans, rice, hold the sour cream please, avocado, salsa, and extra Tali sauce.

I am not a vegetarian, and I definitely consume meat, but there is a time and a place for everything. My master has said, "One should consume a wide variety of food, all of the time." This means that one should not eat the same food multiple times per day. For example, one should not have cheese on one's eggs in the morning, a cheese sandwich for lunch, and cheese as an appetizer at dinner. Diverse foods means a wide and varied diet. Abstaining from certain foods such as meat, pork, substances, and other items are prohibitions that go back for millennia when dealing with beings who are more pure or less pure. Some people fast before rituals, and that is often a good path. However, I had dumped a lot of qi building my protection, and the two main ways to build up qi again are to eat and to breathe.

Qi, while I am on the subject and waiting for my Whole Bowl to be made, can be translated as energy in Western culture, but it is actually slightly different than this. Think of qi as a dense form of potential. It serves as the fuel that propels our physical bodies in the form of movement as well as the chemical processes within our cells. When our qi is exhausted and our body can no longer hold it, we are close to death. Qi, however, is not the most refined potential within our body, nor is it the densest substance. There are substances which are more dense, such as our essence or *jing*, which is a form of compact energy that we are all born with. Essence, however, is finite, meaning we only have so much of it. Qi, in comparison, is relatively infinite. Now, I say relatively, because we can hold as much qi as our container will allow. If our container is the size of a thimble, then we can only hold that much qi. But, if our container is the size of Crater Lake, then that is how much qi we can hold. The container is the lower *dan tian*, or the area two fingers below your navel. Qi is stored here. When we do standing meditation, we build more qi, or we refine the qi which we have consumed in the form of food and breath, thereby digesting it, so that it can be used. Sitting meditation uses this refined food and breath which form the qi, and condenses it, so that it can be stored and used later.

When we live day to day without attending to our qi, it is very much like living paycheck to paycheck, or instantly spending the money we make, the minute that we make it. In this way of living, one never develops a savings account. If a calamity or minor disaster happens, then there are no savings to draw on. When one condenses one's qi to be used at a later time, this is like putting money in a savings account to be used later. The more saved or condensed qi someone has, the larger their container becomes, as there is always more room for storage. However, this is a function that needs to be actively exercised, and it takes will power to actively store qi. When this qi is spent, then more qi has to be refined, then condensed, and placed in the *dan tian* to be stored again.

Restricting or abstaining from certain foods allows the body to process and extract the qi from foods faster. The more complicated the food, the longer it takes to extract the qi from it. Therefore, at times a vegetarian diet can be helpful to replenish the qi more quickly. Yet, in the same way that a vegetarian diet can be helpful for a short period of time, if one eats this way as way of life, it can be harmful (except in certain situations or climates).

The body, for the most part, is an impure machine or, more aptly put, our bodies are machines that are used to running on multiple kinds of fuel, and often, a lot of this fuel is less than clean. If we run more pure fuel in the machine, the body runs better for a while, but at some point we have to use this pure potential, created from pure food, to do a spiritually higher work. If we do not apply ourselves to a higher calling when eating a purer diet, then we run the risk of burning out our container. You might say our container burns gas well, but it does not burn nuclear energy well. We can burn nuclear energy, but we have to move it quickly out of our body, and do something constructive with it.

Let me explain this in a more practical way. When someone becomes vegetarian or vegan, for the first few months, their energy will feel awesome. If they are under thirty, they might even maintain this awesome feeling for a year to five years. During this time of well-being, the body is using its reserves to supplement what the body is missing from eating an omnivorous diet. Reserves in this example can mean essence, qi, nutrients, fat, what have you. Basically, the vegan or vegetarian diet does not provide enough fuel to live a modern lifestyle, and the body attempts to do damage control by pulling the reserves from wherever they are stored, and supplementing or filling in the holes or cracks wherever they are created. In this way, the body can carry on as normal for a while. But, if someone is over thirty, or has been vegan or vegetarian for longer than two to five years, and they are not leading a spiritual life, then we begin to see problems arise in this body. If this weren't a problem, it would not appear to look like a disease. Regardless of the patient, once the threshold of reserve depletion is crossed and all the reserve nutrients are used up, then all the vegans and vegetarians whom I have treated for this have the same symptoms. This is a self-inflicted disease from an ideology, and the symptoms of reserve nutrient deficiency are: anemia, palpitations, anxiety, restlessness, hot flushes or hot flashes, night sweats, low energy, poor wound healing, loss of menstrual period, easily emotional or angry, etc. Some people put on extra weight but can't metabolize it, ending up with pear-shaped bodies. Other body types lose all of their body fat, and can't put on either fat or muscle. Other symptoms may include tachycardia, low blood pressure, coldness of the hands, feet, and buttocks, or other problems with temperature regulation. If the patient tends to eat a lot of spicy food, they will then have chronic tenseness of the muscles, possible mania, or tendency to obsess over things, easily anger, etc. If the patient tends to eat a lot of sweets, they will tend to be overweight, tend to think too much or be very intellectual, tend to get sleepy and lethargic, tend to have more yeast and infections like athlete's foot, etc. These patients will also have problems metabolizing sugar, with a tendency towards hypoglycemia or even diabetes.

The cure for these symptoms at this level is simple. Red meat, about the amount that would fit in the palm of the patient's hand, three times per week, for about three months. Now, if one is committed to eating vegetarian or vegan because of religious beliefs, a heart condition, or an unchangeable ideology, it is possible, but eating then has to be a science. I have met a terrible number of people who think that they are being vegetarian because they eat pizza without adding meat to it, I am sure you have met these people as well. Gabriel Cousins talks about eating as a science in his book *Conscious Eating*, and rather than having me go on about it here, just give that book a look.

I said a vegan or vegetarian would have the same conditions, unless they had a spiritual life, so why does having a spiritual life matter? Generally speaking, meat acts as a ground. Earlier, when listing the prohibitions of acupuncture, I said that food acts as a ground, similar to an electrical ground, or as a grounding force. The same holds for meat, but rather than grounding one's energy as in with food, now we are talking about meat acting as a ground for one's spirit. The human body, simply put, is a combination of body, mind or emotions, and spirit. A spirit without a body (for the most part) does not have the ability to effect physical change on earth. Emotions or mind also do not have the ability to manifest the ideas or emotions in the physical world without a body. A body that exists without spirit, mind, or emotions is inert. Therefore, it takes all three aspects to make up what we are. The spirit and the body are polar opposites, which mutually work together to manifest life. To feed the body grounds the spirit, and to enlighten the spirit elevates the body. This is the push-pull nature of our being, which, when both are nourished, helps to elevate our consciousness and make our mind more clear.

If one then chooses not to eat meat, what can be done? Then one's spiritual practice must be developed in order to actively channel spirit and use our spirit to supplement that which we are not creating with meat. In other words, we have to create a system where our spiritual practice acts as the ground, and this means pursuing stillness through meditation. Stillness is the opposite of action, and when one meditates for long enough, one can sedate the body in the same way that one gets from the eating of meat; however, this stillness has to be cultivated consciously. There are many forms of meditation, but people often get lost in the idea that if they do "x" or "y" meditation, it will give them "x" or "y" abilities. This is a false path. What I mean by this is that your rational mind is putting expectations and goals on the practice. My master says, "The first step to meditation is to know your body." This means that when one meditates, one's first "goal" should be to clear the mind of all goals, all to-do lists, and all random thoughts, and stop the monkey mind from chattering. When one reaches this point, then one simply is, and the mind becomes like a placid pond on a still day. Do this enough, and your unconscious mind will begin to engage with you. Your body begins to come alive in meditation: there are sensations of energetic current moving from one place to another, gurgling in your bowels and lymph, sensations of your skin crawling, and shaking of your abdomen and limbs. The pain you have, whereever it is, will come to the forefront, as the unconscious mind brings the resources, that previously were spent on maintaining the ego, to bear on your wounds. After some time of working on one wound, the unconscious will switch to other wounds, until at some point the wounds no longer hurt, and then the unconscious mind will again be placid. This is completion of the first stage, and at this point one will begin to learn a lot about how one's body functions, and how it truly feels. One will feel qi, and begin to feel the meridians or lines of energy in the body. One will be able to feel and discern the internal organs of the body. At this point, one can begin storing qi in one's lower *dan tian* or the body's container.

This is the minimum level of requirement for a person who is vegetarian or vegan. When eating this way, and practicing a meditation that achieves this, the body will ground itself without meat. Understand though, that the body at this point becomes much more communicative, and one's body may, once it is being listened to, ask that one consume meat. If one ignores the communication of the unconscious to the conscious, then at some point the unconscious will stop communicating. Allowing this disruption in communication will impede one from moving to greater spiritual levels, and so one should always listen to the unconscious mind over the rational mind. The comparison is that the conscious mind processes megabytes of data, while the unconscious mind processes gigabytes of data. This means that the unconscious mind is much smarter than the conscious mind by orders of 100.

Meditation is a simple affair. Find a meditation cushion or *zafu* as they are called. It should be firm, like a futon is firm. Sit on it looking at a blank wall or a wall with a line in it, like a door or door frame. Face in a direction that feels comfortable to you. For example, in my practice, I tend to face south. One's legs should be in half lotus or full lotus position. Half lotus for men is left leg touching the ground with the right leg sitting on top of the left leg. The buttocks should rest on the edge of the *zafu*, in such a way that the perineum hangs in the open space between the pillow and the ground. For women, the left leg should be on the ground with the right leg over the left leg. The hands should sit in the lap, palms up. For men, the left hand should rest in the right palm, and for women the right hand should rest in the left palm. The back should be straight, and the eyes should gaze softly just below what would be considered the line of the horizon. Diffuse and relax the eyes in such a way that they lose focus while looking at the wall. Practice this every day at the same time for twenty minutes, eventually extending it to an hour or two if one desires. The first month will seem like torture for the rational mind. The second month will be easier, but still difficult at times. By the third month, the unconscious mind will begin to take control. This open-eyed meditation should be practiced for at least a year or two before moving on to other forms of meditation. It gives beginners a base from which they can advance.

Abilities that come from meditation rarely occur when one seeks for them. Yet, it is not uncommon for someone who meditates regularly to have more-heightened senses than someone else – think of this as simply having trained oneself to listen to the stillness. In most practices, the abilities that come through meditation are considered to be like the sparkles on a lake when you are thirsty. You cannot capture the sparkles, you cannot bottle the sparkles, and when the sun sets, the sparkles fade. More important, though, is that you are thirsty, and only the lake itself can slake your thirst. In other words, when you are thirsty, the sparkles on the lake are inconsequential – you only notice them as you are bending down to cup the water in your hand and drink. Abilities from meditation could be considered to be much like the sparkles on a lake, and would be considered a false path. A false path is something that distracts the meditation student from that which they need to learn. Being able to see or hear the energetic world is not the end goal. The true path is to still the mind and collect the energy of the body into the *dan tian*.

"Here is your bowl," the woman making my Whole Bowl said. "If you want extra salsa or seasoning, it is to your right."

"Thank you," I said.

I took my Whole Bowl back towards the office, and ate it on the street. After lunch, I went through the exterior door of the office building, and took the elevator up to the office. A nap sounded good, and if I really was going to have to face something down, it would be best to be well rested. I reclined in the La-Z-Boy and set the alarm on my phone for two hours. I woke up before my alarm went off, worked on some charts, and did some billing and other paperwork to keep my mind occupied. The hour of 5 p.m. came and went, then 6 p.m. At 7 p.m. I decided it was time to prepare. I took a standing-horse stance and let my mind relax. I followed my breathing, slowed my heart, and observed my body from within. Standing meditation is a more active form of meditation than sitting meditation. The normal focus of standing meditation is to balance, find stability, and relax. It helps the body to quickly generate qi and hastens the refining of qi from food and breath. I will often perform standing meditation for a while, then do my sitting meditation after the standing. These days, although I often do standing meditation, if given the choice because of time constraints of standing or sitting, I will generally pick sitting. Today, however, I knew I might be in the office all night, so there was plenty of time to do both.

At 8:30 p.m., forty-seven minutes after sundown, I began to feel an imperceptible change, similar to when the sun goes behind a cloud and you feel the absence of the sunlight on your skin. The room first became a little colder, then it became a little darker. The lights were on, but now it was as if the 60-watt bulbs had been reduced to 25-watt bulbs. I could still see, but the interior of my office was beginning to be shaped by something else. I continued in my standing stance. I did not see anything, nor did I sense a presence in my office, so I said, "I know that you are coming. There is no need to do battle with me. I know that you can hear me through time and space. You will not lose face, if you do not come."

A column of black smoke formed from the ceiling to the floor. It was rectangular like a door, and from it stepped the soldier demon. It approached, then stopped about five feet from me. It poked the air between us, and I expanded the sphere of light I had been building since 7 p.m. As the sphere filled the space between us, the demon withdrew its hand from the air, and stepped back a step. It bared its black teeth at me and hissed.

"I have no desire to fight with you or your master," I said, "but neither will I let you in, nor let you have your way with me."

The shape of the demon's face changed slightly. What had been a primitive, beast-like appearance took the shape of the focus of intellect, and I heard a slightly more refined voice in my mind saying, "There is no one here to protect you now."

"I don't need to be protected by anyone, but you know that I also don't have permission to send you to the pit," I said.

"You are afraid," it said.

"I do not fear you. I do, however, respect that you and I have different journeys in this life. I am flesh and blood, and you lack a body; this is why you want Zach – so that you can become incarnate."

The demon continued to move back and forth, poking here and there into the space I had filled with light. "You are mortal, son of God, and I am immortal. You need to continue to take care of your human frame, but I do not," it said.

"This is true. But before long, you will be melded into a human form, and you will not be able to travel or leave the shell of the body which you have selected. You are here now because it will not be long before your transformation is complete, and while your spirit will be in my patient, I actually need not worry about another visit from you, as you will have clipped your own wings."

"Yes, mortal. What you say is true. I feel my spirit owning the weak spirit of the human I have chosen. My master has others like me, and you will need to eat, rest, or sleep eventually. You will not be able to guard yourself from us forever," it said.

"I must take care of my body, mind, and spirit, however, your master will not send any others of your kind, because you have nothing to offer that I want. Everything your masters have to offer is tainted and poisoned. If your master chooses to do battle with me for the sake of doing battle, then we shall see what happens. Until then, I don't have permission to send you to the pit, and you don't have the strength to break me. Therefore this conversation bores me."

"You order me? You taunt me? With one call, I can bring my master and he will come and break you, human."

"Frankly, I doubt that your master will come running to do his servant's bidding, yet both of us know what will happen if you do this, providing he answers your call. If you summon your master, the rules change. If the rules change, the more likely I will be given permission to interfere. Besides, while I have seen your master, you have yet to lay eyes on my master. If your master is called to defend you, then so too will my master be called to defend me. Therefore, it is left to us to settle our fight."

"There are many ways to cause you pain, human, even without involving my master. I will enjoy watching you suffer."

"Demons and their threats, we both know the way this works. There is no opening for you here and you know it. I tire of you, and our conversation is done. You have failed to inspire the fear you intended, and we both know you lack permission as well as strength to actually do harm to me, just as I lack permission to send you to the pit. Leave my office, and take your foul stench with you," I said.

"We will not meet again while I am pure, but I will watch with glee from afar," it said, and then it vanished. The room again grew warm, and the light once again brightened. I changed my position from standing to sitting, re-drew my wards, and embraced the nothingness of my unconscious mind.

Ninety-five percent of the time spiritual warfare is a contest of will. It is not a contest of ego, but a contest of who can hold onto their intention longer. The longer one can focus one's mind on the intention, the better one is at spiritual warfare. If one is easily distracted, how can one build any kind of defense to protect oneself. This is where one's meditation comes into play, as the meditation teaches stillness and concentration. Without the ability to perform both of these unwaveringly, the cracks in one's defense are palpable. "What about the other five percent?" I am sure you are asking yourself. The other five percent of the time, the battle is both spiritual and physical. In these battles, you can be sure, that all sides walk away with physical scars. Try to avoid these, as afterwards, you will find things that are broken in your body which are not supposed to break.

At midnight, I emerged from meditation, once again checked my office for any malevolent interference, then headed home.

Chapter 5

Sending the demon to the pit, or Tartarus as the pit is sometimes called, would be gratifying, but meaningless. For every prince and lord of hell, there are thousands of foot soldiers. Casting one out would only bring another, higher-ranked demon to my office. One would have to banish each demon in turn, squeeze them for information, then wait for the next one to come. No, the voice was right – I should not have interfered with Zach.

The next morning, I woke up at 8 a.m. It was April 8th, and Zach would be going to the witch at noon. I puttered around my house, doing the normal: shower, check email, check social media, see if the world had ended while I was sleeping: you know, the stuff we all do. By 10 a.m., I was ready for a cup of coffee, so I got into my SUV and headed down to the Raleigh Hills Starbucks. Kris was working this morning, and he, like Jake, was familiar with my habits.

"French roast?" he said, holding up a sixteen-ounce cup.

"Yep." You caught me, occasionally I switch between French and Sumatra. It is very impressive that the Starbucks employees can keep up with my predilections, as well as, the other thousand people's habits who frequent this location.

"Are you working today? Or enjoying the rain?" he said.

"A little of both, as usual," I said with a smile.

"Nice," he said.

I went outside to stand on the corner and smoke a cigarette while I waited for my coffee, and I mused. There is some thought among demonologists that because God is all-knowing, all-creating, and all-present, this means that both angels and demons are under God's dominion. The basic premise is that angels are the carrot, while demons are the stick. If humans can be guided to an end purpose, God will use angels to do this, but if humans refuse to be guided, then God uses demons to bring the humans back in line. Now, I cannot remark on the veracity of the truth of this, yet it has the appearance of truth, in that people who have committed much "sin" appear to have more experiences with demons, while people who have less "sin" appear to have more experiences with angels. In this particular instance, one might say, that the truth is subjective.

Now, for the purposes of this muse, let me simply define a "sinner" as one who has strayed from the path of worshipping God to the path of worshipping the self or the ego – or strayed from worshipping the divine in order to worship that which has fallen. The commandments of God, as they were discussed in the Bible, are simply the commandments of human morality, which span all cultures. Strike a few of the commandments, and I think one arrives at the place where the small voice inside us rebels when we commit an action that is innately wrong. I could say more about this, but this isn't a sermon on sin; it is a discussion about how demons perhaps play a functional role in the world of God. To be clear: in my opinion, sin is a human problem. Once one commits a sin, only after that do the demons come. This is because when one breaks one's own moral code, the demons then have a gate of entry, and will act as the stick.

To continue this thought: only if demons are under God's domain can they be bound in God's name. If they were merely free agents, why would they cave if you tried to bind them using the tools of God? For thousands of years, people have bound demons in God's name, so it makes sense that demons have some chain of command that ultimately goes back to God. Angels represent order, or light, while demons represent chaos, or darkness. Darkness cannot be defined without light, and light cannot be defined without darkness. As the Chinese say, "light is yang, while dark is yin." When there is no more duality, then there will only be singularity, and in singularity there is no division, therefore elimination of duality brings one back to God.

To once more touch on this idea of demons being the stick, it is interesting to note that demons or the devil have not always been affiliated with the dark. They were once angels, after all. Additionally, demons have reputedly done good as well as evil. Supposedly, and I think this is hearsay at best, Solomon – as in King Solomon who built the original temple on the Temple Mount in Israel – bound more than seventy demons in order to help him build his temple. A binding is used on something that is outside of one's authority, causing it to come under one's authority. There are a number of *Keys of Solomon* which allude to these methods. There were also supposedly demons who helped with medicine and farming, but I think the religious texts of old sometimes conflate and confuse. Lastly, Phillip Carr-Gomm in *The Druid Way* reminds us that most places on maps that are called "the devil's xyz" were originally places where the native peoples sought out and found power. This led the Christian church to name these places as places of the devil, in order to keep people away from them.

In my case, I wasn't allowed to treat Zach. I wasn't allowed to bind the demon, and the demon was not allowed to go outside of his internal power structure (to call to his master), in order to try to hurt me. Again, this only makes sense if one applies the carrot-and-stick methodology. Zach had lost his way, and so the demon had come to him; therefore, using this reasoning, since Zach was being educated by the stick, I was not allowed to interfere. Lastly, because Zach's education was planned, as one might say, I was not, nor would be, given permission to effect change within him. It is the only real idea that makes any sense. I say this because one does get permission to banish demons. In some cases, this may be because the stick has done its part and taught the lesson that was needed. Also, using this idea, it clarifies how sometimes one comes across people who are on the path of darkness, yet they interact with people who are on the path of light, not as someone to do battle with, but as someone who is acknowledged and then promptly left, each person going their own way to do the work of God as they have been instructed to do it. In a way, this takes the fear out of the idea of demons, but it does not ameliorate the suffering that demons cause people.

I walked back into Starbucks. Kris gave me my coffee, and I went back outside.

There is a parable about a demon that is worth thinking about. It is called *The Demon and the Hair*. This story goes something like this:

In olden times, a man acquired the services of a demon, whether through binding the demon himself, or by a binding from a sorcerer, I have no idea. This demon was able to grant the man anything he wished. Immediately on receiving the subjugation of the demon, the man said, "I want to be rich."

The demon said to the man, "It is done, master," and riches of gold and silver arose all around the man.

The man said, "I want a harem of wives, all shapely and beautiful."

The demon said, "It is done, master," and his house was filled with beautiful women.

Mere seconds had flown by between each wish. "I want the biggest and best sultan's castle in the world, with gazing ponds, inlaid mosaics, and thousands of archways filled with scenic views."

A minute later the demon appeared and said, "It is done, master. How may I serve you now?"

The man asked for wishes upon wishes, and each time the demon appeared moments later to ask how he could serve, through meals, through the night, and on to the next day, and the next. After a week, the man had run out of desires for himself and the world. Yet, the demon continued to ask him how he could serve. The man was not able to sleep or eat a full meal, or smoke hookah – always the demon was there.

"What is your command, master?"

"Take me to the most powerful sorcerer in the world," the man said. Poof, the man appeared in the dwelling of the sorcerer.

The sorcerer looked up from his books and said, "Yes?"

The man said, "I have a demon, and it is ever at my beck and call, but I have run out of wishes, and I don't know what to do. I can't eat or sleep, or relax. It is always asking how it can serve. Can you help me with my situation?"

The sorcerer said, "I can. Summon the demon."

The man said, "Demon, I have a request."

Poof. The demon arrived, "Yes, master?"

The sorcerer plucked a wavy hair from his head and said to the man, "Ask the demon to straighten this," and he handed the hair to the man.

The man received the hair and said to the demon, "Straighten this hair."

The demon replied, "Yes, master," then he straightened the hair. But because the inherent nature of the hair was wavy, when the demon let go, the hair again took its natural form. Then the demon again straightened the hair, and again when he let go, the hair resumed its natural form. The demon did this again, and again, and again. The demon could create in seconds, but he could not change the nature of the physical form in his hands.

The sorcerer said, "Well, right, then. When you need the demon to do something for you, simply remove the hair and make your wish. When it is done with that, then give it back the hair."

"Thank you," the man said. He reached out, took the hair from the demon, and said, "Take me home."

Poof. He was home. "What is your command master?"

"Straighten the hair," the man said giving the demon back the hair. Everyone except the demon lived happily ever after.

This is an old parable with multiple meanings, but each meaning derives from the idea of changing the nature of something. The demon can create or reform, but cannot change a nature to be straight or change a nature to be bent; only we have the power to do this by our choices. One could also apply this parable to any other being that is not in human form; humans affect this world through choices, while gods and other beings can only guide the choices. In other words, a being, whether light or dark, cannot change our true natures, it can only influence and manipulate the decisions that you and I make on a daily basis. This is yet another illustration of how our choices have consequences, and attract or repel the beings we seek to be guided by.

I went back into Starbucks for a refill of my coffee. It was noon, and I would be hearing from Mary Jane, the witch, in a while. Before my coffee was done, my phone rang. It was 12:10 p.m.

"This is Roland Pearce. How may I help you?"

"You sent this to my office?" came the accusatory voice.

"Hi Mary Jane. How did it go?"

"Go? It never even started! This guy is possessed by a demon!"

"I believe I mentioned that?" I said.

"Yes, you did, but this demon is connected to a Greater demon ….!"

"Yes," I said.

"Why would you think I would even work with anything like this?!"

"You said you did dispossessions, and you didn't bat an eye when I said he had a demon .... So, it sounded like you had experience with this sort of thing," I said.

"I do, but I don't do Greaters. That is asking for inconceivable trouble. Sorry, I can't help. I don't think this can be fixed. Please do not ever refer a demonic possession to me again!" With that, Mary Jane hung up the phone before I could respond.

Well, that went about as expected. Five minutes later, Zach called.

"Hey, Roland," he said.

"Hey, Zach. How did it go?" I said.

"It didn't. I walked in and introduced myself, told her that you referred me. She looked at me for a second, then cranked up her music really loud, and started clapping her hands in my face, then told me I had to leave."

"I'm sorry that happened, Zach."

"Why did she do that?" he said.

"Because she was profoundly scared of what is in you," I said.

"Oh. So what do I do now?"

"I saw in the paper yesterday that there are a few East Indian masters coming to town. Maybe they can intercede on your behalf. Look at the *Willamette Week*, and see if you can find the advertisement. When you go, ask for a blessing."

"OK. Can I come back in to see you?"

"I'm sorry, Zach. As I told you yesterday, I am not allowed to intercede for you."

"I know. I was just hoping you would have changed your mind."

"Zach, it is not my mind that needs to be changed. If I could help you, I totally would. However, I am not allowed to help you, and this is completely different. You stand on a precipice of choice; you can either go on as you have been, and in that case you and the demon will become one. Or, you can take the path of utter and devout faith in God, or whatever religion which rings true to you, and give yourself over to that religion completely. I don't think there is an inbetween now. You were given guidance from a number of sources, and you failed to hear. Now, you are getting the stick, and those who tried to guide you are not allowed to intervene. You are here by your own choices. I am sorry that it is this way for you."

Zach sobbed a little on the phone. "You know, Roland, whenever you told me to improve this or that about myself, or told me to get out of service work, or any of the other things you said to me, I thought I would get around to it one day. I thought my growth was on my own timetable, and that there would be no consequences. I wish I could go back to Day One and really hear what you were saying."

"I know, Zach. I know. The window is closing for you, and now your decisions have to be made in a timely way."

"I will seek out these masters and ask for their blessing."

"Good, Zach. Good," I said.

"I loved being your patient, Roland, and I am going to miss you."

"I will miss you too, Zach."

"Thanks, Roland," Zach said and hung up.

I spent the rest of the day doing errands and research. In the background, my mind still reeled with this singular event. Sadly, I knew it wasn't over, and I was waiting for the other shoe to drop. I didn't have to wait long.

I had been dating Stephanie for about six months. She was an engineer; she had no understanding of demons, ghosts, and the like; and she was my weekend solace from the world of the unseen. Our relationship was simple, kind, not dramatic, and full of board games, good food, and trying new pubs. It was the antithesis to my work, and always helped me recharge. We would laugh, and laugh, and laugh, talk about the world, express our ideas, and we never fought or even raised our voices at each other. We had made plans to go try the newish StormBreaker Brewing pub this evening, and so when Stephanie called, I figured it was to discuss our plans. But it really was the other shoe dropping.

I was at home when my phone rang, and I saw it was Stephanie in my caller ID.

"Hey, Steph!" I said.

"Roland," she said vehemently. "I can't go out with you tonight."

"What? Why?" I said.

"Because I hate you," she said.

"What?" I said.

"I hate you!" she screamed into the phone, "And I never want to see you again!"

"Whoa, slow down. Where is this coming from? We had such a good time last weekend…?"

"You need to suffer. I told you I would make you suffer," she said, except I now knew who I was talking to.

"Ahh. Demon. Leave Stephanie out of this."

"No. She has holes. She is not on the path. She is prey, and is fair game. Now, even though I cannot make you suffer directly, I can make you suffer through her. I have changed her memories of you. Even when you call back, she will hate you."

"Demon, you try my patience with you. I ask you again, leave her be."

"Human, do you not know why hunters like yourself have always sought to live a life without deep relationships to your fellow humans? It is because, while my kind cannot hurt those who walk on God's path, we can terrorize all whom you love and hold dear. I will take great joy in watching your suffering as I reprogram this woman you love to seek out vice, sexual wantonness, and the destruction of everything she has worked for, leaving her destitute and penniless, to be used as a common harlot so she can simply eat."

"The logic of your words denies the spiritual laws, demon. Your words attempt to inspire fear within me, but I know that you are primitive at best. You are not all-powerful. While you attempt to scare me with your words, in reality, you cannot inhabit two bodies. For you to leave the one you are being bonded to so you can inhabit this woman's body, you have to break your bond to the other. You are not strong enough to be in two places at once, and each time you leave your original chosen body, you weaken the bond. I am not afraid of you. I know your limitations, and I surmise your master would be disappointed in you for breaking your chain of command. You want this to be personal with me, but to me, your kind are all the same. You are no better than the humans who call you to them. You want, and when you receive what you want, then you want more. The more you receive, the hungrier you get, and because of this you will never find your way back to God. For all of your power and ability to effect change in this world, you will never be able to get what will fulfill you. Regardless of how many bodies you possess over thousands of years, God will never take you back. So, demon, how would you like to spend the limited energy that we both know you have?"

The phone was silent for twenty heartbeats. Then a voice said, "Hello." It was Stephanie.

"Hi, Steph," I said.

"Did I call you?" she said.

"Yep."

"Did we talk about something already? My mind seems all disordered, as if my brain had just been in a blender. I don't feel very good," she said.

"It's OK, Steph. It will be fine. I think we should cancel tonight, and you should stay home, take a salt bath, then go to bed," I said.

"That sounds heavenly. Yeah, if you don't mind? I just don't feel like myself for some reason."

"It's OK, Steph, it will fade. You will feel better once you are in the bath," I said.

"OK. Sorry to cancel on you."

"No, I am sorry. I will call you in a few days."

"OK. Thanks, Roland," she said.

I hung up the phone, went to the refrigerator, pulled out a Chai Societea Ginger kombucha, twisted off the lid, walked back to the couch, and sat down. The world worries about human terrorists, but discounts the true threat, the terrorists of the dark, which can be in anyone at any time. These spiritual terrorists can infiltrate anyone who does not have enough faith in God to overcome their poor choices in life.[15] When the human form is killed, a demon can simply move to another body and continue to fight the same battle. Demons and beings of the dark are immortal; they do not sleep, eat, or focus on anything but their war. They are the true spiritual terrorists, and the only tool humanity has to win this war is to live a path closer to God, and to be consciously aware of one's own decisions on a moment-to-moment basis. Each tool takes years to acquire, but each starts with baby steps. Awareness has to come first. Once aware, one can begin to move closer to God. When I was younger, I had several experiences that taught me the value of awareness, and through these experiences I moved closer to the understandings I have now.

---

15. We all have made poor choices, but as we make these poor choices, we have the opportunity to learn from them. In learning the lesson, we come closer to God, and closer to walking a purer path of life.

Chapter 6
Awareness One

At the end of spring in 1993, I needed to find a job – the dreaded summer job while in college, the kind of job where no one wants to hire you, because they know you will be heading back to school in a few months.

The previous summer I had worked in Bristol Bay, Alaska in a whole-salmon packing plant, and the work was brutal. The pay really wasn't that great compared to the grueling sixteen-hour days, when oftentimes I would simply collapse into bed after my shift, literally falling asleep in my rain gear, guts, slime, and all. The mental fortitude that working this long, day after day, was more than many people could muster. I worked in the freezers, pulling racks of salmon that had been flash frozen at 80 degrees below zero. A cooling system further added to the freezing process by running 80 mph winds through the freezer. The company had twelve freezers that would all be operational at the height of the salmon run. The freezers could flash freeze the fish in about ten hours. When all the freezers were running, we could crack open a new freezer about every hour. During a sixteen-hour shift, we often processed more than 300,000 pounds of salmon.

My position was as a breaker. We entered the freezers once they were turned off, then pulled out the racks of fish, wheeled them to the front of the conveyer belt line, broke them away from the plastic sheeting the fish were frozen on, then dumped the fish on the conveyer belt. Breaking the fish off the plastic trays meant heaving the rack that held the plastic tray onto a table which had five small pilings sticking up from the table, roughly in the same formation as the marking of five on a set of dice. This meant that I and whoever was my partner lifted all 300,000 pounds of fish for that shift. My mind could handle the mind-numbing work, even though at times it was like I was asleep on my feet. It was my body that suffered. Shoulder joints simply were not meant to lift that amount of weight on a daily basis. However, working the freezers was nothing compared to being on the "slime line," where other workers had to do the initial cleaning and gutting of the fish. It was quite common for people on the "slime line" to be standing in a foot or more of fish guts at their feet while they worked, and the smell of the guts and blood was simply overwhelming. While I was there, there were a couple of people who completely lost their mind, and who purposely tried to stab their coworkers who were standing next to them. It was ugly, ugly work.

No, this particular summer I wanted to do something else, preferably, something a bit less taxing. Ideally, I would be able to find something closer to Portland, where I could stay at my folks' house and at least be able to work some kind of normal schedule.

Portland is one of the oddest towns I have ever been to. Don't get me wrong, every place has its own quirks, but for all of our "keep Portland weird," "keep Portland beards," or "keep Portland beered," signs, I have never been to a place where the quality of jobs you can get is so dependent on whom you know. The longer your family has been in town, or the more networking you do, the more likely you are to have a well-paying job. Even as an adult, I hear people complain about this. As long as the city is booming, most have no worries, but when the city goes bust, Portlanders take care of their own first. And trust me, Portland will go bust again. The boom and bust cycles seem to happen about every twenty or thirty years. Portland went bust in the early 1980s after the massive logging operations cut most of the old-growth trees. Saw mills and wood processing plants all over the state closed. Most of the factories and shipyards that were functioning during World War II had already been closed by this point, and this really only left service industry jobs available for blue-collar folk. Up until recently, a good job at a restaurant or hospital was highly sought after by those who did not have an extensive education. Sometimes even with an extensive education, those service jobs were still highly sought after. I have never been to another city with so many Ph.D. graduates working as waiters.

At times, finding a job in Portland is bleak, and this particular summer was one of those times. This left me again looking for something outside of Portland. Alaska was out, as I didn't love my experience there. The question was, where in the United States was the economy not bleak? Even back then, I noticed a pattern in the United States, where music and style generally flowed from Europe to the East Coast of the United States, skipped the Midwest, and then landed on the West Coast. When I looked harder, I also noticed that when the economy was slow on the West Coast, usually it was booming back east. Then, I noticed that when the West Coast was producing more music and style, it tended to flow east, skipping the Midwest again, and when this happened, the West Coast economy was going strong, while the East Coast was slow. I postulated that this was some sort of economic phenomenon, similar to putting water in a square tub; rock it one way, and it creates a high wave on one end and a reduced amount of water on the other end. Leave the tub alone, and these waves will slosh back and forth from one end to the other end with diminishing intensity until eventually the water is flat. Then the process has to begin again. One could also call this the pendulum effect. When the water becomes flat and still, then the entire country would be in a recession or depression. Sadly, it seems that the US uses war as the method to start the economic waves moving again.

Following this rationale, I began looking for jobs on the East Coast. In the back of a magazine, I found a classified ad which read, "Rowers wanted to work as movers in Boston, Massachusetts. If interested, please call (617) xxx-xxxx." I went to the phone and dialed the number.

"Hello, Jogging Giant Moving Company," the voice on the other end said.

"I am calling about the want ad in the rowing magazine," I said.

"Yes. Are you a rower?"

"I am."

"Do you have any experience moving furniture?"

"I don't."

"No problem. Be here Monday at 6 a.m. We will train you and put you to work."

"OK," I said. It was Wednesday. This meant that I had to be in Boston in four days. I gave the Jogging Giant employee my name and social security number, and that was it, I had a summer job. That was so much easier than trying to get a job in Portland, I thought to myself. Well, except now I had to get there, and figure out a place to live for the summer. Buying a ticket was easy, as this was many years prior to the attack on September 11th and the screening for tickets was comparatively benign. A place to live: now that was more of a dilemma.

In January of that year, my sophomore year of college, I had joined the Sigma Chi (ΣX) fraternity. It had been a hard decision, but a few friends had joined this same fraternity and they all had found it rewarding. I had participated in the off-season rush and been accepted. One of the reasons I decided to join a fraternity was the idea that I would have a lifetime bond not only to the brothers within my own chapter, but also to brothers in other chapters, and that this fraternal bond transcended whether one was still in school, a recent graduate, or a longtime alumnus. This had seemed like a very good thing to have in my virtual pocket as I moved forward in life.

Each fraternity has a moral code on which it is based, and Sigma Chi's is called the *Jordan Standard*. It reads:

> The standard with which the Fraternity started was declared by Isaac M. Jordan to be that of admitting no man to membership in Sigma Chi who is not believed to be:
> A Man of Good Character
> A Student of Fair Ability
> With Ambitious Purposes
> A Congenial Disposition
> Possessed of Good Morals
> Having a High Sense of Honor and
> A Deep Sense of Personal Responsibility.

These words were something I knew I could live by, and so I became a pledge to the fraternity. A semester later, in spring, I fulfilled all my requirements as a pledge and became a brother in my own right. Now, each chapter of Sigma Chi has a Greek number to indicate not only the year it was founded, but also to identify us within Sigma Chi's international governing structure. At the University of Puget Sound (UPS), our Greek number was Delta Phi (ΔΦ), showing that our chapter was founded in 1950. The bond of brotherhood transcends the limits of individual universities; if a brother can help a brother, they will. While I had not planned to leverage my membership for this purpose, it turned out to be a wonderful part of my Sigma Chi experience.

Thus, when faced with the dilemma of where I would live for a summer in Boston, when I had to be there in four days, I turned to my brotherhood. I looked in the *Norman Shield*, my pledge book, and found that Sigma Chi had a chapter at the Massachusetts Institute of Technology (MIT). The Greek number of this chapter was Alpha Theta (ΑΘ) as it had been founded in 1882.

I called the chapter number, and a voice answered the phone, "Sigma Chi."

"Hi, I am a brother at University of Puget Sound, and I am thinking of coming to Boston for the summer. I was wondering if my brothers in Boston had a place I could stay?"

"We probably do. Let me get the consul," the voice said. The consul is the president and the pro-consul is the vice-president in chapters of Sigma Chi.

"OK," I said.

Chapter 6

There was a pause on the phone, and then, "Hi, this is Brian. I am the consul," he said.

"Hi Brian. I am a brother at the Delta Phi chapter at University of Puget Sound. I am thinking of coming to Boston for the summer to work, and I was wondering if you have a place where I could stay in your chapter?"

"We sure do. It is $500 to stay for the summer," Brian said.

"Sold," I said. "I will be there Sunday."

"Great. We will see you then!" Brian said.

And that was that. I had a place to stay for the summer. By this time in my life, I was an expert packer. For a summer in Boston, I only needed a few of the things I would generally take when I went back to school or came home. The list was short: clothes, books, bike, camera, and that was it. Three nights later, I was on a red-eye to Boston. I took a cab to Back Bay where the Alpha Theta chapter house is located.

Brian greeted me at the door, helped me bring in my baggage, and said, "You will be staying up on the fifth floor, so on the way up, I can give you a tour if you want."

The Alpha Theta chapter has one of the best fraternity set-ups I have ever seen. They own their own building, a five-story brown-stone in Back Bay, a neighborhood in Boston a stone's throw from the Charles River. The fraternity is conveniently located on Beacon Street, less than a block from the Massachusetts Avenue Bridge, or Mass Ave Bridge, which is also the 2A freeway. This bridge crosses the Charles River, the place where the Head of the Charles Regatta, the Holy Grail for rowers, takes place. The Mass Ave Bridge crosses the Charles in a slightly northwest and southeasterly direction, and this road runs through the MIT campus. Continuing down this road will take you to Cambridge, and about a half mile from Cambridge Central Square is Harvard.

"Let's start with the lower levels, then work our way up. Why don't you bring your bike, and I will show you where we store those," he said.

"OK," I said.

"Alpha Theta has five floors, a basement, and a subbasement," he said as we descended the stairs to the basement. At the the basement landing, Brian turned right. Five paces into the hallway, he pointed to his left, and said, "This is the door to the subbasement. We store our bicycles here." He opened the door, and I looked in. "The light is on your right," he said reaching in and flipping the light switch on. I walked my bike down the stairs, found an empty hook, and hung my front tire on the hook. Climbing the three or four stairs, I switched off the light and closed the door behind me. As I came out of the door to the subbasement, directly across from me was a small room.

"This is the laundry room," he said, turning on the light.

"OK," I said.

We turned left, walked another five paces, and Brian said, "This is our bar." The room had a small wood bar running north to south, like you would see in an old pub. There was a bit of alcohol on the shelves. "We tend to only be in here occasionally, as most of the brothers hang out in the TV room on the second floor," he said. "That door" – he pointed to the south wall – "leads to Beacon Street."

"OK," I said, as we headed back down the hall, past the subbasement door, and passed the stairway back up to the main part of the house. Five paces north of the stairs, he pointed to a door, "There is a bathroom here."

"OK," I said.

Another five paces north he said, "This is our kitchen. During the school year we have a chef cook our meals, but during summer we do our own cooking. The refrigerators are over there," he said, pointing to the far east side of the room. "There is a grocery store about a mile away which we can show you later. That door leads to the back parking lot," he said pointing to the north side of the building.

"OK," I said.

"Now, up the stairs here," he said as we climbed the stairs from the basement to the main floor, "is our main foyer and dining room."

"OK," I said. All of the tables were made of antique hardwoods, and each of the chairs matched the tables. Each chair had a large ΣX carved into the front of its back rest. The foyer had a large crystal chandelier hanging over the empty space where the stairs wrapped around the chandelier, taking one from floor to floor. There were two smaller chandeliers in the dining room. The dining room also had a dumbwaiter for bringing up food from the basement, so the chef would not have to run each dish up himself. This was a kind of "class," which I had not seen in any fraternity house before or after. I was in fraternity heaven.

"We don't eat down here in the summer, as we don't have a formal meal time, and there are only a few brothers around," he said as he walked out of the dining room. "Let's grab your stuff, as we will get to your room in a bit," he said, grabbing my backpack and climbing up the first flight of stairs.

"OK," I said, picking up my duffel.

"This is the second floor," he said hooking left around the chandelier and into a larger room. "This is the TV room and the general lounge. The lounge is where we hang out, eat, play cards, watch TV, and have movie night. This is where most of the brothers will be when they are not doing anything else. Hey, brothers! This is Roland from the UPS Delta Phi chapter. He is going to be staying with us this summer. Make sure to make him feel welcome!"

"Hey, Roland!" the four or five brothers in the room exclaimed.

"Hey, guys!" I said.

"The consul and pro-consul office is on this floor, directly opposite the lounge," Brian said going on with his tour. "If you need me or Matt, the pro-consul during business hours, you will generally find us in there, so just knock on the door."

"OK," I said.

"Now, levels three through five are sleeping quarters for brothers. Each floor has its own bathroom which the brothers share," he said as we climbed to the third floor, and then up to the fourth floor. "We are going to put you in this room here," he said turning right off the fourth-floor landing and entering a moderately sized room. Four beds had been built into the walls, and each bed had a desk underneath it. The beds were tall enough that one could easily stand up under a bed without hitting one's head. On the north wall was a couch and a window looking out at the Charles River.

"This is Peter's room, and he will show you around from here. Peter, this is Roland. Roland, Peter," Brian said.

"Hi Roland," Peter said.

"Hi Peter," I said. "Thanks for letting me share your space."

"No problem," Peter said.

"OK, you know where everything is. Let me, Matt, or Peter know if you have any problems," said Brian.

"OK. Thanks Brian," I said.

Compared to Bristol Bay in Alaska, Boston was awash in cultural and epicurean delights. The dichotomy between the fishing industry and the pristine surroundings of the tundra and Bristol Bay seemed extreme, yet this same dichotomy exists everywhere humans harvest nature in an industrial way. The wild beauty of Alaska had been breathtaking, and the wilds of Alaska should certainly be considered a national treasure. My summer job the previous year had taken me to the remotest place one could imagine, and this summer I would be in the thick of one of the most bustling cities in the United States. Boston is a city with a vibrant heartbeat, and a culture where young and old mix harmoniously. There are over eighteen colleges in Boston, and this breeds not only a little inter-school rivalry, but also a mix of young, academically inclined minds unlike anywhere else I have ever been.

Jogging Giant Moving Company, my new employer, had its office in Somerville, about two miles, as the crow flies, from where I lived. Each evening, I would call and see if they had work for me the next day. If they did, I would get up at 6 a.m., and descend the stairs of the fraternity to the basement. Then I would remove my bike from the subbasement, and ride the two miles to Somerville. If they didn't have work for me, I would wander over to Newbury Street and peruse the small shops there, often selecting a bookstore or coffeeshop to hang out in. This was my routine. Go to work in the morning, if there was work to be had, or hang out on Newbury Street. Come evening, I would hang out with the brothers. There was a bit of a *Groundhog Day* effect, as each day was highly similar to the previous one. I do believe that I said college was an idyllic life, right?

Chapter 6

One morning, I awoke at 6 a.m. to go to work as usual. I showered, dressed, and descended the stairs to the basement. I turned right at the bottom, walked the five paces to the subbasement, and put my hand on the door knob to open it. Then I paused, hand on the knob. I stood there hand outstretched for a minute or so; my mind was puzzled. Something was out of place, and I could not figure out what I had seen which was out of place. I stood there trying to figure it out. It had nothing to do with the subbasement, but had to do with something which I had seen between the stairs and the subbasement. The only other doorway I had walked by was the laundry room, and that was directly behind me. I slowly turned around and stared into the laundry room. It was pitch black as I had not turned on the lights when I came down the stairs. I stared and stared into the laundry room, trying to figure out what I was seeing. Like a flash of light, I realized what I was seeing. I was looking at the whites of someone's eyes, who was about my height. The eyes were staring at me like two small orbs glistening in the blackest night.

I really should have thought this through better, but instead I said, "What's up?"

Out from the darkness stepped a tall, moderately built, African American man. He looked to be in his thirties, and he was dressed from head to foot in black.

"Not much," he said.

I did not know this man. "What are you doing in the laundry room?" I said.

"Man, that party you guys threw las night was awesome! I think I must have gotten drunk and passed out in here. I just woke up when you came down," he said.

"It was an awesome party," I agreed, except both of us knew that there had not been a party the night before. "Well, you know how fraternities are. I have to ask you to leave, if you are not part of the fraternity," I said.

"Yeah. No problem," he said.

I escorted him towards the back entrance, which faced the Charles River.

As we walked through the hall into the kitchen, he gestured towards the kitchen sink, which happened to be right next to the kitchen knives, and said, "Do you mind if I splash some water on my face?"

This was a chess match fueled by adrenaline, and luckily I was thinking as fast as he was. "Sure," I said, "there's a bathroom right here. Go ahead, I will wait," I stood in the kitchen between him and the knives.

He looked at me and smiled a guilty smile. "Thanks," he said, then went into the bathroom, bent over the sink, and splashed water on his face. He dried his face with a paper towel, then stepped back out.

I walked him to the door, held it open, and said, "Thanks for coming to the party!"

He stepped out, and then after a few steps looked back over his shoulder with a large toothy smile. Then he started a light jog toward his next target.

I closed the door and started walking back to the subbasement, when the after-adrenaline rush hit. My knees wobbled a little bit. At the stairs, I picked up the in-house phone, and hit the direct-dial button for Brian. The phone rang five or six times, and finally, a sleepy Brian answered the phone.

"What?" he said with a disoriented yawn.

"Brian, it's Roland. I just escorted some guy out from the basement."

"What?" he said, much more alert now.

"African American, all dressed in black, about my size, but a little slighter. He seemed athletic," I said.

"I think you just had a run-in with the person who has been stealing our bikes," he said.

"Well, you should change the codes on the locks."

"I will see to it, and Roland, beers are on us tonight!"

"Thanks, Brian," I said and hung up the phone.

Five floors down in the basement, I had sent a thief packing with only my wits and awareness to guide me. That could have gone horribly wrong, and it would have just been me and him. Damn, I thought. I am glad my awareness was on point. Now, I am going to use this post-adrenalin rush to get my butt to work!

Chapter 7
Awareness Two-Dot-One

Three years later, in 1996, George Walker, my mentor from college and the psychologist, called me and said, "Hey, Roland. I just came across something you would be interested in."

"Sure, shoot," I said.

"I was talking to a friend of mine in Montana. He is a veteran, and walks the Red Road. He said they are looking for a photographer to shoot the powwow on their reservation, and he called to ask if I knew anyone. I told him I sure do."

"That's great news," I said.

"Do you want me to tell him you'll do it?"

"Yes. Does it pay? I suppose it doesn't matter if it does or not, but it is nice to know up front," I said.

"Well, I doubt they have any money, which is why they asked if I knew anyone. He did say that he would put you up, feed you, and show you around."

"Got it. Sure, tell him I will come on out there," I said.

"Great. Once he agrees, I will email you his contact info."

"Thanks, George! You have come through for me again!"

"That's what friends are for, Roland."

About a day later, I received an email from George. It simply said, "Green light. Here is Pete Youngbull's phone number. Give him a call, and he will give you the details."

I promptly called Mr. Youngbull. After a few rings, a deep baritone voice answered, "Hello?"

"Hi, Pete. This is Roland Pearce. George Walker told me to call you."

"Hey, Roland. How's your day treating you?"

"Good. Good. George said that you were looking for a photographer for a powwow in Montana. When are you thinking?"

"I am indeed. The powwow is July 26th to July 28th, but if you want to come on the 23rd, I can show you around a bit."

"OK, I could do that. Where in Montana is it?"

"We are in Harlem, Montana," Pete said.

"Where is that in relation to Missoula?" I said.

"North and east of there by about 300 hundred miles, near the Milk River, or on Route 2 if you don't know where the Milk is, about thirty miles south of the Canadian border."

"Sounds good, I will be there on the 23rd. I will be driving a big white K5 Blazer."

"We will see you then," said Pete.

Pete gave me his address. I wrote it down, checked to make sure I had it right by repeating it back to Pete. Then I thanked him for allowing me to share my skill with him and his tribe, and hung up.

I had a few weeks to prepare. It would be a long drive from Portland, about 867 miles to be exact, but I would be driving through some of the most beautiful country in the United States. Going a long distance in an old car takes a bit of preparation, and one must always carry a few necessary sundries in case of emergency. These include vehicle things, emergency and first-aid supplies, and things to do. A small list of what I spent my final week gathering includes:

Flares	Various wrenches including a set of vice grips	A medical kit
4 pints of engine oil	Ratchet set	Emergency blanket
Radiator fluid	My knife belt (2 knives, a knife sharpener, and a portable shovel)	
Power bars	Fire-making supplies	Sleeping bag

2 gallons of water	Beads and beadwork	Sleeping pad
5 gallon plastic water container	Leather for making things	Poncho
Water filter	A few sailcloth needles	Books for identifying plants
Water bottle	An awl	General reading books
Portable white gas stove	Artificial sinew	A journal
A liter of white gas	A draw knife	Tobacco pipe and pipe bag
A blue tarp	Various wood and metal files	1 pound of pipe tobacco
Sunglasses	Tomahawk	Camera and film
Clear shop glasses	A bow saw	Tripod
A bandana	Leatherman	A pot and a pan
100 feet of cotton rope	Tent	a fork and a spoon

I planned my trip to include an overnight at my friend Jarrett's house in Missoula, before driving the rest of the way the next day, if all went well. This would make the first leg of the trip 547 miles and the second leg 320 miles. This seemed a lot less stressful than driving the whole way in one jaunt. A week before I was to leave, I called Jarrett. The phone rang a few times, and then "Hello?"

"Hey Jarrett, it's Roland. I am going to be coming through Missoula in a week. Will you be around?"

"I think so. What date are you thinking exactly?"

"July 22nd."

"Yeah, I'll be here. I have to work during the day, though."

"That's OK, man, I won't be there until 6 p.m. at the least. Do you think I could crash on your floor for the night?"

"Sure. How far are you going?" he said.

"Harlem, Montana," I said.

"Man, that is in the middle of nowhere. What are you doing out there?"

"A photo shoot. A buddy of a buddy has asked me to come take some pictures on the Rez."

"Oh, that's cool," he said. "That's the Fort Belknap Reservation, right?"

"I don't know. My host said he was Assiniboine though."

"Yeah, that's Fort Belknap then. The Gros Ventres live there too. You know the messed-up thing about that reservation is that the Gros Ventre and the Assiniboine were hereditary enemies. What was the government thinking when they put those two tribes together on the same land?" Jarrett said.

"I don't know," I said.

"They probably hoped one or the other would kill the other one off," he said.

"That seems pretty brutal."

"Roland, there's something you should know before you come out here. Montana is a strange place. We have cities, but they are not like the cities you have on the West Coast. We also have diversity, but that diversity is more like a few Native tribes, and a bunch of white people. A lot of the white folk don't have the same respect for the Natives that you do, and anti-native sentiment often bubbles just under the surface. The Natives also look at the whites with suspicion. You know that phrase 'someone who is an Indian giver'? Well, that phrase was coined for a white man who gives to an Indian, and then takes what he has given back.

"Take Fort Belknap as an example of this. In 1885 the Blackfoot, Gros Ventre, and Assiniboine agreed to live in area roughly from Glendive, Montana to Browning, Montana, or 477 miles east to west, and from roughly Sweet Grass, Montana to Harlowton, Montana or 249 miles north to south. Then on May 1st, 1888, they were forced to cede an additional 17,500,000 acres. Look up the treaty sometime – it is an interesting read," Jarrett said.

"When did you get interested in treaty law? That is some detailed information you are giving me," I said.

Chapter 7

"I grew up in Havre, Montana, which is in the middle of the original reservation. It was one of the things we were taught in school. The reason I've told you all this is to let you know that there is an uneasy truce between the whites and the Natives out here. The whites for the most part speed up when they see an Indian crossing the road, and a white person who finds themselves on a reservation uninvited could be considered fair game."

"Well, I have an invite, so hopefully, I will be fine," I said.

"OK. Well, I thought you should know."

"Thanks."

"So, I will see you in a week?"

"Yep. I'll give you a call when I get close," I said.

"OK. See you then," Jarrett said.

What Jarrett said did not bother me terribly, at least the part about not having an invite, as I was fine in that department. I was concerned about his "Indian giver" comments, though, so I decided to look up the treaty of 1888. He was right about it being an interesting read. This is how the treaty read, and the italics are mine.

> Whereas the reservation set apart by the act of Congress approved April 15th, 1874, for the use and occupancy of the Gros Ventre, Piegan, Blood, Blackfoot, River Crow, and such other Indians as the President might, from time to time, see fit to locate theeron, is *wholly out of proportion to the number of Indians occupying the same, and greatly in excess of their present or prospective wants, and whereas the said Indians are desirous of disposing of so much thereof as they do not require*, in order to obtain the means to enable them to become self-supporting, as a pastoral and agricultural people, and to educate their children in the paths of civilization: Therefore to carry out such a purpose, it is hereby agreed as follows:
>
> ### Article III
>
> In consideration of the foregoing cession and relinquishment the United States hereby agrees to advance and expend annually, for the period of ten

years after the ratification of this agreement, under direction of the Secretary of the Interior, for the Indians now attached to and receiving rations at the Fort Peck Agency, one hundred and sixty-five thousand dollars; for the Indians now attached to and receiving rations at the Fort Belknap Agency, one hundred and fifteen thousand dollars; and for the Indians now attached to and receiving rations at the Blackfeet Agency, one hundred and fifty thousand dollars, *in the purchase of cows, bulls, and other stock, goods, clothing, subsistence, agricultural and mechanical implements, in providing employees, in the education of Indian children, procuring medicine and medical attendance, in the care and support of the aged, sick and infirm, and helpless orphans of said Indians, in the erection of such new agency and school buildings, mills, and blacksmith, carpenter, and wagon shops as may be necessary, in assisting the Indians to build houses and enclose their farms, and in any other respect to promote their civilization,* comfort, and improvement. Provided, that in the employment of farmers, artisans, and laborers, preference shall in all cases be given to Indians residing on the reservation who are well qualified for such position. Provided further, that all cattle issued to *said Indians for stock-raising purposes, and their progeny, shall bear the brand of the Indian Department, and shall not be sold, exchanged, or slaughtered, except by consent or order of the agent in charge,* until such time as this restriction shall be removed by the Commissioner of Indian Affairs.

Let's first look at a few parts of this treaty: First, the value of a dollar in 1888 converts to about $24.89 in 2017. This means that the Indians of the Fort Peck Agency received $165,000 in 1888 dollars, which would have a value today of roughly $4,100,000. The Indians of the Fort Belknap Agency received $115,000 in 1888 dollars, or the equivalent today of roughly $2,860,000. The Indians of the Blackfeet Agency received $150,000 in 1888 dollars, or the equivalent today of roughly $3,700,000. These payments would be made for a period of ten years, so Fort Peck Agency received a total of $41,000,000 in today's dollars. The Fort Belknap Agency received $28,600,000 in today's dollars. Lastly, the Blackfeet Agency received $37,000,000 in today's dollars. All told, the US government paid $106,600,000 for the ten-year total to all the reservations in this treaty in today's dollars.

At today's prices (as last set in 2016), the average price for land in Montana is about $900 per acre. Multiply the 2016 value of an acre by 17,500,000 acres, and we come to $15.75 billion dollars as the value for the said land, without calculating in additional value such as mineral rights, water rights, or timber rights. (*Values courtesy of the USDA*). There are 640 acres in one square mile, so 17,500,000 acres equals a total of 27,343 square miles of land. Lastly, the entire state of Montana covers a total of 147,040 square miles. This means that these tribes traded roughly one fifth of the state of Montana to the US government in this one treaty alone.

Another thing worth mentioning here is that the money being provided by the US was earmarked for items, as in items of trade. The items listed could have cost anything, and you will note that there is nothing in the agreement which says that trade items and services had to be sold at fair value. This money also could be used to pay Bureau of Indian Affairs (BIA) employees. Lastly, the Natives would be provided with cows and bulls, but they couldn't sell them, exchange them, or slaughter them; oh, except unless they had permission from the Commissioner of Indian Affairs. I also find the first paragraph rather humorous: from the phrase, "*wholly out of proportion to the number of Indians ...*" to "*desirous of disposing of so much thereof as they do not require ...*"

In today's world, who in their right mind is hoping to dispose of land? Additionally, who would do so for trade only, and not cash? Let's just assume that the Natives were not provided with neutral legal counsel, and that the US government was not blatantly lying, but any way I read this, the Natives received the sharp end of the stick, and it did not have a juicy bison steak on the end of it. All of this really did give context to Jarrett's words, and going to the Rez, I would need to walk carefully until I knew just where I stood.

I passed the rest of the week finishing my preparations and hanging out at Powell's Books reading books on Montana. The best roads, hiking trips, national forests, where to eat, what had to be seen, who lived there, the flora and fauna, and the ways and culture of the Native people who lived there. As it always does, the time trickled down to nothing, and finally it was the morning I intended to leave, July 22nd.

When packing the car, I usually make a list and I simply tick it off. The trick is not forgetting anything on the list or forgetting to add something to the list. There is nothing worse than being in the middle of nowhere and realizing that you forgot your jacket, sleeping bag, or flashlight. I set down everything in the driveway and checked it against my list. When I put it in the car, I checked it off the list. It wasn't long, and I was all packed up. I had done well; it only took me thirty minutes to fit it all in. K5 Blazers always seem to have more space than you actually need. I had filled the gas tank the night before, so I simply filled my water bottle, and got on the road.

I headed out Interstate 84, Portland's great and only thoroughfare to the East. What about Highway 26, you might ask. Comparatively, one might as well compare a residential street to a freeway. Let's simply say that 26 does not really meet the expectations of a "great thoroughfare," it is more like a minor thoroughfare.

It wasn't long before I was through Troutdale and zipping by Multnomah Falls. By the time I reached Hood River, one could say that I was properly in the Columbia River Gorge. Don't get me wrong, Multnomah Falls is in the Gorge, and so are the rest of the waterfalls. However, just before Hood River, one crosses the edge of the seismic activity zone, which acts like an invisible border that separates the wet, or yin, side of the Columbia Gorge from the dry, or yang, side. The Gorge from this seismic activity zone to Portland is roughly fifty miles of high cliffs covered with Douglas fir, maple, and, near the flats of the Columbia River, cottonwood. There is plenty of water, which means the trees are large, lush, and dense. In comparison, east of the seismic activity zone, the land is dry, there is more grass, the trees are stunted, and the bluffs appear to rise out of the earth at forty-five-degree angles. One side is not necessarily better than the other, but once I pass Hood River, I feel like I am really going somewhere, and that my trip is beginning.

Twenty miles further, and I entered the Dalles. I pulled over for gas at an Exxon station, grabbed a cup of coffee from Starbucks, and got back on the road. It was hot, easily in the nineties, which meant that it was only going to get hotter as I traveled east. I stayed on Interstate 84, marveling at how the gold of the grass contrasted with the dark brown of the columnar basalt. Past Biggs Junction, I drove up a hill to what could be considered the high desert. The sun beat down mercilessly here, and it became even hotter. I passed through Rufus, Blalock, Arlington, Boardman, and a number of one-horse towns until I arrived in Pendleton. Here, I gassed up, grabbed a bite to eat, then continued on my way. I sped onto Highway 11, past the turnoffs for Athena and Weston, into the small but long town of Milton Freewater. Then I crossed the Oregon-Washington border and entered Walla Walla, home of the famous sweet onion. From here, Highway 12 would take me all the way to Missoula. I passed Dixie, Waitsburg, and Huntsville, all with no problem. Then, I passed Dayton. The electronic sign at the bank in Dayton blinked and read 115 degrees, and I felt like the wax was going to melt out of my ears. The Blazer began to feel like it was going to die. I was going the speed limit, but my big K5 felt like she was stuttering. When I increased my speed to seventy-five miles per hour, she began to feel like she was driving normally again. I passed Delaney and might as well have been in the middle of nowhere.

Chapter 7

I kept on at seventy-five, well above the speed limit, intuitively knowing that to slow down meant the Blazer would quit.

"Come on, baby, we are about halfway there," I thought to myself. "You can do it."

Then from behind me, out of nowhere the flashing of red and blue lights appeared. As I pulled over on the two-lane road, heat waves rose off the ground. It seemed like they would melt the tires right off my rig. I sat there, dripping massive globules of sweat, while the police officer ran my plates, and otherwise checked out my car.

Five minutes later, he approached my driver's side window, and said, "Did you know that you were speeding, and that the speed limit here is 60 miles per hour?"

"I did, officer. I believe that my SUV has vapor lock, and I was afraid if I drove slower, my engine would die."

"Hmm. License and registration please?" he said.

"Sure. Here you go," I said handing him my documents.

He stepped away from my driver's side, and went back to his cruiser. While he pulled up my record, I continued to sweat. Since this interaction had begun, not a single vehicle had passed us. One has to remember that this occurred in the days before cell phones, and being stuck on the road meant that you were at the mercy of good Samaritans passing by for help.

The officer walked back up to my Blazer, and said, "I am not going to issue you a ticket today, as your driving record is clean, and I don't want to be the one to mess that up. However, I am going to issue you a warning. Slow down! The speed limit is 60 miles per hour." He gave me back my documentation, went back to his cruiser, waited a few seconds, then pulled away.

I turned the ignition on the Blazer, but she wouldn't start. I tried several times, as I watched the officer slowly drive off. I didn't know what to do. I got out of the Blazer, walked into the middle of the deserted road, and started waving my arms in the universal sign for distress. Way in the distance of this flat, barren stretch of road, I saw the cruiser slow down, then hook a u-turn. He drove back and stopped his cruiser in the other lane opposite my Blazer, "What's the problem?" he said.

"My rig won't start. As I said, I believe I have vapor lock."

He looked at me, shook his head, and said, "I can call you a tow truck."

"Thank you. I would appreciate that."

"The next town is twenty miles up the road. There's a shop there, and maybe they can help you figure it out."

"Thanks," I said.

The officer drove past me a bit, then hooked another u-turn, and pulled up behind me again. Ten minutes later, the officer stepped out of his cruiser and walked up to my driver's side window. I was covered in sweat.

"I have put in a call for a tow truck. They are busy, and said it could be up to an hour before they get here. If you want to sit in the back of the cruiser, I have air conditioning."

"That would be heavenly," I said. "Thank you."

The officer turned around and went back into his cruiser. I reached behind the driver's seat, grabbed my half-full water bottle, and stepped out onto the frying pan currently called a highway. As I walked back to the cruiser, I took a drink from the bottle and had I not filled the water bottle myself, I would swear that someone had filled my bottle from a Jacuzzi. I opened the back door of the cruiser, and got in. It was cramped, and I felt a little claustrophobic and trapped. It is not every day that I will willingly enter anything with bars on the windows and no working inside door handle. Had it not been so hot, I probably would have declined his offer. The officer acknowledged me, but otherwise did not speak to me. Every once in a while his radio squawked as the dispatcher announced an event. I had begun to cool down, and while I was still wet, I had quit sweating. Time passed, and I let my eyes close. After a while, the officer said, "Here comes your tow truck."

"OK," I said.

The officer stepped out of the cruiser, walked around the back of the car and opened my door.

Chapter 7

"Thanks," I said.

"No problem," he said.

I stepped out of the cruiser and watched as the tow truck pulled up in front of my Blazer. An older man with grayish-brown hair, a beard, and a bit of a pot belly opened his door, stepped out on to the asphalt, and walked up to us. "What seems to be the problem?" he said.

"I think I have vapor lock," I said.

"Have you tried to start it again?" he said.

"No, but I can give it another try."

"Yep. Do that, and we will see if she starts," he said.

"OK." I walked back to my rig, took out my keys, opened the door, put the keys in the ignition, and tried to start the Blazer. She still wouldn't turn over. I looked back at the tow truck driver and shook my head no.

"OK. Well, I can give you a tow to a shop in Pomeroy. They have an additive which you can add to your gas tank for this kind of thing."

"Thanks. That would be great," I said.

The officer nodded his head, and said, "OK. Well, I am off then."

"OK," I said.

The tow truck driver nodded, and we took a step or two back into the ditch while the officer climbed back into his cruiser and pulled away.

The tow truck driver talked as he messed with the levers of his truck, lowering the lift, and adjusting it so that the arms of the lift lay under the front of the Blazer. He added running lights to the roof of the SUV, and prepared the vehicle for transport.

"Vapor lock is a real problem with these older rigs. When it gets hot like this, the fuel literally vaporizes as it moves from the tank to the engine. Once the fuel gets to the engine, it is nothing but fumes. The only way to get the engine to start again is to cool it off, and get the gas to condense into liquid. But, that is not going to happen in this heat. They may be able to give you an additive in Pomeroy, but I don't think it will solve your problem long term. These older vehicles just do this, it is a flaw in their design. Then again, most places in the country don't have the kind of heat we do," he said.

"OK," I said.

"I'm ready. Are you ready?" he said.

"I am."

I opened the passenger door of the tow truck and scrambled in. He climbed into his seat, took out a pack of Marlboro Reds, and said, "Smoke?"

"No, thanks," I said.

"Mind if I do?"

"No problem. Go ahead."

"Thanks," he said, as he lit his cigarette and took a drag. He looked in his rearview mirror for traffic, then he pulled out. "Where are you off to?"

"Montana. First Missoula, then to a small town called Harlem."

"Have you ever been?"

"No," I said.

"Montana is truly God's country. You will love it. I think everyone would want to live there, if there was some way to make a living there."

"I have heard it is beautiful," I said.

Chapter 7

"It is. Nothing sends a chill of awe up your spine, than seeing the Rockies thrust out of the ground. It is breathtaking."

"Do you have any recommendations of places to visit?" I asked.

"You really can't pick a place which is bad. Glacier is magnificent. The Bob Marshall Wilderness Area is filled with pristine streams, and below Missoula is the Bitterroot River valley where you drive between the Bitterroot Mountains and the Rockies. Down by Clearwater and Darby, the Bitterroots steal the show. I haven't spent too much time east of the Rockies though."

"Once I pass through Missoula, I will be heading north to Kalispell, then through Glacier to get to Harlem. Any recommendations for this part of Montana?" I said.

"Well, if it were my trip, I would take the slightly longer route, and head up Highway 209 past Seely Lake. That will take you to Kalispell, and it's a beautiful drive."

"I think I will do that. Thanks for the recommendation!" I said.

"No problem," he said. Ten minutes later, we pulled into the mechanic shop at Pomeroy. "I am going to put you down here. These guys deal with this all of the time and they will get you moving again."

"Thanks," I said.

The tow driver reversed all his motions and unhooked the Blazer from his towing apparatus. "Do you have AAA?" he asked.

"I do."

"All I need to do is see your card and I will be off," he said. I pulled out my membership card and showed it to him. "Good thing you have the plus membership. You know they only cover a three mile tow on the regular membership?"

"I didn't know that. I have always had the plus membership," I said.

"Well, that's all I need. Have a good rest of your trip!" he said.

"Thanks!"

He pulled away, and I stepped into the mechanic's shop. A man with short blond hair and a navy blue jumpsuit with the name Bob sewed on it stood behind a small counter with an old green-screen computer on it. Piles of Chilton manuals were stacked behind him.

"Good afternoon," Bob said.

"Good afternoon," I said.

"I see that Harley dropped you off. What seems to be the problem?"

"I think I have vapor lock."

"Oh. Well, that is easy enough," he said.

Bob squatted and looked for something under the counter, then stood up with a bottle of additive. "Add this to your gas tank, and it should make your gas denser, so it won't become an aerosol as it is running through your gas lines."

"OK," I said.

"It is a quick fix. You will need to buy more if you are running through hilly areas or places where it is hot. This is the most cost-effective option I have to offer you."

"I'll take it. I am on a schedule, and I need to get back on the road. How much?" I said.

"$7.95," he said.

"I will take three then," I said.

"Let me see," he squatted down again looking in his cabinet. "Yep, I have three. Here you go."

I paid for the bottles, walked back to the Blazer, and put two of the bottles in the back seat. Then I opened the door to the gas tank, unscrewed the gas cap, and dumped the remaining bottle in. I waited for it to stop pouring, then took it out, careful to not drip any on the Blazer. I put the gas cap back on, closed the door to the tank, then threw the

Chapter 7

bottle away in the garbage can. I walked back to the Blazer, took out my keys, and inserted them into the ignition.

"Here goes nothing," I thought to myself. I turned the ignition. Nothing.

"Come on Creator. I have to get moving," I said to myself. I waited a few seconds, and tried again. The engine roared to life. "Yeah. Come on, Baby!" I said out loud. I put the transmission in drive and the engine kept purring. Back on the road!

I turned out of the mechanic's shop, and onto Highway 12. A few seconds later I was out of town and watching the flatland of grass waving in the wind as I rolled through the high desert, doing speed limit. Highway 12 is the same route Lewis and Clark traveled on their way to Astoria. I asked myself what was going through their minds at this point of their journey. What did the land look like then? Now, it is flat plains that roll off in the distance, and to the south, one can see the beginnings of the Umatilla National Forest. Ten miles or so past Pomeroy, the road twists and turns through some small hillsides, and just north of the road, one can see parts of the old wagon trail road that the early settlers trod on their westward journey. In the valleys, scrub cottonwood, willow, and black locust could be seen growing along the water. In another ten miles, I picked up the Snake River, as the highway hugged its banks. Before I knew it, I was passing through Lewiston, and the fork where the Clearwater and Snake Rivers have their confluence.

Twenty miles past Lewiston, my rig started having vapor lock again. I guess the additive was not going to help; it was a quick fix after all. There wasn't a cloud in the sky and it was hot. If I wanted to make Missoula on time, I needed to figure out another way to make this work. I reached behind me to my pipe bag. The pipe was nothing special, a bamboo stem with a rough corncob-like bowl. It was the pipe I use to pray with when I am in the woods, though, so it has a certain feeling that has been imbued in it from offering up prayers. I pulled the pipe from the bag, loaded it with tobacco and pulled my lighter from the same bag. I lit it, taking a long drag, held in the smoke, and exhaled. I began to pray aloud.

"Great Spirit, Grandfather of all life. I know that you have your own way. I know that nothing you create does not have meaning. I know that this heat makes the grass grow longer and feeds the plants and trees around me. I am humbled by your wisdom in the creation of life. But, I ask a boon. I try not to ask for much and accept that which you provide for me. I am grateful to be on this journey. I fear though, that my Blazer will not make the journey. I have utmost faith in you, Great Spirit."

I took another long drag from the pipe, held it in, and exhaled. "I wouldn't ask this of you if it was not important. I ask that you change this situation, so that I can make it to my destination. Please hear my call. It is with great respect for you that I ask this. If in your wisdom, you think I need to continue to have this problem, I accept your wisdom. But, if you want to clear this obstacle, I would very much appreciate it. As always, I am your humble servant. Thank you Grandfather. My life would be nothing without you."

I took another long inhale of my pipe, held it in, and exhaled. "Thank you, Grandfather," I said. Then I knocked out my pipe on the windowsill of the Blazer, put the pipe and tobacco back in their bag and continued down the road. Ten miles later, blowing quickly from the south, I saw the darkest thundercloud I had ever seen. Ten miles before, the sky had been perfectly blue, and now racing towards me was this dark gray bank of clouds. The trees bent under the force of the wind. Two miles later, the cloud converged on the road I was on. Thunder exploded above me, and lightning lit up the sky. Then. right over me, it began to hail. Hail so large, it was like golf balls coming from the sky. The hail covered the road and beat down on the Blazer like a hammer. The road cooled, and the Blazer started running normally. The hail then turned into massive droplets of rain.

As I drove the bends of the Clearwater River, I saw anglers and boaters huddling under what cover they could, as this un-forecast rain poured down on them. "Sorry about that," I said to myself. I passed Orofino, and thirty miles later arrived in the town of Kooskia, where the South Fork of the Clearwater joins with the Middle Fork of the Clearwater. I needed gas. As I drove into Kooskia, the rain began to abate, and blue sky once again became prevalent. "Thank you, Creator," I said to myself.

After I gassed up, I drove back through Kooskia, and turned again onto Highway 12 for the final 143 miles of my trip to Missoula. Near the town of Lowell, I joined up with the Lochsa River, which I would follow almost all the way to Lolo Pass.

There is something special about small tributary rivers. They represent neither the origin nor the destination, but the beginning of the journey. They are often more shallow and less deep, as if they represent when the journey has just begun, where one is not yet wise and the going is relatively easy. Of course, in tributaries, there are always rocks sticking out of the water, but if one is aware, these rocks generally pose few problems. Tributaries also generally start somewhere high and flow towards the ocean, at least when the tributary comes from a mountain chain. This is representative of where we all come from, and where we are all going.

Chapter 7

The Lochsa flows through the middle of a small valley in the Bitterroot Mountains. The road that adjoins it is a simple two-lane affair with pullouts from which one can absorb the scenic views of the river and steep canyon it flows through. Fluffy light clouds misted over the hillsides like thin cotton gauze covering the lush forest of Doug fir. Near the riverbank, aspens leaves quivered, cedars hung low over the river, and sphagnum moss covered the Doug fir nearest the river. Every once in a while, an angler could be seen out in his waders fly fishing for trout. It was a picturesque scene and similar to Thoreau's *Walden*. Eighty miles from Kooskia, the road slanted upward and I began my climb to Lolo Pass. It would not be long now. The Blazer purred as I drove, enjoying the much cooler temperatures of the mountains. I passed by Lolo Hot Springs, thinking I might take advantage of their hot springs on my way back. The sign said $7 for use of their facilities, and I imagined sitting in their tubs on a cool October night.

Crossing the pass, I began the slow descent towards the town of Lolo. Hills of trees and the small rivulet of water called Lolo Creek greeted me when I had fully descended the pass. I was already in love with what I had seen, and from what I had heard, I probably would leave besotted with Montana. Thirty minutes through the Lolo Creek Valley, I entered the town of Lolo and I turned right to get gas at the Conoco station. I only had eight miles left and I was eager to see Jarrett. At the Conoco, I used the pay phone to call him. I put in fifty cents, dialed the number, and waited for an answer. It was 7:30 p.m. I was a little later than my anticipated arrival because of my vapor lock issues. The phone rang a few times, then Jarrett answered the phone, "Hello?"

"Hey, Jarrett. It is Roland. I am in Lolo. Where do I go from here?"

Jarrett gave me directions to get to his house on Skyview Drive in Missoula. When I had repeated the directions back to him, I hung up the phone, walked back to my rig, opened the door, and started the ignition. I then pulled up to the pump, filled up the Blazer with gas, paid, then turned right out of the Conoco station and made a quick left at the light. Twenty minutes later, I pulled up to his house, parked on the street, went to his door, and rang the doorbell. After a minute or so, Jarrett opened the door, and said, "Hey, Roland! Great to see you!" Then he gave me a big hug.

"Good to see you too, Jarrett! It has been years!"

"It was too long, in my opinion!" he said.

"I agree."

"Do you need help getting your stuff out?" he said.

"Sure. That would be great."

While we unpacked the Blazer, and took my stuff into the guest bedroom, Jarrett and I chatted about old times, who we still were in contact with, and what we had been doing for the last ten years.

"Are you hungry?" Jarrett asked.

"I am. Do you know a good place to grab a burger?" I said.

"I do. Let's go to the Double Front. It is about ten minutes away. I can drive if you want."

"Sure. Let's go."

We left the house, and piled into Jarrett's silver Toyota V4 truck, then headed down to the establishment.

Missoula is a three-horse town compared to Portland or Seattle. It is not a village, but a small town with a population of about 56,000 people. The city itself was founded in 1860. The French referred to the area of Missoula as "Hell Gate," because it was a central route for the travel of both early settlers and Native tribes. Because each of these groups was not necessarily friendly to the other, this led to a number of skirmishes. So many skirmishes, in fact, that it was very common to find human bones strewing the narrow valley which served as the corridor from east to west. Now, just so you don't think the Natives, in this case the Blackfeet, were racist, they also killed other tribes who were not part of their trading pact. The tribes from the west of Hell Gate wanted to travel to the east side of Hell Gate to hunt buffalo, and certain tribes would wait in the hills for these western tribes to come through the narrow pass. If the ambushers felt like they had overpowering numbers, then they would attack whatever group was coming through. If the group passing through Hell Gate was either better armed or had more numbers than the ambushers, then they would be allowed to pass.

In 1866, the name for the town of Missoula became official. It is a Salish name for the Clark Fork River, which runs through the northern part of Missoula. The Northern Pacific Railway was constructed and finished in 1883, allowing the export of lumber from the surrounding areas, and in 1893, the University of Montana was founded. In the early

1980s, Missoula suffered from the same timber crash that affected the rest of the Pacific Northwest. Mills closed, and one of the staples of Missoula's economy (roughly 40%) simply disappeared.

"Here we are," Jarrett said.

"I am starving," I said.

We got out of the truck, then stumped up to the door. Inside we were greeted with the smells of an old bar, diner, and pool hall. As we bellied up to the bar, a number of people greeted Jarrett. The bartender gave us a couple of menus and Jarrett asked to be put on the list for a pool table. We ordered a beer apiece, I ordered a burger, and Jarrett ordered fried chicken. Then we got down to our version of a friendly conversation.

"Did you look at the treaty I was talking about?" Jarrett said.

"I did. Think what it must have been like to be there at that time," I said.

"I wouldn't have wanted to be either a settler or a Native American at that time. I think it would have been a hard life, and hard to make good decisions as those two cultures clashed," he said.

"I agree. Although it seems to me that the Natives received the raw end of the deal," I said.

"Definitely, but America was expanding westward, and these weren't the only tribes who had to sign treaties or lose their ability to live their customary life," he said.

"Well, I think they still lost their customary life. The treaties didn't stop that," I said.

'True, but the Natives probably didn't know or were not able to predict what signing the treaty would do to their tribe," he said.

"Probably not. It would have been a true 'between a rock and a hard place' situation," I said.

"I agree. Do you have any trepidation about heading to that part of Montana, knowing what you know now?" he said.

"No. I think that I will be OK," I said.

"Good."

Our food arrived, and the burger was standard. Nothing to write home about, but it was food and I was hungry.

"What are you going to do after your trip?" Jarrett said.

"I don't know. Go home. Get a job. Try to figure life out, I guess."

"Yeah. It all seems more complicated as we get older, doesn't it?"

"It does. How does one create a meaningful life is something I ask myself. How does one work for the benefit of more than just oneself? How does one move past simply surviving to thriving?" I said.

"Not by living in a small town, certainly, and probably not by living in Montana in general."

"Perhaps one simply has to have faith that God will provide," I said.

"God helps those who help themselves," he said.

"That is a Benjamin Franklin quote, right?"

"Actually, it was originally coined by Algernon Sidney, the political theorist. But Benjamin Franklin made it famous in his *Poor Richard's Almanack*," he said.

"Your ability to retain facts like this amazes me sometimes, Jarrett."

"I know. I am an idiot savant sometimes," he said, laughing.

"But do you really think it is about helping yourself? Or is it really that man must learn to ask God for help?" I asked.

"Do you think that God has the ability to hear us as individuals? Or are we heard collectively? How many people pray to God, only to have their prayers go unheeded?" he said.

Chapter 7

"I think God can hear individuals, because it is said that God is omnipresent – meaning God is everywhere at once."

"OK. Then why do people's prayers go unheeded?" he said.

"I don't know. Maybe because the sense of time for humans and God is different? Humans tend to be rather immediate, and God, it would seem, would be able to see the continuum of a person's life. Additionally, how do we know that prayers go unheeded? Perhaps it is that the prayers are heeded, but simply answered at a later time, one which is better for a person's growth?"

"I guess that is as good of a reason as any," he said.

"Hey Jarrett, your table is up. Do you still want it?" the barkeep asked.

"Do you want to play a couple of games, Roland?" Jarrett said.

"Sure, let me finish the last bite of my burger," I said.

"Yep. We still want it," Jarrett told the bartender.

"OK. Here are the balls," the bartender said as he put a tray of pool balls on the bar. "You are number five."

"I think I will have another pint. Roland, do you want another?" Jarrett said.

"Sure," I said.

"I have these," he said.

The bartender poured out two more Moose Drool Brown Ales. Big Sky Brewing had released the Moose Drool a few months back, and it was all the rage.

I stood up, picked up the pool balls, walked to table five, and spilled the balls onto the table. Jarrett brought the two pints over, set them on a small table next to the pool table, then racked the balls while I mused. Jarrett was a good and long-time friend, who accepted me even though I had idiosyncrasies. However, it did not feel remotely acceptable to talk to him about my own prayer experience just this day. It seemed like this had been a conversation between God and me and that sharing it would lessen the sense of this powerful thing that had happened. It was not that I feared Jarrett would not believe me, or tell me that it must be coincidence. No, it was more that the conversation or prayer which I had been a part of, was a private thing, and not to be shared. The truth is, when unexplainable things happen, they are actually difficult to share with other people. While sometimes one might feel a sense of permission around discussing something, even in these cases it is difficult to share. I suppose one of the main concerns when sharing spiritual stories, is this idea of "why me versus you?" The listener has a tendency to react with, "What makes you more special than anyone else?" or "Maybe it was all in your head?" or "Really? I just can't believe that." Regardless of the response, when something mystical happens in your life, unless the person you are talking to either was there, or has had a similar experience themselves, it is hard for them to fathom. Worse, they may think you want attention, or want to feel special, or want to feel powerful. But the truth is, when these things happen, in the moment it seems as natural as watching the trees blow in the wind. The greater the wind, the more awesome the spectacle, yet, it is still what we would consider natural or of nature.

One thing that seems consistent with prayer is that asking for yourself, or praying for yourself, often does not yield results. However, praying with love and compassion for others often yields great results. If one does pray for oneself, one has to pray with an understanding of what the larger picture is. It seems that when God answers your prayer for yourself, God does it, so that you can effect a greater good, bigger than yourself. One also has to pray for things that the spirit world can understand. Power, protection, love, guidance, understanding, these are all things that spirit understands. A fast car, a house on the lake, a roll of hundred-dollar bills in your pocket – these are things that have no value in the world of spirit, and so they are often not granted.

For example, when you ask to be healed or for God to intercede in your disease process, God certainly weighs out the cause and effect of giving you what you want – meaning that the disease which has come to you has come for a reason. I know that this is hard to hear and hard to accept, but the reason one becomes sick is often because of our own choices, whether they seem like choices or not. We know that too much stress causes a whole host of diseases. When smoking cigarettes, drinking alcohol, using drugs, eating too much sugar, or a diet full of junk food and carbs, we know that all of these choices have an effect on our body. It defies logic to think that our lifestyle choices do not affect us. The question God must decide when you pray for healing is, has the lesson for which the disease was provided been learned? Has one changed their life, their mind, and the way they interact with the world? Has this change been great enough, in such a

Chapter 7

way that it has reformed the way one sees one's life? Or upon healing, is one going to go back to one's old way of being? If one does not continue forward on the new way of life, acknowledging all that one has learned from being sick, and continue down this path, why would God answer the prayer for healing? In other words, God won't steal away the lesson for you by taking away the disease.

Why is it different if someone else prays for our healing? Simply that the love and compassion we feel for our brothers and sisters can move the spirit world to be compassionate on the person who is ill. The more people who pray for our well-being, the more likely the person who is ill will have a serendipitous awakening to the lesson which their illness is about. Think of this in terms of a spark. A single spark flashes and is out, but a number of sparks together can create a sustained light. The prayer itself acts as the container for this light. The more prayers, the more people, the more light. The more light, the more change can be effected. Compare this to praying for oneself which is a single spark and then goes out. Using this analogy, we can see why praying for others causes greater change. In Max Freedom Long's book *The Secret Science Behind All Miracles*, he mentions a Catholic priest who says that people who routinely pray for others tend to be sick for less time than those who only pray for themselves, when both people have disease. As with the earth, we are not supposed to be overlords of each other, but are supposed to be caretakers of each other.

"Do you want to break?" Jarrett said.

"No. You can if you want," I said.

Jarrett went to the wall and looked for a twenty weight cue, then pulled it off the wall and sighted down it to see if it was straight. Satisfied, he came back to the table, placed the cue ball slightly off center from the racked balls, and took his shot. I went to the rack of cues, also found a twenty weight cue, and sighted down it. I had to look at a couple of cues before I found one that looked straight. We played a few games, neither of us really trying to win, and simply playing for fun, talking about old times, and slurping our Moose Drool.

After the third game, Jarrett said, "There is a decent nightclub here called Mustang Sally's. Do you want to go dancing?"

"I don't think so. I have to hit the road early-ish tomorrow. I think I am done for the night. It is 11 p.m. after all, and it's been a long day for me. Playing some stick has been grand, though," I said.

"Yeah. I wouldn't mind staying out, but I have to be at work at 4 a.m. tomorrow, so getting to bed is good, too."

"4 a.m.? And you wanted to stay out?! Man, when would you sleep?" I said.

"It would have been a no-sleep night, but at least you would have been able to see some more of the town," he said, smiling.

I pulled the pool balls out of the pockets and put them back on the pool ball rack while Jarrett grabbed our empty glasses, and we walked back to the bar. The bartender was putting the finishing touches on a Spanish coffee for one of the other patrons.

"I will be right with you, Jarrett," he said.

"No problem, Roy," Jarrett said.

The bartender added a shake of cinnamon to the drink while it was still on fire, and little sparks sparkled up as he shook the cinnamon on.

"Here we go, miss," Roy said as he put the drink on the bar in front of a woman in her thirties. She paid, took a drink of her hot Spanish coffee, then licked the sugar off the rim, her eyes twinkling mischievously at the bartender. Roy looked at Jarrett and said, "All done? You are out of here early tonight."

"Yeah. I have to get up early tomorrow, and we are both tired. Can you tab us out?" Jarrett said.

"Sure. Here you go," Roy said as he gave us our ticket.

"Roland, as I said, I have the drinks and the pool."

"Thanks, Jarrett," I said as I took cash out of my pocket for the burger plus a tip, which I gave to Jarrett. Jarrett settled up with the bartender, and then we left out the way we had come in. We walked to Jarrett's truck, opened the doors, and squeezed into the small cab. Jarrett turned the ignition, and he started driving us back to his house.

"As I said, I have to be at work at 4 a.m. So, I am going to try not to wake you before I leave. You can leave whenever you want, and sleep as late as you want. There is cereal in the cupboard, and eggs in the fridge. Feel free to help yourself," he said.

Chapter 7

"OK. I appreciate that. I would like to get a solid eight hours in before I get on the road again," I said.

"No problem. All you have to do is push the button on the door knob when you leave," he said.

"Simple enough," I said.

We pulled up to his house, he turned off the ignition, and we both opened our doors, and got out of the car. We walked up to the door to the house, and Jarrett unlocked the door. On stepping into the foyer, Jarrett said, "It has been great spending some time with you, Roland."

"Likewise, Bro. It is like the last ten years fell away as we were together," I said.

"I feel that way too. Let's try to do this before another ten years have passed," he said.

"Agreed," I said as I gave him a big hug. "Thanks again for letting me crash at your house."

"My house, is your house, Roland, always," he said.

Neither of us wanted to wind down, but we both knew we had to. If God was willing, we would see each other again in the near future. He was a special and dear friend, and I would have to be better at being in contact.

"Good night, Jarrett," I said as I let go of my hug.

"Be safe, Roland, and have a Grand Adventure!" he said, eyes slightly misty.

"I will, man. I will."

I went to the guest bedroom, brushed my teeth, undressed and climbed into bed. "Tomorrow, it's into the unknown!" I thought as I shut my eyes.

Chapter 8
Awareness Two-Dot-Two

The next morning, I gave myself permission to wake up naturally, and chose not to set the alarm. It was July 23rd, and I would be driving the second leg of my trip today, God willing. I woke up at 10 a.m., wandered down to the kitchen to have a bowl of cereal and a couple of eggs. Yesterday's sun had been replaced with damp clouds and a light drizzle of rain, which definitely worked in my favor. I washed my dishes, left Jarrett a quick thank-you note, and schlepped my pack and camera gear out to the Blazer. I looked at my maps, and found the road which took me to Highway 209 past Seeley Lake to Kalispell, as the tow truck driver had recommended yesterday. I looked around for anything I might have forgotten in Jarrett's house, then clicked the button on the lock and shut the door. I walked down the slight hill of the driveway to the street, took my keys from my pocket, unlocked the Blazer, climbed in, put the key in the ignition, and turned it. The engine roared to life. "God is willing," I said to myself with a smile.

I drove down Skyview Drive, turned right on Hillview Way, and followed that until it became South Russell Street. At the intersection of South Russell Street and Brooks Street, I turned right, then followed Brooks until it became South Higgins Avenue. Here, I turned left, crossed the bridge over the Clark Fork River, then turned left on West Broadway Street. A few blocks later, I turned right on Orange Street, and turned onto the on-ramp to Interstate 90, just after North 3rd Street West. No more than fifteen minutes had passed. As I said, Missoula is a small town.

A mere four miles east of Missoula, I entered the infamous Hell Gate, which is the small valley that lies between Mount Jumbo to the north and Mount Sentinel to the south. At mile five from Missoula, I turned off on the exit for Highway 200 at West Riverside and promptly passed through the towns of Milltown and Bonner. At Milltown, the Clark Fork and the Blackfoot River have a confluence, so as I left Milltown I parted ways with the Clark Fork and began my day's adventure on the Blackfoot River. For roughly ten miles, the Blackfoot cuts its way through the Lolo National Forest, forming a deep and beautiful canyon. Highway 200 snuggles against the bank of the river, first on the south side, and then on the north side. After ten miles of following the Blackfoot, Highway 200 enters the grassy ranchland of the seven-mile-long Potomac Valley, with views of the rolling hills of the Garnet Range Mountains to the south and more immediately, ponderosa pines to the north. As I entered the Potomac Valley, rain began to fall. Through the

Chapter 8

valley the rain was a slow drizzle, but by the time I reached the junction of Highway 83 (also known as Highway 209) the rain had become a downpour. I stopped in the town of Seeley Lake to gas up at the Sinclair station, then got back on the road.

Highway 83 truly is a scenic byway, or the road of the hundred lakes, each beautiful in its own right. I passed by Seeley Lake, Lake Inez, Lake Alva, Rainy Lake, and then Summit Lake. The rain beat down so hard that even with my windshield wipers at maximum, I still couldn't see. I was speeding along at 70 miles per hour, as I needed to make time, but visibility was a problem. Luckily, this road had very little traffic, or at least today it didn't, as I hadn't seen another car since I passed through Seeley Lake. Through the driver's side and the passenger's side windows, I could see the ponderosa pines, Doug fir, and larch blur by as I drove. I passed the sign for Holland Lake Lodge, then slowed down through the village of Condon.

Ten miles past Condon, an odd feeling came over me. I took my foot off the gas pedal, and the Blazer immediately slowed down. There were no other cars on the road in front of me or behind me, and no other cars in the other lane. I had already learned that odd feelings are meant to be listened to, and that when I do listen to this small, sometimes indecipherable voice, I can expect something profound to happen. A K5 Chevy Blazer is a big, heavy SUV, so heavy, in fact, that it had to have a small block 400 engine in it simply to move the weight of the vehicle. Therefore, when I removed my foot from gas pedal, she slowed down quite rapidly on her own. Following my gut instinct I watched my speedometer fall from 70 miles per hour to 50 miles per hour, then to 30 miles per hour, then 10 miles per hour. Then I rolled to a stop. The rain still beat down on my windshield, but without the addition of speed, I could now actually see in front of me, as the wipers quickly moved back and forth flicking off the rain.

Ten feet in front of where my Blazer had naturally come to a stop, a large doe stepped out of the forest onto the road. She looked at me as she walked to the center of the road. Her big eyes gazed into mine, one ear flicking off the rain as it came down. The Blazer purred, and my wipers moved back and forth, then she looked back the way she had come, and from the forest two white-spotted baby fawns stepped forth. They were still a little wobbly and ungainly, lacking their mother's preciseness of movement. They stepped across the west side of the road to where their mother stood in front of my vehicle. When they reached her, they pranced around a little bit. Then they both looked at me. When her fawns were by her side, the doe looked at me once more, then continued crossing to the other side of the road, fawns by her side. As they stepped into the forest, the doe looked back once more, then disappeared into the trees.

"Huh. How did that happen?" I thought to myself. Since I only applied my brakes when the Blazer had finally come to a stop, how could that have been any less than miraculous? I would say that it took about a mile for the Blazer to come to a complete stop. This meant that whatever unconscious communication had occurred between the doe and my still self, had to occur far enough in advance so that this moment could simply be this perfect. Or perhaps it had nothing to do with the doe and myself, but simply was an act of God? Surely, the doe doesn't understand the physics of how long it takes for a K5 Blazer going 70 miles per hour, to come to a stop without the use of brakes. Frankly, I couldn't have explained the physics of this if you'd asked me. So, disregarding an understanding of physics on both our parts, that leaves either some form of communication, which I didn't understand, nor could I have initiated it, which means a one-way communication from the doe – or it was an act of guidance by God or another unseen being, which again would have been a one-way communication from it to me. Having the feeling that I needed to let my foot off the gas, certainly at this point, with this result, could not be considered random. Huh. In many Native American tribes they refer to that which connects all of us as the "Spirit which moves through all things." This experience certainly validated that way of thinking. It also showed that a mother's love for her children spans through all creatures. We as humans often think that other things on Earth are below us, because they are animals or vegetables, but if a doe feels the same love for her children as a human mother feels for her children, one might ask: Are we really that different? In the same light, I don't know many human mothers who can broadcast a psychic communication out over a mile-plus to be cautious, because her children are crossing the road. No, I think for the most part that we humans mistake our place in the world, and that we are neither greater nor lesser than the other beings who live on our, all of our, great Earth.

"Well, right, then," I said to myself. "Show is over." Certainly, sitting stopped on a state highway when visibility is low is probably not a good idea, even when I had not seen any other cars on the road. I definitely did not have the confidence that another driver would intuit that I was stopped here, a mile before they slammed into my tailgate. I lifted my foot off the brake, and applied pressure to the gas pedal, starting forward again, this time keeping my speed to 50 miles per hour. Twenty minutes later, I was hugging the east side of Swan Lake. Another forty minutes or so, and I entered Kalispell. I drove onto Main Street, and just before the crossing of East Idaho Street with Main Street, I found Moose's Saloon. I liked the old wood siding and the rustic batwing swinging doors on the outside that reminded me of the saloons in the Old West. I parked on Main Street, and walked through the swinging doors, half expecting to see a bunch of cowboys playing cards, or a gunfight mid-progress, but instead the fragrant smell of baking pizza filled the air. "Look at that! Sawdust on the floor! You don't see that every day," I said to myself.

I bellied up to the red bar and wondered if I ordered rye, would they offer me the type of whiskey which in the Old West used to be cut with turpentine, ammonia, gunpowder, or cayenne? I wondered if the bartender would know what I meant if I asked him for a shot of Coffin Varnish or Taos Lightning, both names of custom products of rye whiskeys in the saloons of the Old West. The whiskey in the old days was often nothing more than a mix of grain alcohol, caramelized sugar, iodine, and chewing tobacco. Modern connoisseurs of whiskey probably not only would not recognize the whiskey from the Old West, but would think the swill they were drinking would literally rot their gut. Of course no modern bar could offer such a thing. This adulteration of whiskey was officially denounced with two laws, one in 1897 called the Bottled-in-Bond Act, which created a system where the federal government would guarantee the authenticity of the whiskey. In order for distillers to participate in this system, the spirit had to be produced in the United States, during one distillation season (about six months), by one distiller, at a single distillery. Additionally, the spirit had to be aged for four years in a warehouse which was federally bonded, and it had to be bottled in its pure form, meaning that it could not be blended or mixed, and this resulted in 100-proof alcohol. Each bottle had to include a label of the distillery and where it was bottled.

I will get to the second law in a second, but to add another thought here. What is this thing we call proof? Essentially, proof is an antiquated way of determining how much alcohol was in a spirit by adding the alcohol to gunpowder and then trying to light the gunpowder. If the gunpowder caught fire, the alcohol had more alcohol and less water in it. If the gunpowder did not catch fire, then the alcohol had more water and less alcohol in it. This might explain why saloon owners might cut a whiskey with a substance like turpentine, which is highly flammable. If a patron did this test in a whiskey-turpentine mix, their gunpowder would definitely catch fire. Interestingly, the Native Americans used to call whiskey "fire water," and most likely the liquor given to Native Americans was more adulterant and less alcohol, so it truly was fire water.

The second law was put forth by President Theodore Roosevelt, a Republican, in 1906 and was called the Pure Food and Drug Act. This act required that drugs such as alcohol, cocaine, heroin, morphine, and cannabis had to be labeled if they were contained in a drug, medicine, food, or beverage. Additionally, the proper dosage of every medicine, as well as the ingredients, had to be printed on the label. This meant that a drug or alcoholic beverage could not have secret ingredients. After the passage of this act, drug companies could no longer illicitly add opiates to their drug recipes, which led to a decrease in opiate consumption and addiction. Can we, the people, really have been fighting the corporate attempt to get the public addicted to opiates since 1906? This Act's truth-in-labeling concept also cut down on the amount of toxic preservatives that were used at this time, and subjected any company that was found to be making, selling, or transporting poisonous or toxic drugs to be subject to search, seizure, and disposal of their product. This single penalty made it unprofitable to continue in this line of business. This Act, created at a time when Republicans were looking out for the people of the United States, paved the way for the Food and Drug Administration, and was the first official consumer protection law. Thank you President Roosevelt for keeping our drugs safe, our whiskey free of contaminants, putting over 230 million acres under federal protection, and establishing 121 forest reserves in 31 states!

"Howdy," said the bartender.

Howdy, as most people know, is Western slang for "how do you do?" or "how do ye?"

"Good," I said. "One for lunch please and bar seating is fine."

The barkeep waved his hand at the empty bar, suggesting that I pick a seat, and then when I sat down in a stool, he placed a menu and an ice water in front of me.

He said, "Would you like a drink?"

"No, just water for me today. I still have a fair amount of driving to do."

"OK. Where are you headed to?"

"Harlem," I said.

"Well, you certainly do have some driving in front of you. About five hours or so would be my guess, unless you mean Harlem, New York," he said with a chuckle.

"No. I am definitely driving to Harlem, Montana," I said. "What do you suggest for lunch?"

"Well, we are known for our pizza, but I am also keen on our Reuben sandwiches," he said.

Chapter 8

I have a mini-love affair with Reuben sandwiches. How can one beat rye bread, sauerkraut, corned beef, Swiss cheese, and Thousand Island dressing all in one place?

"Yep. I'll have the Reuben," I said.

"Anything else?" he asked.

"Looks like it comes with chips and a pickle. How about a side of pepperoncini as well?"

"Sounds good. I will put your order in."

"Thanks," I said.

The bartender walked a few steps away and entered the order into his computer. Then he returned with a rag and wiped the bar down around me.

"I assume you are going to take Highway 2 or Route 2, as we call it around here, through Glacier?" he asked.

"I am," I said.

"Have you ever been to Glacier?" he asked.

"Nope. This will be my first time."

"You are in for a treat. It is one of our state's crown jewels," he said.

"I hear that it is phenomenal, but I won't be able to stop to enjoy the woods this trip."

"That's too bad, but the drive through the park is also very pretty."

"I am looking forward to it," I said.

"Order up!" came the call from the kitchen window.

"That's your food. I will be right back," said the bartender.

When he came back, he presented me with a Reuben generously stacked with corned beef, stuffed with sauerkraut, pickle and chips on the side, and a small bowl with ten pepperoncini in it.

"Here you go!" he said.

"Thanks. That looks perfect, and I am hungry," I said.

I gingerly picked up half of the sandwich, eyed it to figure out where I could get my mouth around the whole sandwich in one bite, and deciding the corner edge was best, chomped my first bite. The corned beef was juicy and dripped into my goatee. The sauerkraut tasted homemade, and all the flavors blended well with the Thousand Island dressing. I would give it an eight on a one-to-ten scale. Definitely on the higher end of palatability. It wasn't long before I had destroyed the sandwich and chips, consumed the pickle, and downed the pepperoncini.

The bartender walked back over and said, "It looks like that went down quickly. How did you like it?"

"It definitely hit the spot," I said smiling.

He produced my check and assured me there was no rush. But for me the clock was ticking and I was feeling the urge to get back out on the road. I pulled $4.50 for the sandwich, 50 cents for the pepperoncini, and a $3 tip out of my cash and laid them on the bar.

"Thanks for the recommendation," I said as I headed for the door.

"No problem. You be safe out there, and have a good drive!" he said.

"I will. Thanks," I said. I stepped out the swinging saloon doors, walked the few steps back to my Blazer, and climbed in. I started the ignition and the engine purred back at me. The rain was still coming down, but I didn't mind, as rain meant no vapor lock. I pulled ten feet up to West Idaho Street, turned right, and now was on Highway 2, the road I would be on for the rest of my journey. Two blocks later, I pulled into the Conoco on 2nd Avenue East North and filled my tank. When I went in to pay, I grabbed myself a cup of coffee from one of the coffee pumps, then paid for my gas and the coffee. It was 2 p.m., and if all went well, I should arrive at my destination by 8 p.m. My mid-back was getting a bit stiff, and I could tell that the mileage was starting to take a toll on my body. I got back into the Blazer, started her up, and turned right out of the Conoco lot, which headed me in a slightly northeasterly direction. In another two miles, Highway 2 became LaSalle Road, as the road I was driving turned to head due north. The sign on the road said thirty-two miles to West Glacier.

Eleven miles later, at the Flying J, I turned right to follow Highway 2 through the town of Columbia Falls, then crossed the Flathead River. Large cottonwoods grew along the river, then as I moved past the bridge and the river proper, the cottonwoods began to be interspersed with ponderosa pine, lodgepole pine, and larch. The towns of Hungry Horse and Martin City blew by like a short breeze, and I rounded the bend of the four-lane highway towards Glacier. The road narrowed down to two lanes again just past the village of Coram, and I was in Big Sky country once again. All along the highway were trees of cottonwood, aspen, ponderosa pine, and lodgepole pine interspersed with grassy meadows, and in the distance on three sides the mountains were capped by rain clouds. The scenery of Montana easily compares with the grandeur of Yosemite in California, except that the majestic scenery of Montana spans the whole western edge of the state. The epic downside of Montana compared to California, of course, is that Montana winters are brutally cold.

Past the sleepy village of West Glacier, I passed the Belton Chalet and started my climb into the mountains of Glacier proper. The rain drizzled off and soon the sun broke through the clouds. To the north, bordering the road, the Middle Fork of the Flathead River gently flowed in its course. On a hotter day, I could imagine rafting guides drifting the river with their boats full of tourists. "Someday, I will have to come back here and give Glacier its full due, when I'm not on such a tight schedule," I thought to myself as I drove. For now, though, the rugged beauty I could see from the road filled me with wonder and curiosity, as I continued to look forward, left, and right as I rounded each new bend of the road. My mind was like that of a child taking in a place which was completely new. I had no idea what was going to be around the next corner, a stunning view of the river, rock striations of red and gold in the cliffs, or a cluster of cottonwood and lodgepole pine where the leaves of both trees glistened as the trees shed the rain and the sun sparkled overhead. Perhaps, I would even be lucky enough to see a grizzly bear.

The chain of parks which Glacier is a part of is one of the largest continuous wilderness areas in the United States. This massive area is a combination of the Waterton Lakes National Park in Canada, Glacier National Park, the Flathead National Forest, and the Bob Marshall Wilderness Area. All told, these four areas together cover 7,113 square miles, which is roughly two times bigger than Yellowstone National Park which is 3,417 square miles. Now, unlike most other national forests and parks, the majority of Glacier, the Flathead National Forest, and the Bob Marshall Wilderness Area is virtually inaccessible by car. This means that if you want to see the interior of these parks, you either have to have a horse or backpack in. Therefore, much of these wilderness areas are pristine, in a way that parks with many logging roads or major thoroughfares are not. Having this massive, virtually roadless forest in the northern part of Montana meant that I only had two ways to get to my destination. The first route was the one I had chosen: over Highway 2 through Glacier. The other route was to take Interstate 90 from Missoula to Butte, then Interstate 15 through Helena and Great Falls, then Highway 87 to join back up with Highway 2 just before Havre.

I would rather drive down a two-lane road, if I can see beautiful scenery, than choose an Interstate. The drive from Coram to East Glacier is roughly fifty-four miles, and it winds through the largest valley in Glacier. Within this valley are tiny farming communities, which might as well be simple outposts. At roughly mile marker 167, I again picked up the Middle Fork of the Flathead River, and was astounded by its turquoise-green blue clarity which I have since learned is characteristic of Montana's high-mountain rivers. The cottonwoods, ponderosa pine, and Doug fir reflected from the surface of the river as if it was a mirror. I was obviously driving through a flood plain, where the river on the north side of the road flowed through one channel, but another channel had obviously flowed to the north in the recent past. The glaring white of the rocky beach of the old channel could only be from the caking of minerals from the mountain. The contrast between the turquoise-green blue water and the white rocks was stunning.

Highway 2 continued in a southeasterly direction through this valley. I passed the villages of Pinnacle, Essex, Single Shot, and Snowslip, each little more than a few houses, maybe an inn and a tavern. After the Bear Creek Guest Ranch near Blacktail, the valley spread out a bit. The trees were more stunted and the hills while still observable in the distance, did not directly dwarf the cars on the road. I passed the obelisk at Marias Pass, which is the marked summit of the Continental Range. At 5,213 feet, this pass and valley were "discovered" in 1889 by John Frank Stevens, and proved to be a key link for the Great Northern Railway. Had Lewis and Clark stumbled upon this pass and valley through the Rockies, it is likely that they would have saved substantial time on their great journey. For myself, this marked the end of the climb through this valley, and the gateway to the Great Plains was a relatively short distance away.

Chapter 8

Eleven miles later I entered East Glacier Park Village, and stopped to get gas at the Cenex on the north side of town. After I filled my tank and paid, I climbed back into the Blazer, started her up, and headed north to continue on Highway 2. Just out of the village, I passed over the small valley formed by the Two Medicine River. Ten miles later I passed through Browning. The landscape had dramatically changed from one of rolling hills with vast forests and rivers to a great sea of brown grass which contrasted with the azure of the sky. The Great Plains were beautiful, but plain. Now the measure was of small villages and small streams which broke the monotony of the drive. Cutbank, Shelby, Chester, Joplin, Inverness, Rudyard, all passed by like exhaled smoke, visible for a second, then gone. Every ten to twenty miles, there was a small village with a small population, and only the necessities to survive the long winters. There was no need to stop unless I needed gas or a bottle of water. 160 miles from Browning, I stopped in Havre to gas up and give Pete Youngbull a call and let him know that I was forty miles out. The call was short. He gave me directions to his house and told me that they would have some food prepared for me when I arrived. I thanked him, paid for my gas and got back on the road. It was 6:30 p.m., and while I had not made great time, I couldn't complain about the scenery on the road here. The continental divide really was a division in my mind, between the area of wet and dry, forest and field, mountains and flatland, cities and villages. Now, don't get me wrong, I am not saying these are absolutes, only what the appearance was. Yet, where Missoula's population was 56,000 people in 1996, comparatively Havre's population was 10,780 people. So, in a sense, we are talking about a significant difference in the size of towns between the west and the east of Montana. At Havre the Milk River joined up to snake along the side of Highway 2. The bends reminded me of the small tributaries I had flown over by bush plane on my way to Bristol Bay, Alaska in 1992. For the forty remaining miles to Harlem, the Milk River would be the eye candy that kept me interested in the final leg of my trip, as it played hide-and-seek first winding towards the road, then winding away from it.

The towns of Lohman, Chinook, and Zurich sped by, and then there it was: Harlem, Montana. I was 897 miles from where I called home, in a small town I had never heard of before this gig, and I was in love with the adventure of it all.

Just before Harlem, I followed Highway 2 on its southeasterly course, and five miles later I crossed the Milk River for the last time. A few minutes later I passed the small village of the Fort Belknap Agency, then turned right onto Highway 66 to head due south. It wasn't long before I turned into the quarter-mile-long gravel driveway to a small yellow house on a small knoll. It was 7:15 p.m. I pulled up next to a big black Ford truck with an extra cab and parked. As I stepped out of the Blazer, an older Native man wearing a flannel shirt, jeans, and cowboy boots stepped out the door.

"Roland?" he asked.

"Yep. Pete?" I said.

"Yep. How was your drive?" he said.

"Long, but interesting," I said.

"It's a pretty drive. Did you go through Glacier?" he asked.

"I did."

"Then you were able to see some of the most beautiful country Montana has to offer," he said. "Do you need help hauling everything in?"

"No, I will just grab my camera gear and my pack for now."

"OK. I will tell Donna to get the food warmed up," he said.

"Great. I am hungry," I said.

"Just come on in," he said as he disappeared inside, leaving the door cracked open.

I opened the back hatch of the Blazer, shifted a few things around to fish out my camera gear and pulled out my day pack, shouldered it, then walked up on the porch. Crickets sang all around me, and the wind gently blew the grass. I opened the door, put my stuff in the entryway, and stood there for a second.

"Shoes on or off?" I asked.

"You can leave them on," a voice said from behind a wall in another room, which I would soon see was the kitchen.

Pete stepped around the corner and said, "You will be staying in my daughter's room. Let me show you where."

I picked up my gear and followed him off to the right and down a narrow hall.

"This, is our bedroom here." He pointed to a door on the left. A few steps later, he said, "This is our grandson's bedroom," gesturing to a door on the right. In a few more steps, he said, "This is the bathroom," and he gestured to a door on the left. At the end of the hall, he opened a door on the right. "And this is where you will be sleeping."

"Great," I said.

"Go ahead and put your stuff down, wash up if you want, then come to the kitchen," he said.

"Sounds good," I said. I plopped my stuff down, looked around the small room which had a feminine touch, noting the twin bed, the simple chest of drawers, and the images of Jesus on the wall, along with pictures of cats and a map of the United States. It was simple, and looked like a teenager's room. I crossed the hall to the bathroom, washed my hands, and washed the travel dust off my face, then walked down the hallway to the foyer. On the left was the living room, and on the right was a small dining room with a table for four, which was unset. I took the few steps into the dining room, then a left into the kitchen. Pete was standing next to the sink, and Donna was ladling pasta out of a pot on the stove into a colander. A round table sat about five feet from the stove, with a red-and-white checkered table cloth and three place settings.

"Donna, this is Roland. Roland, Donna," Pete said.

"Nice to meet you, and thank you for having me into your home," I said.

"Nice to meet you too, Roland," Donna said.

Donna then put a hot pad and extra plate in the center of the table, placing a bubbling pot of marinara on the hot pad and the colander of pasta on the plate.

"What kind of dressing would you like on your salad, Roland? We have Italian, blue cheese, and Thousand Island." she said.

"Italian would be great," I said.

"OK," she said as she took bottles of Italian and Thousand Island dressing from the pale yellow refrigerator and set them down on the table. She then set down a large bowl filled with iceberg lettuce, tomatoes, green peppers, celery, and cucumbers.

"I hope you didn't have to wait too long beyond your normal dinner time for me?" I said.

"It's OK. We gave Jojo, our grandson, some chicken strips at five p.m. He's the only one without food patience," she said smiling.

"Roland, why don't you sit here," Pete pointed to the chair closest to the dining room wall.

"Sounds good," I said.

I sat down, unfolded my napkin and set it on my lap. Pete and Donna did the same. I waited to see if Pete or Donna would say Grace.

Pete said, "If you don't mind, I would like to say Grace."

"No problem," I said.

Pete closed his eyes and Donna did the same, then Pete said, "Creator. God of all peoples, I would like to thank you for bringing Roland safely to our home. Thank you for my daughter, and our beautiful grandson Jojo. Thank you for this bounty of food on our table, and the shelter under which we sleep. It is because of your grace that we have enough. Amen."

"Amen," both Donna and I said.

"Please help yourself, Roland," Pete said. "There is plenty of food."

I picked up the pasta, ladled several spoonfuls onto my plate, then passed the dish to Pete who sat to my left. Pete spooned some out, then passed it to Donna, who sat on Pete's left. In this way, we made our plates from the dishes of food.

"Would you like a soda, iced tea, or water, Roland?" Donna asked.

"Water is fine, thank you," I said.

Chapter 8

Donna stood up, pulled a pitcher from the cupboard over the counter and filled it from a Britta water filter. Then she poured me a glass, then herself a glass. She sat the pitcher on the table, then opened the refrigerator, pulled out another pitcher with iced tea in it, and poured Pete a glass of iced tea. She set the pitcher of iced tea on the counter and sat back down.

"So, Roland, George Walker speaks quite highly of you. How did you guys meet?" Pete said.

"I met him while in college. One of my professors introduced me to him," I said. "He became a bit of a mentor to me, because of his deep interest in dreams and the Red Road."

"Did you know of his work with veterans before you met him?" Pete asked.

"Frankly, I was so preoccupied with my college life prior to meeting George that I might as well have stumbled upon him. In other words, my professor knew of my deep interest in Native American culture, and when he suggested that I should meet George, I simply followed my professor's lead. Since then, George has been a good friend and almost a father figure for me," I said.

"He's a good man," Pete said.

"How do you know George?" I asked Pete.

"I worked with him at American Lake when I was having a particularly harsh bout of post-traumatic stress disorder," he said.

"Was he able to help you?" I asked.

"Yes. Immensely. It was nice to work with a psychologist within the Veterans Administration who respected my spiritual traditions, and who was willing to go so far as to offer treatment for myself and the other Native Vets in a way which worked with our spiritual practice," he said.

"What did he do that was different for you?" I asked.

"Well, primarily he organized sweat lodges for us. I don't think that they had ever been organized at American Lake before George did so. He also gathered together other Native vets, or vets who wanted to walk the Red Road, so that we could process our trauma in our own way," he said.

"I have found George to both insightful and wise," I said.

"He is indeed," Pete said. "How long have you been doing photography?"

"Since I was fifteen or sixteen, so about nine years now," I said.

"What do you expect from it? Do you see it as a hobby or a profession?" he asked.

"I would love to see it as a profession," I said. "But I think that times are changing. At this point, I don't really see it as a viable business, as much as I love it. So, to answer your question, it is probably more hobby than business at this point."

"It is good to understand your own limitations," Pete said.

"I was hoping to get my masters in photography at Brooks in Santa Barbara, California, but in talking to the professionals I have been exposed to, they have advised against it. From what I have experienced trying to get photography gigs, I am beginning to believe that their advice is legit," I said.

"So, when you are not doing photography, what do you do for an income?"

"I am still figuring that out," I said. "I graduated from college, but that didn't give me a profession. I guess I am still trying to figure out what I want to be when I grow up," I said.

"How old are you?" Pete said.

"Twenty-four," I responded.

"Well, I was already in the military for three years by that age, but kids these days have a different life trajectory. I simply can look at my daughter, who is in your generation range, to see that," Pete said.

"What is she doing with her life?" I asked.

"Traya?" Pete said, morbidly chuckling. "Nothing. Bringing shame to her family. Being the stereotypical drunken Indian and taking no responsibility for her life. She isn't even reliable enough to raise her own son, which is why we are doing it," he said, sighing.

"I am sorry to hear that," I said.

"This is the Red Man's burden," he said. "How do we educate our children and grandchildren as to the nobility of their race, when rather than having fortitude, they can go to the minimarket, buy their booze, and live a life of apparent freedom from responsibility? Without being offensive to you, Roland, your people have taught us to be our own jailer," Pete said.

"No offense, Pete. I know a lot of people back home who feel jailed by our culture, too," I said. "As long as everyone pays their taxes, the US government is happy if all of the people destroy themselves."

"I am Assiniboine. My people once were one of the tribes who essentially ruled the Great Plains. Then the Great White Chief boxes us up on this small piece of land with our traditional enemies, the Gros Ventre. Perhaps it is no wonder that our children cannot see themselves."

"My whole generation chaffs at the same bit, Pete. Modern culture seems to be tired of the Old Ways, but rather than pluck the gold out of the sluice box, people seem content to throw out the Old Ways, in exchange for the temporary success of a new way," I said.

"Well, I wish I didn't have to be a direct observer to my daughter's implosion. A parent shouldn't have to watch their child slowly kill themselves. It is a cruel punishment."

"I agree, Pete, it is. The only thing you can do is be there when she needs you," I said.

"You're right, of course. Except sometimes you can't let yourself be there when they need you. Sometimes, they learn more from falling on their face," Pete said.

"That is tough love," I said. "Kudos if you can make that work long-term."

"Well, we have already failed. Traya lives in Harlem with the boyfriend of the month. She moves from boyfriend to boyfriend, whoever can give her the most, while she works as a waitress at the local diner. She just turned eighteen a few months ago, and Jojo is four, if that gives you any idea of what we have been living through."

"I don't know what to say, Pete," I said.

"I tell you this, Roland, not for your sympathy, but to tell you that you will have to find a direction in life which you can believe in. Otherwise, life will simply chew you up, spit you out, and one day, you will realize that your life is a cycle of getting a fix, then sobering up, simply to get the fix again. So, if photography isn't doing it for you, find something which satisfies you and delve into that," he said.

"I understand Pete, but I don't always think that it is this simple. I believe that the Creator has more control of my destiny than I do. Well laid plans do not always come to fruition, and sometimes if I think I am supposed to go right, the Creator will direct me left. I also believe that suffering is directly tied with growth, and that it is rare that growth can happen without suffering. Therefore, when we appear to be suffering, we almost always are learning, even if we don't understand the lesson. If one acknowledges that wisdom comes from one's collected experiences, then if the Creator removed my sufferings, would he also not be removing my ability to gain the wisdom which comes after I have suffered? With your daughter, I would say that perhaps the conclusion to her chapter on why she has suffered has not yet been written, and no one can tell us what the Creator has in store for her. Also, I don't think you can hold yourself completely accountable. If the Creator is the one who writes all of our stories, couldn't we say that Traya's story was written for her on the day she took her first breath? We all make choices that affect our story, but even with these changes, would it not be acceptable to say that the outline of each of our stories essentially stays the same?" I said.

"Hmm. How old did you say you were again?" Pete said.

"Twenty-four," I said.

"I can see why George Walker likes you," he said.

"Pete," Donna said, "you are always so serious. Roland just got here, and he doesn't even know you, yet you are already giving him advice on his life? At least let him warm up to you a bit, honey."

"Well, what's the point of being an elder, if I can't dispense wisdom where I see it can create good? Young warriors are generally rash and it is the advice of elders like myself that can help temper the metal of the rashness," he said.

Chapter 8

"Yes, honey," Donna said. "But it doesn't sound like Roland here is rash."

"It's OK, ma'am I have been known to be rash at times, and there is no such thing as being tempered too much. I enjoy listening to the perspectives of my elders, and invariably I learn from their stories. I try to live my life without having regrets, and one way I can do this is by listening to the stories of people older than I am, listening to the choices they made and the choices they wish they'd made. When a similar situation comes up in my life, I can remember the elder's story, and if their situation applies to my situation, I can learn from it in the same way one learns from a parable. In short, I don't mind listening to Pete's advice," I said smiling.

By this point, everyone's plate was empty, and there were still leftovers for tomorrow. Donna said, "Roland, I have a blackberry pie I made this morning, if you would like to have a piece for dessert. I can also make coffee if you like?"

"A piece of pie sounds delightful. Thank you, Donna," I said.

"Donna makes the best pie, and she also knows that bringing her pie out is always a good way to change the course of a conversation," Pete said, smiling. "Count me in for a piece and a cup of coffee, honey. I have been trying hard to keep my fingers out of that pie all day."

Donna pulled the pie out of the refrigerator, turned the oven to low, and put the pie in. "It will just take a few minutes for this to warm up a bit," she said.

Next, she ground some coffee beans, placed them in a round, pleated filter and put that in the automatic coffee maker. Then she filled the glass pot that sits underneath the drip spout with water. Lastly, she poured the water into the drip machine, and turned it on.

"By the time the coffee is done, the pie will be warm," she said as she sat back down.

"Roland," Pete said. "I told you I would show you around, but my schedule has changed a bit. I am going to have to work tomorrow, but I can give you a little tour of the Rez on Thursday the 25th. Then the powwow starts on the 26th. Do you think you can occupy yourself tomorrow?"

"I can. I brought some projects and some books to read," I said.

"Great. I have to work a half day on the 25th, so we can have lunch, then go wander around after that," Pete said.

"Sure. No problem," I said.

"My sister Ellen is getting married on the 26th at the powwow. We have invited a medicine man we know to officiate. Do you think you can take some pictures of that for us?" he said.

"My camera and I are at your disposal," I said.

"Great," he said.

The coffee pot gurgled as it dripped the last of the water. "Coffee is done, and the pie should be warm now. Roland, would you like a cup of coffee with your pie?" Donna asked.

"Yes, please," I said.

Donna stood up, took three plates and three mugs from the cupboard and set them on the counter. She then pulled a hot pad from a drawer, opened the oven, pulled out the pie using the hot pad, and placed the pie on the counter. Next, she plucked a knife from the knife block, cut the pie into eight generous pieces, used a pie server to lift three pieces of pie from the pie dish and placed them on the plates, one by one. She reached over to the full coffee pot, then poured out two cups of coffee.

"Do you take cream, Roland?" she said while she was pouring.

"No ma'am," I said.

Donna then filled the last mug. She picked clean forks from the silverware drawer and first brought the pie and forks to the table, then the mugs of coffee.

"Thank you, Donna," I said.

When everyone was sitting again, Pete said, "Have at it, Roland!"

We all picked up our forks and dug into the pie. It was wonderful, indeed. The blackberries were tart and Donna had purposefully not added too much sugar, so the tartness of the berries really zinged as the front note on the tip of the tongue. Then the sweetness came through, as the back note, once the pie was fully in the middle of my palate. There was a slight element of warmth to the pie. I could taste a little bit of cinnamon, but what was that other spice?

"This is some of the best blackberry pie I have had in a long time," I said.

"Thank you, Roland," Donna said.

"I taste a little bit of cinnamon, but what is the other spice in here, it seems so familiar, but I can't name it," I said.

"Ah, you are tasting my secret ingredient," she said.

"Shall it remain secret?" I asked.

"No, I will tell you," she said. "The secret to a good blackberry pie is to take whole cardamom pods, then dehusk them. The seeds that come out are then sautéed briefly in a bit of butter and brown sugar, then this is added to the berries."

"It adds such a wonderful complexity to the pie. I am surprised more people don't add this," I said.

"Well, it is my secret recipe," she said smiling.

"Your crust is great as well. Flaky but solid. I never am able to make a good pie-crust," I said.

"You have to use lard. That in my opinion makes the best pie-crust, even if lard is not the best fat for people."

"Well, I am impressed. I am amazed that Pete isn't fat, because if I had someone who could cook like you, I definitely would be," I said smiling.

Donna blushed, then said, "I don't make Pete pie every day and if I want my husband to stay trim, I make him eat at home, so that he isn't out eating at fast food restaurants. This way I can keep lean and healthy food on the table. Left to their own devices, men do not always make the best decisions around food. You know, it is as they say around here, behind every great man, is a good woman making them great food," she said giggling.

Pete rolled his eyes. "If you weren't here, Roland, dinner would be a salad, or maybe if I was lucky, a thin cut of beef with lots of vegetables. How does a man live on salad?" he said with sarcastic exasperation.

"Well, from the looks of it, thinly," I said.

We all laughed. The sun had set at 9:04 p.m., and now it was nearing 10:00 p.m. I was tired, the pie and good food made me more so, and I suppressed a yawn.

"Looks like you are winding down, Roland," Pete said.

"I am. It was a long drive. That plus the stellar meal, are a recipe for bed," I said.

"You can hit the hay, if you want. Donna and I will clean up here," he said.

"OK, I will in a few minutes for sure. What do you do for work, Pete?" I said.

"I work for the postal service in Fort Belknap," he said. "When you serve in the military, if you work a federal job when you get out, you keep the pay grade you had in the service, so for a veteran like myself, it was a good job to be able to come back to," he said.

"Do you like it?" I asked.

"Truthfully, it is a bit monotonous, but it is steady, and it leaves my mind free to pursue my hobby of working with horses," he said.

"I saw a corral as I drove up," I said.

"Yeah. I moonlight as a farrier on the side. It provides extra income and keeps my passion for horses alive," he said.

"A farrier?" I asked.

"Putting on horse shoes, trimming hooves, and analyzing the gait of an animal to see if the shoes they have on are the best fit for them," he said.

"Oh. I see," I said. "Do you have a job, Donna?"

"I do. I work for the Bureau of Indian Affairs in human resources. It also is a little mind-numbing, but it pays the bills," she said.

"Will you be going to work tomorrow as well?" I asked Donna.

"Yes. Unlike Pete, I don't have any days off this week," she said. "We both leave at 8 a.m. and we will take Jojo with us to daycare. You will have the house to yourself. I will leave the coffee on, and there are eggs in the refrigerator. There is also some deli meat, cheese, and bread if you want to make sandwiches for lunch," Donna said as she stood up. Then she said, "Frying pans are in this cupboard and the bread is in the freezer. Feel free to eat whatever you want and make sure to have another piece of pie tomorrow. If you don't eat it, Pete will, and then I won't be fulfilling my wifely duty of keeping him thin," she said with a chuckle.

"Do you see how it is for me, Roland?" Pete said looking a trifle pained.

"Got it. Eat more pie, so Pete can't have more than one piece tomorrow," I said.

"You learn quickly, Roland," Donna said smiling.

"Well, I think I will hit the hay. It has been a long day," I said. "So, I will see you tomorrow evening?"

"Yep," said Pete.

"Thanks for dinner, pie, and the conversation," I said.

"Well, we really wouldn't be very good hosts, if we didn't make sure your belly was full," Pete said with a smile.

I pushed away from the table, picked up my dishes and put them in the sink, then said, "Good night."

"Good night, Roland," Donna and Pete said in unison.

I stepped into the living room and little Jojo was asleep on the floor with the TV flashing images of some show I had never seen before. I walked down the hallway, dug through the pouch of my backpack holding my toiletries until I found my toothpaste and toothbrush, then went to the bathroom and brushed my teeth. My eyes were getting heavy, and I knew that once I lay down and shut them, I would be dead to the world. I finished brushing my teeth, opened the door to my bedroom, stripped down to my T-shirt and boxers, and lay down. Ten breaths later, I was asleep.

Chapter 9
Awareness Two-Dot-Three

July 24th passed by like a warm summer breeze. I woke up at 10 a.m. to an empty house. I got up, fixed some breakfast, ate, took a shower, and dressed, maybe not all in that order. I pulled a few ongoing projects from the Blazer, and when 5 p.m. rolled around, Pete and Donna came home to me sitting on the floor surrounded by seed beads of a number of colors, while I worked on a beading project that I had been in progress with for several years. Seed beads are of course, tiny glass beads, which come in a variety of colors. By Donna and Pete's arrival, I had been at it for four or five hours. This project was a large rosette of a mandala with the colors of the four directions: black representing west, white representing north, yellow representing east, and red representing south. These four colors spiraled inward from the outside to the center, so to build it conceptually, I had to start with the most inner spiral, and work my way outward.

When building a rosette, a good finished piece will have no stitch marks on the back of the piece, as the stitching all is performed through the horizontal plane of the leather. Because of this, rosettes are most commonly created on leather that is very soft, such as buckskin, or specially prepared deer skin. The finished dimensions for this project were quite large as rosettes go, as I had designed it to be eighteen inches wide by eighteen inches long, or as a perfect circle of eighteen inches in diameter. One important thing about rosettes is that in order for the spacing between each line of beads to be correct, one has to start in the center of the piece, and carefully stitch each line of beads so that it is held down fast in spiral concentric rings from the center. The other important thing for this piece was that, in order to have the look I was going for, the concentric spirals of beads rotated in a counter-clockwise spiral, much like doing a coiled basket or a coiled ceramic pot when doing pottery. The beauty of this pattern with this design was that while the beads' physical structure spiraled counter-clockwise, the actual colors of the beads in the pattern spiraled clockwise.

Now, another thing to note is that in most Native cultures, beading is considered to be "woman's work," in the same way that most Western cultures of a certain time would designate sewing or quilting as "woman's work." So, to come home to see me doing such a thing was surprising for both Pete and Donna.

"Heya. How was work?" I asked as they came into the house.

"Long," Pete said.

"Interesting," Donna said.

"Long and interesting, sounds like together you had a great day," I said with a chuckle. Jojo trailed in through the door silently, a minute or two after Pete and Donna had entered.

Donna set down the groceries she was carrying and walked over to stand above me. "Beading?" she said.

"Yep," I said. "Just a little project I have been working on here and there."

"Can I see?"

"Sure," I said, tightening my last stitch and handing her the piece.

Donna inspected the spirals of beads, running her thumb over the rows to check their tightness, then flipped it over to look for stitches on the back side. "You bead the Native way. Where did you learn how to do this?" she asked.

"Oh, here and there," I said, "I read a lot."

"Your work, it is good. The best I have seen in a long time," she said.

"I try to make each piece the best that I can."

"Is that buckskin?" Pete asked.

"It is," I said.

"Where did you get that?" he asked.

"I made it," I said. "In the old way, using brains to tan the hide."

"Huh," he said, surprised. "You know, that's kind of a lost art. Even Natives don't make buckskin that way very often anymore."

"I know, but well-made buckskin is a superior product to commercial leather for most applications. Beading on it is far superior to using a dense commercially tanned leather," I said.

Pete bent down and smelled the buckskin in Donna's hands. "You even smoked it?" he asked.

"I did. It took about a day, but I wanted it to last. If you don't smoke it, the buckskin doesn't have the ability to repel water," I said.

Donna handed me back my piece, and said, "How long have you been working on this piece?"

"Oh, collectively about six months or so. Here and there as I have time. I like the meditative nature of the work," I said.

"I think you are the first white man who has done beadwork in our house," Pete said while Donna nodded.

"Well, I can put it away, if it offends you?" I said questioningly.

"Oh, no. We are not offended," Donna said. "It's actually nice to see a young man like yourself expressing himself through an art form which we would generally see as a purely Native mode of expression."

Pete nodded, looking thoughtful. "What are you going to do with it when you finish?"

"I thought I would make a buckskin jacket, and sew it on the back,'" I said.

"That would be beautiful," Donna said.

"My sewing skills are not as good as my beading skills, but I am persistent, so I should be able to figure it out," I said.

"I am sure you can figure that out, if you were able to figure this out," Donna said. "Well, I am going to get dinner going. You boys hang out and chat."

Jojo signed to Pete.

"Roland, will it bother you if Jojo watches TV?" Pete said.

"Definitely not," I said.

"OK Jojo, you can watch TV," Pete said, picking up the remote and handing it to Jojo.

"Thank you," Jojo signed.

"Is Jojo mute?" I asked.

"No. He can talk, but he doesn't talk much. He still prefers to use sign language. In our culture, a child can take his or her own time to mature, and if they don't feel comfortable using their voice, that is OK. The sign language lets him communicate in a way that is comfortable to him and as long as we can understand him, that is enough," Pete said.

"Jojo is an odd name. Is there meaning for this name, for your family?" I asked.

"No. Jojo is his baby name. At age seven, he will receive his adult name. This has been a tradition for hundreds of years, in part because for many of those years, we had many children die before age seven, whether due to disease, famine, birth complications, raids, animals, etc. Once a child reaches the age of seven, we think that there is a good chance that they will survive, so at that time, it is appropriate for them to be given their adult name," Pete said.

"That makes sense," I said.

I made my last stitch for the day and folded up my rosette. I stacked the cups of beads together and put the vials of beads in a Crown Royal bag, which I used to store the beads which were in regular use. Then I picked up the stacked containers of beads, the Crown Royal bag, and the rosette, and put them in the gray tackle box I used for keeping my beadwork in. I could hear the sound of sizzling and the smell of cooking meat coming from the kitchen.

"Are you done for the day?" Pete said.

"I think so. It smells like dinner will be ready soon," I said.

"I think I will have a cigarette before dinner. Do you smoke?" Pete said.

Chapter 9

"Not usually. Only ceremonially at this point," I said.

"Good for you. It is a nasty habit I picked up in Vietnam. You know the military, we might run out of food and soap, but wherever we were, they air-dropped us our weekly ration of cigarettes and beer," he said.

"I didn't know."

"Yeah, I think they knew we could survive without food, but if they had withheld the things we were all addicted to, there would have been platoon-wide revolts. Do you want to sit with me on the porch?"

"Sure," I said.

Pete walked from the living room to the foyer, opened the door, and stepped out. I stood up and followed him. On the porch, to the left of the door, was two folding chairs. Pete sat in the one farthest from the door, picked a pack of Marlboro Reds out of his breast pocket, shook the pack until a cigarette popped out from the cigarette-sized hole on the top of the pack, and held it in his left hand while he took a lighter from his right front jean pocket. He put the cigarette between his lips, and flicked the lighter held in his right hand with his thumb, until a small flame ignited. Then he moved the lighter to the end of the cigarette and inhaled until a coal formed on the end of the cigarette. He drew in a deeper inhale and the coal became bright. Pete leaned back in his chair, cigarette held in his left hand to the side and below the seat of his chair and blew out a cloud of smoke directed at the roof of the porch. All of this had taken no more than the second or two, while I was sitting down. From the porch, I could see Highway 66 running through the acres of grassland. The only remarkable feature was a butte that rose above the grass a couple of miles away.

"Has George talked to you about his experiences in Vietnam?" Pete asked.

"Some. I have heard a few stories from a number of vets," I said.

"It was an ugly, gruesome war, with much senseless violence and bloodshed. What I saw there really made me question humanity. In many ways, I lost much of my faith in man while I was there," he said.

"I have heard from a number of people that it was awful. What did you do there?" I asked.

"I was a gunner with the 1st Air Cavalry. We flew the Bell UH-1D Gunships, or what is commonly referred to as Hueys."

"I bet what you saw was about as bad as it comes," I said.

"You don't know the half of it, and the worst was that the brutality I saw was not just from the Việt Cộng against us, or us against the VC, but also how certain elements of our own force treated other parts of our own forces. I think a lot of soldiers simply lost their humanity in that war."

"You said last night that you had met George while dealing with some PTSD. Do you still have it?"

"It never goes away, Roland, only sometimes you are better at managing it and sometimes you are not. At the worst times, it is like my mind is playing a slide show of the same five or six images over and over. Everything stands out in graphic detail, the smells, the colors, the blood, the noise, the emotions of myself and the people around me. Almost like I can see every bullet that came out of my M60 machine gun, see the blood erupt out of every target I killed, and see their facial expressions as parts of their body were literally sawed off by my gun. Then these images play over and over again. It is exhausting and many of my brothers from the war have taken to finding peace in the bottle, or in taking their own lives."

I watched the pain wash over his face as he talked.

"I used alcohol to cope when I came back, but quickly realized that if I wanted to keep my family together, I would have to medicate in a different way. After a few lapses, I finally decided that I wasn't handling it well on my own, and I checked myself in to the Veterans Administration Hospital. I was sent to the American Lake facility, and that is where I met George. He helped me to face my survivor's guilt, and named it. It is like a demon inside of you, poisoning everything in your life and you don't know how to rid yourself of it," he said.

"Survivor's guilt? Did you feel like you should have died instead of someone else?" I asked.

Chapter 9

"We all have it, or all vets have it. But yeah, I lost someone. The way the military works for the most part is: first they break you, then they remold you in their image. Part of this remolding is that your team, whether that is your crew, your squad, your platoon, or your company, are all to be considered as your brothers, and that when one of your brothers is killed, then there is a hole. This is like when you lose a relative – there is a hole in your family. Unlike a family, the military would always provide more soldiers, but inevitably these recruits would be green, and often they would last no more than a week or two before they were killed. So when your unit had survived enough skirmishes, then bonds of brotherhood became even tighter, because you knew that, hell or high water, these men would have your back, and you would have theirs. There is no other option when you are in war," Pete said, taking another long drag from his cigarette, then exhaling.

"In the 1st Air Cavalry, we either provided troop transport or air cover as needed, but mostly our job was to get the troops to the landing zone or LZ, so that they could push the war forward. We were initially stationed at Camp Radcliff in the Central Highlands in 1965, then in January of 1968, we were moved to Camp Evans near Hue. On April 19th, my crew participated in Operation Delaware in the A Sâu Valley. Our mission was to carry troops from Camp Evans to landing zone Tiger. The other gunner, who was the crew chief and I had flown every mission together since we arrived, and both of us had under six months left in our tour. Other Hueys would fall out of the sky, but our chopper was known as the one that the troops wanted to ride in, because by this point we had flown hundreds of mission without ever taking serious damage. Until this day, the Creator had watched over us. Perhaps we had grown a little reckless due to our continued survival, I don't know. The way a Huey crew worked was we had a pilot, a co-pilot, the crew chief, and the door gunner. We could carry eleven soldiers in addition to our crew. The soldiers we were transporting would either sit behind the pilots on a bench seat that held four people, or a bench seat that held five people, or next to me and the chief in the two-man bucket seats that faced the sliding bay doors. While we were in motion, everyone sat. When we came close to the landing zone, Tom, the crew chief, and I would stand at the open sliding doors. We wore harnesses that were attached to the cabin so we wouldn't fall out, and the M60s we used were attached to the cabin with bungee cords so that we both had a full 360-degree range of fire, and so if something happened, we wouldn't lose our guns," Pete inhaled another long drag on his cigarette.

"This was the first day of the offensive, and we had already flown round trip five or six times bringing in troops. It was only nineteen miles, or thirty-eight miles round trip. We were not the only Huey doing this, so every twenty or thirty minutes another Huey would come in to drop off their troops. The landing zone, which was quiet on our first two or three trips, started to get hotter as the day progressed. Our Huey would take scattered fire now each time we landed, whereas initially no one was shooting at us. But the sound of Hueys flying is unmistakable – for many of us who survived, the sound of the Huey is both the sound of salvation and the sound of war. As we unloaded our most recent load of troops, the bushes near us, about fifty yards out, started moving, and I saw several rifle muzzles protrude from the jungle. Most the troops who had been unloaded were on the other side of the Huey about a hundred feet away. Everyone had been disembarking on the chief's side, and it was my job to watch the jungle, as Tom did not have a clear field of fire on my side. I opened fire as the VC guns also started firing. The bullets from the M60 began falling below me as I used the machine gun to cut down everything in front of me. Every few shots, I could see the fine spray of blood, as the bullets found the hidden targets in the jungle."

"After a bit, I could not see any movement, and I stopped firing. I think I said something cliché over my shoulder to Tom, like, "I got them," but Tom didn't answer. The pilot looked back at me, then started lifting back up into the air. All the troops were off, but Tom's body hung in the door bay from his harness. Where his helmet stopped and where the back of his head should have been was a large hole. I pulled his body in and got him onto the floor of the Huey. As I lay his body face up, I saw that his face was gone, exploded outward – the only thing keeping his head together was the chin strap of his helmet. Tom had less time left in his tour than I did – he was supposed to leave in less than a month. I cried and howled because I knew that the bullet that killed Tom came through my door, missed me, and hit him. He never even saw it coming," Pete said as he took a final drag on his cigarette and snuffed it out.

"We flew back to Camp Evans, and seeing my state, the pilot relieved me of duty for three days, or until I was airworthy. I went back to the bunkhouse, showered, then just sat on my bunk staring out into space. I sat like that for twelve hours or so; then one of the lieutenants came in to see me.

The lieutenant said, "Youngbull. Pull it together. This is not the first soldier we have lost, and won't be the last. While you have been vegetating in here, we have lost five Hueys and all of their crews. With the losses we sustained at Khe Sanh, we don't have the luxury of having our gunners being catatonic. I don't care what you have to do, but get moving."

"An hour later, I was still sitting there crying. There was a commotion outside my barrack, and I heard the lieutenant shouting at someone, "I don't care if he was made of gold or made of glass! Get that gunner back on a chopper!" There was a commotion again,

Chapter 9

and the sound of the lieutenant's voice fading away. Tom was all around me. He had been my bunkmate and my brother, together we had survived all of this craziness. Tom had shown me pictures of his wife and baby daughter. He had read me the less personal stories his wife shared with him from home. When his wife or parents sent him care packages, he would split his chocolate bars with me, and I would do the same for him. I knew about his childhood in South Carolina, his desire to be an engineer, and which university he wanted to attend when he was discharged. He had been reading me the letters of acceptance or denial from universities after he applied – because we were on active duty, most of the letters were ones of acceptance. We had drunk beer and smoked cigarettes on our bunks, dreaming and talking of home. Now, I would have to pack his stuff up and send it back with his body to his wife and the daughter he would never see grow up," Pete said. Then he lit another cigarette.

I watched his memories flit over his face like the moving shadows of the sun behind a maple tree. Each word evoked shadow after shadow, as Pete was caught within the spider's web of his memory. He took a drag and exhaled.

"Twenty minutes or so later, the lieutenant came storming back in to the barracks. He shouted at me, 'Youngbull! I gave you an order. Get up, and get on your Huey! If you can't go without your crew chief, then you can take him with you!' And he threw something at me. I lifted my hands to block what he threw at me, and Tom's helmet hit my arms showering brain and blood all over me and my bunk. I looked at what was covering me and I lit up in anger. White hot rage. I stood up and went to punch the lieutenant, and he said to me coldly, 'Soldier, hit me and I will have you in solitary in the brig for the rest of this war. Or you can use that anger, get on your Huey, and go out and kill some VC, your choice.' I stopped mid-swing. It is the closest I have ever come to wanting to kill one of my own officers …," he said as he took another drag of his cigarette, then put it out half-smoked, and flicked it off the porch in disgust.

"Dinner's ready," came Donna's voice from the kitchen.

"It never goes away, Roland. I see it all like it happened today. War wrecks a man. We come back like broken glass, shattered and sharp. You can put it back together, but it will never be whole again," he said as he stood up and walked into the house. I stood up and followed him in.

As we walked into the kitchen, Donna looked at Pete's face and said, "You were talking about that day, weren't you Pete?"

"I was," he said.

Donna quietly set the food on the table, then said, "Jojo, come in and eat dinner, now."

Dinner was a quiet affair, and after eating, Pete pushed away from the table and said, "I am going to go for a walk," to no one in particular. He put his plate in the sink, and slipped outside.

After a minute or two, Donna said, "He has gone out to be with the horses. When he gets like this, that is what he does. Don't worry, he will be fine tomorrow. He just needs to let the memory wash out of him."

"He didn't need to tell me the story. He could have simply said he didn't want to talk about it," I said.

"He told you because he wants young people to know that war is horrible. He hopes that in telling your generation some of what he went through, it will curb the desire for war which many people have, whether that is war within yourself, or war in the world. I think his main message is, that his generation lived through it, so yours doesn't need to. On the way home, he told me that he would be showing you around at 2 p.m. tomorrow. You can expect him to be his normal self by then," she said.

"OK," I said.

"You know, he must like you. I haven't seen him tell that story to someone he just met before. Pete doesn't like to feel vulnerable like that, generally," she said.

"I am honored then," I said.

"I think that he feels like you respect our people, and because of that, he thinks you will understand his, and our, sacrifices," she said.

"I don't think I will ever be in his or your shoes," I said. "But that doesn't mean I can't see his pain. I do respect the First People of the Americas, and I understand that their lives can often be harder than other people's. I also have talked to enough veterans that I know that what they sacrificed by fighting in war has allowed me to grow up in peace," I said.

Chapter 9

"Pete would be happy to hear that," she said. "We will probably go to bed early tonight. Tomorrow, I will have coffee on again, and you can make yourself breakfast. I will look forward to seeing how far you've come on your project when I get home tomorrow."

"I may be able to get a few hours in tonight and tomorrow morning."

"Great. Well, I will clean up here. Don't think us rude to retire early. Pete just needs some space and I will probably go out and sit with him when I finish cleaning."

"Don't worry, Donna, I understand," I said.

I went to my bedroom, took out the beads and rosette, and started to bead. As usual, the hours flew by, punctuated only by putting three beads on a needle, a horizontal stitch, come back through the buckskin, then stitch back through two of the beads, then three beads on the needle, horizontal stitch, come back through the buckskin, then stitch back through two of the beads. Over and over and over this pattern played itself out as I created my pattern from nothing. My mind stilled, being absorbed with only what was in front of me. There was peace, my body relaxed, and eventually it was time for bed. I stood up, put the beads and rosette away, opened my day pack, and found my toothbrush and toothpaste. As I walked to the bathroom, I stretched my arms, legs, and back, then stood over the sink and brushed my teeth. The house was quiet; all the bedroom doors were closed. Everyone else was either in bed or asleep. I went back to my bedroom, disrobed, and lay down in bed. The moonlight came through the window and shined on one of the pictures of Jesus on the cross. "They broke your body, and yet you survived and became a legend. Creator, please give Pete the strength to overcome his struggles and dissipate his demons," I said silently, then closed my eyes to let sleep wash over me.

The morning of the 25th, I woke up at 10 a.m., showered, dressed, and made some breakfast. I was alone in the house. My back was a little sore from sitting on the floor beading the night before, so after breakfast I did my basic stretching routine. Then I took out my beadwork and lost myself in my project. A few hours later, a car came up the driveway. The clock on the wall said 1 p.m. A few seconds later, Pete opened the door with Jojo bouncing behind him.

"Good afternoon, Roland," Pete said. "Have you had lunch yet?"

"I haven't," I said.

"Well, let's have a sandwich, then we can start showing you around."

"OK. How did you sleep, Pete?" I asked.

"Like the dead," he said smiling. "Roland, I am sorry about yesterday. Sometimes, when I go into the past like that, I get stuck there."

"No problem, Pete. As I mentioned, I brought plenty of things to entertain myself," I said smiling.

Jojo sat on the couch and signed that he would like to watch TV.

"Jojo, we are only going to be here for a bit, but you can watch until we leave," Pete said.

Jojo signed "Thank you," and Pete gave him the remote. It wasn't long before Jojo found a station that was playing cartoons. He sat back on the couch, mesmerized. It seemed like this was an ongoing interplay between Pete and Jojo.

Pete went to the kitchen and started taking condiments, deli meat, cheese, lettuce, and a tomato from the refrigerator. "I am going to let you make your own sandwich," he said.

"No problem," I said.

"Do you want regular yellow or Dijon mustard?"

"Dijon, please."

"Shall I toast the bread?"

"Yeah, frozen bread isn't so tasty," I said chuckling.

"True," Pete said as he put two slices in the toaster. "So, my plan is this: I have to go down to the powwow grounds in Fort Belknap to see if everything is ready for tomorrow, then I can drive you around the Rez a bit. Then, if you want, we can head over to Snake Butte, which is the butte you can see in the distance from the porch. How does that sound?"

"Sounds fine. Whatever you want to do, as 'I am along for the ride,' as they say."

Chapter 9

We made our sandwiches and had a quiet meal, then left the house, Jojo in tow.

"I'll drive," Pete said.

"OK."

Pete opened his door, sat down, put on his seatbelt, and Jojo scrambled onto his lap. I opened the passenger door, stepped into the truck, sat down, and put on my seatbelt. Pete drove down to the powwow grounds. There was an ordered chaos to it as people put up tents, parked their RVs, and built 'shades' out of cottonwood. A 'shade' looks a lot like a grape trellis. The posts and the horizontal beams stay up all year, then people cut leafy branches to go over the top horizontal poles. Pete's shade was already up next to his RV, and he was checking to make sure the rest of his family did their part, bringing plastic chairs and such to be used under the shade. We parked near the RV, climbed out of the truck, and Pete went to talk to some folk, leaving Jojo and me to wander around. Near Pete's RV a few people were setting up a teepee. I motioned to Jojo to follow me, and stepped closer to watch the teepee going up. All of the poles had been set up in a circle about four feet between each pole. These created a pyramid of sorts, as they leaned against each other; then these poles were tied at the top, forming an almost circular ring of poles at the top of the teepee. Now, the people were midway through putting up the canvas of the teepee. They had bundled the canvas over one pole. They leaned this against the top circle of tied poles, then unfurled the canvas and stretched it around the ring of poles until the side they were working with completed the 360 degrees around the rest of the poles to reach the edge they were not yet working with. Then they tied these two edges together with straps they inserted through grommets that were sewn into the canvas, much like along the sides of a tarp.

Pete walked up to me and said, "Have you ever seen one being erected before?"

"I haven't," I said. "I have seen them up a number of times, but I have never seen one being put up."

"It is a special thing. A lot of Natives still use teepees for a variety of needs. It is one constant which keeps us connected with the old ways. This teepee will be used by the medicine man tomorrow."

"Cool," I said.

"I have checked out what I needed to. Do you want to drive around a bit?" Pete said.

"Sure."

We walked back to the truck, and as before, Pete climbed in, and put his seat belt on, then Jojo climbed into his lap. I climbed in and clicked my seatbelt in. Pete put the key in the ignition and started up the truck.

We drove around the small community of Fort Belknap. Truthfully, there was not much to see. What struck me was the outstanding poverty of the reservation and the large amount of trash piled everywhere. I felt like I was in a third-world country. Pete pointed out the school and the Bureau of Indian Affairs, but most of what he had to "show" me was the history of his people.

"The Assiniboine never called this piece of land home, traditionally. Our people would come over here to hunt buffalo, but we lived east of here. The Assiniboine are part of the Sioux peoples, and amongst them, we were known as the Nakota. This land is Gros Ventre land, and the Gros Ventre were sometimes our enemies, and sometimes our trading partners, but never our friends. We were a proud people and we are still proud, but it is hard to be proud when we have been chained to one piece of land, and also when that land was never our home. Think of it as if you had a four-wheel-drive truck and you could go anywhere you wanted. Then one day you walked outside to climb into your four-wheel truck, but instead there was a Volkswagon bug sitting there, and worse, it was missing the motor and the fuel line. In other words, it was a simply an ill-fitting vehicle that didn't run and barely kept the weather off of you," Pete said.

"How do you think living on a reservation has affected your tribe?" I asked.

"In our culture, the status of a man was not determined by the wealth one had, but by how one had attained that wealth. To have more, young men went out on raiding parties and took from other tribes and later from the white man. A successful man had been on many raiding parties and had taken horses and wives. We were not a culture of merchants or traders, but of warriors. Then the treaties were signed, and we not only couldn't war against other Indians, but we also couldn't war against the white man. Without a way to externally express our bravery, our warlike spirits turned against ourselves. In the hundred-plus years after the first treaty was signed, I think we have seen a general breaking of the Native spirit, and this has been intensified with the introduction of alcohol. In some ways, I think that the three generations of peoples after the first treaty was signed thought that the Creator had forgotten about them. All around them, their neighbors, brothers, and sisters were falling victim to alcoholism. We survived the diseases the white man brought, the destruction of the vast buffalo herds which were our main source of food, the fencing of our lands so that nothing could roam free, and asking us figuratively to trade over our buckskins for white man's clothes. Yet it is the alcohol and later the drugs that have killed us. When warriors have no place to wage war, then they wage it at home, on their family, and against themselves. Roland, when you look around, what do you see?"

"Honestly?" I said.

"Of course. I wouldn't have asked if I didn't want to know."

"I see poverty, more trailer homes than not. Houses and properties in disrepair, fences broken and not mended, lots of children, many broken-down vehicles on people's property. Trash everywhere, blowing in the wind, piled on the sides of the roads – it is like people don't care," I said.

"Exactly. People on the Rez are poor. When a whole community is poor, it is hard to aspire to be any different, because everyone you know is in the same place you are. If your dad or mom is a drunk, and all of your friends' moms and dads are drunks as well, it becomes normal. If the parents of all of your friends beat their children, and your parent doesn't beat you, you call yourself lucky, but it is never called what it is, abuse. I am not saying that poverty is only a Native thing, but unlike other people in America, our wealth and our land was taken from us, with the choice of 'sign our treaty or die.' I think that in most court systems these days, this would fall under the category of duress."

"When people are poor for generations, and they are bombarded by other religions, ways of life, ways of speaking, technology, etc., they forget who they were and who they are. Compound this with the many ways the white man has attempted to eradicate Native culture, and it is a wonder that we actually remember any of our ways at all. At the turn of the century, the government through the proxy of the religious organizations, and paid for with the money we had been given for our land, took our children from our homes. They cut the boys' hair, placed them in white man's clothes, forbade them to speak our Native tongue and renamed them with white people's names. They used our children as slave labor, abused them with words, emotions, punishment, and with unconscionable sexual acts on children. They didn't ever attempt to break our warriors, they simply broke us by breaking our children. Our children could not come home after the missionaries took them away and their parents were not allowed to visit them. In other words the missionaries treated our children like orphans and the adults like a virus who would only contaminate the children. I have read the Bible, and nowhere does it say that Jesus and God will reward man with heaven, if man will force themselves and the words of God on another man's children. I could acknowledge going out and selling your religion to adults who felt they were spiritually poor, but taking children from their parents, and molding them in your image, which is not even the image of God, but the image of men and women who could barely be considered holy by their behavior – it is unconscionable.

"US Army officer Richard Henry Pratt in 1892 said, 'A great general has said that the only good Indian is a dead one. In a sense, I agree with this sentiment, but only in this: that all the Indian there is in the race should be dead. Kill the Indian in him, and save the man.' Well, what they didn't realize was that to kill the Indian, was to kill the man. When the white man stripped us of our beliefs, they destroyed us as a people, but then wasn't that the point of all of this anyway? They beat our children at these schools, overworked them, didn't feed them enough, forced them to convert to Christianity. Were they not surprised that the mortality rates for our children were 6.5 times higher than with other races? Yet they called us savages. When our children came home from these 'mind-control' centers, they couldn't speak the same language as their elders, they didn't understand the Native culture, and they suffered depression, anger, rage, and PTSD. The 'educated' children often would leave the cultures that birthed them, because they could not function with health within their tribe. Soldiers when they go to war know there is a chance that if they are captured by the enemy, they will be tortured. No person should be subjected to torture simply because they are born, yet the Christians who did this to our children were praised as doing the work of God – they were awarded more of our money, plus money from the government, and from their parishioners, as well as prestige. I don't know if there has ever been a group that has attempted to cleanse the ethnicity from a people more than the church-run Indian schools who came to our reservations. These schools existed from 1890 to 1990. The white man stole a hundred years worth of our children. Is it any wonder that we are impoverished now?"

"I am sorry, Pete."

"You didn't do this to us, Roland."

"I know, but I, as well as every other person in the United States, has benefitted and continues to benefit from the sacrifice of your people. In the same light, since we benefit from the sacrifice of the Native Americans, we are also all responsible for the destruction of your culture. So, I am sorry."

"In that case, apology accepted. It is enough for me that you see all that was ours and all which is yours now, because it is no longer ours and the reason why we are who we are today. The history of a people matters," he said.

"It does. Or at least it should. If our own personal history of our lives is any indication of this, then the history of groups of peoples also defines us, just as much as our own personal history. The tough question is if my own choices have consequences, then what of my family's choices, and my community's choices, and my town's choices, and my state's choices, on up the political food chain. Do I not bear some responsibility for all of those choices as well? I guess this is how one comes back to the idea that we are all brothers and sisters in the end," I said.

"My people, in prayer, speak of 'all my relations,' and I think Roland, that you are explaining this. But in our belief, it goes beyond just man, to the animals, plants, rocks, sky, and earth as well. I think I want to take you up to Snake Butte now. How does that sound?"

"Sounds good," I said.

Pete drove through Fort Belknap, and turned left back onto Highway 66, past the second village south of Fort Belknap proper, then turned right onto Snake Butte road. As we drove, Pete said, "Snake Butte is about eight miles from town. This is a place which was sacred to the Gros Ventre, as well as other tribes. It was long a tradition that when braves were traveling through this area, they would go up on the bluff and quest for medicine or power. We called it Rattlesnake Butte then. The tribes who would quest up there believed that there was a male side and a female side. On the male side lived a big male snake and on the female side lived a big female snake. The male side offered more power but it came at greater cost. The female side offered less power but at less cost. Each giant snake had hordes of small or regular-sized snakes which attended the larger snake and who the larger snake considered its children. Therefore, one is always respectful of the snakes on the bluff, as if they are harmed, they will tell their mother or father. When braves came up here, they would often offer flesh offerings to the snakes. As one might expect, the male snake would expect more flesh. Do you know what a flesh offering is?"

"I have heard of it, but tell me how it is for tribes around here," I said.

"Well, sometimes people would offer a part of a finger, say from the most distal joint of the little finger to the end of the finger, or from the flesh of the arm, or a toe. The offering had to be suitable to what the request was. The problem some people had is that sometimes what they offered was not enough, and then they would have to offer more, either another joint of the finger, or more flesh from a part of the body. The blood, was said to draw the snakes, but if the quester's heart was not pure, sometimes the snakes would consume the whole person. These days, the butte is closed at night, but people say that they often see lights on the butte and occasionally they hear drumming from the top of the butte."

I watched as the butte became closer and closer. Then we rounded a final bend in the road and drove along the base of the butte. The butte stands about forty to fifty feet above the road, and I could see columns of stone rising out of the ground almost like the way an accordion would look. This feature is called columnar jointing and happens when lava rises out of the ground, then shrinks as it cools.

"From 1933 to 1940 the Army Corp of Engineers mined the stone that you see here on the east end of the butte, to be used as an abutment for the Fort Peck Dam on the Missouri River. This dam created the largest man-made lake in the United States – 130 miles long and 200 feet deep. This dam was built to create hydroelectric power, and to be used for flood control and water management. The place where they mined was there, just above the escarpment," Pete said pointing to a gradual hill which became steep about a hundred feet south of the road.

"There, right near the bluff, they built a railroad track that ran back to Harlem. They would mine the rock, then load it into the railway containers, then haul it first to Harlem, then on to Glasgow, Montana, which is about a hundred miles east of here. They ended up taking about 880,000 square feet of rock from here."

The mined area looked like someone had taken a bite or two off of a popsicle.

"When they were done, they removed the track of the trains, at least," Pete said.

Just past the mine, the road ended and turned into more of a four-wheel-drive track.

"We will continue on this and it will take us to the butte," Pete said.

Chapter 9

The rock formation next to the road had a very craggy, bouldery appearance, almost like a cluster of moles on the skin. Then in about a half mile, all of those bouldery areas turned into a grassy knoll with no visible rocks on it.

"The east side, closer to where the mine is, would be considered the male side, while this more grassy side would be considered the female side," Pete said as he made a left turn and started driving up the gentle slope of this side of the bluff. The track made a couple of twists and turned through a small depression in the grass and stone bluff. When we came to the top, Pete said, "We will go look at the east side first."

"OK," I said noting that there was a fork in the track of the road, one which led east, and one which led west. I would guess that we had come up about in the center of both ends of the bluff. All through our trip, Jojo had mostly sat quietly in Pete's lap, looking around at things as we drove. We turned east, heading through a small rut which had probably been carved out by a glacier, as it certainly was not man-made. The top of the bluff was beautiful.

"Those mountains in the distance to the south are the Little Rockies," Pete said, pointing as he drove, with his elbow hanging out of his window. About three-quarters of a mile later the rut ended, and we turned south-east, heading to the south-east corner of the bluff.

"Candy?" Jojo signed.

"Sure, Jojo, you can have some candy," Pete said as he reached behind his seat and pulled out a variety bag of candies, the kind one would use for Halloween, with some hard candies and some chocolate. Jojo reached in, pulled out a candy, unwrapped it, and started sucking on it.

Towards the east end of the bluff, the rocks again appeared on the surface, and one could see that these rocks were mainly columns set into the ground, but where one could not see the sides of the columns. The track ended, and Pete stopped the car.

"Do you want to get out and take a look?" Pete said.

"Sure," I said opening the door. I walked towards the edge of the cliff. Even without the rattlesnakes and bull snakes that lived up here, one could see how it was named Snake Butte, as the stone columns set into the ground almost looked like scales of a snake's skin. The columns formed decent crags on the part of the cliff I stood upon. It looked as though some of the original topsoil between the columns had been washed away over time. There was a small depression near the edge of the cliff, which looked to be part of a natural drainage system from the top of the butte. I stepped through the depression and up onto a small rise. At this point, it seemed like I was almost a hundred feet from the floor of the plains.

"It is beautiful, isn't it?" Pete said walking up to me.

"It is," I said.

"The tribe hopes to one day have a herd of buffalo and graze them up here," he said.

"That would be fitting," I said. "The perfect place to graze a sacred animal is on a sacred place."

"My thoughts exactly. We have been trying to find a pure strain of buffalo which we can breed. We need enough bulls and cows so that the genetic strain remains pure and they are not inbred. I think that one day it will happen," he said.

"Who better to caretake a pure strain of buffalo, than the people who the buffalo were everything for. I wish the tribe success in this," I said.

"It would give us back some of our roots. Even if the buffalo are not wild, it would remind us of who we were and who we are," he said as we stared out on the Great Plains below us and the Little Rockies farther away.

"Do you want to see the west side now?" Pete said.

"Sure," I said.

We climbed back into the truck, clicked our seatbelts on, and Jojo again scrambled up on Pete's lap. Jojo reached into the candy bag, picked out a piece, unwrapped it, and put it in his mouth. As we bumped along the road I admired the view from the butte. One could see how the Natives saw this as a sacred place. I looked to my left at Pete, and as I did so, I noticed Jojo unwrap another piece of candy, and throw the wrapper out the window. I asked myself, "Did the wind blow that out?" Then, twenty seconds later, he unwrapped another piece of candy, and threw that wrapper out the window as well. I

Chapter 9

watched Pete, and he seemed unfazed. I puzzled over this, as the whole trip out we had been talking about the sacredness of this land and how it was spiritually active. Jojo unwrapped another piece of candy, and again threw this wrapper out the window. I wanted to say something, but truthfully, I felt very uncomfortable doing so. As we reached the fork in the road, where the road to the right would take us back on to Snake Butte road, and going straight would take us to the west end of the bluff, Jojo threw out another wrapper. I decided that I had to say something.

"Pete," I said.

"Yeah."

"Did you know that Jojo was throwing his candy wrappers out the window?"

"I guess I did. I wasn't paying too much attention though."

"Well, I am just some white kid from the city, but if I knew that this place was sacred, and I watched my grandkid pollute it by throwing his garbage out the window, I would be pretty upset. Whether the place was sacred to me or not, it would seem greatly disrespectful of the land and the spirits who live here. I would also think that the spirits, if this place is as active as you say, would take notice, and that there might be repercussions. But, like I said, I am just a white kid from the city, so I might not know what I am talking about," I said.

Pete slowed the truck to a stop, and gave me a long penetrating look. It was that kind of look where you know mere seconds are passing by, but it feels like minutes. Then he said, "You are pretty smart for a white guy," and he opened the door to the truck, climbed out, and started walking back the way we had come. I watched him walk all the way back to the east end of the butte, every once in a while picking a wrapper out of the grass. When he came back to the truck, he had a handful of wrappers in his hand. Pete didn't say a word, he simply put the wrappers in the candy bag, put the candy bag behind his seat, and then put the truck in drive. I wasn't particularly surprised that Pete didn't say anything to me. The surprising thing was that he didn't scold or reprimand Jojo.

We continued west on the track of the butte, then turned left to wind around a higher part of the bluff which was a mound of rock, roughly 200 feet high.

Pete looked at me and said, "You are wondering why I didn't scold Jojo about the litter?"

"A little. It is none of my business, though."

"The Native tradition has been one of raising boys to become braves. In order to be a brave, you have to be fearless. If I punish Jojo for something, and then he fears me or the act, it instills fear into his future actions. Then rather than simply acting, perhaps in the future he remembers a punishment, and he hesitates rather than acting. To not be able to act when you need to can be the difference between life and death. So, in a traditional household, we don't start to educate until a child has received his or her adult name. From birth to age seven, children are allowed to make their own mistakes without punishment. After age seven we begin the mentoring process and gently teach them. This way, they come into adulthood gently and retain their fearlessness, where the decisions they make come from understanding our ways, and do not simply come from fear," Pete said.

"That makes sense, although it might make a child unruly until they are seven," I said.

"Not really. Children will be children, regardless of how much they are punished. But if one breaks a child too early, their innocence will not survive. It is similar to breaking a horse too young. If you break them too young, they are not good mounts who retain their own spirit and intelligence. A horse that is broken too young is usually only good as a pack animal, as they were never allowed to develop who they were versus who you want them to be."

"I understand. I think the white culture tends to try to break children the minute that they start walking," I said.

"And why do they do this?"

"Probably so that they are easier to control by the parents," I said.

"Exactly, and a child who can be easily controlled by the parents can easily be controlled by anyone else. In other words, breaking a child too young turns that child into a servant of sorts, because as long as they ever could remember, they had to follow someone else's rules. We want our people to be able to remember what freedom is, and make the choice which they want to and not to make their choices for anyone else. I think this is one reason why many Natives prefer their own people. We don't assimilate well simply because we continue to want to think for ourselves," Pete said.

Chapter 9

"Interesting. You know I bet most people in white culture have never thought of raising children in this way. In western psychology this is something which people continually work on, and where the psychologist would say that all the problems of a psyche originate from the individual's childhood trauma. I wonder how much childhood trauma the white culture would have, if they allowed their children to be ruled by only themselves until age seven," I said.

We rounded the mound of rock and were in a small flat area that was about a quarter of a mile long and about a quarter of a mile wide. At the far west end was another mound of rock, about twenty-five feet high. Close to the base of the larger mound was a small natural wall. Pete stopped the truck and we climbed out. It is hard to quantify it, but this end of the bluff felt more peaceful. Perhaps it was because everything was rounded and smooth, whereas the east side was cracked and broken. Comparatively, this side of the butte felt more soft, while the other side felt hard. I walked over to the natural wall and saw that there were many petroglyphs of hands on the wall. The hand prints were all sizes, and I wondered who had made them, and why.

Pete walked up to me and said, "It is said that Chief Joseph of the Nez Perce, or the Watopala as we call them, along with 2,900 men, women, and children, attempted to reach the Canadian border after refusing to be confined to a reservation. In this prolonged escape they were chased by 2,000 soldiers of the US Army, and traveled over 1,100 miles. In this band, there were 800 braves who defeated or held off these 2,000 soldiers in eighteen battles. Chief Joseph, as you probably know, surrendered on October 5th, 1877 after the Battle of the Bear Paw Mountains. In your history books, it says that the entire band of Chief Joseph surrendered there, but in our tradition, these hand prints represent the people who actually made it to Canada. One might say that Chief Joseph understood that not all of his people would be able to make it, so he split off a few small groups from the main tribe, and while the main band acted as a diversion, the smaller groups could make it across the border. Or, that is our version of the story."

"That would be an act of honor and extreme self-sacrifice," I said.

"I hear that Joseph was a good man, although I only heard that from my grandparents when I was a small child. It was they who first brought me up here. They would point at the wall and say, 'Grandson, Chief Joseph knew that he couldn't save everyone, so he chose to save who he could. This is the difference between a brave and a chief. The brave fights to defend and raid. The chief tries to make the best decisions for all of his people. Remember the example Chief Joseph set.'"

"Do you think I could take pictures of this?" I asked.

"Sure. None of these people would be alive now and for you to preserve this memory helps our story to stay alive."

"Thanks," I said, unsnapping the clips on my camera bag, taking out my camera and snapping a few pictures. I took pictures of the wall, then I walked around the flat, and took a few pictures of the panorama surrounding the butte.

While I took pictures, Pete had taken out a cigarette, unwrapped part of it and put the tobacco on the wall. Then he smoked the other half of the cigarette. He was silent, and he smoked with his eyes closed, lips silently forming words. After a while, he opened his eyes, then walked over to me. "Did you find what you were looking for?"

"I think I took a few nice shots," I said.

Pete looked at his watch, and said, "Are you ready to head back? Donna should have dinner ready."

"Sure," I said.

We climbed back into the truck, Pete and I buckling up while Jojo waited for his seat on Pete's lap to be secure before climbing up. Pete drove down the butte, then turned right onto Snake Butte Road and followed that back to Highway 66. It was a quiet drive back. At Highway 66, he turned right, and five minutes later, we turned into his driveway. Donna's car was in the driveway. Pete pulled up, parked, turned off the ignition, and opened his door. Jojo scrambled down to the ground, then Pete and I both unbuckled our belts and climbed out of the truck. Jojo and I followed Pete into the house.

"Honey, we are back. Something smells wonderful!" Pete said.

Donna said from the kitchen, "Did you boys have fun looking around?"

Pete shrugged his shoulders, then said, "I showed Roland around town, then took him up to the butte. Did you enjoy yourself, Roland?"

"I did. Your husband is quite knowledgeable. I particularly enjoyed hearing Pete's take on some of the history of this land."

Chapter 9

"That's great,'" Donna said. "You boys wash up, as dinner is ready."

"OK," Pete and I said in unison.

Pete took Jojo into the kitchen to wash up, and I went into the bathroom, washed my hands and face, then put my camera gear in the bedroom. I walked to the kitchen and on the table was a chuck roast laden with juice in a black roasting pan. Potatoes, carrots, onions, and sweet potatoes had been added to the roast to soak up the juice. There was also a green salad.

"I put out Italian dressing for you, Roland," Donna said.

"Thank you ma'am."

"I love my wife. Pot roast is one of my favorites," Pete said, smiling with twinkling eyes at Donna.

"Well, not only do we have a great guest, but tomorrow your sister is getting married, so you will need your strength," Donna said with a chuckle. "Pete, if you would do the honors?" she said, handing Pete a carving knife and fork.

"Most definitely," he said as he started cutting the meat.

When he was done, we all sat down and Pete said Grace. It was a quiet meal full of chit chat about what still needed to be done for the wedding and what Pete was doing with the powwow. A few times Donna and Pete tried to engage me about photography, but I was strangely exhausted. If my mouth weren't chewing, I think I would have fallen asleep right there.

"You look tired, Roland," Pete said.

"I am. I don't know why. It isn't as if I had an exhausting day."

"Sometimes the butte does that to people. Don't worry, it will pass."

"OK. All the same, I think it will be an early night for me. What time do we start tomorrow?" I said.

"We should be down at the grounds by 10 a.m. to make sure everything is ready for the wedding at noon. So, breakfast will be ready by 9 a.m. How does that sound?

"Good," I said.

After dinner, I picked up my plate, set it in the sink, and said, "I think I am going to go to my room, if that is not impolite. I think I need to lie down."

"7:30 p.m. is early for bed, but do what you need to in order to shake it," Pete said. "We will clean up dinner and if we don't see you again tonight, have a good rest."

"Thanks, Pete," I said. I walked to my room, closed the door, and sat on the bed, looking blankly at the wall. It was odd. I was fine on the drive back, then the minute I sat down for dinner, I was exhausted. If it had been simply a matter of low blood sugar, eating should have fixed that. No, this felt energetic. The only thing that made sense was that this was due to something that happened on the butte. But, I had been respectful, and I hadn't done anything disrespectful. My mind drew a blank. Well, I thought the only way to figure out what is going on is to sleep. If I am still like this in the morning, then I will have to decide what to do then. I reached in my pack, pulled out my toothbrush and toothpaste, and went to the bathroom. I brushed my teeth, then walked back into the bedroom, disrobed, and climbed into bed. Ten breaths later I was asleep.

At 12 a.m., I woke up. Something was off. I lay there trying to figure out why I was awake, then I heard it. From Jojo's room I heard a voice. Except the voice didn't make any sense. It was electronic and speaking rapidly. I had heard this voice before from my own childhood. With sudden clarity, I realized that what I was hearing was a Speak and Spell, but it was talking faster than anyone could push the buttons. Then I heard other electronic toys moving and talking all at once. The hairs stood up on the back of my neck. I tried to get out of bed, but it was as if there was a massive weight on my feet.

Then I heard the voice of a young woman, "Oh, he is awake."

Then the voice of a young man, "You talk to him."

Then the female voice, "OK."

Their voices were understandable, yet had the same sound as doves.

Chapter 9

The female voice said, "Man-child. We thank you for the respect you showed today. Your people have not always been respectful to us. To honor your respect, we want to tell you a few things about who you will become. You will be a hunter of demons, and the path you are on now will lead you to be able to help people who feel helpless. Be wary of the demons, as they are cunning, and they will often try to lead you astray. Be wary of the many forms which they come in. A demon may use anything within its power to seduce you and will often come in the form which you are least resistant to. Your communication with spirit, as well as all human medicine and power, does not come from a name or a title, but from the way you breathe. In our world, this is how we recognize those who have power, and those who don't. I will now show you how to breathe."

I felt a rush of energy like a wave starting at my feet, then expanding to my torso, then up to my head. My breathing slowed, and I inhaled deeply and exhaled deeply.

"There. Now, you will be ready when it is time. Go with peace, man-child," and her voice became the sound of a dove. The two doves cooed reassuringly for a minute, then faded. Once again I could move my feet, and all of the electronic noises in Jojo's room had stopped. I continued to take long deep breaths and I quickly fell back asleep.

The next morning at 8:30 a.m. Pete knocked on my door. Through the door, he said, "Breakfast in a half hour. If you want to shower, you should get up now."

Groggy, but refreshed, I crossed the hall and took a shower. Then, I went back to my room, dressed, and walked out to the kitchen. Pete was sitting at the kitchen table, sipping on a mug of coffee, and reading the local paper. Donna was making batter for pancakes.

"Good morning, Roland. Do you feel better?" Pete said.

"Yeah …" I trailed off.

"Would you like coffee?" Donna said.

"Sure."

Donna poured a mug of coffee and handed it to me. I sat down at the table with Pete and said, "Did you hear any of that last night?"

"Any of what?" Pete said.

"The electronics in Jojo's room going crazy at about 12 a.m.?" I said.

Donna and Pete looked at each other rather intensely.

"I didn't hear anything," Donna said.

"Neither did I. Tell me what happened," Pete said.

"Well, first I heard the sound of the Speak and Spell going crazy. Then, other electronics doing the same. I heard the sound of two doves talking to each other. Then, I felt like my legs were pinned to the bed. The voices of the doves became human voices, one male and one female. It was the female voice who spoke to me."

"Roland, I have to be honest with you. I take Trazodone to sleep, and Donna takes Ambien. When we are asleep, we are out cold. This isn't to say that this didn't happen, but we didn't hear it. There is an old, old legend in our culture that says two young lovers died and were buried on this hill, where our house sits. When we built the foundation, we did not find any evidence of a grave."

"Has this ever happened to anyone else in this room?" I asked.

"Occasionally, our daughter would talk about spirits when she was younger, so you are not the first to have a problem in that room. However, we thought it was simply our daughter making things up, because she knew the legend of the young lovers," Pete said.

"What they told me was interesting, and food for thought, but not necessarily bad. Beyond the strange speaking of the electronic toys, I didn't feel afraid of what they said to me."

"OK. Donna, while you finish breakfast, I am going to make a phone call."

Pete stood up, picked up his mug of coffee and went outside. Donna poured the pancake batter onto the griddle. While the first pancakes sizzled, she broke six eggs into a frying pan and started to scramble them.

"Roland, as a people, we are used to things like this. Don't worry, Pete will take care of it," Donna said.

Chapter 9

"I don't know if I am worried about it, but it certainly was a unique experience," I said.

Pete walked back into the kitchen and said, "OK Roland, I have made arrangements with Ed, the medicine man who will be officiating the marriage ceremony, to give both you and Jojo a blessing after the wedding. Just in case this came from what happened on the butte yesterday."

"OK," I said.

"Breakfast is ready," Donna said as she set a plate of pancakes and scrambled eggs on the table. "Do either of you want bacon?"

"Yes please," Pete said.

"Sure," I said.

"OK. That will take an extra minute or two, but go ahead and start," she said as she pulled a package of bacon from the refrigerator, then put it into a pan. She turned the heat on under the burner, and poured another round of pancakes on the griddle.

"Do you want syrup, butter, or jam with your pancakes, Roland?"

"Just butter ma'am," I said.

"Syrup and butter for me," Pete said.

Jojo came out of the living room, crawled up into his chair, and signed, "Like Grandpa, please."

"That's my grandson," Pete said.

Pete took a minute, said Grace, then we piled food on our plates. Two minutes later, Donna sat down with a plate of bacon. Pete picked up the plate and offered it to me. I used my fork to spear two pieces, then Pete offered the plate to Donna, who also speared two pieces. Then Pete speared three pieces onto his plate and one onto Jojo's plate.

"After breakfast, we will drive down to the powwow grounds, and get ready for Ellen and Tom's wedding. They will have the ceremony, then we will have lunch down at the grounds after the wedding. After that, Ed will work with you. The powwow will start at 2 p.m. or so," Pete said.

"About how long should I expect to shoot for?" I said.

"The dancers generally go until daylight ends. Today the sun sets at 9:21 p.m. is what I read in the paper, but my guess is you would be using a flash regardless. The actual dance area is indoors in the powwow building. So, you should probably count on about six hours, but of course you can shoot what you want, and take breaks as you want," Pete said.

"OK. I will bring a bag of film and my flash," I said.

"Would you like another cup of coffee, Roland?" Donna asked.

"Yes, please," I said.

"Pete?" she said as she stood up, picked up the coffee pot and returned to the table.

"Yes, please. Thank you, Donna," he said as she filled his cup, then mine.

When we had all eaten our fill, Pete pushed back from the table and said, "I am going to feed the horses. Roland, get your gear together, and I will drive us down."

"Actually, I think I will take my Blazer today and follow you down. That way I'll be able to do projects in the down time," I said.

"OK, suit yourself. I will be ready in about twenty minutes," Pete said.

"OK. I will be ready."

I went to the bedroom, picked up my camera gear, and hauled it out to the Blazer. Then, as an afterthought, I went back in and picked up the tackle box containing my beads and beadwork. Packing up didn't take long at all, so I lounged on my front bumper and watched Pete feed the horses. He had three horses in a decent-sized corral. From the looks of them, they were Appaloosas. Now, I am not a horse expert, but the Appaloosa is pretty easy to spot, as they are known for their distinct spotting, called leopard spotting. They are also distinct because of their striped hooves and their white sclera. Leopard spotting generally means a horse has a coat which is a dark-under layer of skin with a lighter coat on top. While oftentimes an Appaloosa is light-colored with darker spots, it does not have to be so, as an Appaloosa may be a bay, a black, a chestnut, a palomino, a buckskin, a cremello, a perlino, a roan, a gray, a dun, or a grulla. The spotting is most common around the muzzle, eyes, anus, and genitalia.

While Appaloosa are not unique to the Americas,[16] they are commonly associated with the Nez Perce. The Nez Perce were and are dedicated horse breeders, who in the past as well as today have very strict breeding practices. As a breed, Appaloosas tend to be fast, agile, and hardy. There are a number of spotting patterns that identify an Appaloosa. These are: spotted, a blanket or snowcap, a blanket with spots, a leopard, a few-spot leopard, a snowflake, an Appaloosa roan, a marble or varnish roan, a mottled, a roan blanket or frost, and a roan blanket with spots. Pete's three Appaloosas displayed different spotting patterns. The first was spotted, with a brownish base coat and white spots that dappled its hind end. The second was a leopard, that is, a horse with a white base-coat and brown spots covering its hind end, flank, back, and head. The third was an Appaloosa roan, who had an intermingling of lighter hairs on the surface and darker hairs on the undercoat, giving the top coat an appearance of frost-covered coal.

I watched as Pete gave each horse a full pat down, running his hands along the horse's mane and flank, then down each of its legs to check the hooves. The horse he was working on huffed and puffed, leaning into Pete as he found an itchy spot. It was obvious that the Appaloosas loved Pete as much as he loved them. Each horse was "naked" as one might say, without bridle or ropes. As Pete found tender or itchy spots on their body, he would work the area with his hands. These horses had spirit, they held their heads high, and they were alert. They did not have the look of a horse which had been broken of its spirit, nor were they spiteful. They did not display any signs of skittishness or anxiety to Pete's presence or touch. I could feel the love radiating off the three horses and Pete from a hundred feet away. Inspection and petting over, Pete went just outside of the corral nearest the house, picked up a bale of hay mixed with alfalfa, and carried the bale to the front of the corral, setting it down by the water trough. He then went back out the gate and picked three apples out of an old wooden barrel. The horses nuzzled up to him, each waiting their turn to have their apple from his hand. When the first horse had its apple, it strutted forward and took a bite off the hay on the ground, munching it quietly. The second and third horse soon followed suit. Once all the horses were eating hay, Pete checked the water in the trough, and finding it wanting, he walked to the side of the

---

16. Appaloosas have been depicted in prehistoric cave paintings in Europe. Drawings of this horse were also found in ancient Greece, ancient Persia, and in Han dynasty China.

house, and picked up a coiled hose. He turned on the spigot, and filled the tough with fresh water. When the trough was full, he brought the hose back to the house, turned off the spigot, and wound the hose back up. Then he walked back into the corral, put his head next to one horse, and said things I could not hear. The horse's ears were upright listening to Pete as he talked while the horse chewed the hay. He then did the same thing for the other two horses. He gave each horse a final pat, then stepped out of the corral, locking it behind him and walked towards me.

"OK. The horses are fed," he said.

"What did you say to them?" I asked.

"I thanked them for being part of my life, I thanked them for protecting me, and for being there for me when my heart needs the solace which only they can provide."

I nodded my head in appreciation, thinking to myself, "We all have an animal which nourishes our spirit."

"Are you ready to head out?" Pete asked.

"I am."

"OK. We are heading to the powwow grounds, where we were yesterday," he said.

"Sounds good."

"Donna will follow us down once she has finished a few of the dishes she is making for lunch, and she will bring Jojo with her."

"Great," I said, and opened the driver's side door of the Blazer, climbed in, and buckled my seatbelt. I put my keys in the ignition, turned it, and the Blazer roared to life. "I love my car," I thought to myself. I watched Pete climb into his truck, start the engine, back out, and turn around. I did the same, and followed him down the driveway to make a right-hand turn onto Highway 66. We drove the five-plus minutes to Fort Belknap, turned right off Highway 66 onto White Eagle Road. Roughly a block later we turned right on Blackbird Trail and entered the powwow grounds on the south end. We parked next to the large "shade" Pete's family had made. Both of us stepped out of our trucks and walked up to the shade.

Chapter 9

The ordered chaos of yesterday, had turned into a full encampment of people who had done the majority of the work and were now prepping last-minute details. Jingle dancers were putting finishing touches on their regalia, older people were lounging in chairs under shades drinking coffee and talking to neighbors, and children were running around occupying themselves with play until the festivities started. A few groups near us were hooking up BBQs to propane, adding a few more branches to their shade, and a few officials were going around to the different encampments checking in dancers.

Pete's sister wasn't there yet, but her soon-to-be husband was already there practicing his vows.

Pete walked up to him and said, "Today's the day!"

Tom said, "It sure is."

"Are you nervous?" Pete said.

"A little," Tom said.

"Don't be. You will make each other very happy."

"I know. I couldn't have found a better wife," Tom said.

"She is a great woman. Tom, I would like to introduce you to Roland. He will be taking pictures for us today."

"Nice to meet you Roland," Tom said stretching out his hand.

I shook his hand and said, "Nice to meet you Tom. Congratulations on your day."

"Thank you, Roland. I hope you get some good shots."

"I will, Tom. This is not my first wedding rodeo," I said smiling.

"Well, I hope it goes more smoothly than a rodeo," Tom said smiling.

"Roland, I want to introduce you to Ed, and we will see what he needs from you," Pete said.

"OK," I said.

We walked twenty steps to the teepee, and Pete said, "Ed, are you here?"

A voice from inside the teepee responded, "I am."

"I would like you to meet Roland, the photographer," Pete said.

"OK. One minute, I will be right out," came the voice. I heard Ed speaking in a low voice in Nakota. Even if I knew the language, his words were too low to hear. This went on for three or four minutes, then a tall, thin Native man stepped out. He was wearing jeans, boots, a turquoise vest, and a red button-down shirt.

"Good morning, Pete," he said as he stepped out.

"Good morning, Ed," Pete said. "Ed, this is Roland Pearce. Roland, this is Ed Blackwolf."

"Nice to meet you," we both said and shook hands.

"Ed, I have a few things to do, and Roland won't be doing anything in particular until the wedding starts. If you need him to do anything for you, I am sure Roland would be happy to help you," Pete said.

"Definitely," I said.

"I could use a fire. I have some cut cottonwood rounds there," he said pointing to a stack of wood. "But, I haven't had time to make it. Do you think you could do that for me?"

"Yep. No problem," I said.

"Great," Pete said. "Roland, now that you have a task, I am going to go get a few of my chores done."

"OK, Pete," I said.

"Do you need an ax, Roland?" Ed asked.

"No, I have one in my Blazer."

Chapter 9

"OK. The fire pit is there," he pointed to a fire pit which had been dug into the ground and lined with fist-sized rocks. "I appreciate you being the fire keeper today."

"I am happy to help," I said.

"I am going to go back into the teepee and finish my preparations," Ed said.

"OK. I will get going on this," I said.

I walked to the place I had parked the Blazer, opened the door, found my tomahawk buried under some other items, my knife belt, the canvas bag which I keep tinder in, and the other supplies I use to make fire. Then I closed the door, locked it, walked back to the fire pit, and put my tools down. I picked my tomahawk back up, unsheathed it, and walked to the cottonwood rounds. They were about one foot in diameter by about eighteen inches long. Nothing that would be a problem for my tomahawk. As I split ten rounds or so in half, I mused on the use of cottonwood.

Cottonwood is a large tree, which in its native habitat grows roughly fifty to eighty feet tall and some say a hundred feet tall. The bark tends to be an ash gray and is deeply fissured. Cottonwood has deciduous green leaves with toothed edges, a wide base, and triangular leaves. The stem that attaches the leaf to the branch is flat. In spring, it produces male and female flowers separately in catkins that appear before the leaves bloom out from the tree. The seeds formed by the catkins are downy, which allows them to easily become airborne. The cottony seed down can make good tinder when combined with coarser materials. Cottonwoods are commonly found in areas with a lot of water, such as rivers and stream beds. Due to their love of water, they have a tendency to tolerate flooding, erosion, and flood deposits that could kill other trees. The trunks of the trees were used for dugout canoes, the bark can be used as a tea, and the leaves and bark can be used as forage for horses and mules. The inner bark, when dried, can also make good tinder when combined with other materials. The wood itself is soft, and burns fairly quickly.

In the Siouan culture, the cottonwood tree is seen as the tree of life, and it is the tree that is used in the venerable Sun Dance ceremonies as the main center pole. Traditionally, the medicine man would select a tree to be used, then a man would be chosen to chop it down with an ax to count coup on the tree. The tree trunk was not allowed to touch the ground, so traditionally braves were chosen to catch the tree as it fell. Now, I can't confirm or deny this catching of the tree, because I have not witnessed it myself, but this is what I have been told by more than one old medicine man.

I picked up two half rounds of wood and split these into twelfths to be used as kindling. I chose another two half rounds and split these into thirds. Then I chose another two half rounds, and split these in half. I picked up all of these pieces in several trips and set them down by the fire pit. I walked back to the wood pile, picked up four half rounds, and set these near the fire pit, but separate from the first stack. I put my tomahawk back in its sheath, then unsheathed my large carbon steel knife, which is roughly ten inches long by an inch wide, and then I sat down next to the pit. I used my large knife to further split some of the smaller pieces until the pieces were about the width of my pinky finger. I stacked these smaller pieces to my right. When I had what I thought was enough of the pinky-sized pieces, I split more pieces to the size of my ring finger. After I had enough of these, I split pieces to the size of my thumb. I separated each pile by diameter and put each pile in its own place on my right. After getting my kindling prepared, I picked up a couple of half rounds and stripped off their outer bark with my knife. Once the outer bark was off, I shaved the inner bark from the side of the round. When I had what I thought was enough of this inner bark, I placed it on top of my kindling pile. Now, I was ready to start building the fire.

I picked up three of the thumb-sized pieces of kindling, and poked them in between several of the fist-sized rocks which lined the base of the fire pit, and pushed the pieces into the earth about two inches. Once they were placed, I angled the upright ends so that they touched each other, forming a sort of triangle. I picked up the inner bark of the cottonwood, and rubbed it between my two palms, as if I were trying to warm my hands. I wanted to break down the fibers of the inner bark to make them softer, so that the fibers within the inner bark started to tease out of the strips. I had shaved off enough of the inner bark that I had to do this part in several repetitions. Once this inner bark began to resemble something like a bird's nest, I then combined each bundle, and rolled it in my hands in a circular motion to lock the different bundles together, then I once again rolled this larger bundle back and forth in between my hands. Once I again had something which looked like a bird's nest, I placed this under the point which was formed by the three sticks in the fire pit. This was not my tinder, but would act more like when someone would traditionally use paper when making a fire.

Now, I picked up a handful of my smallest-diameter sticks and began placing them around the pyramid that had been formed by the initial three sticks. I started closest to me, then worked around the circle of the pyramid clockwise, but I left a three-and-a-half-inch opening within the circle in front of me, where I could see the cottonwood inner bark underneath the peak of the triangle.

Chapter 9

"What are you doing?" a Native boy said as he walked up to me and sat down on the ground on the other side of the fire pit.

"I am building a fire," I said.

"Why are you building it like that?" another boy said as he came up and sat down on the ground next to the first boy.

"This is called a teepee fire. It is the way your people used to make fire. Have you ever been in a teepee when it rains?" I asked as I now added my next-thicker set of sticks to the pyramid of sticks.

"Yeah," the first boy said.

"Do you get wet?" I asked.

"No. Of course not," he said indignantly.

"Why don't you get wet?" I said still placing sticks.

"Because the teepee blocks the rain," the second boy said.

"What happens to the rain when it hits the teepee?" I asked.

An older boy who was maybe ten, who had been listening a few feet away, walked up and sat down. "The rain runs down the sides and away from the center of the teepee," he said proudly.

"Exactly. And when you build a fire in a teepee, where does the smoke go?" I said.

"Out the top," the youngest boy said.

"Out the smoke hole," said the older boy.

"You are both right. Why does the smoke go out the top?" I asked.

They had to think about this for a second, and then the older boy said, "Because fire and smoke go up, and not down."

"Yes. Because heat rises, so fire and smoke would both burn upwards. Additionally, the small spaces left between the earth and the edge of the teepee canvas let in air. As the fire burns, it pulls in more air from the bottom sides of the teepee, and this helps fire burn cleanly, thus helping it not smoke so much, and helping the smoke to rise," I said.

"Why did we used to build fires like teepees then?" said the younger boy.

"Because when the wood is stacked precisely like this, the top of the wood keeps the tinder dry, like a boy in a teepee, and the rain drips down these outer pieces of wood without letting the inside get wet. Further, because the top pieces are closer together than the bottom pieces, air can still get through to help feed the baby fire," I said.

"Ohhh …." all three of the boys said together.

"It really is a teepee," said the youngest boy.

I sat down, reached inside my canvas tinder bag, and pulled out a mish-mash of tinder which I had been gathering for several summers. There were elm shavings from the last bow I had made, thistle-down from berry picking on Sauvie's Island, paper birch from a place I had camped in Idaho, the inner bark of cedar from some knife sheaths I had made, down from cottonwood seed I had gathered at a rest stop on my way to Montana, and other woody chips and shavings from various projects. I scooped up a handful of this and started rubbing my hands like I had done with the inner bark of the cottonwood.

"What are you doing now?" said the middle boy.

"I am preparing my tinder," I said.

"What is tinder?" said the youngest boy.

"Tinder is the smallest and softest substances mixed with small paper-like substances, and small coarse substances. The recipe is about one-third of each mixed together. This is how I will start the fire," I said.

Once the tinder was prepared, I placed the tinder bundle on a rock on the edge of the fire pit. Then I reached back into my canvas tinder bag, and plucked out my hand drill and fireboard. I checked the notch and the hole to make sure there was enough wood left in this hole to get a fire.

"What is that?" said the middle boy.

"It is how I am going to make fire," I said.

"You mean like rubbing two sticks together?" said the older boy.

"Yep. This is the way your people made fire originally," I said.

"Why don't you use a lighter?" said the middle boy.

"Because fire is something which has to be respected. If we didn't have fire, life would be less pleasant. Fire gives us its gift of warmth, heats our bodies, and cooks our food. It is sacred to all people, and using a lighter, when I know how to make it the old way, seems disrespectful to me," I said.

"How does it work?" said the younger boy.

"Well, this," I said, holding my hand drill up, "is a yucca flower stalk. And this," holding up my fireboard, "is a piece of alder. First, I make a small hole, then I rotate the drill between both my hands like this," I said making the motion of rubbing my hands together as if to stay warm. "Then, once I have a hole drilled, I cut a triangular notch so that the pointy part of the triangle is inset to almost the center of the hole. Once I have done that, then as I twirl the hand drill, it makes dust, which falls into the notch. When there is enough dust, and it is hot enough, it will make a coal. Do you want to see me do it? I already have the hole and notch cut, so when I do this, I will be making fire," I said.

"Yes please!" all three kids said in unison.

"OK. Then I will begin," I said.

I placed the hand drill in the hole, and I began "floating" my hands on the top of the drill. Floating means that rather than simply rubbing my hands back and forth to twirl the drill, I instead made counter-clockwise circles with my hands as I twirled the drill, so in an exaggerated view I would be making circles with my hands, and the circles would be rotating towards my body. Floating is a way that one uses to warm up both the drill and the fire board. As I did this, I prayed silently, "Thank you Creator for giving me this opportunity to make fire in the old way, in this place, and to give back to these children, at least the idea of a skill which their people knew intimately. I am humbled by this opportunity, and I thank you too, fire, for sharing your gift with me at this time, and in this place. Thank you, Creator."

Now, normally making fire takes a fair amount of work, mainly in applying downward pressure on the fire drill. It takes a huge amount of concentration and a fair amount of stamina. This means that when I begin to make fire in this way, my attention becomes pin pointed to this task, as there is no paying attention to anything else. Fire demands your attention, as to create the spark is to create life. As if from far away, I heard a voice say, "He's making fire the old way." Then another voice, "He's making fire the old way." But these voices were as if from a far off place, as I was one with the drill and the fire board. I stopped floating, and started in earnest. I applied massive downward pressure on the drill, twirling it as fast as I could, letting my hands twirl all the way down the shaft until I was two inches above the fire board. The fire board had a billowing cloud of smoke coming from the hole. I placed the thumb of my right hand on the top of the drill to hold it in place, then brought my left hand up to the top, and again I twirled my hands as fast as I could. Halfway down the stalk, I saw that a big coal had formed from the dust created by the friction. I gently lifted the stalk of the drill out of the hole so as to not disturb the coal. Then, I picked up my knife, and gently held it over the coal while I lifted the fire board, and hence the notch away from the coal. I then lifted the small piece of bark with my left hand which I had rested underneath the fire board to catch the coal, and picked up the tinder bundle which I had created earlier with my right hand. I gently nudged the coal from the bark into the center of the tinder bundle. I let go of the bark, and using both hands moved the tinder bundle towards my face. I then blew on the coal. On the first breath, the bundle started to smoke, and on the second breath, flame burst out from where the coal had been. I gingerly placed the burning tinder bundle into the opening I had left in the wooden teepee I had built onto the bed of cottonwood fibers. Within seconds the wood of the fire started to crackle and burn, then the fire licked its way to the top of the teepee. I have never before or since made fire so easily.

"Wow!" said the middle boy.

I looked up to the boy, and I realized that I was surrounded in many concentric rings by the entire tribe, young, old, women, men, children, all silently looking at the fire, then at me. The adults nodded to me, then everyone began to disperse. As the crowd cleared, I saw Ed standing outside his teepee looking at me and the fire. When he noticed me looking at him, he nodded and stepped back into the teepee.

"I think," I said to myself, "that I was just the vehicle for a miracle."

Chapter 9

The fire crackled and I sat there watching it, feeding it more wood as it needed it, nourishing it, and honoring it. "I think I will remember this experience for the rest of my life," I thought to myself.

About a half hour later, Ed stepped from the teepee with a large abalone shell, and using two pieces of left over kindling as chopsticks, picked up a couple of coals from the fire. As he placed them into the abalone shell, he looked at me and smiled. "Thank you for making the fire," he said. But I knew what he was really saying was, "Thank you for reminding us of who we are, and what we are capable of." He didn't have to say that, as we both felt the specialness of the whole experience. I smiled back and nodded respectfully.

"We are going to start the wedding in a few minutes. I will watch the fire if you want to get your camera gear," he said.

"Thank you," I said.

I stood up, leaving my tinder bag, walked to my Blazer, unlocked it, fished my gear out, and brought it back to the fire pit. Ed sat silently staring into the fire. I sat down, unzipped my camera bag, put color film in the camera, checked to make sure my battery had enough power, then nodded to Ed. Ed looked up at me, nodded, then stood up. He walked over to Pete's shade, and announced, "We are ready. Shall we begin?"

Tom stood up, and Donna went into the RV and asked Ellen to come out. Donna stepped out first, then Ellen walked out. She was wearing traditional Nakota wedding garb. The ceremony was a simple affair, and consisted of vows by Tom and Ellen with Ed observing and bearing witness. I shot as many photographs as I could within the short ceremony. Then it was over. Ed pronounced Tom and Ellen man and wife, and the couple walked between two rows of guests out to the parking lot. It was hard to mistake the mutual love that beamed off both their faces.

As Ed walked by me, heading back to the teepee, he said, "Pete said you had an experience up on the butte, and that he would like me to bless you and Jojo. They will want to break for lunch to celebrate the wedding, then we will do it afterwards. If you wouldn't mind keeping the fire going, that would be much appreciated."

"OK," I said.

I looked to the right hand side of the shade and saw that Pete was firing up a gas grill while Donna had opened a Tupperware container of hamburger patties. Donna then went back into the RV and brought out several more Tupperware containers and set them on a table about five feet from the grill. Donna went in and out of the RV, bringing out more food each time until there was a whole spread of food set out on the table. Next, she procured paper plates, plastic ware, cups, drinks, and napkins. When the grill was hot, Pete started placing the hamburger patties on the grill. They immediately began to sizzle. Donna went back into the RV and brought out hamburger buns, mustard, ketchup, and relish. She placed the buns next to Pete and the condiments on the table.

It wasn't long before Pete said, "Burgers are ready."

The family and guests filed up to the grill. Pete had a number of buns toasting, and as each person would come up, he would ask them if they wanted cheese, and if they did, he would melt a piece on their burger. Then he would place a burger or two on their plate. After this, people moved to the spread of condiments, fixed their burger, loaded their plate full of potato salad, three-bean salad, or mac salad, and potato chips. Then they went back to their chairs to eat. In a bit, Ellen and Tom came back to the party wearing casual clothing. It was a simple, low-key affair. When I was in front of the line to get my burger, Pete said, "Thanks for being here, Roland."

"Thanks for having me, Pete," I said.

I fixed up my burger at the condiment stand, loaded up my plate with potato salad and three-bean salad, went back to the fire pit, and sat down. I added another half round of wood to the fire, then ate my lunch. When I was done with that plate, I went back for seconds. I had been hungry.

When I was done eating, I sat by the fire, watching it consume the wood. I wasn't necessarily feeling anti-social, simply being in the moment with the fire. There would be plenty of time over the next three days to socialize, but today I wanted to be quiet. After a while, Ed walked over and said, "I will work with Jojo first, then work with you. Pete will be bringing Jojo over in a few minutes after he cleans up a bit."

"OK," I said.

Ed went into the teepee, and I heard him speaking in Nakota again for a bit. Then he came out with his abalone shell, picked up a few coals and went back into the teepee. A

Chapter 9

few minutes later, Pete returned to the fire with Jojo and called out to Ed, "Are you ready for Jojo?"

"I am," Ed replied. "Send Jojo in."

Pete gave Jojo a little nudge, and said, "Jojo, go in and see Ed."

Jojo looked up at Pete, and signed, "OK." Then he stepped into the teepee. I heard Ed say a few things in Nakota, then a few minutes later Ed appeared at the door of the teepee with Jojo. Jojo walked out and smiled at Pete and Pete smiled back.

"Pete, do you mind attending the fire while I work with Roland?"

"No problem, Ed," Pete said.

"Roland, if you would step into the teepee?" Ed said.

"Sure," I said. I left my camera gear with Pete and followed Ed into the teepee. It was dark inside. Not gloomy, just shaded. In the center of the teepee was a table with the abalone shell, an eagle feather, a bowl of water, a bundle of sage, and a bundle of sweet grass on it. On one side of the table were two chairs and on the other side was another chair. Within the abalone shell, the coals still glowed and smoked.

"First, let's clean you up," Ed said.

"OK."

Ed picked up the abalone shell, stripped some sage off of the bundle of sage and placed it into the abalone shell onto the coals. He then picked up the eagle feather and walked around the table to me.

"Hold your arms out as if you are going to give me a hug," he said.

I held my arms out so that I looked like a cross or a "T".

In a low, quiet voice, Ed spoke in Nakota, as he began wafting the sage smoke over me with the eagle feather. He started with my face, and worked his way down the front of my body, underneath my armpits, around each of my arms, then down to the groin, and over each leg. Then he moved behind me, and started from the back of my head, down my back, down to my waist, then down both legs.

"Lift your right foot," he said, then wafted smoke under my foot when I lifted it.

"Lift your left foot, he said, then wafted smoke under this foot. The whole time he spoke in Nakota, except when he asked me to move.

Next, he lit the sweet grass. Ed spoke in Nakota and faced north, then east, then south, then west. He stood still and looked up, then down. Then he rested the sweet grass on the abalone shell so that it continued to burn.

"Please sit," he said, "and tell me what happened."

I sat down and described going out to the butte with Pete, then the voices I heard at Pete's house.

Ed stood by the table and his eyes went slightly distant and unfocused for a minute or two. Then he said, "This is a true thing. These spirits were not malicious. They followed you back from the butte, and these were the male and female snake spirits of the butte. Your being there, and what you said to Pete, have set something in motion which will begin as you come into your true power. In other words, you showed respect for the butte, and the butte respected you back. You can now consider the butte as one of your power places, just as other braves of the Plains people do. These spirits simply delivered you a message of your future. They did not cause harm, nor did they intend to cause harm. You are lucky. The butte is not always kind and it certainly is not kind to many outsiders. The good spirits move in mysterious ways. Do you have any questions for me?"

"I don't," I said.

"OK. If you would stand up please? We will finish with a blessing," he said.

I stood up. Ed picked up the eagle feather and the cup of water. He began speaking in Nakota. As he was speaking, he dipped the tip of the feathered end of the feather into the water just enough to have a single bead of water form on the end of the feather. Then he used the feather to flick the bead of water at my forehead. He dipped the feather again, and flicked the bead of water at my chest. He repeated this procedure for my waist, each leg, each arm, then the back of my head, my back, and the back of each arm and leg, all the while speaking in Nakota. When he was done, he did the same for each direction, the sky, and the ground. Then he looked at me and said, "OK. You can go back outside."

I nodded, and said, "Thank you."

"No problem, Roland," he said.

I stepped outside into the light. Pete was sitting by the fire, and he stood up as I walked out. The fire had died down, and was only coals now.

"How'd it go?" Pete asked.

"Good," I said.

"OK. I will leave you in charge of the fire, while I go take care of a few more things."

"OK," I said, and sat down next to the fire. I stared into the coals and let my mind be still while I watched the coals slowly turn to ash. When the fire was out, I gathered up my fire-making equipment, put my camera bag over my shoulder, and walked to my car. I opened the tailgate, reordered my gear, and put the fire-making equipment in its designated place. As I closed the tailgate, I noticed Ed a few cars away getting something out of his car. I walked to my driver's side door, opened it, and reached back to my pipe bag. In it was a pound of pipe tobacco I had brought in case I needed to give offerings for one reason or another. I pulled out the bag, shut my door, and walked over to Ed's car. Ed was looking for something in the back seat, so his feet and legs were on the ground, while his torso and head were in his car.

"Ed," I said.

Ed bobbed his head out of his car and turned around.

"I want to give you this … for the blessing," I said.

Ed looked at me and the bag of tobacco in my hand. Then he looked deep into my eyes, and said, "You know our ways quite well, Roland. This is good. I accept your offering."

I placed the tobacco in his hands and said, "I respect what you do and the tradition it comes from."

"I know you do, Roland. I will pray for you."

"Thank you, Ed," I said. We both smiled, then I turned around and walked back to my car. It was 2 p.m., and hot as it was, I thought to myself, "A siesta would be nice before all of this gets going." I climbed into my passenger's seat, cranked the seat back, pulled my hat over my eyes, and took a nap. I woke up an hour later to the rhythmic beat of a pow-wow drum beating as the drummers began to warm up. I grabbed my camera gear, shut and locked my passenger door, and walked to the powwow arena. Everyone was warming up. The dancers walked around in their bustles and bone frontal pieces. With every step they took, the bells on their feet would jingle and their costumes were in all the colors of the rainbow. People were filing into the bleachers, and I stood to the side of the floor of the dance grounds. After about ten minutes, the MC walked to the drum group and talked quietly with them. About a minute later, the drumming stopped and the MC let all be quiet for a moment.

Then he said into the microphone, "Hey now! Hey now! I want to welcome all of you to the 1996 Fort Belknap Powwow! Before we get started, I would like to invite anyone who has fought in the armed forces to come down on the grounds to be recognized. Whether you are a vet, or currently serving, we would like to honor you. Come on down, regardless of whether you are of the tribe or not!"

I watched as Pete and a number of other men and women walked onto the powwow grounds and stood in a line. Some were crippled on the outside, missing a limb, or they walked with the slow but steady pace of someone who has suffered terrible injuries, and had recovered, but still had pain. Others were crippled on the inside, like Pete, who had no obvious wounds, but who suffered from PTSD.

"Veterans and current troops! We want to honor you for your service to our great country! You are our warriors! You have suffered in unimaginable ways! Yet, here you stand amongst us. Without you, we would be a scattered people! Your sacrifice has given us our freedom, and our peace of mind. Because of you, we can live our lives without fear. Your sacrifice is seen, and you bring honor on us all. Come on, folks. Give our military people a round of applause!" said the M.C.

The entire community gave these men and women a standing ovation. The clapping went on and on. People thumped the bleachers with their feet, the drummers beat their drums, the jingle dancers stamped their feet, and the veterans seemed to stand up a little taller.

Chapter 9

After about five minutes of clapping, the MC said, "Thank you, veterans! Now, are you ready to see some dancing!?" The crowd let out another roar. "Then, let's get this pow-wow underway!"

It was time to get to work.

Chapter 10
Awareness Three

I was waiting in the Maui airport, all checked in, and simply awaiting the boarding of my flight back to Portland. I had taken a small spring break with a few friends, but now it was time to head home. The year was 2003, and I was in my third year of acupuncture training at Oregon College of Oriental Medicine, or OCOM. My trip had been both for pleasure and for work. You see, I was considering relocating to Hawaii to finish school. The reasons were complicated but unimportant. Let's just say that while OCOM had a perfectly stellar program, I was looking for something that delved more deeply into the classical and obscure traditions of Chinese medicine. I was also thinking about where I wanted to be after graduation and Hawaii seemed like the perfect place to recover after the rigors of school.

Any way I look at it, Chinese medicine school is difficult and not for the faint of heart. The rigors of Chinese medicine school are different than Western medicine school, for sure. For one thing, Chinese medicine schools will generally take people who are eligible for student loans and who have a bachelor's degree. It does not have to be a specialized bachelor's degree, like a bachelor's in science. There are also no standardized entry exams that one has to pass to gain entry, but we do have a comprehensive exit exam to obtain national licensure, just as Western medicine schools have. So how could this be difficult? you ask. I would like you to imagine that you are going to learn how to do complicated procedures on people, but all of the instruction and reading material is based in another language and culture. This is the difficulty in learning Chinese medicine. All of the medicine and its theoretical components are taught in a wholly different language and philosophic tradition than most of us in the West are used to. Unfamiliar terms like qi or energy, yin, yang, blood, spirit, etc., are the fundamental building blocks to diagnosis and treatment. All of this is mostly taught to a population of students who, for the most part, have absolutely no experience with Asian philosophies and worldviews. Given these limits, the schools actually do a pretty good job at turning out knowledgeable graduates. However, the understanding of Chinese medicine is often in direct opposition to the tenets and beliefs of Western medicine and Western society in general. This dichotomy can often leave graduates of Chinese medicine schools struggling with their own identity and values. Graduates generally choose to embrace Chinese medicine and make it a part of their way of life, or they choose to amalgamate their core beliefs with Chinese medicine, and throw out that which they cannot believe or understand.

Chapter 10

My experience was perhaps different than other people who have gone into Chinese medicine in the West, as I grew up getting acupuncture from the time I was eight. When I was young, if I was sick or hurt, I was taken to the acupuncturist rather than the pediatrician. In some sense, I was courted with my current understanding from this young age, even before I was found by my master. As an example, one time during my early twenties, I went in to see my family acupuncturist, Hok Pang, who was Chinese. He asked me what I was coming in for, and then had me lie face down on the table. As he inserted the needles, he said, "Roland. Do you believe in ghosts?"

"Sure," I said.

"What would you do if you encountered one?"

"I don't know. Normally, I would think to talk to them, but beyond that, I don't know what I would do," I said. At this point, I was still a veritable novice in the ways of the spirit world.

"What would you say if I told you I'd had a direct experience with a ghost?" he said.

"I would be curious as to what your experience was," I said.

"When I lived in China, during the Cultural Revolution, my family was ostracized by the Maoists, because we were related to the old Qing royalty. When the Maoists took over, they broke up my family, burned all of our certificates of accomplishment and degrees, then took my brothers and sisters and dropped us in the rural areas of China. They left us naked, without clothes and without money or any means of survival."

"I had to survive by my wits and intellect. If I made waves anywhere, I could be rounded up and put in a work camp. So, I learned to disguise myself, and changed my mannerisms, in order to appear to be much older than I am. I did this because no one in any country sees people who are older than sixty as any kind of threat. I did not have a home, and I was essentially a vagrant. I did not have a Work Unit ID card, so I could not work, and because I was not allowed to work, I had to beg for food, or trade my medical knowledge for food. It was a life where I felt I was on the run, and when I could find shelter out of the elements, I often couldn't sleep there long for fear of being caught. My possessions were simply the clothes on my back and what I could carry in my backpack. It was a brutal existence, and I very quickly decided to escape China, somehow."

"One day, I was in a small city, the name is unimportant, and I was walking through what had once been a wealthy neighborhood. All of the houses had red placards on them and red ribbons over the gates. This would be the equivalent of the yellow tape police use here which says "Do Not Enter" on it. It was autumn, and I was cold. I looked in at the houses, longing for a bit of shelter. Entering a house with the red mark on it was breaking the law, but I was already treated as if I had broken the law, although my only crime was being born. Because I had already been judged, I decided I didn't have a whole lot to lose and at least I would be warm for a bit. I threw my backpack over the fence of one of these compounds and told myself that I was now committed. Even though I was 'on the run,' I practiced my martial arts and exercised every day; therefore I was in good shape. I jumped up, caught the edge of the wall with my hands, and pulled myself up, then hopped over. This whole neighborhood was deserted, so I wasn't worried about being seen, but you never knew, because the Maoists had eyes everywhere. I waited an hour in the courtyard to see if there would be anyone coming, but no one came. I made my way to the door and turned the handle. It moved, but the door did not open. I looked around the edges of the door frame and saw that it had been nailed shut. The nails had been applied from the outside; therefore I simply had to move the door inward. I stood in horse stance position, drew up qi from the earth, and leaned into the door with my shoulder applying qi. The door slid off the nails, and opened.

"The house was covered with dust. The door opened into a foyer, with a wall along the right side of the door, and to the left of the door was a receiving room. Beyond the door, about ten paces away, was a stairway leading to the upstairs. I was tired, so I sat down against the wall and decided to take a nap. I would explore the house when I awoke. A couple of hours later, I woke up feeling like I was being watched. The sun had set, but it was not fully dark, and I could still make out the furniture of the room in front of me. Something caught my eye to the right of me, on the stairs. I looked right, and at the top of the stairs was the glowing white form of a young woman who was maybe in her later twenties. The glow she emitted was soft, not blindingly bright. I stood up, focused my yang into my eyes, and stared at her. In a few seconds she disappeared.

"This was not my first encounter with a ghost, nor would it be my last. Ghosts are pure yin; they feed off yang, but if the yang is strong, it is too much for them. Think of this as if in the morning and evening your shadow is longer and darker, but at the peak of the day, your shadow is small and faint. The peak of the day represents yang at its strongest. Ghosts are often benign, but they can be dangerous. It depends what they are trying to achieve. A ghost can infect you and make you very sick as it steals all of your yang qi.

Chapter 10

"I berated myself that of all the houses in this neighborhood, I had to pick the one with the ghost in it. This was another example of how bad my luck was. I sat back down and went back to sleep. A little while later, I woke up again with the feeling of being watched. I opened my eyes and the ghost was halfway down the stairs. When she saw that I was awake, she turned around, glided up the stairs, turned right, and disappeared into a room. I was rested enough now, so I thought I would see where she had gone. I went up the stairs and turned right into a room that looked like it had been a nursery. In the center of the room was a crib with the skeleton of an infant in it. Next to the crib was the skeleton of a woman.

"OK," I said to myself, "this is too much." I left the room, picked up my backpack and put it on. Then I went to the door, opened it, and went to walk out, but something grabbed my backpack. I pulled hard to break the grip, but it held me firm. I leaned into the doorway – still it didn't budge. I started to run and pulled as hard as I could. Then there was a cracking, as the entire frame of the door pulled out and I stumbled into the courtyard. When I looked back, an envelope fluttered down from where the doorframe had been. I walked back over and picked it up. It was not sealed, so I opened the envelope, and read what it said:

" 'My name is Li Yu. The Red Guard are coming. They have already taken the neighborhood to the east of me. My husband was taken months ago, and he never returned. I do not want to be used as chattel, and I have no intention of being away from my newborn child. Today, I have given both of us rat poison. We will die free, and by our own hand. I will take the honor which I can during this time of great suffering. To whomever finds this letter, please deliver it to my family in Shiyan. I would like to say you will be rewarded, but the truth is, if my family are alive, they may not have anything left. The only reward I can offer is my thanks that, by helping me, you will allow my family to know what has happened to me. To my family, do not miss me. I have been brave, and I have been strong. I do honor to our name by not surrendering. I hope that you too have not surrendered. I will love you always. Li Yu.'

"I put the letter into my backpack, hopped over the compound wall and was glad to be leaving that sad place," Hok Pang said.

"Did you deliver the letter?" I said.

"Of course. To not do so would be to invite more bad luck. A few weeks later, I had walked myself to that part of the country. I asked around as to where the family residence was, and slipped the envelope under their door. I didn't want to be there as they read of their daughter's suicide."

"To be clear, did you say that to get rid of ghosts, you focus your yang in your eyes?" I asked.

"Yes. That is one way, when you come across something unexpectedly. If you have more time, you can draw talismans on a long scroll. Then go to the house, unfurl it, step on the end of it, then project your yang to the ends of the scroll and make it flutter like it is blowing in the wind. Wuists or shaman, as well as Daoists, also used something called a coin sword to exorcise evil spirits and demons. This sword consisted of Qian coins from the reign of Emperor Sheng Zu who ruled between 1662 and 1722. The coins are tied with red thread or cord to two iron rods, roughly two feet long. There are about a hundred coins on the sword, or fifty on each side. Then a pommel or handle is crafted to hold the rods. Another common tool for killing evil ghosts and demons was a sword made out of peach wood. Peach was used because it symbolizes immortality. Therefore, because a demon or ghost is not immortal in life, they are warded off by this."

Thirty minutes had passed and Hok Pang began plucking out the needles in order from the top of the body to the bottom.

"Have you used these talismans here, in North America?" I asked.

"I have not. Firstly, because I have not needed to use them here. Secondly, because I don't know if these talismans would work here," he said.

"Why is that?" I asked.

"Because, Roland, one has to think of a talisman as a tool. The tool works because of the energy you put into it – much like a hammer is a tool, but without someone to lift it up, it simply lies there, inert. Therefore, not only do these talismans work because of the energy we put into them, but they also work because of the energy which is imbued in them by a culture, and more importantly the beliefs of a culture, and who that culture worships. In other words, using the talismans of a certain civilization in a place outside of the dominance of that civilization does not always yield results, or at least, not the results that one would expect. It is almost like spirits and demons have a governance or a chain of command. If I want to appeal to or exorcise a spirit or demon, I first figuratively have to know what language it speaks, or what it fears. Then I have to know what celestial organization is in charge of that spirit or demon. Now, I am not saying that if I call on Zhong Kui, who in Chinese culture is a fierce slayer of demons, that he won't respond, but perhaps his power is not as strong in North America, because he is not worshipped here," he said.

"The question one has to ask oneself is: do deities derive power from being worshipped, and is their power limited in places where the deity is not worshipped? Here, in North America, Jesus Christ is worshipped, and the angels of the Christian God are shown great respect, so when I am dealing with a demon or spirit here, would I not be better calling for help from the Christian Pantheon? Lastly, and I can't answer this one, but is our name for Zhong Kui simply another name of the angel Michael or Gabriel, or vice versa? And to get the best results, do I have to invoke the name of the being who deals with these kinds of things from the dominant religious powerbase? One other thing to consider is, does the belief of the person who is being bothered by a demon or a ghost matter? And do I have to work within their belief system, or do I work only from my own belief system? I also can't answer this. So, the simplest way I have to think about this is that I know my yang qi wards off demons and ghosts, but the talismans and words may vary depending on where one is," he said.

"So, you are saying that geography and the demographics of worship matter in the world of energy?"

"I think that this has to be so. In magic, proximity matters. It is much harder or takes more energy to effectively curse someone from far away than someone who is right next to you. Think of this like throwing a ball. If I want to throw a ball a short distance, it takes very little energy, but if I want to throw a ball farther, I have to expend more energy. Sorcerers can enhance their power to "throw" by being on "Dragon lines," or what your culture would call a "ley line," but even this has limits. So, if someone is being cursed by someone in China, it is relatively easy to break this curse because the distance the sorcerer has to overcome is great, and it takes a significant amount of their power simply to maintain the curse. Again using the ball analogy, if the thrower is trying to hit a target from a great distance, they have to be able to aim well, but if the target is moved or obscured after the sorcerer has thrown the ball, they will certainly miss the target. But in a short throw, if the target is moved or obscured, the sorcerer will still likely be able to hit the target, as they can correct their throw while they are throwing. For a curse that is cast from a distance, I simply have to move or obscure the person who is the target, and the curse will not only break, but likely rebound on the caster. It takes a very strong sorcerer to maintain a curse at a long distance, because they have to show up to do spiritual battle if I take the person who is the object of the curse under my protection. In this same way of understanding, I think that when I call for help with my own pantheon of beings from China, their ability to help is less here in North America. I do know, however, that my qi and yang within my body are the same as they are anywhere in the world, so I can always count on my own abilities and what you should remember is: that even though the tools and beings you call on for help may change, the energy within you remains constant."

"I think it is interesting that you wonder whether the names of deities may be called different things in different cultures, but may actually be the same beings," I said.

"This is only common sense. Because each culture has a different language, different cultural mythologies, and different traditions, it would be natural to have different names for spiritual beings. After all there are very few names in any language that are similar to the same name in another language, even for the most mundane objects, let alone spiritual beings. If one believes that there is only one God, regardless of the name that is used for him, her, or it, how many messengers and helpers would that God actually have in totality? Of course there could be an infinite number of helpers, but do you think that the Celestial emperor, as we call God, and the God which the Christians or Muslims call God are different gods? If there is only one God, how could the God of different nations and cultures be different? Lastly, do the names we, as humanity, use for God and his helpers synchronize with the names God uses for his helpers? Would it not make sense that a helper only has one name – that which God gave it, but in the world of humans, we have named that helper in a way which we can pronounce and understand?" he said.

"When you put it like that, it definitely makes sense," I said.

A bell rang.

"That is my next patient. Maybe we can talk about this more on your next visit, Roland," he said.

"I would like that," I said.

"OK. Make an appointment a week from now and we will see where our conversation leads us."

"I will. Thank you for sharing your story of the ghost, Hok Pang," I said.

Chapter 10

"No problem, Roland. You will find that over the course of your life you will come across the unexpected, and when you do, you need to understand the basics of how the world really works. I am glad that I can share my experience, so that you have some knowledge when that unexpected situation finds you," he said.

"Thank you for sharing your wisdom with me," I said.

"OK. See you next week, and Roland, always trust yourself," he said as he left the room.

As you might see, even from a young age, the people around me began teaching me the tools I would use later, even when I didn't know that I was being taught.

"We are now boarding Hawaiian Airlines Flight 305 non-stop direct to Portland, Oregon. Please have your ticket and ID available while boarding," said the voice on the intercom.

I slung my carry-on bag over my shoulder and joined the line by the ticket counter. One by one, the people in front of me showed their IDs and tickets. Compared to my flight here, this plane seemed not to have that many passengers. My turn in line quickly approached.

"Ticket and ID?" said the middle-aged woman taking tickets.

I handed them over.

"Good afternoon, Mr. Pearce," she said. "Did you enjoy your stay in Hawaii?"

"I did. Thank you," I said.

"You are in the emergency exit row. We have a lightly booked flight, so you will likely have the whole row to yourself," she said.

"Great. Maybe after I am done studying for my test, I will be able to stretch out for a nap," I said.

"Just make sure your feet don't hang out into the aisle," she said, smiling.

"Duly noted," I said, smiling back.

"Here you are," she said handing me back my documents. "Have a good flight."

"I hope to," I said. I received my documents and tramped my way down the hallway to board the plane.

The flight attendant as I entered the 747 said, "Watch your head."

"No worries. I am used to planes not being tall enough for me," I said.

As I walked back to the emergency exit row, I noted that there were three seats on either side, and five seats in the middle of the plane with two aisles on either side of the five seats. As I walked down the aisle nearest the door, I realized I was going to be in the aisle opposite the entry door of the plane or on the starboard side. At an opening, I crossed to the correct aisle, and counted rows until I found my seat. I plucked out my test notes from my pack, then stored it under the seat in front of me. People were sitting in various rows, and others were still boarding. A young blond woman sat in my row, but she was in the furthest seat to the left or port side of the five seats in the middle section. Looking forward I counted fewer than fifty people on the plane. "It is a light flight," I thought to myself.

The flight crew generally prepared the plane for flight. One of the pilots came back and talked to the young blond woman for a bit. They knew each other, but I couldn't tell if they were lovers or family. Eventually, the pilot returned to the front of the plane and I looked at my notes in my hand. It was Sunday, I had a test Monday morning on herbal formulas, and it looked like I had a lot to cram into my head. I began to study in earnest, and as is my way, I blocked out all around me.

"We are waiting on one person to arrive at the gate. So, we will have a slight delay, then we will be on our way," said a voice over the loud speaker.

Fifteen minutes or so passed, then the voice on the loud speaker said, "Our final guest has arrived. Thank you for your patience. Flight crew, begin final preparations for departure."

I felt the plane shift slightly as the blocks were removed from the tires. I looked up briefly from my studies to see whether there was anything I needed to observe. What I saw sent a chill up my spine. I could see the naked and bare skull of every single person in front of me, as if someone had replaced the head of every person in front of me with a dried skull

Chapter 10

from a tomb. There was no flesh on any one of these people's heads. I couldn't believe what I was seeing. I blinked, hoping that it was just some trick of my eyes. I opened my eyes, and the skulls were still there. I shut my eyes for five or ten seconds, then opened them again. Yep, still skulls.

"This can't really be happening, can it?" I thought to myself. I looked to my left, and the young blond woman looked normal. I looked back in front of me, and the skulls were still there. An image of the young blond woman and me floating on a round orangish-yellow inflatable raft in the middle of the ocean flashed into my mind.

The real clincher for me was that I started to feel my soul begin to separate from my body, meaning that I began to think of all the connections I had made in my life, and my soul, outside of my conscious mind, was saying goodbye to those connections, as it prepared to leave my physical form. Think of this as a will of sorts, like signing a will that tells your heirs how to dispose of your assets. We all have an energetic will as well. It consists of the work we have left undone and the work which we have completed. The work that is unfinished will need to be completed by someone else, and therefore, as we begin the death process, we let go of that "mission," or task as you will, so that it can be completed by the next person in the line of inheritance. This does not mean that it need be completed by one's family members per se, even though that is often the case. No, it could be willed to someone you have never met, but whom your soul knows from a previous time, and your soul knows that they have already been born. This energetic will feels as if you are shaking off the shackles of your physical body. As I said, this was going on completely separate from my ego, or what I think of as myself. It was an automatic process, which when switched on, simply begins to run on autopilot. The only way to shut this process off is to change what is happening right now, not three minutes from now, or a day from now, or a month from now, because when this process begins, I can assure you, your death is imminent.

"Oh, hell, no!" I said to myself. "I don't know what is going on, but I am getting off this plane."

I grabbed my backpack and rushed to the front of the plane. They were closing the front door as I got there.

"Sir. You need to return to your seat. We are closing the door, and will be taking off shortly," the stewardess said.

"I have to get off this plane," I said.

"What?" she said. "You can't. See, we are closing the door." The door was about one-eighth closed.

"I am sorry. I am getting off this plane," I said as I moved forward to the door. Someone grabbed me by the arm. Sometimes, I thank God that I am a big man, and seeing as how I was full of adrenaline, it was like a fly grabbing me. I stepped through the closing door, bringing the surprised attendant with me.

"Sir! What is going on!?" said a third attendant who had been standing outside the door in the hallway of the ramp.

"The truth is, you wouldn't believe me if I told you," I said.

"Try me," said the third attendant.

"Security! We have a situation at Gate 3. Please come immediately!" I heard the first attendant say into her walkie-talkie.

"On our way!" came the response from the walkie-talkie.

"This plane is going to crash somewhere over open ocean," I said.

"What?!" said the third attendant. "How do you know that?!"

"I know," I said.

Three security guards rushed up.

"What is going on here!?" said a heavyset guard, who looked to be native Hawaiian.

"He says the plane is going to crash!" said the third attendant.

"Why do you believe that?" said a lanky Caucasian security guard.

"As I told this attendant," I said gesturing to the third attendant, "You wouldn't believe me if I told you," I said.

Chapter 10

"You would be surprised at what I believe, so tell me," said the Hawaiian guard.

"I will need your ticket. Did you have any other luggage than your carry-on?" the third security guard, a Hawaiian woman, said.

I fished my ticket out of my pocket and my ID out of my wallet, handed her both, and said, "Only my carry-on."

The female security guard said to the male Hawaiian guard, "I will go pull the manifest." To the third attendant, the woman guard said, "Can you go thoroughly check his seat and row, and make sure to lift the cushions, and check under the seat."

The third attendant waved to the rest of the flight crew to follow her to look at my seat and the rows in front and behind my seat.

As the woman security guard started to walk up the ramp, she said, "Bring him up to the gate."

As we walked up the ramp, the lanky guard said into his walkie-talkie, "Dispatch, can you send a police unit to Gate 3? We have a suspect. He seems cooperative and non-threatening at the moment, but he is big."

"Copy," said the dispatcher's voice on the walkie-talkie.

"I am still waiting to hear why you think the plane will crash …" said the male Hawaiian guard.

"Well, I was sitting in my seat preparing for a test, and I looked up, I don't remember why, but everyone in front of me had a death's head. The only person who didn't was the woman sitting in the same aisle as me. If everyone has a death's head but myself and the woman in the same row as me, this means that something is going to happen to the plane," I said.

"A death's head. What do you mean by that?" he said.

"Meaning, I could see their skull through their head. This means that their death is imminent, as if they are already dead, but no one has told them that yet."

"I see. Are you psychic?" he asked.

"Not generally," I said as we walked into the waiting area of the gate. Two police officers walked up. One was short and stocky with blond hair. The other was tall and thin but muscular, with a bit of a military bearing, and brown hair. "Hey, Jerry. We will take it from here," said the dark-haired officer with a bit of an accent.

"He thinks the plane is going to crash because he could see everyone in front of him as the walking dead," said Jerry, the Hawaiian security guard to the brown-haired officer.

"Have you checked the manifest for extra luggage?" the blond police officer said with a slight Jersey accent.

"Tina's pulling that now," said Jerry.

"OK. We will write this up," said the brown-haired officer.

"OK, Steve," said Jerry.

Jerry and the lanky security guard walked off down the concourse.

"Let's start from the top. What's your name?" Steve asked as the blond officer took notes.

"Roland Pearce," I said.

"What are you doing in Hawaii, Mr. Pearce?"

"I have been on vacation with a few friends," I said.

"What part of Hawaii were you in?"

"I flew in to Kona, was there for three days. Then, I flew to Kauai, and was there for two days. Today, I left my friends on Kauai and flew here to catch this flight back to Portland," I said.

"So you are traveling alone now?" Steve said.

"Yes."

Chapter 10

"Did you check any baggage?"

"I did not."

"What do you do for a living?"

"I am training to be an acupuncturist," I said.

"Do you live in Portland?"

"I do. My address is on my license, or I can tell it to you," I said.

"Please say it, so that we can record it," Steve said.

I stated my address.

"Are your friends still on Kauai?"

"They are."

"May I have their full names?"

"Bonnie Turner and Melia Harcourt."

"Where are they staying?" Steve said.

"At the Hilton at Wailua Bay."

"Room number?"

"I don't know. They moved to that hotel this morning, after I left."

"OK. Tell me why you think this plane will crash?"

"Because, as I explained to the security guard, I saw something which was unprecedented," I said.

"And that was?" Steve said.

"Everyone in front of me had skulls of death's heads rather than their normal heads," I said.

"Did you notice this on first boarding the plane?" Steve said.

"No. Everyone looked normal at that point."

"So, what changed?" Steve asked.

"I don't know," I said.

"Did anything outside the normal happen while you were sitting there?" Steve asked.

"There was a delay, as we waited for a late passenger," I said.

"Did what you 'saw' happen after that?"

"Yes."

"Would you say that you are psychic?"

"Not generally, no. I would not describe myself that way."

"I have pulled the manifest, and he did not have any other luggage. Also the flight crew said that they did not find anything around his seat," said Tina the security guard as she walked up and handed me my ID and ticket.

"OK. Go ahead and give the green light for the plane to take off," Steve said.

"Danny, do you have any other questions?" Steve said to the blond officer as Tina walked, off talking into her walkie-talkie.

"I do. Do you fly regularly?" Danny said.

"A couple of times per year," I said.

"Are you afraid of flying?" Danny said.

"I am not."

"Do you have any phobias, like claustrophobia?"

"I don't."

"Do you have any diagnosed mental illness?"

"I do not."

"Has anything like this happened to you before on a plane?"

"It hasn't. It is my first time."

Danny and Steve looked at each other, then Steve said, "As far as we can tell, you have not committed a crime, and we don't have reason to arrest you. We will simply note this as an oddity. You are free to go."

"You guys seem to make a good team. Maybe one day you will be promoted to detectives," I said with a smile.

"Is that supposed to be funny?" said Danny.

"Just an observation," I said.

"Maybe he is predicting our future, Danny," said Steve with a chuckle.

"I doubt it. Come on Steve. We have more important things to do," Danny said as he turned around and walked away.

"I would advise you not to do this again," Steve said as he turned to walk away.

"Advice taken," I said.

"Well, I have missed my bus," I said to myself. I walked to the representative at the ticket counter and said, "Is there another flight to Portland today?"

"I am sorry sir, there is not."

"Can I use this ticket to get on another flight?" I said.

"Yes sir," she said as she accepted my ticket. "I will need your credit card as well, as there will be a $50 fee to change your flight."

I handed her my debit card. She charged it, then printed me a new ticket. "We will see you back here tomorrow at the same time."

"OK." I said, taking my new ticket. It seemed that I was going to miss my test tomorrow. Hopefully Dr. Wong would be kind and allow me to take it a bit later. However, I had more pressing things to think about, such as an unexpected twenty-four hour layover in Maui. Also, what had I just witnessed? It was real. I had checked and rechecked, and I was sure of what I had seen. There was an urgency to what I was seeing that I don't often experience, as if I were being shown something important. I had that feeling like I get when my "spidey-senses" tingle. No, I could only trust my decision, hope I was right, and move forward.

I sat down in a chair at the gate and called Bonnie. The phone rang a couple of times, and then Bonnie's bleary voice answered, "Hello?" It sounded like she had been crying.

"Hi, Bonnie. It's Roland," I said.

"Roland? Thank God!" she said.

"What's going on?" I said.

"I don't know. After we dropped you off at the airport, both Melia and I started crying, and we couldn't stop. Nothing happened to make us start crying, it just happened and we couldn't stop. Melia said that she felt like one of the lights on earth had winked out. I felt like suddenly there was a void, where before you left that void was not there. What is going on? And where are you? I thought you would be over the ocean by now?" Bonnie said.

"I am not. I am on Maui. I got off my plane," I said.

"Why did you do that?" she said.

Chapter 10

"Everyone in front of me had death's heads, except the person in the same row as me," I said.

"Skulls? You saw skulls on the people in the rows in front of you?! Jesus, Roland!"

"I know," I said. I loved my friends, they knew exactly what I was talking about.

"Then what happened?" she said.

"Who is that?" I heard another weepy voice in the background of the phone.

"It's Roland. He says he got off the plane because he sensed it was going to crash," Bonnie said to Melia.

"Jesus!" I heard Melia say in the background.

"Roland, I am going to put you on speaker, so Melia can hear," Bonnie said.

"OK," I said.

"Then what happened?" Bonnie said.

"I grabbed my stuff and forced my way off the plane. Then security came, and later the police came. I think they thought I had planted a bomb on the plane," I said.

"You're lucky they didn't throw you in some kind of detention cell," Melia said.

"I guess so. I didn't even think of that. I was simply focused on getting off that plane," I said.

"What are you going to do now?" Bonnie said.

"I don't know. I am booked on a flight for tomorrow, but I guess I have to find a hotel for the next twenty-four hours," I said.

"Hold on a second. I have an old friend who lives on Maui. Maybe she would be willing to let you stay with her?" Melia said.

"It's worth a shot," I said. I reached into my pocket and fished out my pen.

"Here's her number," said Melia. I wrote it on my hand.

"Call her. Her name is JoAnne, and she is an old woman who talks to crystals. She has awesome rock magic stories!" Melia said.

"OK. I will do that," I said.

"I am so glad you are OK, Roland," Bonnie said.

"Me, too," said Melia. "I guess we were crying about you, because I don't feel like crying anymore."

"I don't either," said Bonnie. "How is that even possible, that we would both be mourning something which hadn't even happened yet?"

"I don't know," I said. "Maybe it was one of my possible windows," I said.

"Windows?" Bonnie asked.

"Yeah. A possible death in my thread of destiny," I said.

"Possible death?" Melia said.

"Yeah. A window is a possible exit point from life, where a person has an opportunity to make the choice about whether they want to die at that time or not. This is different than the actual 'set in stone' time of death, which we all have. Think of it as being presented with five doors, where you know that door five is the true end of your life. Then doors one to four are other opportunities when you can essentially choose to die early, without the karmic consequences of suicide," I said.

"I have never heard of such a thing," said Bonnie.

"But of course we all have heard of this, Bonnie, just not in this language. Whenever someone says, 'I don't know what happened, but I should have died in X or Y situation,' what they are really saying is that they were presented with a window to die, but a part of them chose not to," I said.

Chapter 10

"I have definitely heard people say that before," said Melia.

"Window or no window, I am glad you are alive," Bonnie said.

"Me, too, Bonnie," I said.

"Call JoAnne and let us know what happens," said Melia.

"I will do that now," I said.

"OK, then we will let you go," said Bonnie.

"OK. Bye," I said.

"Bye," they said in unison.

I hung up the phone, then dialed the number Melia had given me. After a few rings, an older woman's voice said, "Hello?"

"Is this JoAnne?" I asked.

"It is," JoAnne said.

"Hi, JoAnne. My name is Roland Pearce. I am a friend of Melia Harcourt's. I am in a bit of a jam, and she thought you might be able to help me," I said.

"Anything for a friend of my beautiful friend Melia. What is going on?" she said.

"I was supposed to fly to Portland today, but while I was on the plane, I saw the skulls of everyone in the rows in front of me, except the woman in the same aisle as me. So, I got off the plane. Now, I am stuck on Maui for twenty-four hours, and need a place to crash until my plane leaves tomorrow," I said.

"We can definitely take you in for the night, Roland. I live about fifteen minutes from the airport. Meet me at the departures gate under the first sign. I will be in a silver Honda Accord and my daughter will be driving. She has red hair."

"OK. I am tall, have a black vest on, and am wearing a blue baseball cap," I said.

"Great. We will see you soon," she said.

I picked up my pack, walked down the concourse, past the screening area, past the front desks of the airlines, and out into the Maui heat. I found the first sign on the departures level, put my pack down, and waited in horse stance. I definitely needed the grounding right now.

Fifteen minutes later, a silver Honda Accord pulled up with a red-haired woman driving, and an older woman in her seventies in the passenger's seat.

"Roland?" The older woman said through her open window.

"Yep," I said.

"Get in," JoAnne said.

I opened the back door, threw my pack in, then climbed in behind JoAnne.

"On our way down here," JoAnne said, "I called a psychic friend of mine in New Mexico, and told her what you told me. She said that your plane was supposed to crash because it would hit something mid-air over the open ocean. Because you got off the plane, and they took the time to search your seat, the delay which was caused meant that that plane would not be at the same place when whatever it was supposed to hit passed. In other words, the plane was behind in schedule, so it didn't collide with the object it was supposed to. You not only saved all of those people's lives, but you changed all of those people's destinies," she said.

"Huh," I said to myself, "I guess it is true then, that one person can make a difference."

Chapter 11
Awareness Four

I was sunning myself on a bench at the Traditional College of Chinese Medicine of Hawaii (TCMCH) at the beginning of September in 2003. It had been an eventful six months. After finishing my spring semester at the Oregon College of Oriental Medicine (OCOM), I had contacted TCMCH on Kona, the Big Island of Hawaii, and asked if they would take my credits from OCOM so that I could transfer schools. They said they would. I found an apartment in the small community of Hawi, and I set about the process of uprooting my life. I called a trans-continental shipper and asked what the process was to ship my stuff to Hawaii. They said that it would take about six weeks for my stuff to arrive. Therefore, six weeks before I intended to be in Hawaii, I gathered all of my books and things I thought I would need while I was there, packed them in a crate, and shipped them to Hawaii. I then drove my little V4 Toyota truck to Seattle, and had the truck put on a container ship to be shipped to Hilo. Four weeks later, I bought my ticket to Kona, so that I would leave Portland at the beginning of August. I arrived on the Big Island a few days after my stuff had already arrived. I rented a car, drove to Hilo, and picked up my truck and my crate of stuff.

My lease in Hawi was month to month, so after I was semi-settled, I began looking for another place closer to the school, which was in Waimea. By the end of August, I had secured another place to live in Waimea, about a mile from the school, on the dry side. I then moved all of my stuff to this location and worked on getting settled.

I built a temporary desk, set up my computer, then built a bed frame so that it sat over the desk. I then used my desk as a partial footstool to climb into the bed at night. The frame of the bed was built so that the mattress sat about a foot from the ceiling. Now I was settled, and already studying away. TCMCH was a much smaller institution than OCOM, and overall, the program was less rigorous than what I had been used to. This meant that I had quite a bit of free time to meditate, do martial arts, and intensely review what I had already been taught. At this time, the requirements to be an acupuncturist in Hawaii, were merely three years of schooling, the requisite clinical hours, and passing the national boards. This meant that I had already fulfilled the majority of my core classes at OCOM and spent most of my time treating patients under the watchful eyes of my supervisors.

On this day, I had a patient in an hour, so I was soaking up some of that great Hawaiian energy. As I was sitting there, a man walked up and sat down beside me. He was about five foot eight inches or so, Caucasian, husky, and had a shock of black hair.

"Good morning," I said.

"Good morning," he said in a deep and husky voice.

"Are you coming in for treatment?" I said.

"Yep. I have an appointment with Rob in ten minutes," he said.

"Great. Have you ever had acupuncture before?" I said.

"No, but my wife Aurora goes to school here. Maybe you know her?"

"I sure do. Aurora is a great woman. You are a lucky man," I said.

"I am. My name is Elliott," he said holding out his hand.

"Roland," I said giving his hand a shake.

"You're new here, right?"

"I am. I transferred in from the mainland," I said.

"From where exactly?"

"From Portland, Oregon," I said.

"Oh! I love Portland. Not as much as I love this island though. Why did you transfer?"

"I was looking for something different and I wanted to be in a place where I could recharge a bit," I said.

"I think you picked the perfect place for that. The energy on Kona is healing, if Pele doesn't kick you off the island."

Chapter 11

"Pele? You mean the goddess of the volcano?" I said.

"Yeah. She's a real presence here, and if she doesn't like you, you won't last long."

"I will try to mind my P's and Q's and keep my head down then."

"They say that the Islands of Hawaii represent different chakra centers. Kona, for example, is the chakra for the heart," he said.

"Interesting. Do you believe that?" I said.

"Maybe. I have been here fifteen years and I have seen a lot of people come and go. Maybe they leave because they couldn't open their heart to the island energy. Either way, Hawaii has a lot of transients, people who come here for a year or so, then leave. It also could be because people have a hard time making a living here," he said.

"Oh. You would think that there would be plenty of money to be had here," I said.

"There is, but it is all money from tourists. This means that most of the jobs are in the tourist industry, and these don't pay very well," he said.

"What do you do?" I asked.

"I paint houses," he said.

"Do you like it?"

"It pays the bills. Since we pretty much have an endless summer, I can work year-around, except during hurricane season."

"That seems like an ideal profession for this climate. What are you coming in for?" I said.

"I have numbness in my feet. Or, it started in my feet, and has been creeping up. Now, it is in my ankle as well," he said.

"That is odd. Did you have an injury?" I said.

"A few months ago, I fell off a ladder, but I have done that before and never had this happen previously," he said.

"It is an odd sequela of a ladder injury," I said.

"What's your astrology?" he asked.

"I am a Sagittarius," I said.

"I thought so. I am as well," he said. "You know, I don't like doctors or medicine in general, as I am a Christian Scientist, and we believe that prayer should be able to fix all things. But, I like you. I think when I come back in, I will make an appointment with you," he said.

"If you want to," I said noncommittally, as I didn't want to "steal" another practitioner's patient. "Maybe see what Rob can do for you first."

"We will see. Aurora introduced me to him last year at the Christmas party. He is the only person I have met and know something about here. So, I requested him, but he seems a little bit hippy and grungy for me. I am also concerned about whether he is professional or not."

Elliott's concerns were not unwarranted. Rob was known for going out to get high on marijuana prior to treating patients. He had asked me if I wanted to go smoke when I had first arrived, and when I figured out that he was talking about marijuana, which he called Da Kine, I was not only repulsed, but actually went and talked to the president of the school about it. Completely unprofessional and dangerous in my opinion. I heard the president talked to him about it, which meant that Rob avoided me like the plague. Then a few weeks later, news came down from the clinic supervisor that a few patients had contracted lice after coming to the clinic. As the clinic narrowed down the vectors and pored over the schedule, it turned out that all of the infected patients were Rob's patients. The clinic asked Rob to be checked for lice, and sure enough he had then. Apparently, the lice were jumping out of Rob's long hair onto patients. It was utterly disgusting that patients with their own problems had come in seeking help from the clinic, and then caught something from the practitioner.

Rob walked out of the clinic, head bald, and said, "Elliott?"

"Yep," Elliott said.

"I am ready for you now," said Rob.

"OK. Nice to meet you, Roland," Elliott said.

"Nice to meet you too, Elliott," I said.

Rob, as usual, ignored me, and walked back into the clinic. Elliott followed him. An hour later, I was still sitting on the bench, as my patient had been a no-show, when Elliott walked back out.

"How'd it go?" I said.

"I will see you in a week, Roland," Elliott said.

"That bad, eh?" I said.

"Waste of money," said Elliott.

"Well, I hope I am better for you," I said.

"I know that you are. Perhaps, I had to come to this appointment, simply to meet you," Elliott said.

"Perhaps," I said.

"I will make an appointment. See you in a week," he said.

"OK. See you then," I said.

A week passed by. As I get older, I notice that time races by quicker and quicker, whereas when I was younger than sixteen, each day seemed to take forever. Nowadays, a week goes by and it feels like a day. Maybe it is because when you are young, you have yet to be deeply interested in anything particular, or maybe as adults we have too much to do, but the week between Elliott's visit with Rob and when I noticed he was on my schedule for the day, was one of those weeks that passed in the blink of an eye, as they say.

I was sitting in the sun when Elliott walked up.

"I am beginning to think that you spend more of your clinic time in the sun than seeing patients," Elliott said.

"Hey," I said. "I am simply storing up sunshine for when I go back to Oregon. You know we live in perpetual darkness and rain there, right?" I said with a smile.

"Oh. You are filling your sun piggy bank then?" he said.

"Yeah. Hopefully I don't have to smash my body to get all of this energy out," I said with a chuckle.

"That wouldn't be pleasant. How are you doing today?" he said.

"Good. The time just whips by," I said.

"Tell me about it," he said.

"How are you doing, Elliott?" I said.

"Ostensibly, good. Although the numbness in my right foot continues to creep."

"Let's go in the treatment room and officially see if we can diagnose this," I said, standing up. We walked into the clinic and my assigned treatment room. I shut the door and took a seat on the black rolling medical stool, while Elliott sat in a folding chair. I placed a new chart on a clipboard, rolled over and picked up Elliott's chart from the counter. I had pulled it from the patient files before he arrived. I flipped through the file and saw that Rob had not done a thorough intake.

"It looks like Rob didn't ask you as many questions as I would like, so let's start from the top," I said.

"OK," Elliott said.

"Are you having any headaches or dizziness?" I said.

"No."

"Any ringing in the ears, problems hearing, or any other problems with your ears?"

"No."

"Are you having any stiffness of your neck, or other problem with your neck?"

"No."

"Any shoulder pain, or stiffness of your shoulders?"

"No."

"Any chest pain, speeding up or slowing down of your heart, irregularity of your heart beat, or feelings of anxiety?"

"No."

"Any rib-side tenderness, or pain over your liver, here?" I pointed to the right side of my body just below my ribcage.

"No."

"Any pain over your spleen, here?" I pointed to the left side of my body just below my ribcage.

"No."

"Any gastral disturbance, acid reflux, feelings of gas or bloating, or that you don't digest food well?"

"No."

"Any problems processing alcohol or metabolizing pharmaceutical drugs?"

"No."

"Do you use illicit drugs?"

"I smoke marijuana on occasion and I drink beer," he said.

"Any rumbling in your intestines or excessive flatulence?"

"No."

"Any problems urinating, with dripping urination, hesitancy while urinating, problems getting an erection, or premature ejaculation?"

"No."

"Any problems with your bowel movement, such as constipation, diarrhea, or floating stool?"

"No."

"Can you describe your bowel movements for me? How often, color, consistency, and shape?"

"Once a day, brown, formed," he said.

"Long like a log, short, or balls?"

"Like a log," he said.

"Do you have any cravings for sweet, sour, salty, spicy, or bitter?"

"Sweet and spicy, maybe."

"Do you drink coffee?"

"Yes."

"How often?"

"One sixteen-ounce cup a day," he said.

"Would you say that you drink enough water?"

"Yes. About a gallon a day, while I am working."

"Would you say that in general, you are thirsty?" I said.

"No more than what the temperature and my work dictates."

"Do you feel abnormally hot or cold?"

"No."

"Do you have night sweats or spontaneous sweats?"

"Night sweats, occasionally."

"Can you correlate the night sweats to after you have consumed sweet, spicy, or alcohol?"

"I hadn't thought about it, but I can going forward," he said.

"Any tenseness of your legs, tendency to easily sprain joints, or problems with your feet, besides the numbness?"

"No."

"When was the first onset of the numbness in your right foot?"

"About six weeks ago."

"You said that you fell off a ladder at that time? How far did you fall?"

"About eight feet."

"Did you land on your right foot or hit your head?"

"No. I landed on my side."

"Did you injure your ribs?"

"Not that I am aware of."

"Do you feel like the numbness is getting worse?"

"Yes."

"How is it getting worse?"

"It started in the sole of my right foot, and over the past six weeks, the numbness has crept up to about two fingers above my ankle."

"Does anything make it better or worse?"

"No."

"OK. I am going to take your pulse and look at your tongue," I said as I rolled my stool over to him.

"OK."

I placed my first, second, and third fingers just medial to the radial stylus of his right hand, with my third finger in line with the stylus, to feel his radial pulse. His heartbeat was strong and regular. It had a slippery quality to it, meaning that it felt like a small marble which slightly spun as the pulse hit my fingers. I pressed down deeply until my fingers touched his radial bone, then backed my fingers off a bit, so that I was just above the bone. The pulse was consistent. Then I backed off more, so that I would be in about the middle between the surface of the skin and the bone, and felt the pulse here. Then I backed my fingers off more, so that my fingers lay lightly on his skin. The pulse was slippery in each position. I repeated the same procedure on his left radial artery and found this side to be slippery as well.

"Can you open your mouth, relax your tongue as if you were a dog panting and slightly lift your head?"

"OK," Elliott said as he did what I asked.

I picked a small flashlight out of the breast pocket of my lab coat, turned it on, and looked in his mouth. There was a whitish-yellow coating on the back of his tongue, closer to his uvula than to his teeth.

"Can you lift your tongue, so that it touches the roof of your mouth?"

"OK."

His sublingual veins were swollen and enlarged.

"OK," I said.

"There were no red flags for the questions I asked you. Therefore, I will treat you according to the objective signs of your tongue and pulse. You can take off your sandals and lie on the table face up," I said.

"OK."

I stood up, walked to the counter where the needles were kept, and as I picked out packs of single use needles, I thought about what was going on with Elliott. His pulse told me that he was spleen-deficient, as we would diagnose this in Chinese medicine. Yet, according to the answers to his questions, the only thing that matched this was that he craved the sweet flavor. He didn't have any of the usual signs of gas, bloating, distension, or soft stools which would normally indicate a spleen-deficient diagnosis. His tongue told me that he had dampness in his kidneys, which was creating a bit of heat, but again none of his answers to the questions confirmed a kidney diagnosis. Normally, with a diagnosis of dampness in the kidney, I would expect to see urination problems, such as urine retention, burning urination, or hesitancy while urinating. He also didn't have any back pain or soreness of the back which would generally indicate a kidney diagnosis, such as kidney qi or yang deficiency. Was there any other system which I had forgotten to ask about? Ah, there was, but did it matter to this case? Well, to be complete, I would ask.

I turned and looked at Elliott, "I forgot to ask you about your eyes. Are you having any visual disturbance such as floaters, changes in vision, recent near-sightedness or far-sightedness, or any other visual disturbances?" I said.

"It's funny that you ask that. Every now and then I have kaleidoscoping vision," he said.

"You mean like looking out of a kaleidoscope?" I said.

"Yeah," he said.

"And then what happens?" I asked.

"Then, I have a seizure," he said.

"When did this first start happening?"

"About a year ago. I was walking through Hilo, and had this kaleidoscope thing happen with my eyes. Then the next thing I knew I was writhing and spasming on the ground."

"Oh, man. Elliott, does your wife know about this?" I said.

"No. I didn't tell her."

"How many times has this happened?"

"About five or six times," he said.

"When was the last time?"

"About a week ago," he said.

"I think I need to talk to my supervisor. Go ahead and lie there for a minute. I will be right back," I said.

I left my treatment room, and walked down the hallway to the clinic supervision room. Keith, my supervisor for the day, was sitting on a massage table with his back to the wall.

"What do you have, Roland?" Keith said with one eyebrow raised. I usually didn't have to confirm my treatments with Keith. After he had observed a few of my treatment plans when I had first began at TCMCH, he told me that I should think of him more as an advisor than a supervisor. He had told that I was already a skilled-enough practitioner, so I didn't need to consult him about every single treatment. Thus, when I came to consult, he knew to expect something complicated.

"My patient says that he is having kaleidoscoping vision, and then a few moments after that, he has a seizure. This has happened five or six times, with the latest being last week. Initial onset one year ago. Six weeks ago, he began having numbness in his right foot, which has been creeping up his ankle since the initial onset of the numbness. Tongue is whitish-yellow at the root, pulse is slippery in all positions."

"What do you think is going on?" he asked.

"I think he might have a brain tumor," I said.

"Why do you think that?" he said, wanting me to explain my deductive process.

"I asked him the full range of system questions. Nothing stood out until he spoke of the kaleidoscoping vision and then the seizures. None of the viscera would cause a visual change like this. The only thing that would make sense is something pressing on the optic nerve. If he had a clot in his brain, then he wouldn't have a seizure, but a stroke. The numbness in his right foot could be from a stroke, but I have never heard of the damage from a stroke getting progressively worse over time. Usually, a stroke does the initial damage, then that damage remains static unless there is another stroke. He also doesn't display any facial droop or hemilateral or unilateral dysfunction, as a stroke would cause. The tongue tells me that he has dampness, which I would generally attribute to the spleen, but the dampness could be potentially anywhere in his body. A tumor or mass could be considered dampness or phlegm," I said.

"Thorough as always, Roland. Ask him to get an MRI or CT scan as his MD sees fit, and ask him to come back in a week. I concur that this is likely a brain tumor," Keith said.

"OK," I said, then turned around, walked down the hallway, and stepped back into the treatment room.

"OK, Elliott. I think I have a plan," I said.

"OK," he said.

I walked back to the counter, picked up the packets of needles, then walked back to Elliott who was lying face up on the table, and began inserting the needles in the places which I had already selected during his intake. As I did so, I said, "Do you have insurance?"

"I do," he said.

"I would like you to make an office visit with your primary care provider and ask them to do an MRI or CT scan, whichever they feel is appropriate. You need to tell them about the kaleidoscoping vision and the seizures right off."

"Roland, I don't like doctors."

"Do you trust me?" I said.

"I do. You are different somehow," he said.

"Then this is what I think you need to do. I am not saying that you need to accept their form of treatment, but they are the only ones who have the technology to look inside your skull. I think your foot numbness is a symptom of something larger, and until we know what is really going on, I don't think we will make great inroads with your foot," I said.

"I will make an appointment, if you need it to better treat me, but I will only do this for you, because I trust you. I have avoided Western medicine until now, because I don't trust them," he said.

"I know you don't. This will help me rule out and make the best differential diagnosis I can. The better the diagnosis, the more effective I can be with my treatments of you."

"OK," he said.

"I will be back in twenty-five minutes. Close your eyes and relax," I said as I walked to the door, opened it, and gently shut it behind me. I walked back to the clinic supervision room and sat in a chair.

"How did he take it?" Keith said still sitting on the massage table.

"I didn't tell him what I think it is. I asked him to get an MRI or CT scan, though. I don't want to worry him if I am wrong," I said.

"I don't think you are wrong, Roland. However, I agree with your decision. Officially, we are not supposed to diagnose these kinds of things. Better for him to hear it from an MD, and if you are wrong, then he doesn't have a week of anxiety."

"You know, this is Aurora's husband. He hasn't told her about the seizures."

"Oh, man," Keith said. "What do you want to do about that?"

Chapter 11

"Nothing. I can't do anything because of patient confidentiality," I said.

"Of course, but you know it will be a shitshow when she finds out," he said.

"I know. The only thing we can do is be there to comfort her when she does find out, but until then, I think this has to stay between you and me," I said.

"Agreed. The ethical and professional thing is to treat her husband like any other patient, and not as the husband of one of your peers and my student. This happens sometimes, Roland. Our ethics sometimes bind us, as we have to protect our patients' privacy. To not do so would make us hard to trust. You wouldn't believe some of the horrible things I have heard from patients who were also my students, but I still have to show up to class, and treat them the same way I would treat any other student – with no more or less compassion," he said.

"Do you ever feel like the burden we carry as practitioners is too great?" I said.

"Often, but who else can people talk to? If they talk to their friends, their friends judge them, and if what a patient is going through is terrible, and too much, their friends will distance from the patient. If they talk to their family, often the family is either ambivalent, or cares too deeply, which then impairs their judgment. The patient should talk to a counselor, which is the best option, but many people associate mental health therapy with mental health issues, and don't see that going to a counselor can give them the tools to work through their emotional trauma. They could talk to their doctor, but doctors see a new patient every three to five minutes. How can a patient even unpack their issues in that time? They could talk to their barber, their massage therapist, or their bartender, but none of these people can actually help treat their emotional issues. That leaves us. We lie somewhere in between all of the disciplines, yet we use needles and herbs to move these emotional issues out, and thus clear them; this is something that none of the other professions does. Thus, if we don't carry the burden, it doesn't get carried. You will find that this profession is very difficult Roland, and before you retire, you will cry the tears for thousands of patients. You can't save them all, and you have to realize at some point that many patients really have not come to be saved. That is another hard lesson in itself. New graduates think that they can save every patient, but you won't be able to. When you lose your first patient to death, you will awaken to this reality as well. The trick is not to get jaded or feel failure for those you can't help, but find hope in those you can help," he said.

"I don't know what I will do when I lose a patient," I said.

"You will figure it out. You will cry a lot and feel grief. When you lose the ability to cry and feel sad about the loss of a patient or a life, it is probably time to retire. Medicine is a business, but when you lose your moral compass, you are simply a ship adrift. Connect with your patients, bond with them, see them as family, and always work on being more compassionate. If you can't do this, refer them on to someone who can. Then, when a patient passes, feel and grieve, but remember that we do fifty percent of the work, and they do fifty percent of the work. If they don't do their fifty percent, you can't do one hundred percent of the work, as it is impossible for you to do all of the work."

"I understand, Keith, or at least I think I do," I said.

"Good. These are hard lessons and over time we all must learn them and figure out that this is a part of our profession. In a sense, when each patient comes in, we have to assess whether we are helping them transition to a healthier life, or whether we are helping them transition to having an easier death. Ninety-five percent of the people you see will be transitioning to a better life, while about five percent will be transitioning to death. It is these five percent who will make you question why you chose this profession. Lastly, you have to remember that in the end, our profession works best as a mode of prevention, not intervention. We better people's lives by moving them in small increments over time. If there is not enough time, or a patient has a life-threatening illness, we are ethically bound to refer them to our Western medicine counterparts who specialize in intervention, but don't do as well with prevention. This is how we fit within the medical ecosystem. An ounce of prevention is often worth more than a pound of cure, as they say," he said.

I looked at my watch, and noted twenty-five minutes had passed. "I have to remove the needles," I said.

"OK, I am going to go have a cigarette. I will be back in fifteen or so."

"OK," I said as I left the clinic supervision room, walked down the hall, and knocked on the treatment room door, then opened it.

"Is it time already?" Elliott asked.

"It is," I said as I walked to the massage table and began plucking out the needles.

"That went fast," he said.

Chapter 11

"It always does," I said. "How do you feel?"

Elliott sat up, swung his feet to the ground, and took stock of his body. "I feel good. I have a feeling of more energy, and I felt a lot of movement with the treatment."

"Good. Talk to the front desk and make another appointment in a week. In the meantime, try to get to your PCP promptly, and get those tests run, if you would," I said.

"OK. I will. Thanks, Roland."

"No problem, Elliott," I said.

Elliott stood up, slipped on his sandals, opened the door and walked out. I cleaned up the room, threw the packaging for the needles away, changed the sheets on the massage table, then stepped back outside to the bench and resumed sunning myself.

A week later, I was sitting on my bench, soaking up the sun, lightly meditating, and feeling the sun fill up areas of my body that felt like they had been in the depths of a great ocean for a long time. It was not about being cold; it was more as if these areas had not felt the energy of the sun for long stretches of my life. I envisioned the water and damp draining out, to be replaced by the sweet nectar of the golden sunlight. Hawaii is a special place, as the energy of the land is alive and vibrant. This is semi-common in many places in the tropics or on the equator. Some say that the energy is so palpable because Hawaii is the umbilicus of the world. Others say it is because Hawaii is directly opposite the Giza plateau in Egypt. I cannot verify either of these opinions, but I can say that each breath I took in Hawaii seemed to fill me up with energy and recharge my body.

Climate and geography are interesting. The Willamette Valley, where I was born, was referred to as the valley of death by the local tribes, because if they stayed in it too long, they would develop a croupy cough, which could end up being fatal. This is because the Willamette Valley is very damp, with not much sun in comparison to other places. Every place has its own pathology and qi. Think of it simply as a metric of how much sun a place receives. The more sun a place receives, the more yang it is, and the less sun a place receives, the more yin it is. Therefore, a yang climate is more dry, arid, hot, or moist and hot, and there also tends to be more wind in these areas. The ground has a harder time absorbing moisture, or when it does easily absorb moisture, the moisture quickly disappears, like in a desert. A yin climate is damp, rainy, cold, and cloudy. The water easily absorbs into the ground, and the whole environment has a wet quality to it, such as the Pacific Northwest, or a rain forest.

These qualities affect the people who live in yin or yang climates. A more yang climate influences the personality of a person to be more extroverted, more gregarious, less shy, more bold, more angry, more argumentative, more of a leader and less of a follower: in other words, more masculine. A more yin climate influences the personality of a person to be more introverted, more quiet, less outspoken, shy, more passive-aggressive, more restrained, more of a follower and less of a leader: in other words, more feminine. Don't get masculine and feminine confused with the ideas of what a male or female should be, or the roles they should play, as I am speaking about the archetypes of masculine and feminine, which is what yang and yin translate into. Now, the caveat with these characteristics is that all of these qualities are greatly enhanced if you are born in these climates, and influence people more the longer they live there. Thus, if you are born in a sunny place, then move to a cloudy place, and are concerned that your "take-charge attitude" will be affected, don't worry: it will take many years before that happens.

Another factor to consider is the elevation of the place you live. The higher in altitude, the closer you are to the sun. The lower in altitude, the farther you are from the sun. The closer you are to the sun, the more yang the place you live in is. The farther from the sun, the less yang and more yin the place you live in is.

Climate and elevation are important to think about, because maintaining one's equilibrium is fundamental to reducing the possibility of disease. If you understand who you are at the core, you can choose a climate that offsets your negative traits, therefore balancing them, which leads to less chance of disease. Imagine that you have a strong tendency to "fly off the handle" in anger. This anger has created problems in your work, with your partner, and with your children. Regardless of any other factors such as stress, family-of-origin issues, drug and alcohol abuse, etc., if you live in a hot and sunny environment, your anger will be greater. However, if you live in a damp and cloudy environment, your anger will be less. This is because the climate either enhances your negative traits or balances your negative traits. If we know that food can make subtle changes in our body, is it so strange to acknowledge that climate can also create changes in our body? After all, are not climate and food both products of solar activity? Chinese philosophy would say that "all life is yang, while all decay and death is yin."

When one transitions to being in a state of disease, then one has to make greater changes to one's life. This may include changing jobs or letting go of working altogether, cutting off interactions with family or friends who are continual negative influences in our life, understanding and working through one's family-of-origin damage, changing one's habits, looking at one's ongoing emotional process, changing one's diet, changing exercise habits, dealing with stress in alternative ways, embracing some form of belief, etc. But one of the factors which one may also consider changing is what climate one lives in.

Truthfully, these ideas are not far-fetched by any means. For example, it is quite clear that multiple sclerosis is a disease that occurs more frequently in someone who was born north of forty-one degrees north latitude.[17] These people have a three-and-a-half-times higher chance of developing multiple sclerosis than a person who is born south of thirty-seven degrees north latitude.[18] This is believed, at the moment, to be because those who live farther north than thirty-seven degrees north latitude have decreased sun exposure, and therefore a lower absorption of vitamin D. Another opinion is that the gradient of disease is between forty-five degrees north and sixty-five degrees north.[19] According to this view, if someone who lives below forty-five degrees north moves anywhere between forty-five and sixty-five degrees north prior to the age of fifteen, they have a much greater risk of occurrence of multiple sclerosis. It is to be noted that the southern hemisphere has the same level of risk between forty-five and sixty-five degrees south. Lastly, the occurrence of multiple sclerosis is quite rare near the equator.

Another example of this is tuberculosis. It appears that when someone is deprived of sunlight for too long, or if they live in a northern climate, that the resultant vitamin D deficiency reduces the ability of the macrophages to kill the *Mycobacterium tuberculosis* which lives in cells.[20] A common way to treat tuberculosis prior to the 1950s was to send someone who was infected to live in a warmer, dryer climate. It was said that this would help with the cough, but the actual process more likely was that the patient's increased exposure to sunlight increased the vitamin D within the body, thus enhancing the macrophages' effectiveness at killing bacteria within the cells. These are simply two very common, known diseases that are affected by climate. Maybe someday I, Roland Pearce, will write a dissertation on such a thing, that is when I graduate from school and finally have some free time.

---

17. "Latitude is Significantly Associated with the Prevalence of Multiple Sclerosis: A Meta-analysis," Simpson S. Jr. et al. *Journal of Neurology, Neurosurgery, and Psychiatry*. 2011 Oct;82(10)
18. "Temporal Trends in the Incidence of Multiple Sclerosis: A Systematic Review," Alonso, Alvaro and Hernán, Miguel A. *Journal of Neurology*, 2008 Jul 8;71(2)
19. "Spatial Analysis of Global Prevalence of Multiple Sclerosis Suggests Need for an Updated Prevalence Scale," Wade, Brett J. *Multiple Sclerosis International*. 2014.
20. "Effect of Latitude on Seasonality of Tuberculosis, Australia," 2002–2011, MacLachlan, Jennifer H. et al., *Emerging Infectious Diseases* 2012 Nov; 18(11)

"Hey, Roland," Elliott said as he walked up.

"Hey, Elliott. You don't look happy," I said.

"I am not. I went and had the tests you asked for and I received the results this morning. It appears that I have a brain tumor next to my optic nerve," he said.

"Man. I was really hoping it wouldn't be something like this," I said.

"I don't know what to do," Elliott said.

"I will do anything within my power to help you, Elliott," I said.

"Thanks, Roland, I really appreciate that."

"How did the doctors say that they wanted to treat it?"

"They gave me some pills," he said, "but I don't know if I want to take them."

"Did they say what the pills are for?"

"The doctor said that it is chemotherapy and will help reduce the swelling of the tumor."

"Did they talk to you about side effects?"

"Yeah. They basically said that I would feel like death warmed over: nausea, headaches, dizziness, vomiting, upset stomach, lack of appetite, lack of sex drive, inability to focus, etc., etc., etc."

"Have you started taking the medicine?"

"No. I wanted to talk to you first," he said.

"I can't contradict an M.D., Elliott, so you have to do what feels right to you," I said.

"But, do you think I should take them?"

"I think we need to do what we can to reduce the tumor, and if their recommendation is chemo, then I think you should listen to them. Have you told Aurora yet?"

Chapter 11

"No, but she is beginning to be suspicious, as I never go to doctors."

"Elliott, you need to tell her. She is your wife, man!" I said.

"I know, but once I do, you know, I can never put that cat back in the bag. What if it ruins our relationship?"

"If she truly loves you, it won't. On the other hand, if you don't tell her, and have a seizure in front of her, then tell her how long this has been going on – well, that will certainly ruin your relationship."

"Aurora is everything to me. I don't know what life would be like without her. I will suck up my fear and tell her," he said.

"I think that is the best decision, Elliott," I said.

"I appreciate you not saying anything to her, until I have a chance to speak with her. I know you are friends, as I talked to her about my visit with you last week. She said that she thinks you are a good practitioner and knowledgeable," he said.

"It goes without saying that anything you tell me is confidential Elliott," I said. "Shall we go in the treatment room and get started?"

"Yep," he said.

I stood up and walked down the hallway to my treatment room of the day, with Elliott following. We walked through the open door, then I shut it as Elliott sat in the chair. I picked up my clipboard and the chart, then sat down on the rolling chair, and fished my pen from my pocket. I dated the chart, then scratched down what Elliott had already told me.

"Did the M.D. give you a prognosis or a course of treatment?"

"Sort of. They said if the tumor doesn't decrease, then my seizures, kaleidoscoping vision, and numbness will get worse. They didn't say that I would die, but implied that if the tumor continued to grow, I would lose other functions, or perhaps end up paralyzed. It all depends on which way it grows, they said."

"Well, these kinds of things are generally slow growing, so we should have some time to work. Did they offer you any alternative ways of treating this?"

"Yeah, but it is horrible. I don't know if I would be strong enough to do it," he said.

"What was their suggestion?"

"They said that they could remove the top of my skull and surgically remove the tumor," he said with a look of sheer horror on his face.

"That definitely seems like a last resort kind of situation. Let's try not to think of that as an option," I said.

"I agree. If they made any mistake at all, I could essentially be lobotomized. Then my relationship would truly be over, and worse, if Aurora stayed with me after that, she basically would be reduced to being my nursemaid. I don't know how I would be able to stand that."

"Let's think about what we can do right now," I said as I felt his pulses, which had not changed. "I can make some herbs for you which will strengthen your digestion, and help reduce the potential side effects of the chemo such as nausea and vomiting. This will make taking the chemo a little easier, hopefully," I said.

"OK."

"I will also look at potential diet changes that can help reduce the tumor growth."

"OK."

"It goes without saying that you should stop all recreational substances and alcohol."

"I figured as much."

"Until I know more about tailoring your diet, I think it is safe to say that you should cut out all sugar and carbs, and essentially eat a diet of high-quality meat with organic vegetables and fruits. Sugar is a known food which tends to feed cancer, and hence eating it facilitates the cancer's growth," I said.

Chapter 11

"OK."

"My phone number is 503-XXX-XXXX. I want you to call me if you need anything. If you have nausea or vomiting which is uncontrollable, or if you need help and can't get hold of family or friends."

"Thanks, Roland."

"I am hoping that we can manage this with the chemo and Chinese medicine alone, without any more dramatic treatment. If you can afford it, I would like to see you more times per week, like three times per week would be good. I can make up the herbs and give them to you on your next visit," I said.

"I can afford it for a while, but if I am not able to work, then money will start to disappear really quickly. We are in debt, and we owe money to creditors and the IRS," he said.

"If we cross the threshold where you can't afford to come to the school to get treated, perhaps we can work something else out," I said.

"I appreciate that, Roland," he said.

"Let's treat your back today. I want to do a number of points on your scalp, near the top of your neck, and on your back. If you would remove your shoes and take off your shirt?"

"Sure," he said, removed the requested items, then lay face down on the table.

I inserted needles in the places I had chosen, then said, "OK. Take a nap. I will be back in thirty minutes."

"OK," he said.

I picked up the chart, opened the door, and shut it gently, then walked to the clinic supervision room. Keith was sitting on his massage table, his favorite spot. "Is it a brain tumor?" he asked.

"It is. On the optic nerve," I said.

"Congratulations for being a good diagnostician," he said.

"I don't feel very happy about being right," I said.

"Think of it this way," he said, "you were able to use differential diagnosis to identify a condition that an M.D. would generally confirm using an imaging machine. This is something to be amazed about."

"It doesn't seem that amazing. It was simply a product of deduction, eliminating which systems were not affected, looking at the systems which were, and applying the pattern of knowledge of the medicine which is stored in my mind. It is like doing simple arithmetic," I said.

"Sure, but have you ever treated a patient with a brain tumor before?" he said.

"No," I said.

"That sir, is my point. Without any previous experience with a disease, you were able to narrow down the possible diagnosis and predict what the outcome would be. For me, this means that your training has been solid, and that you have integrated this training to become second nature, or part of the operating system of your brain. You should be proud of yourself," he said.

"I don't know if I will ever take pride in being able to diagnose. I would rather take pride in a patient who leaves my treatment room disease-free," I said.

"Well, someday that may happen, but for now, realize that being able to accurately diagnose informs the ability to pick a successful treatment strategy. If your diagnosis is off, your treatment will be ineffective at best and harmful at worst. Students want to think they can misdiagnose, then stick needles in and give herbs, and if they are wrong, there are no consequences. But this is definitely not true. Remember, anything that is strong enough to effect change is also strong enough to effect harm," he said.

"I understand your point," I said. I opened one of the formula books in the room and began looking for formulas that could help Elliott. I knew what I wanted basically, so it didn't take me long to find the formula, then modify it with some other herbs. I then wrote the entire formula as I wanted it to be in Elliott's chart. For this case, I would use bulk herbs, which Elliott would then have to make into a decoction. This required different dosing than using something like a granule or a pill. I calculated out how much raw herb he would have to take on a daily basis, then wrote down the entire weight of the formula based on these figures. Next, I took the combined weight of the formula and divided it into three. Each of these three divisions would be weighed out separately and put into its own bag; thus each bag would contain enough herb to make one decoction and hence three days of preparation per division. Lastly, I calculated how much of each single herb would go into each bag, and wrote this down in the chart next to the formula, so that on weighing the herbs, I could simply put a check next to each herb and quickly move on to the next herb. I looked at my watch and I saw that the thirty minutes had passed.

I stood up, tucked the chart under my arm, and walked down the hallway to my treatment room, gently knocking on the door before opening it.

"OK, Elliott," I said as I began plucking out the needles. "I have a formula designed, and I will have it ready for you on your next appointment. I would like to see you in three days, and please consider what we talked about outside. The medication they gave you may help, but you definitely need to tell Aurora," I said.

"OK," he said. "I will and I will also make an appointment."

I finished removing the needles and said, "That's it."

Elliott pushed himself upright, swung his legs off the table, and stood up. "Oh. I feel a little dizzy," he said.

"That's OK. It is common after lying face down on the table, it will quickly pass. Sit down, put your clothes on, and wait a minute or two," I said.

"OK," he said sitting down.

A minute or two after putting his clothes on, Elliott stood up and said, "You're right, I feel better."

"Good. See you in a couple of days," I said.

"See you then."

Three days later I was getting my requisite vitamin D on the bench outside the clinic when Elliott walked up.

"Hey, Roland," he said.

"Hey, Elliott. How are you doing today?"

"I feel awful," he said.

"Let's talk in the treatment room," I said.

"OK." Elliott followed me into the treatment room and I shut the door.

"What's going on?" I said.

"I started to take the medicine the doctor gave me, and within twelve hours of taking it, I began throwing up. I can't hold food down and I had another seizure yesterday," he said.

"I have your formula made, so hopefully that addresses the nausea and vomiting."

"I also have started having terrible headaches," he said.

"Are you drinking enough water? The headaches could be from dehydration, if you are vomiting a lot," I said.

"No, I have been conscious enough to do that, at least. The biggest problem is that I feel incapacitated. I have had to cancel a number of jobs because I couldn't function."

"Sounds like the side effects of this chemo are terrible. Have you called your PCP and asked them to switch you to a different chemo?"

"No, but I will do that after I see you," he said.

"Did you tell Aurora?"

"Yeah. She didn't take it very well. We cried a lot, and she said she was my wife and that we had to face this together."

"Did you feel relieved by that?" I said.

"In a way, but I also feel like I will be a burden on her. How will she finish school if she is stressed about me?"

Chapter 11

"Aurora will figure that out. This is a small school and I am sure that her teachers will make exceptions for her," I said.

"I appreciate your helping us, Roland. I told her that you knew and that she could talk to you if she needs to. I give you permission to discuss anything we have talked about, with her."

"Of course. I am happy to talk to Aurora, with your permission," I said.

"Can you help me with the nausea and headaches today?"

"Definitely," I said.

"I simply want to feel better. I have been considering stopping the medication," he said.

"Let's see if we can mitigate the side effects with the acupuncture and herbs. Then if that doesn't work, you should probably consult with your PCP before you stop taking the chemo."

"OK. Front or back today?" he said.

"I am going to have you lie face up today."

"OK," he said, taking off his sandals and lying on the table.

"How is the numbness?" I asked.

"Worse. It is up to the base of my calf now. It seems to be moving faster, and I am having a little difficulty walking, because I can't feel my foot and ankle now."

"OK," I said.

"I am definitely not happy about how this is going, Roland."

"I wouldn't be either, Elliott," I said as I opened packs of needles and started placing them in the points I had chosen.

When I was finished, I said, "OK. Take a nap, I will be back in thirty, and I will have your herbs."

"OK."

I picked up the chart, opened the door, and gently shut it, then walked down to the clinic supervision room.

"How is he?" said Keith.

"Suffering. The chemo side effects are bad," I said.

"The herbs will help."

"I know. I hate treating the side effects of drugs with herbs," I said. "It always feels like I am plugging up a hole in a dam with a finger, and then another hole starts leaking."

"Chemo is poison. The basic idea behind it is that by poisoning the body, one can poison the cancer. Unfortunately, for most patients, by the time the chemo has killed the cancer, it has also killed the body. As they say, 'you can win the battle, but still lose the war,'" Keith said.

"I wish that Western medicine would figure out how to bolster the immunity to kill the cancer, rather than destroying the cancer and the immunity with it," I said.

"Someday, maybe. I think Western medicine is still in a pretty barbaric and primitive phase. Someday, it might become more enlightened, but probably not in our lifetime, and certainly not as long as the two main ways of making money in Western medicine are to do surgery or to give drugs. If doctors were paid for healthy patients, and weren't paid for sick patients, meaning that there was no financial incentive in doing surgery or prescribing drugs, then I think Western medicine would become highly focused on prevention," he said.

"I hope money is not the only reason people become doctors. I hope they have a more altruistic reason than money," I said.

"Some do, and some don't, probably. The system creates the problem and the doctors are part of the system. As long as it costs between $200,000 and $500,000 to attend school to become a doctor, there is going to be a financial consideration to their practice.

Chapter 11

Imagine if going to medical school was free for all who wanted to attend, provided that they could meet the requirements. Do you think the doctor would still charge several hundred dollars for a few minutes' consult?"

"I don't know," I said.

"My guess is, if getting an education in medicine was free, we would both have more doctors and a less expensive medical system," Keith said.

"Too much for me to think about Keith. I am just concerned about my patient at the moment and getting through school," I said.

"I understand, Roland. Someday, you will think about this, though, as you watch family, friends, or lovers struggling with mounting debt of medical costs, for something that could be less expensive," he said.

"I guess I will have to think about it at that time, because right now, I don't have any ideas to contribute," I said.

"Call me in thirty years and we can revisit this conversation," he said, chuckling.

"You got it," I said smiling.

I took a seat and picked up a book on the bookshelf called *Neurology for Non-Neurologists*, by Wigbert Wiederholt MD, and thumbed to the pages discussing brain tumors. Before too long, it was time to take Elliott off the needles. I walked down the hall, turned right into the medicinary and picked up his formula, then continued to the treatment room, where I gently knocked on the door. As I opened the door, I said, "OK, Elliott." Then I stepped up next to the massage table and plucked out the needles.

"You can get up now," I said.

"OK," Elliott said. He pushed himself off the table, swung his legs down and stood up. He walked a few feet to the chair, sat down and slipped on his sandals.

I handed him a grocery bag full of herbs, told him how I wanted him to prepare them and how he should split up the doses.

"Thank you, Roland. I appreciate you doing everything in your power to help me," he said.

"Always, Elliott," I said. "See you in three days?"

"Yep," he said.

"OK. See you next time," I said.

"See you," he said, and he walked out the door.

Three days later, I was sitting on the bench, waiting for my appointment with Elliott. The time of his appointment arrived, but he did not come. Twenty minutes into his appointment time, I called his cell phone. No answer. The appointment time expired; still no Elliott. I filled out a no-show slip, tucked it in his chart, and gave the chart to the clinic staff to be re-filed. As I walked into the clinic supervision room, Keith, in his usual place, said, "How did it go?"

"It didn't. Elliott never showed up," I said.

"That's odd," Keith said.

"I know. I called his cell, but there was no answer. Hey. Have you seen Aurora lately? I don't think I remember seeing her around for a few days."

"Now that you mention it, she was absent for the last couple of classes I have taught," he said.

"Weird," I said.

"It's probably nothing," he said.

"Sure," I said.

Three days later, there was still no word from Elliott. I called Elliott and Aurora's house and left a message on the message machine. A week later, I still had not seen or heard from either of them. I was getting a little anxious. It is not unusual for patients to disappear. Usually their disappearance is around the holidays, however, generally most patients will tell you ahead of time that they will not be around.

Chapter 11

Five days later, I called the house again. The phone rang three or four times, then a voice answered, "Hello?" It was the voice of a woman, but it was not Aurora.

"Hello? Is Elliott or Aurora home?" I said.

"Who is this?" said the woman.

"My name is Roland Pearce. I am a student at TCMCH, and I have been treating Elliott here at the clinic, but about two weeks ago he stopped coming to his appointments," I said.

"Hi, Roland. I am Aurora's mother, Nancy. Did no one call you?" she said.

"Call me? About what?" I said as my anxiety ramped up a notch.

"Roland. Elliott died last week," Nancy said.

My breath caught mid-exhale. "What? How did that happen?" I said as my voice squeaked a bit.

"Aurora should really be the one to tell you, but she hasn't been very functional since it happened. Ten days ago, Elliott went to the Honolulu General to have surgery to remove the tumor from his brain. Aurora went with him. The surgeons performed the surgery, removed the top of his skull, then the tumor. They put his skull back together, and the next day he seemed OK – he even talked to his parents on the phone. Then when he hung up with them, apparently he hemorrhaged, and they couldn't stop the bleeding in his brain. He died that night, nine days ago," she said.

"I don't understand. Why was he in surgery?" I said as tears leaked from the corners of my eyes.

I thought to myself, "Elliott had said that he didn't want to go the route of surgery, and he should have had plenty of time before he needed to have surgery, or so my research told me. This doesn't make any sense."

"Aurora told me that she had asked Elliott to do it for her, and Elliott said he would face his greatest fear for her, if that was what she wanted him to do. Aurora found a neurosurgeon who had an opening and they scheduled it," Nancy said.

"Can I talk to Aurora?" I said.

"She is not here. I haven't seen her in a few days. She promised me that she wouldn't harm herself, so I am letting her take her time to come to grip with her loss," she said.

"That is so sad," I said. "Elliott was a great guy, and I was looking forward to helping him manage through this. Sometimes, tumors like this take years to become dangerous …."

"He was a great guy, and he loved my daughter with all of his heart. That is all a mother can ask for her child, is that she find a partner who loves her."

"I just can't believe it," I said.

"Sudden and unexpected death is always the worst, Roland. I will tell Aurora you called," she said.

"Please do, Nancy. Thank you," and I heard the phone hang up on the other end.

I sat there, looking at nothing for hours, tears rolling down my face. I was not sobbing or wailing, simply feeling the loss of a life that seemed to be snuffed out before its time. Then I thought how Aurora must feel hundreds of times worse, than I did. Worse yet, she had asked him to do it, despite his own trepidations and now she had to be feeling guilty. A day turned into two, and two days turned into four days. My routine was constant. Wake up, shower, ride my bike to school, attend class or treat patients in clinic, ride home, do my martial arts, meditate, and study. Day in, day out, four days turned into eight, and eight days turned into two weeks.

One evening, two weeks after I had learned of Elliott's death, there was a knock on the door to my apartment. I was not expecting visitors. In fact, I never had any visitors, as I wasn't very social at this time. I stood up from sitting in front of my computer, walked ten paces to the door, and opened it. Aurora was standing there. She looked small, alone, and disheveled.

"Hi, Roland," she said.

"Hi, Aurora. How are you doing?" I asked.

Chapter 11

"Not so well," she said. "I asked student services for your address. I hope you don't mind?"

"Not at all. Would you like to come in?" I said.

"May I?"

"Of course," I said opening my screen door so she could come in.

She walked a few paces in and looked at my one-room apartment. "Austere," she said.

"I am not really into stuff," I said. "But I have everything I need here. I only have one chair, but we can sit on the floor if you want. Are you hungry? Or would you like a beer?"

"Both, if that is OK? I haven't been eating much," she said.

"I have some stew cooking in my crock pot," I said as I walked to the mini-fridge, took out two Kona Brewing Long Board Lagers and popped the tops off. "Do you need a glass?"

"No. In the bottle is fine. Stew would be fabulous," she said.

I handed her the beer after she had sat down, then plucked two bowls from the kitchen cupboard and ladled out stew for both of us.

"It's hot," I said.

Aurora took a small bit in her spoon, blew on it to cool it down, then stuck the spoon in her mouth. "Oh. It is good," she said. "The meat is so tender."

"That's all the crock pot's doing. I can't take any credit for that," I said smiling.

She took a few more bites of stew, then said, "I'm sorry I didn't answer your calls."

"It's OK, Aurora. I understand that all of this was unexpected."

"It's all my fault," she said with tears forming in her eyes.

"Do you want to talk about it?"

"Not really, but it is all I can think about. I feel so guilty," she said setting her bowl down with the spoon in it, then wiping the tear running down her face with her fingers.

I put my bowl down and walked to the bathroom, which was on the east side of the apartment, opposite the front door. I grabbed a roll of toilet paper, walked back to her, sat down, pulled off about two feet of tissue, and handed it to her, then set the toilet paper down between us.

"Thank you," Aurora said.

"No problem," I said, picking up my bowl of stew and dipping my spoon in for another bite. Aurora cried and I stayed silent, knowing that she would talk when she was ready. My part was to simply be and let her know I was there for her.

"I have been in Hilo for the last two weeks. I didn't want to be at home and I still don't want to be. I see him everywhere in my house and I miss him so much," she said.

I nodded, wanting her to know I heard her, but still creating the space so that she could speak as she needed.

"He really liked you, Roland. He said that he felt better after each treatment and that the herbs you gave him were helping him with the nausea," she said.

"I liked him too, Aurora," I said.

Silence and more tears, then she said, "Are you wondering why we did surgery?"

"A little, but every patient has to make the choices they feel are best for them," I said.

"He didn't want to do it. He said he wanted to give your treatment and your herbs a chance," she said.

"What changed?" I asked.

"Nothing for him. Everything for me. After he told me, I simply wanted it to all go away. I was happy with my life and with my husband the way that he was. I asked him if he would consider getting the surgery. He said that he didn't want a doctor cutting into his head. I asked him if he would do it for me and he said that of course he would do anything for me. I can't believe I asked him to do it for me, even when I knew he was deathly afraid of doctors," she said.

"He bravely told me, I will go wherever you want me to go, and do whatever you want me to do. I called his primary care physician here, and they put me in touch with a neurosurgeon in Honolulu. The neurosurgeon's office said that Dr. Takeda, the neurosurgeon, would be going on vacation for a month, in seven days, but that he did have an opening where he could do the surgery two days before he left. They asked us to come for an initial visit in three days, so that Dr. Takeda could assess Elliott. We gave Dr. Takeda Elliot's doctor's name and number, and I faxed in a patient release of records, so that Dr. Takeda would have the records before we arrived. Two days later, we took an Island Hopper flight to Honolulu, and rented a hotel. The next morning, we showed up at Dr. Takeda's office, and after a stack of paperwork, vitals, and an intake by Dr. Takeda, he concurred that this tumor was on Elliott's optic nerve. He counseled us that these things could take years to grow, and that while the symptoms might get mildly worse, it was likely that nothing would worsen immediately. I asked him if surgery was an option, and he said it was, but that it didn't need to be done right now. I asked him, if Elliott elected to have surgery now, would he do it? He said that of course he would, but he didn't think it was the best first move. I told Dr. Takeda that if Elliott couldn't work, we could quickly be consumed by our debts and that Elliott's contracts were the only thing keeping us afloat."

"Dr. Takeda said he didn't think this was the best reason to move down the path of brain surgery, but he also said that he couldn't argue against Elliott wanting to maintain his contracts. Elliott, my brave man, then said he wanted to pursue surgery as soon as possible. Dr. Takeda said that if we were set on our decision, that he had time to do the surgery in two days. Elliott asked him to schedule us in. We never came home. We went back to the hotel. The next day at 3 p.m. Elliott checked into the hospital to be observed overnight. His surgery was set for 6 a.m. That night, I slept in the hospital with Elliott as he was poked and prodded, measured and weighed. At 4:30 a.m. they came and wheeled him away to prep him for surgery.

"If I were a little less selfish, perhaps I would have seen the writing on the wall. I was trying to hold onto my old life, and I never thought about the consequences if something didn't work out. After all, the neurosurgeon said that often with this kind of surgery, the prognosis can be excellent. Like everyone else in the world, I told myself that the worst-case scenario would not happen to me.

"His surgery went on for eight hours. Rather than doing some form of laparoscopic surgery, the surgeons elected to remove a part of Elliott's skull. The surgery was a success. They removed the tumor and replaced the portion of the skull they had removed. That evening, they allowed me into his room. He looked awful. All of his beautiful hair was shaved off. But he could sit up, and he had his fine motor control. He asked the attendant if he could make a call to his parents. He rang them, told them he was fine, and that the surgery had been a success. His parents, of course, were ecstatic. He hung up with them, gave me the sweetest smile, told me he loved me and then he coded. His brain just started bleeding. They couldn't stop it, and within hours he was dead. It had been six days since he had said he would do this for me. Obviously, with my concern over how his illness would affect our lives, it never occurred to me that he would be utterly wiped from my life," she said sobbing.

"Did you arrange a funeral?" I asked.

"My mom helped me. Elliott wanted to be cremated and have his ashes dropped in the ocean. His parents came, my mom was there and a couple of his close friends. We chartered a boat, floated out into the ocean and dropped his ashes. It was so solemn. After the funeral, I couldn't stay home. I admit, I have been finding my solace in the bottom of a bottle, many bottles in fact. Roland, I don't know what to do. I don't think I can stay in Hawaii without him. Not only would all of this remind me too much of him, but finances will soon trickle down to nothing. I don't know where I will go. I certainly don't think I can focus enough to be in school. I feel like my life has been a windshield, where a month ago, I was protected and could see it all clearly. Now, the windshield looks like someone threw several bricks into it. The windshield is cracked, porous, I can't see out of it, and I know that if one more bad thing happens, the whole thing will shatter," she said. Then she reached out and tore off another two-foot section of toilet paper. She dabber her eyes, picked up her beer, downed it, then picked up her bowl and spooned out a few more bites of soup.

"You are safe here, Aurora," I said.

"I feel safe with you, Roland," she said.

"You can come over any evening that you want, when I don't have a late clinic shift. I generally will have food on and beer in the fridge," I said.

Chapter 11

"I appreciate that, Roland. Do you think that I could come back tomorrow night?" she said.

"Sure. I have a few games around: scrabble, cribbage, cards, that kind of thing. We can eat, drink, play games, and listen to music. In other words, we can have fun. You don't have to share any more about Elliott, if you don't want to, or you can share your memories of him, as you want. The important thing is that you don't have to be alone, and you can grieve in whatever way is appropriate for you," I said.

"Frankly, I am tired of crying. It seems like all I've been doing for the last few weeks. I want to be able to laugh again. I almost feel like I have forgotten how!" she said.

"What time would you like to come over tomorrow?" I said.

"Is 7 p.m. too late? I can be pretty functional in the day, but as it gets dark, and I am home, that is when I feel trapped. The house almost starts to feel like everywhere I go, I see his dead body. I sleep in our bed and I smell him. Maybe at another time it would be comforting, but right now, I simply feel guilty and sad," she said.

"7 p.m. is fine," I said.

"OK. Thank you for opening your home to me, Roland, feeding me, having a drink with me, and listening. I am going to go home, but I will be back tomorrow at 7 p.m.," she said, standing up.

"OK," I said as I stood up.

"Roland? Do you think I can have a hug?"

"Of course," I said as I stepped next to her, put my arms respectfully around her, and drew her in for a hug. She encircled her arms around my ribs and pulled me close to her. She held me like someone who is afraid of drowning clings to something floating by them. After a few minutes like this, she slowly let go. Wiping tears from her face, she reached down tore off more toilet paper, and said, "Some for the road." She smiled a little smile.

"There are smiles hidden in there, see?" I said.

"Maybe I just have to dive deep enough to find the pearls. Thank you, Roland," she said.

"Good night, Aurora," I said.

"Good night, Roland," she said.

She opened the door and closed it behind her. I heard the engine of her car start, and the tires crunched on the gravel as she pulled out. I picked up the bowls, washed them, and put them on the counter. I boiled some water and made a cup of Dragon Well tea. I took the pot out of the crock pot and set it on the counter to cool, then turned off the crock pot. I had enough stew for tomorrow night; I hope Aurora doesn't mind leftovers, I thought. I picked up the bottles and put them in the recycling. Once the kitchen was clean and my tea was steeped, I sat back down at my desk and put in a few more hours of studying before climbing into my bed, which was seven feet off of the floor. I shut my eyes and fell asleep.

The next day, I rolled out of bed, made breakfast, then rode my bicycle to school, had my morning classes and my afternoon of clinic. At the end of the day, I rode home and mused on the education I was receiving at TCMCH. In many ways, this school was not as rigorous as I wanted. It paled in rigor compared to OCOM, which I had transferred from. This is not to say that TCMCH didn't have its own merits, but the professors and staff had adopted more of an "easy-going" approach – not a lazy approach, but more following the thought of "it will get done when it gets done." My approach as a mainlander was much more like "let's get this done and move to the next thing." Compared with the locals, my way didn't really fit in very well. I wanted to have my mind bent in all directions due to rigorous study and copious amounts of relevant information. It is as if I wanted to create a three-dimensional structure with my education, like making an origami flying horse from a piece of colored paper, while in my opinion, my peers were simply content with an education that was like a flat white piece of paper. My desire for a different standard of education chafed against my peers, and in the back of my mind, I began to wonder whether I should reconsider my move to Hawaii.

In most education systems, it is quite common that many classes are taught to the group who could be considered the lowest common denominator. I mean that the teachers tailor their classes, not to the dumbest person, but to the person who has the least amount of knowledge. This allows the lowest common denominators to "catch up," and is a hallmark of public education. Yet, this way of educating is always at the price of people who have more education. This is not about privilege, or about being smarter, but about aptitude. There are always going to be skills which some are better at and skills which some are worse at. The mark of a good teacher is one who realizes that their students have different aptitudes, and the teacher will tailor a class to take these different aptitudes into account. This means more work and more advanced information for those who have a stronger aptitude and less work and less advanced information for those who have a weaker aptitude. In this way, a teacher can continue to challenge the different aptitudes within any given class. When the teacher takes a one-size-fits-all approach, the students with the least aptitude struggle and the students with the best aptitude quickly become bored, quit studying and tend to be more rebellious. In most education models, it is apparent that the teachers are underpaid and overworked. In order for teachers to devise better lesson plans that accommodated students with different aptitudes, they need to be able to teach fewer students and earn a better income. The more secure the teacher feels in their ability to earn, the more energy they will have to invest in their students. The more investment, the better the education. Of course this is why the wealthy often send their children to private schools – to get this very experience. I have often wondered, if teachers made the salary of lawyers and lawyers made the salary of teachers, how would this change our society?

In my situation I was concerned that if I wasn't pushed to excel, it would be all too easy to "go with the flow" of my peers. In my opinion, the cost would be a worsening of my skill as a practitioner, and this was not a price I was willing to pay. In many ways, I had been naive to assume that all Chinese medicine schools would teach the same information. At the moment, there was nothing to do about any of this. All I could do was pray to God to direct me; then I let this train of thought go. I would get an answer at some point, and if I didn't, then I would know that it would be appropriate to stay in Hawaii. As always, I believed that I had been brought to Hawaii to learn something. Perhaps it was simply to meet Elliott, observe the end of his life, and help Aurora through the aftermath. Who knows? Only time would tell.

I arrived home at 5:30 p.m., brought my bicycle in, turned on the crock pot, put the pot in the warmer, and looked at my beer supply. I had ten beers left and that should be more than enough for the two of us. I turned on my computer, sat down, and continued my studying. At 7 p.m., there was a knock at my door. I opened the door and Aurora stood there with a six-pack of Kona Brewing Longboard Lager.

"Hey, Aurora," I said.

"Hi, Roland. I brought beer!" she said, holding up the six pack, smiling.

"Good smile!" I said opening the door for her. As she walked in she handed me the beer.

"For some reason, it seems I have to dive less deep for the pearls around you," she said.

"Are you ready for some fun?" I said.

"I definitely am!" she said.

"How do you feel about leftovers?"' I asked.

"Stew is always better on the second day," she said. "Anyway, 'she who complains about the cooking, has to cook next time,' is what we say in my house."

"Agreed," I said. "Would you like a beer?"

"Please."

I removed two bottles from the six-pack, put the rest in the refrigerator, popped the tops, and handed her a bottle.

"To good cheer!" I said and clinked her bottle.

"To good cheer," she said, and took a drink. "Now, you promised fun. What is the agenda, game master?"

"I have a deck of cards. Do you play gin rummy?" I asked.

"Oh. I love that game!"

"Then, that is the first game on the agenda!" I said.

Every couple of evenings, for a few weeks, this is how it went. Aurora would come over, we would have a couple of beers, play games, talk about our lives, laugh, cry, have dinner, and then she would head home around ten or eleven. It was innocent, and even though she still had moments of grief, overall I watched her mood began to lighten. Then one night, after our usual games and dinner, Aurora changed our flow.

Chapter 11

On this night, around 11 p.m., Aurora said, "Roland, can I sleep here? I don't want to go home tonight."

We had been behaving as friends, so I said, "If you want to. I can give you a pillow, and a few blankets, but all I have to offer you is the floor."

"OK," she said. "The floor is fine."

I took a few blankets and a pillow off my bed and made her a little nest on the floor. "How's that?" I asked.

"That will be great," she said.

"OK. I am going to brush my teeth and change in the bathroom," I said.

"OK," she said.

I went into the bathroom, closed the door, put on some shorts, brushed my teeth, and washed my face, then came back out, leaving the door open. Aurora was already curled up in her nest.

"Are you ready for bed?" I asked.

"Yes," she said.

"OK, I will turn off the light," I said. I walked to the wall, turned off the light, walked back, climbed onto my desk, and crawled into bed. I could hear her breathing begin to slow.

About fifteen minutes later, as I was beginning to drift off to sleep, she said, "Roland? Can you give me a hug?"

"I can," I said.

I crawled down from the bed, lay down next to her and gave her a hug. She clung tightly to me in the dark room. I was facing west with my face towards the bathroom, and she was facing east with her face towards the front door. Again, she clung to me as if she were drowning and I was her buoy. I held her gently, the hug of a friend giving support to another friend. She didn't disengage, and neither did I, so we lay there. The darkness of the room was thick. I could see the light from the electrical power bar and such, but there was not enough light to make each other out, or otherwise see. I was gazing at the darker black rectangle of the bathroom doorway, listening to Aurora breathe and sob a little bit. I closed my eyes for a second, then opened them. In that blink of my eyes, the dark rectangle of the bathroom doorway changed, and upon opening my eyes the dark rectangle had changed to a rectangle of brilliant, pure white light. Framed in the doorway stood a man.

"Roland," I heard my name in my head in the distinctive deep and husky voice of Elliott.

"Elliott," I said in my mind.

"I would like to ask something of you," he said.

"OK," I said.

"I would like to make love to my wife one more time, before I pass on."

"Is that wise, Elliott?" I said.

"Maybe, maybe not, but it is what I want. You said that you would do anything within your power to help me and is this not within your power?"

"It is not quite what I meant, but you are right, it is within my power," I said.

"I will need your permission to take control of your body. I will not linger afterwards. You do not need to fear for your spiritual health. You have great work to do, Roland, beyond this moment of time between Aurora and me. I was given permission to come and ask this of you, but I was not given permission to stay, nor to interfere with your life in any way. I was told that it had to be your choice. It would mean a lot to me, and I know it will mean a lot to her," he said.

Aurora gripped me a little tighter. I knew that she couldn't see Elliott in the doorway to the bathroom. I also suspected, but could not be sure, that she was not party to this conversation.

"Elliott, my concern with this is, what will she think of me? And how will this damage our friendship?" I said.

Chapter 11

"It won't. Even now, you are being called someplace else, as is Aurora. Neither of you will be in Hawaii by the end of the month. As to your friendship, what you have done for my wife will be remembered, and she will always respect you for having helped her, but after tonight, you will not see her again. She will be off the island in a few days and this is why it has to be tonight. When she leaves the island, I will have already been called back to God, and I will no longer be able to walk by her side, as I have been," he said.

"You have been here all along?" I said.

"Of course. I asked her in the subtle ways we have of communicating, to stay with you tonight. You are different than Aurora, though, because you and I can communicate directly. I don't know if that is because of your promise to help, or because of who you are, but I was told that I could communicate with you directly, and that you would hear, and you did."

"This is all odd, but OK, Elliott, I give you permission to use my body for the next hour, and since words have the power to breach the place in between life and death, I will add that you are not allowed to linger beyond the hour, or interfere in my life in the future," I said.

"Do not worry, Roland. Your body will be safe in my hands. I have the utmost respect for you, brother, and I hope that in some future life, we will have the opportunity of really getting to know each other and being friends," he said.

"How does this work, Elliott?" I said.

"Relax. I will only be able to use your body. I will not be able to interfere with your mind. So, once I enter you, I will not be able to use your mouth to speak or communicate. Your will and spirit are currently the driver of your body. When I enter you, I will not displace your spirit, but it will be as if I become the driver and you become the passenger. As the passenger, you will witness, but not be a participant. Then, once I have made love to her, I will leave. Thank you for allowing us this parting gift," he said.

"As you said, 'it is within my power.' I suppose I am as ready as I ever will be," I said.

"Goodbye, Roland. You have many adventures in front of you, and know that God is with you, always," he said. Then he walked the few steps from the bathroom to where I lay and entered my body.

This conversation had taken mere seconds. When he stepped into me, there was a small feeling of warmth and a small sensation of electricity. At the same moment he stepped in, I felt Aurora began kissing my neck. I watched as my hands moved of their own volition. My lips spoke no words, but my eyes looked deeply into her eyes. Her eyes widened slightly, her breath quickened, and I could hear her breath begin to pant.

"Make love to me?" she said.

My hands removed her clothes, then my own. No words left my mouth. The only way it seemed that Elliott had to communicate was with the intensity of my gaze, but it was enough. Aurora's body responded, not as one does with someone one has never made love to, but as intimate partners who have made love so many times that the connection between their bodies was theirs and theirs alone. My hands touched her, and she moaned. As my lips kissed her, I could feel her heartbeat quicken and she inhaled and exhaled in small pants. She grasped my body tightly, and as her body trembled, she said, "Please. I want you inside of me." My body obeyed and my hands placed my penis inside of her.

She looked into my eyes, the intense staring eyes, and she said, "I love you." Then she orgasmed and my body ejaculated into her. I was surprised at the speed of it all. Frankly, I would have expected a longer time of making love on the part of both parties, but the thing about spiritual energy is that it adds a spark of energy to the whole process which acts as its own kind of lubricant. My body lay there with her for a moment, holding her, loving her completely, then I felt Elliott step from my body. I turned my head towards the bathroom and saw the door of light open up. As he reached the doorway he turned, raised his hand towards me, and said, "Thank you Roland." Then the doorway of light closed and he was gone.

We didn't talk, and simply lay there, eventually falling asleep. Around 6 a.m. Aurora got up, thanked me, and left. True to Elliott's prediction, I never saw her again. Also true to his prediction, a few days later, I decided that what I had been called to Hawaii to do, was done. I dismantled my room, packed up my stuff, took incompletes in my classes, and within ten days I was back in Portland. It was all very surreal, odd, and not like anything I had ever done before.

Showing up back in Portland without any advance planning was a bit chaotic, but I had family and friends to stay with, and as it turned out, I would not be in Portland long. Apparently, I had not filled out all of the requisite paperwork prior to leaving OCOM, so the soonest they could readmit me back into their program was in fall, a year from my return from Hawaii. A little sleuthing later, I discovered that Five Branches University in Santa Cruz would accept me into their program as soon as January 10th. That gave me about a month in Portland, and then I moved to Santa Cruz.

Six months later, I was studying in my apartment in the Santa Cruz mountains when my cell phone rang. I looked at the caller ID and didn't recognize the phone number. I answered, and said, "Hello, this is Roland."

There was a pause, then a woman's voice said, "Roland? It is Aurora. From Hawaii?"

"Wow. Hi, Aurora," I said. "How are you doing?"

"I'm OK. Still grieving, but I am living with my sister in Utah, and she is helping me to keep it together. What are you up to?"

"I am in school at Five Branches in Santa Cruz," I said.

"How's that going?" she said.

"Good. I miss Hawaii though," I said.

"Me too. Roland? I told myself I wasn't going to ask you, but I have to know, because it is making me a little crazy," she said.

"Go ahead and ask," I said.

"I just need to know. The night … the night that we made love …. I feel crazy asking this, but the night that we made love, was it you? Or was it Elliott?"

"That was all Elliott. He wanted to make love to you one last time," I said.

"That is what I thought," she said. "I kept telling myself that it was crazy, but I could feel him inside of you. When you looked at me, it made me feel the same way that I felt when I made love with him. It was like I could feel all of that same love emanating from you. It is one of the reasons that I left Hawaii, I didn't know what to do with those feelings that awoke in me after we made love. Only Elliott had ever stirred those deep feelings in me before," she said.

"It's OK, Aurora. He asked to use my body and I let him. It was the most compassionate thing that I could do for the both of you. I am glad that you could feel him. I told him I was concerned that you would think I was taking advantage of you, and he replied that you wouldn't feel that way. That somehow you would know it was him," I said.

"Thank you, Roland. Thank you for telling me. I miss him terribly still, but one day I will get over it. You will be a great practitioner, Roland."

"Thank you, Aurora," I said, then there was a long pause.

"Have a good life, Roland," Aurora said.

"You too, Aurora," I said. Then she hung up.

Never again have I promised anyone that I would do anything in my power for them, as words apparently matter greatly.

Chapter 12
Continuation of The First Law

I drove to work on May 1st, 2017 at 3:00pm, coming down the hill of Highway 26, past the Washington Park Zoo, driving in the middle lane, warily watching for the zigzaggers who have a tendency to cross lanes at high speed when their lane on the left or the right is not going fast enough for them. It is a little like running the gauntlet. You know what I am talking about – all major cities have zigzaggers. Avoiding these crazies, I took the off-ramp onto Market Street, stopped at the red light, then on the green drove one block to Twelfth Avenue and turned left. I drove four blocks, intermittently stopping and going as lights changed from red to green. At Salmon Street I stopped at the red light and looked left and right as I started hunting for the day's parking and my daily tithe to the City of Portland. Down Salmon Street to my right, I saw a crowd gathering a few blocks east of me. As I sat at the light, three white vans with "Portland Police" emblazoned on the side drove past me to the park. Hanging on rails placed on the top of the van and standing on the base boards at the foot of the van were twelve officers per van, bedecked in flak jackets, helmets, batons, and clusters of zip ties hanging off their belts, along with their normal gear.

May 1st, International Worker's Day. This was going to be another crazy day in downtown Portland, it seemed. I hoped it wouldn't make parking a pain. The light turned green, and I watched as hordes of Portlanders headed east from each street I passed to converge on the Park Blocks. I am all about free speech, and the ability to protest, but more often than not, the protests in Portland turned into riots, and well, that was always bad for business. I drove another block and found my tithing spot between Taylor and Yamhill. I paid my tithe, put my ticket in the passenger window, grabbed my bag, and walked to the office. I passed the Mexican cart, where the owner was sitting on the hood of his truck talking on his cell phone. At the Indian cart, I turned right and Harvey, its owner, yelled out, "Hey, Roland! Have a good day at work!"

"You too, Harvey!" I called back.

I walked past the older black gentleman smoking outside the parking garage and we nodded at each other. I turned left, walked north on Eleventh, and turned right onto Morrison. Billy and Marla were outside in their thrones, smoking cigarettes and holding court.

"Good afternoon," I said.

"Hey, Roland," Billy said.

I paused for a second, then said, "What do you think, shitshow today, or no shitshow?"

"Shitshow, I think," Billy said while Marla nodded.

"Yeah. That is what I think too," I said. "I hope my patients don't get blocked by the protest route."

"Freeways are clear," Billy said.

"Yeah, true," I said. I turned left, went into the building, and rode the elevator to the third floor, then walked down the hall to my office, fumbled with my keys, and opened the door. I set my bag down, then went back out the door, walked down the hallway to the bathroom, washed my hands, then walked back to my office, opened the door, crossed the treatment room, and sat in my La-Z-Boy. My patient was scheduled for 3:15 p.m., and she arrived promptly.

"Any problem finding parking?" I said.

"More difficult than normal, but not terrible," she said. "What is going on?"

"May Day protest," I said.

"Well, hopefully we can do this rather quickly, so that I can get on the road and escape downtown," she said.

"Agreed," I said. "I hate being downtown during these things."

"Me, too," she said.

We went through the questions, and I had her lie face-down to treat her shoulder pain. At 4:15 p.m. we were done, she paid and scooted out the door. As she left, I said, "The protest started at 3:30 p.m. It shouldn't be too nasty out there yet."

"I hope so," she said. "See you next week at the same time?"

Chapter 12

"Yep," I said.

"OK. Be safe out there, Roland," and she left.

My next patient was waiting outside the door and walked in after the first patient left.

"Can we make it a quick treatment today?" she said.

"Yep. Story of the day," I said.

We went through the questions, then I asked her to lie face-up in order to treat her for her multiple sclerosis.

"Can we only do a few needles today, Roland?"

"It's your treatment," I said. "You're the boss."

"It feels really chaotic downtown today. I want to get home as soon as possible."

I inserted six needles into her, then sat down to wait the half hour for her treatment to be over. When the time was up, I plucked out the needles, and like the first patient, she paid, booked her next appointment, and scooted out the door. It was 4:55 p.m. and I could hear megaphones, and the bangs of flash grenades.

Curious to see what was going on, I left my office and walked east on Morrison Street. At the corner of 10th and Morrison, I looked south up the slight incline of 10th to see a fire burning in the middle of the street a couple of blocks up. There were a number of police officers attempting to put it out. I walked four blocks east to 5th Avenue, where there was a crowd of people, stoodd on the edge of the crowd, and looked at the chaos. Over the megaphone, I heard the police say, "This is now a riot! Disperse, or be arrested!" Police were using flash bang grenades to move crowds of protestors, and the protestors were throwing Pepsi cans and other things at the police.

"Yep, shitshow," I said to myself.

"It's glorious isn't it?" a voice said from my left.

"What?" I replied, turning to look to my left.

"The chaos. It is glorious," the man on my left said. He looked to be in his thirties, about five foot eight inches tall. He had a light accent which I couldn't place, but what really made him stand out was the white Armani suit he was wearing, complete with a white tie, a white waistcoat, a white pocket square, white Italian leather shoes, and white socks. He was moderately muscled, but not in a body builder way. Without the white attire, he could have been built like any other thinnish person his height. He was particularly handsome for a man, with crystal blue eyes, a perfect nose, and rosy lips that set off his slightly tanned skin.

"That is not what I would call it," I said looking back at the riot. Except now, rather than being chaos, everything was stopped as if I was looking at a still photograph. About ten paces in front of me, I could see a Pepsi can about three feet from an open hand completing a throw. The can, which had been tumbling end over end, was perfectly still in the air. Fifty yards in front of that, I could see the powder leaving a police officer's gun, and a rubber bullet about ten feet in front of the gun, which, had it not been perfectly stopped, was on a trajectory to hit the man who threw the Pepsi can. A flash bang grenade was stopped mid-explosion about twenty-five feet in front of me. It was like being in the middle of a mosh pit, but where everything was simply stopped, and it was utterly silent. To the left and right of me, the crowd was caught in the awkward positions of half ducking while moving away from the grenade, their mouths open in silent yells. Time has simply stopped.

I looked at the man in white and he simply shrugged his shoulders. It appeared that we were the only ones moving.

"Is this you?" I asked.

"Which?" he said. "The time or the riot?"

"Both," I said.

"Just the time, I am afraid, but these are my people, and the kind of show I enjoy best," he said.

"What show?" I said.

"Why man destroying himself, of course."

"I would think this would be beneath you," I said.

"Oh, it is, certainly. Have you ever gone to a movie simply to be entertained by the spectacle? Well, this is my spectacle. Not as fun as those riots in Egypt a while ago, but still enjoyable. Makes me hungry for popcorn. I will go back to doing more important things shortly. The difference between Egypt and here is that everyone thinks Egypt is rotten and corrupt, but this riot is worth savoring, because here is an otherwise 'good and peaceful' city destroying itself through the chaos of the people's making. I didn't even have to push or prod for this, it is free entertainment. Wars and destruction get boring after a while, but this – this is heavenly. It doesn't get much better than watching mankind eat itself," he said.

"So, Trump. Is he your man?" I said.

"Little Donald? No, I can't claim him. He is more like Beelzebub's toy,[21] but really I am just a big fan. A big fan. I love how he calls people who sow chaos 'losers,' but I think you humans have a phrase like the 'pot calling the kettle black?' No, I prefer people like that Bannon fellow, someone who can hold to an agenda. Now, that guy knows how to bring the chaos to the party.[22] You understand, certainly, that the real joy is not making a bad man worse, but to take a good person and corrupt them. That is like American cherry pie, as you might say."

"So, why come and talk to me?" I said.

Satan walked forward through the crowd to the man who had thrown the Pepsi can, and made a slight adjustment to his position while looking at the trajectory of the rubber

---

21. Beelzebub is one of the princes of hell. It is believed that he rules over the sin of pride. Another opinion is that Beelzebub rules over the sin of gluttony. Gluttony often means the over-consumption of food, but it can also simply "mean abuse of." In the *King James Bible, 2 Timothy 3* describes this: "1 This know also, that in the last days perilous times shall come, 2 For men shall be lovers of their own selves, covetous, boasters, proud, blasphemers, disobedient to parents, unthankful, unholy, 3 Without natural affection, trucebreakers, false accusers, incontinent, fierce, despisers of those that are good, 4 Traitors, heady, high-minded, lovers of pleasures more than lovers of God, 5 Having a form of godliness, but denying the power thereof: from such turn away....7 Ever learning, and never able to come to the knowledge of the truth...."
22. In Hebrew, Satan is a noun meaning "the adversary." Ancient writing suggests that he is the great deceiver and the teller of lies. Satan is also known as the divider, in that he attempts to separate the followers of God from God through temptation, chaos, and confusion. As to the hierarchy: Satan directs and Beelzebub follows.

bullet. He then walked to where the grenade was exploding, and gently kicked it towards the crowd. As he walked back, he kept gently kicking the grenade, so that now instead of being twenty-five feet from the crowd, it was now only two feet from the crowd.

"There. That's better. This is so fun! What did you say again?" he said as he walked back through the crowd adjusting them so that they were clearly off balance.

"Why talk to me?"

"Why, because, you can also see it all and you know, sometimes after a movie it is fun to talk about it."

"Surely, you could find one of your minions to talk about this with …" I said.

"I could, but they are all 'yes' minions. They are used to doing what they are told. You, on the other hand, are a 'no' man in my book."

A book appeared in his hands. He thumbed through a few pages, saying, "P, P, P, Pear, Pearce, Yep. See, Pearce, Roland, 'no' man." He held the book out where I could see an ordered list of names with 'yes' man and a box, and 'no' man and a box on the same line as each name. By my name, the box marked 'no' man was checked.

"What? You didn't think we kept lists of who was naughty and who was nice? That Kringle guy is not the only one who keeps lists, you know," he said as he waved his hands and the book disappeared. "Anyway, you being a 'no' man, it makes the discussion more lively."

"You have nothing I want. In fact, you are the task which I am set against," I said.

Satan yawned, then said, "If I had a mortal's soul for every time one of you true believers said that to me, I would be so much closer to ascending my throne in heaven. Anyway, think on your words. You have decades of life left and I am immortal. How much damage do you really think that you can do to me? For every one of my weak peons which you cast out, I have another who is willing to do all that that peon did and more. In a way, I should thank you for weeding out the sick and weak demons, which simply makes my corporation a stronger entity. Call my visit what you like. I just came to enjoy the movie, and you were the only one who was interesting to talk to here," he said.

"I would prefer talking to a wall," I said.

Chapter 12

"OK. Let's change the subject. Have you heard how I was cast out? Let me catch you up on how it really happened," he said.

I crossed my arms and looked straight ahead.

"Would you like me to make it so that you are literally 'all ears'?" he said.

"I can hear you loud and clear," I said.

An iPhone appeared in his hand. "One second. Oh right, there is no time right now, so I will take as long as I want to write this mental note. Maybe we should add a box marked 'trainable' in the list," he said as he typed. "I love Apple products, but of course I would. I love a company that produces products that people learn to rely on, then with every update causes the product to be less and less reliable. Such a great invention, I had to have one. Have you had your iPhone 'brick' yet when it was fully charged and you were in a remote place and couldn't charge it back up? That was my idea. So much fun. Do you mind if I take a selfie with us? Don't worry, you won't ever see it, but I can text it to all of my minions."

"No. I would rather not," I said.

"Too bad. I don't really need your permission, as I have already taken it. That's the great thing about being outside of time. I simply left you in this moment of time, and took a selfie of us in another moment of time, then came back to this moment. See?" he said as he held up the iPhone with the version 666 on it. There was a picture of Satan standing next to me. My arms were crossed, and his hands were behind my head creating devil's horns.

"I am afraid this version of the phone won't be out for a while. Or, maybe it is, just in every single operating system Apple produces. Let me text this out," he said, typing again while reading what he typed. "To Beelzebub, Asmodeus, Mammon, Leviathan, Lucifer, Belphegor, Belial, and Astaroth .... You know, it's hard to manage our texts and emails. You humans have so many names for us. I really can't keep up, and we often get a number of duplicate messages to each other .... Anyway," he said, texting again. 'Look who I bumped into. Yep. Can you believe it? Oh, and WATCHLIST .... You know what that means ....' There. Sent. Belial is our network administrator. He will make sure this gets to the right places. What network? I can see you asking yourself. The Satanic network, of course! What other network is there?"

"Oh sorry, one more text. Actually, you know that I am not really sorry. I love that figure of speech, though. It is like I can say it, and everyone knows that I didn't mean it. Yet, they will then give me permission to do what I want to anyway…." Satan said, then read what he was typing. 'Asmodeus. Is this the guy you and your minion encountered a little bit ago? ….' Really, this time thing is very confusing for us. We tend to use words like a little bit ago, a while ago, and ages ago. So a few weeks ago is like an instant for us. Oh, the difficulties of being immortal and enslaving humans. I breathe in, you are born; I breathe out, you die. It really is all that fast for us."

Satan's phone issued a blood-curdling scream. "Do you like my ring tone? I had to get a minion to repeatedly torture some little man to get that one. So hard to get the timing right. I was like, 'Minion. Wait until I hit record, then chop off the finger.' But no, all it could hear was, chop off the finger. It took us eight tries to finally get the damn thing recorded. Yep, as I thought, Asmodeus says you are the guy he saw. Asmodeus is my prince of porn. He loves to seduce humans into committing adultery and enthrall them with the idea of receiving and administering pain on each other while they fornicate. It is he who whispers the thoughts of lust, jealousy, and violent passion. But of all things that he is involved with, he loves pornography most of all. He says it is the best two-for-one you can get. Make one sexual partner addicted to porn, then have them lose sexual interest in the other partner, or better yet, try to change their partner into becoming a porn star. He loves Portland with all of its many strip clubs. You could almost say he is a patron of the sexual arts. All of those lovely ladies who booze and do drugs while they are stripping love it when he comes in. You know, he is hung like a bull, and he boasts about what he can do with that bull snout of his. Frankly though, I don't know how he texts with those cloven hooves. Sometimes, just for giggles, I turn off his ability to change his form, just because it makes me laugh to watch him struggle to write with those hooves. I gave him an iPhone too, simply because the keyboard is smaller, and it makes it that much more fun to watch. But I digress. So, where was I? Hmmm. Oh yeah, my supposed fall. Do you have the time for my story?" Satan chuckled, then said, "But of course you do!"

> God is a real bitch, you know that? She, yes, I said she, was always micromanaging us. Do this, do that, go here, go there. Of course I was the most beautiful, and my job was guarding the throne, but was she content with that? Hell, no!
>
> It was always, "Satan, the humans are trying to break the fence again. Can you fix it? Satan, can you walk with the humans? I don't have time. Don't look at me like that, I have worlds to create. While you are watching the throne, I am out

creating and building. Satan, I am disappointed in you. You are not meeting my expectations!"

"But God," I would say, "You didn't tell me what you wanted?"

"Satan, you are supposed to know what I want and need!"

"But God, I am not omniscient."

"I don't care," she would say. "Figure it out!" And then,

"Satan, have you told all of the Angels what to do yet?"

"I am working on it, God, but there are a lot of them."

"Well, work faster! I have a million more tasks for you before the sun sets!"

And she meant it. I would have to comfort her when she failed, stroke her hair, rub her ethereal feet, and feed her heavenly chocolate. Then, while I was trying to be the best Seraphim I could, she would start yelling at me, telling me it was all my fault! God never makes linear decisions, she is always all over the place, and I had to simply say, "Yes, God. Whatever you want, God," while continually stroking her ego, telling her, "You are the most magnificent God. You are the most beautiful. All are enthralled by your beauty. Glory to she who is the most high, etc., etc." Do I really look like a "Yes, God" kind of guy to you?

On and on it went. "Satan, the humans are shitting in the orchards again, can you go remind them where they are supposed to defecate again, and please pick up all the shit while you are there. Satan, the humans can't remember how to feed themselves. Can you go and remind them? Oh, and pick up the shit while you are down there. Satan, the human forgot how to talk. Please go and teach them again. Don't forget to pick up the shit."

This went on for millennia. At some point a Seraphim needs a break, you know? And it's not like the trip from heaven was a second away. Anyway, one day I was picking up the shit in the orchards for the millionth time. It's not like you were eating meat at that time, so the shit was all runny and goopy, nasty vegetarian poo. I was walking through the orchards, and there was Eve shitting by a tree.

I said, "Eve! Hey! Get away from there! How many times do I have to tell you? God doesn't want you shitting in the orchards!"

Eve got out of her squat, picked up a fig leaf, wiped, and looked at me like I was ruining her fun. Who knows what goes through these human minds? I watched her walk towards the river, which was twenty paces away, and I noticed that her back side had a nice sway to it as she walked.

"You know," I said to myself, "I think I am going to have a little fun."

I followed Eve to the water and watched her bathe herself. The nipples of her breasts turned into hard little rocks while she was in the cold water. As she walked out, I noticed the sensual slope to her breasts.

"Eve, come here. I want to show you something," I said.

Eve walked over to me.

"Sit down," I said, and she did. Humans were much more compliant back then. "Open your legs, like this," I said spreading my legs and she did as I commanded her.

I reached between her legs to touch her vagina, spread her labia, and moved her clitoris up and down. She moaned a little bit. "Eve, this is your apple," I said.

"Apple," she repeated back to me.

I removed my finger, and said, "Find your apple."

Eve stuck her fingers between her labia and found her clitoris. She poked around a bit, then flicked it with her index finger. "Oh," she said. She flicked it again, "Ah," she said. Then she began rubbing herself in earnest. As she neared climax, she began to say, "Snake. Satan, snake, please. Snake, I want the snake."

What's a Seraphim to do? Now, you know that we are really neither he nor she, but on occasion, when the mood suits us, we could manifest whatever body part we wanted. So I lifted the hem of my robe, as I manifested a thick penis, pointed, and said, "This snake?"

Chapter 12

"Yes. Yes. Yes, Satan, please. Snake, please."

I mounted her, and tore it up a bit, if I do say so myself. Eve's hands were all over me. She couldn't get enough, and frankly having sex with a human actually was quite pleasurable. She climaxed with her hips bucking into me quite hard and fast. It is all quite erotic when I look back on it. As she slowed down, I ejaculated into her.

"Who knew I could ejaculate?" I thought to myself.

We lay there for a second, and then I rolled off of her, knowing that God would come looking for me at any moment. Before I left, I said to her, "Eve."

"Yes, Satan …," she said, hoping, I think that I would enter her again.

"Share your apple with Adam and have him gently bite it. It feels even better than this."

Eve stood up, and said, "Yes, Satan. I want Adam to bite my apple." She then ran naked to find Adam to teach him how to bite her apple.

When I arrived back in heaven, after figuratively taking the slow bus, God said, "What did you do?!"

"I picked up the shit, like you are always telling me to do," I said.

"What did you do after you picked up the shit?!"

"Oh. Well, I talked to Eve. You know, I think it is mostly her shitting in the orchards. She seemed to take a certain pleasure in not following the rules," I said.

"Then what did you do?!"

"Well, I gave Eve the knowledge of her apple."

"And then?!"

"I shook her tree for a bit," I said. "Oh, and I told her to have Adam bite her apple."

"You go too far, Satan!" God said.

"You know, God? You work me to the bone. You never come to bed. I can't remember the last time I knew or mated with a female. All because I constantly work my ass off for you. A Seraphim needs a little rest and relaxation every now and then."

"You ejaculated into her?!"

"Now, I didn't know that could happen. I don't think I have ever ejaculated before," I said.

"Satan! You have tainted Eve. Through sex, she will now know disease of her genitals. She is no longer pure."

"Wait. You are saying she will now have a disease which is transmitted by having sex with me?"

"Yes. She will now manifest warts on her vagina, as a sign of her shame for having sex with you. It will be painful and look like the knobby scales of a snake's head. You have brought this upon Eve!" God said.

"Well, I had fun. I think I will tell Beelzebub and Leviathan that they should give it a try," I said.

"I forbid it!" God said.

"Geez, God. Cut a Seraphim some slack," I said.

Well, as you might guess, God is a wrathful, jealous bitch. From this point on, I was sent to pick up not just the human shit, but all of the animal shit, too.

Michael and Gabriel would make fun of me, saying, "Our most beautiful brother. He used to be the bringer of light. Now he is simply the bringer of shit."

Chapter 12

Oh, that would make me so angry. My pure white robes started to take on a brownish color and I couldn't get the smell of human shit off of me. No matter how much I bathed in the rain, I would still find pieces of shit in my beautiful hair.

A few days after I had sex with Eve, I was in Eden scouring the ground for shit, because if I missed a single piece, God would send me back to find the glop in the veritable haystack of Eden. Anyway, I was in the orchard and I saw Eve peek from a bush at me.

"Eve," I said.

"Satan," she said. She came forth from the bush with Adam behind her. They both looked ashamed, and they were wearing fig leaves over their genitals.

"Adam," I said. Adam looked down. He was always a weak little man. I never understood what God saw in him. You know, I don't really think God created Eve from Adam's rib. I think God took half of Adam's brain, and gave Eve the smarter half of it. Anyway, Adam was lucky I didn't enjoy Eve right there in front of him. If I commanded him to, he would watch and do nothing. That actually would be fun, at least more fun than picking up shit.

"Eve," I said. "Why are you wearing a fig leaf? Take it off." Eve did as she was told, but looked embarrassed doing it.

"Sores, Satan. Around the apple hurts," Eve said.

"Come. Let me look," I said. Eve walked forward to within a foot of me. "Sit," I said. She did. "Open your legs like before," I said. She did. Sure enough, just as God had said, she had warts on her labia trailing down to her perineum. "Adam, come here. Remove the fig leaf and show me your tiny snake," I said. Adam approached, removed the fig leaf, and held his penis in his left hand, so I could look at it. There were warts up and down the shaft of his penis and trailing to his perineum.

"Put your leaves back on and Eve, you can stand up," I said.

Eve pointed at my waist and said, "Your snake?"

"No, I don't have warts, Eve," I said.

"You give me … warts?" she said.

"Yeah. Not intentionally. You can thank God for this gift," I said.

"Satan bad. Satan give Eve warts and blame God!" she said.

"OK. I have had enough of this, I literally have shit to do. Go away," I said.

Anyway Roland, you know the rest of the story. God kicked humans out of Eden, which actually worked for me, as I didn't have to pick up Eve's shit anymore. Then, that jerk Michael threw me and my friends out of heaven. They say that I wanted to overthrow God, and maybe I did, but mostly I wanted to become the Light Bringer again, instead of the shit bringer. That was really the whole point. A day came where I just couldn't take the shit any longer.

God said, "Go to Earth and pick up shit."

I said, "No."

God did her vengeful, wrathful act and said, "You defy your God?!"

I said, "You created things that shit. Why don't you take some personal responsibility for the never-ending shit you created."

Oh, man. She was livid. Lighting and thunder cracked all over heaven, the wind howled as if in a hurricane, and the sun disappeared. All of heaven trembled, and she yelled, "Satan! You will do as I command, or I will cast you out!"

"I will not pick up any more shit!" I said.

She stamped her foot causing a massive earthquake, and screeched, "Michael!"

Of course, Michael was there in an instant.

"Michael! Throw Satan out! Cast him to Earth, so that he smells the stink of human shit forever!" she said.

Michael came over, grabbed me by the elbow, and said, "Now you have done it. You should have just kept picking up the shit."

"You know," I said, "when I am gone, God will need a new shit bringer. Maybe you will be so lucky."

"Not likely," he said. He hauled me to the heavenly gates, and before he shoved me out, he said, "From now on, you will be known as the Lord of Darkness. But we, in heaven, all know that this means you are the Lord of Shit." Then he pushed me out. I fell, and fell, and fell, and yes, sure enough, when I hit the ground, I landed in shit.

"That will be the last time, God!" I yelled at the heavens. "I will raise an army and I will continue to teach your human children to find their darkness within. I will dethrone you one day, and when there are billions of shitters on this Earth, I will make you pick up every single piece!"

I haven't seen that bitch since. Every once in a while, Gabriel and Michael come to rough me up and try to smear shit in my wounds, but I avoid them."

"Dawn Bringer, Teller of Lies. Do you lie to yourself as well?" I said.

"You don't believe me? Well, I was there and you weren't," Satan said.

"I was not, but I see humanity continues to exist and I don't see you having an army with you," I said.

"Oh, I have an army, but they are hungry and would consume all humans if given the chance. So, I keep them in Hell, until I need them. And humanity, sure it continues to exist, but it is more in my image than in God's. I have kept myself busy these last several thousand years," he said.

"I can't deny that I see your presence in the world," I said.

"I control it all. I am making the world great again. I actually do you a great honor by taking selfies with you. Most of your world doesn't get to see me; I send my minions instead. It is hard running the world, but someone has to do it," he said.

"Perhaps, if it is so hard, you should take a vacation?" I said.

"Believe it or not, I do take vacations, but they are often working vacations. I like the Mar-A-Lago at the moment, as all my people tend to stay there. You know, as they say, 'you don't have to control the big dog, if you know what it eats. Keep putting the tasty scraps on the table and eventually all the pigs come to the trough.' I don't need to toot my own horns, but where there is money, power, and influence, there I am."

"Do your patrons understand that your gifts are always tainted?" I said.

"I am sure they do, but as you know from interacting with your fellow humans, people always want something they don't have. I actually have never met a more short-sighted being than a human. We call your species a little short-term, high-yield investment target species, or little shits, as I like to abbreviate it. Catchy, isn't it?" he said smiling.

"Witty," I said disdainfully.

"Everyone in the corporation laughs about it. I think it is funny. Let me explain it to you. Short-term: Not only is your life span extremely short, but humans often can't project themselves beyond their desires. They want to be powerful, wealthy, beautiful, healthy, or famous. They will unabashedly do anything to fulfill their desire. My marketers fill many of the rungs of middle-level bureaucracy, whether in government (war and global instability), Hollywood (sex and drugs), the Fed (currency manipulation – love it!), the banks (more people in debt every day. What's not to love there?), technology (how else would I get my custom phones?), business (a new stripper created every minute in Portland.), etc. Anyway, to get what they want, the deal is simple. I get the part of their soul that is their God light, and in exchange they get my light. This means that when they pray to what they think is God, they get me instead. I really should figure out how to put one of those phone messages: 'Dee Dee Dee. I am sorry, your call to God has been re-routed to the only place your prayer goes – to Satan. Have a shitty day!'"

"You know, your humor is really quite off," I said.

"Really? I admit, it has been a while since I did stand-up at the Improv…." The iPhone was in his hands again. "'Note to self. Pearce thinks humor is off. Convert more comedians. Offer them drugs, prostitutes, happiness, fame, and money. Only come through with the drugs.' Duly noted," he chuckled. "Do you really think I give a shit about what you think? As long as I laugh, that is enough."

Chapter 12

"Anyway, I digress. You really should quit interrupting me, otherwise when I let you out of this time loop, you may spontaneously shit yourself, and you will have to walk back to your office with 'brown robes' as we used to say…. As I was saying, they get my light and hence my influence, and I can bring them into our sister company, the human corporate world.

"They are high-yield, because once we control the steering wheel, we can influence them to do any damage we want. We can cause them to hurt themselves, or to hurt others. I love those guys and gals in the House and Senate of your country. They keep getting elected, but never get anything done. We just keep playing them off of each other. It's like betting on a rigged game – no matter what, we win and humanity loses. I especially love those Christians who want to take rights away from women, make the poor suffer more, deport immigrants, increase military spending, decrease spending on education and social welfare, increase the cost of health care, and eliminate abortion. All of this they do in God's name, but really they do it for their ego, which is all wrapped up in their beliefs. It is funny that they justify these things in God's name – they really should justify it in the name of the one they work for, me. These guys and gals are my star team – everything they do makes humans more vulnerable to me. When a soul is broken, tired, overworked, or addicted, I can send the lowest minion and claim another human soul. 'Thank you, both Democrats and Republicans,' I always say. 'Give me a call when you need more money!' The best thing about these relationships is that when I get a parent, I inevitably get the children, and the grandchildren, and the great-grandchildren, etc. It's part of the deal, you see. I give to you and I take from all that is you, as long as any part of your DNA exists in anyone else you birthed. If that isn't high-yield in a number of ways, I don't know what is.

"Investment. Shall I repeat the part where I consume your whole family for generations? No? Moving on. Targets. Every human who has any light left in them is a target. I will be happy when the only people left are people who are in my corporation, or who are slaves to my corporation.

"Species. As far as that goes, you get your weakness and tiny penises from Adam. Don't blame yourself. Or I could phrase that differently. Thank God for your limitations. Here at club Satan, we thumb our nose at the limitations of God, that bitch."

"You seem to still be upset about all that after thousands of years. Do you get tired of being angry?" I said.

"Not really. As they say, 'Revenge is best served cold,' or for God as a shit sandwich. I would love to see that. Something humans should think about is, when you pray, who do you think you are praying to? Do you want money, beauty, fame, power, influence, a nice house, a beautiful mate, the perfect job, etc.? Who do you think answers those prayers? Do you think God gives a damn about those things? No, she doesn't. It is I who answer those prayers, and if you are mad at God because your life hasn't turned out the way you wanted, all the better for me. Hone that anger, channel it, curse God, and turn away from the bitch! I will give you your dream house, which is a money pit, and will break your finances. I will give you your beautiful and wealthy spouse, who beats the shit out of you when no one is paying attention. I will give you fame, and break your mind with depression, drugs, and lack of privacy. I will give you power, but steal it away when you need it most. I will give you physical beauty, then give you an incurable health condition. I will give you health, but take away all of your family members through violent deaths. I will give you influence, but make you attracted only to little children. I will give you money, and take away your dreams. Any way I look at it, I will answer your prayers and you will get what you want."

"As I said, all that you have to offer is tainted," I said.

"Well, I have wars to attend to, as well as murders, rapes, muggings, and political meetings that need my personal attention. I would love to stay and chat with you, but there really isn't any point. Now, if you would be so kind as to step back ten or twenty paces, that would be excellent. I can't have this grenade going off near you, as I am mildly excited about the challenge you offer."

I stepped back twenty paces.

"Good. When you can see the consequences yourself, you do as you're told." The iPhone was back out, "Pearce. Make consequences obvious," he said as he typed. "You should be good there." Satan walked fifty paces in front of the crowd and picked up the rubber bullet that was hanging in the air ten feet in front of the gun. Then he walked close to the man who had thrown the Pepsi can. "Head, eye, or chest?" he said.

"None of the above," I said.

"OK, finger it is, then," he said as he moved the man's throwing hand up about a foot, to where it would have been if the man had just released the Pepsi can. He then placed the bullet an inch from the man's ring finger. "This is so fun, and frankly I am just not as

Chapter 12

patient as I used to be. This is going to be messy, Pearce – I wouldn't criticize you if you left now," he said.

"You're morbid," I said.

"I am a fallen angel. What do you think we do for fun?" he said, and time started again. The bullet hit the man's finger, completely shearing it off. The finger flew through the air and hit a woman in the face. Blood sprayed over people all around him, while the man screamed in pain. His face went white, and at the same time the people in the crowd who had been adjusted by Satan fell over each other, putting them only a foot from the flash bang grenade. Blood rushed from their ears as the grenade exploded and they tried to cover their ears with their hands. Satan looked at me, gave me a big, toothy grin, and said, "Until next time, Pearce." Then he disappeared. The chaos of the riot hit a crescendo, and I backed away, then walked up the street to my office.

This ends The Coiled Needle – Yin Water: True Stories of a Demonologist: A Novel.

Stay tuned for further adventures of Roland Pearce in The Coiled Needle – Yin Wood.

What? You're still here? It's over. Oh. You say I promised I would tell you about my master? You are right, I did. I suppose I have time for one more tale. But, as you can see, things are dire and the people in the world like myself are few. We have much to do, and our time is short. However, I am a man of my word, and I promised to tell you this. Therefore, you will have to satiate your curiosity on this small, but significant, story.

At the end of spring in 1998, I was asleep in my bed. There was nothing remarkable about this day, or this period of sleep. I simply had finished my tasks for the day and had gone to bed at a not-so-reasonable time, as usual. I was dreaming and then I was aware of the dream – that moment when you are lucid and asleep, but not so deep that you can't remember. I was nowhere, simply floating in time and space. Then he appeared, and the space became dense, forming into a room. I quickly realized that while I was present and aware, I was not the one in control.

"Roland." A middle-aged Asian man stood in front of me. He radiated so much power, it was like liquid gold shined from his body. His eyes were gold, and he had a gold ring over his head. "It is time to set you on your path. I have come to tell you that in two weeks, you will have an injury. It will appear to be grave and devastating, but I have come to tell you that it will not be so. You will recover and there will be no lasting damage. This has to happen, as it is a catalyst to your path in this life. Do not worry, I will be here for you," he said in perfect English.

"What? How will I be injured?" I said.

"I cannot tell you how. It is enough for you to know that this change is coming. Be ready, as your life will change. It is time for you to come back to the fold."

"Who are you?" I said.

"I am a servant of God, and I am the watcher who will train you to be a hammer in the army of God," he said.

"You are my master?" I asked.

"On your world, you give it this definition, but I prefer to call it what it is. I am your older brother in spirit. This time, we will be successful with your training. It has been ordained," he said.

"This time?" I asked. "Have there been other times?"

Post Script

"Our spirits are immortal, Roland, and your destiny and my destiny have been intertwined since the world began. I know you and you will remember me. The time on Earth for the heavenly war is nigh, and soon you will began to be a player in this war. I am with you always. When your hope is crushed and you despair, simply call to me, and I will be there. When the world around you seems the most chaotic, I will manifest my physical form and begin your training in earnest. But for now, I will see you in two weeks. Do not worry, Roland, this is the will of God."

The room exploded in golden light, and I sat up in bed. "That was very odd," I said to myself. "Why do I have to be injured to begin my path? I don't like that at all." I lay back down, then fell into a dreamless sleep.

The next morning the dream was hazy. I could still remember parts of it, but it was all foggy. I climbed out of bed, meditated, made some breakfast and some tea, then went out to the garage to work on my project of the moment. I had been slowly molding an elm limb from its native shape into the shape of a bow. I was doing this using hand tools, or about as primitively as you can do it in this day and age without taking a whole year to do it using stone tools. Bow making is like crafting any other thing: there is a lot of failure, and a little success. One has to observe it as a journey. The beginning and the destination are a lot less important than what is learned in the here and now. I opened the garage door, pulled my chair out, picked up the bow staff, sighted down the staff to figure out where I was going to work next, and started flicking off small pieces of wood. After a while of whittling, I took a wood rasp and smoothed the area I had been working on, then picked up my knife and began flicking more shavings of wood off the staff. Back and forth, I switched between these two tools, careful not to shave off more than was necessary, while staying within the grain of the wood.

The technology of a primitive longbow works because of the growth rings in the wood. Each growth ring provides support to the part of the bow that flexes. A bow staff is roughly shaped out by taking a whole limb, then splitting it in half lengthwise, with the grain of the wood. Thus, one has a staff that is rounded on the back side of the bow (this is the side that faces the target), and flat on the belly of the bow (or the side that faces the user). It is the belly of the bow that receives all of the whittling and carving as one thins the bow. This leaves the growth rings on the back of the bow as complete as possible. Slowly, as one carves and thins the ends (or ears) of the staff down from the center outward, the bow ears will become bendable. When the ears of the bow can bend, then the next step is to figure out how much draw weight one wants to achieve with the bow. The draw weight is a measure of how many pounds of pressure it takes to draw the string back on the bow when it is strung. The draw weight also tells you how far you can shoot an arrow accurately.

The higher the draw weight, the more force the ears will release through the string into the arrow. The greater the amount of force, the farther the arrow will fly and be true; the lesser the amount of force, the less far the arrow will fly. So, for example, a twenty-five to thirty-pound bow would generally be considered a child's bow. A thirty-pound bow can kill, but you have to be closer when you use it. A seventy-five to hundred-pound bow is a common measure for a compound bow. A hundred-pound bow will shoot an arrow that travels at three hundred and seventy feet per second; therefore if one is a hundred yards from a target, the arrow should arrive at the target in one second. Mongolian recurve bows made from horn were said to have a draw weight of one hundred to one hundred and fifty pounds, and were said to be capable of hitting a target a mile away.

When one works with draw weight, then one also has to work at balancing the tension or pounds of force between the two ears. Ideally, these are equal, so if the bow is a forty-pound bow, each ear will carry twenty pounds of pressure. However, often when making bows in a primitive situation, one ear might carry more pounds of pressure than the other. Then the ear that carries more force has to be worked on more than the other ear to, as best as one can, balance the pounds of pressure. Otherwise, there is a high chance that the ear that carries more force will end up breaking the ear that carries less force. Thus, in adjusting the draw weight of a bow, one must make a number of small adjustments and refinements. I had been at this refinement stage with my bow for a few weeks now.

Why was I making a bow, you might ask? Well, practice, of course. I had made ten bows or so, and if one wants to excel at something, one has to keep practicing. As with anything else, one has to do something enough in order to master the principles, and when one has the principles, then one can put that project down and move on to another skill or discipline. I had done the same thing with fire by friction, leather work, bead work, clothes making, the weaving of nets, making and using slings to hunt with, flint knapping, primitive shelter, etc. It was all part of my interest in aboriginal skills, or the skills which "primitive" man had used through several hundred thousand years to not just survive but thrive in harsh conditions. In a way, it was like practicing the skills that are humanity's birthright.

During this time, I also happened to be teaching classes with my friend Aaron on these subjects. Aaron and I had met while studying with Tom Brown, Jr., who is also known as "The Tracker." Tom Brown runs a school in the New Jersey Pine Barrens called Tom Brown's Wilderness Survival and Awareness School, or as it is affectionately called by its students, Tracker School. Tom Brown, Jr. has had an interesting life journey, some of which he has documented in his book titled *The Tracker*. This book was the original spark that piqued my interest in understanding more about nature and its patterns. It also inspired me to study Native tribes and their cultures intensely. One could almost say that making this bow represented the continuity of my life, from my first exposure of reading *The Tracker* with my family at the age of eight, to this time in my life.

Tom Brown emphasizes continuous and regular practice of everything you want to be skilled at, and that this practice should also be carried out in different climates and terrains. Therefore, my days were very similar. I would get up, walk out to the garage and practice a skill. Sometimes I would go gather materials like willow suckers for making baskets, cedar bark for making rope, or occasionally a deer hide would find its way into my hands and I would tan it. None of these was a quick project and they often took a fair amount of time. Luckily, at this point in my life, I had plenty of time.

The days slipped by. One day Aaron and I decided to go to the Woodstock Wine and Deli for a bite to eat, then head over to Mickey Finns to have a pint and go over our course schedule for the next month. Aaron arrived at my house promptly. He was always on time; me, not so much. I was in the garage testing the draw weight on my bow. He pulled into the driveway, got out of his car, and walked into the open garage.

"How's it coming?" Aaron said.

"Slowly," I said.

"Looks like you are pretty even," he said noting how the string was drawn on the tillering stick. A tillering stick is a stick with notches cut into it that allows the bow maker to check how the two ears are bending without drawing the bow. The bow string is tied on the two ears of the bow and is nocked into the notches of the tillering board. By using a tillering board, one can determine where one needs to work an ear to make it bend better and more smoothly. The tillering board can also be used to figure out the draw weight of a bow. One does this by putting the end of the tillering board on a scale, then drawing a finished bow to its full draw. The pounds of pressure that the bow at its full draw applies to the scale equals the final draw weight of the bow.

"Yeah, but it still needs to be smoothed out here, here and here," I said, pointing to marks I had made on the ears, on the belly side of the bow.

"You will get there," he said.

"I know, slowly. The tortoise wins this race," I said.

"Definitely," he said. Aaron had made a number of his own bows, and frankly he was better at it than I was. We can't all be perfect at everything.

I put the bow staff and the tillering board down and said, "Let me go get my notebook, then we can head out."

"OK," he said.

I stood up, walked into the house from the garage, grabbed my notebook which was just inside the door, then walked back out the garage door.

"I am ready. I just need to lock the garage," I said.

"Great!"

I pushed the button for the garage door and watched it shut. As we walked out the side door of the garage, I said, "I can drive man."

"Sounds good," he said.

We walked across the front lawn to my trusty K5 Blazer parked on the street, I unlocked Aaron's door, and he climbed in as I walked around the front of the Blazer and unlocked and opened my own door. I put my keys in the ignition and started her up, then drove down SE 32nd Avenue to the blinking red light. I turned right on Woodstock, then drove a mile or so up Woodstock Hill. At 39th Avenue I stopped at the light. Yes, I said 39th Avenue. I am sure César E. Chávez was a great guy, but to locals, 39th will always be 39th, not César E. Chávez Boulevard, regardless of how many signs the city of Portland posts trying to rename the street. When the light changed at 39th, I continued straight and turned right into the parking lot of the Woodstock Wine and Deli at 42nd Avenue and Woodstock. I parked in the lot, killed the engine and we stepped out of the Blazer.

Post Script

"Did you lock it?" I asked Aaron.

"I did," he said.

"Thanks," I said.

We walked ten paces north and five paces south to enter the double glass doors of the Woodstock Wine and Deli, or just "The Deli" as my family always referred to it. It was 5:30 p.m. As we walked in, Tak, the owner, was sitting at one of the tables with a customer while drinking coffee out of a standard-sized ceramic cup.

"Hey Roland," Tak said as I walked in.

"Hey Tak. How's it going?" I said.

"It's going. Growing old is not for the weak. You young folk will see what I mean someday!"

"Your hip is bugging you again today, I take it?"

"What makes you think that?" he chuckled. "Of course it is, Roland. I am going in for a cortisone shot next week. Maybe that will fix it."

"Maybe it will," I said. "Hopefully, you will get some relief."

"I hope so," Tak said.

Tak and I were old friends. When I was twelve, I used to save up my allowance in summer, then walk up the long Woodstock hill to the Deli to buy a sandwich and a New York seltzer. Before Nature's, Wild Oats, Whole Foods, and New Seasons, the Woodstock Wine and Deli was slinging great sandwiches at a reasonable price. I like to think of myself as one of their original customers. Now, while the Deli does have great food, it is also quite well known for its stellar selection of wines. The entire west wall of the establishment is stacked from floor to ceiling with wine. They offer regular wine tastings to purvey their wares and initiate people's palates to the subtle notes of different wines.

"Are you here to have a bite with Adam?" Tak said.

"I am," I said.

"You know where he is," Tak said.

Adam, my brother, happened to be the chef at the Deli. This was his job as he worked his way through paramedic school. His dream was to become a firefighter, but getting into the fire department in Portland was apparently difficult. If one had an additional skill, such as being a paramedic, it was easier to get an interview.

I walked through the Deli with Aaron following me, past the payment counter, between a deli case holding meat and another deli case holding the salads. Behind the salad case is the sandwich-making station where the guys and girls take your sandwich order. Between these two cases is a walkway that is part of the public space of the Deli. This walkway leads to a ten-by-twelve-foot storage area with a shelf of boxes on the north wall, the bathrooms on the south wall, three steps leading up to a back doorway on the east wall, and the kitchen on the west wall. Thus, as I walked into the storage area, I could pop my head in the kitchen doorway on my right to say hello to Adam.

"Hey, Bro," I said.

"Hey, Bro," he said. "Hey, Aaron."

"Hey, Adam," Aaron said.

"Are you guys grabbing food?" Adam said.

"We are," I said.

"Why don't you put your order in, and you can sit off to the side there while I work," Adam said.

Off to the side meant a small table opposite the storage room where there was another open door and a table for paperwork with a calculator on it. This way Adam could still do his food prep, but we wouldn't be anywhere near his workspace. I think Adam enjoyed the break from monotony when people came to visit. As the Deli's chef, he made all the salads, the soup of the day, and Tak's famous chili. (I would assume that he had other duties, but I am simply noting what I saw him preparing most often.)

"Sandwich?" I asked Aaron.

"Yep," he said.

We walked back out through the storage room, to the deli cases to put in our sandwich order. Chris was the sandwich jockey of the day, and he had his pad and pen ready as we walked up.

"Hey, Roland. The usual?" Chris said.

"How did you know?" I said with a smile. I had my own sandwich you see, on the secret menu. It was called the Brother Roland, and was made with corned beef, pastrami, roast beef, dill havarti, lettuce, tomatoes, pickles, pepperoncini, olives, mayonnaise, and Dijon on sourdough. It was heavenly and I had it every time I went to the Deli. Occasionally, if I was feeling wild, I would switch out the roast beef for ham or turkey, but the corned beef and pastrami had to stay.

"I will also have a pint of the Greek salad, please, Chris," I said.

"No problem, Roland," Chris said as he scribbled my order on his pad. "And for you?" he said to Aaron.

"I will have a Number Two, the roast beef and provolone, please," Aaron said.

"Toppings?" Chris said.

Aaron didn't know the drill as well as I did, obviously.

"Lettuce, tomato, pickles, and onions," said Aaron.

"Condiments and bread?" Chris said.

"Mayonnaise, mustard, and rye please," Aaron said.

"Dijon or yellow?" Chris said.

"Dijon please," Aaron said.

"Whole or half?" Chris said.

"Whole please."

"Anything else?" Chris asked Aaron.

"How about a cup of Tak's chili?" Aaron said.

"Cheese and onions?" Chris asked.

"Both," Aaron said.

When Aaron was done ordering his sandwich, we walked to the cooler to inspect the imported and domestic bottled beer.

"Do you want to split a twenty-two ounce beer, or do singles?" I asked Aaron.

"I don't know. What are you in the mood for?" he said.

"A porter?" I said.

"I think I want something lighter than that," he said.

I picked out a sixteen-ounce bottle of Black Butte Porter, and Aaron reached in the cooler to grab a MacTarnahans Amber Ale. We walked up to the cash register with our sandwich tickets and bottles. Chris stepped over to the cash register, took our money, offered us glasses which we both declined (we are primitive after all), and popped the tops on our bottles. Picking up our bottles, we walked back to the kitchen and sat with Adam while he did his food prep.

"What are you guys up to?" Adam said.

"Working on our class plan for the next month," I said while taking a drink of my porter.

"Breaking down the responsibilities of each lecture, who will talk about what, what skill, and what plant we will cover, etc.," Aaron said.

"How's it coming?" Adam asked.

"We haven't started hashing it out yet, but we will get it done before the end of the night," I said while Aaron nodded.

"Anything else going on?" Adam said.

"Not really for me," I said.

"The usual routine," Aaron said.

"I have the Number Two and the Brother Roland special," announced Chris as he walked into the business side of the kitchen where we were sitting, then placed our food in front of us.

"Thanks, Chris," I said.

"Thanks," said Aaron.

Adam had been peeling cucumbers when we arrived. Now he was deftly chopping them into small chunks.

"Anything going on with you?" I asked Adam before taking a bite of my sandwich.

"I graduate from paramedic school in two days. Well, my last class is in two days, then official graduation is in two weeks," Adam said.

"Congratulations!" Aaron said after swallowing a bite of sandwich.

"Congratulations, bro!" I said.

"I am not done yet, but the light is very clear at the end of the tunnel," he said.

"When do you think you will transition away from the Deli?" I asked.

"Not for a while. I am applying to firefighter positions, but that is going slow, as there are not that many openings. While I am waiting for a position to open, I will probably apply to be a paramedic somewhere. Any way I look at it, it will be awhile before something comes through," Adam said.

"At least you have a plan," I said.

"The initial plan is to finish school first," he said smiling.

Aaron had quietly been eating his sandwich and chili while we were talking. I sipped on my Black Butte and thought about Adam's journey and how it had taken him first to culinary school, and now through paramedic school. Over time, I had watched Adam grow from an undisciplined teenager to a disciplined man. I was proud of my brother, as he had faced the challenges of his life head-on. It had not been a quick process, but he was now relaxed in a way which for most of his life, he had not been. God was watching over my brother, and I could see God's influence, even though Adam and I only rarely spoke of such things.

"What kinds of things do you guys want to teach this month?" Adam asked.

"Fire by friction or primitive fire is high on the list," Aaron said.

"I think moccasin making would be good as well," I said.

"A few plants such as dogbane, dandelion, pineapple weed, nettles, and thistle are likely in there as well," Aaron said.

"How will you set up each class?" Adam asked.

Aaron was done with his food now, so I let him talk while I ate my sandwich.

"We like the idea of teaching one skill and one plant per class. Something like fire by friction will take a couple of classes to teach, so each class we teach will have a different plant. To illustrate this, let's say that fire by friction is broken into three classes, a fire one, fire two, and fire three. In fire one, we might talk about primitive fire and dogbane, then in fire two, talk about primitive fire and dandelion, etc. There are many plants to teach that grow in this area, so the next step is simply deciding which plants to teach, then figuring out what kind of handouts we want to give out to go with the teaching of the skills," Aaron said.

"It sounds interesting," Adam said.

"Primitive skills are the science of how all humans lived for hundreds of thousands of years. There is so much which we can teach," said Aaron.

"How do you think people will use these skills?" Adam asked.

I ate the last bite of my sandwich, swigged the last of my Black Butte Porter, then said, "I think we both hope that through the classes people will engage more directly with the Earth, and become more aware of what is around them all the time. The Earth is bountiful, but the bounty which the Earth produces naturally has to be studied. Hopefully, when people have learned enough, they will see that they are part of nature, and if they are aware and have a few tools in their belt figuratively, I think it is our hope that people will respect nature instead of fearing it."

Aaron swilled the last of his beer and said, "These skills also can let someone feel more comfortable in situations such as being 'lost,' or if there is something like a natural disaster. The skills answer questions like: how does one get water, how does one stay warm, what can one eat, what is a medicine, a tool, or an indicator of other things. For example, if one is lost in the woods and has diarrhea, if one knows how to identify the plant ocean spray, one can find an astringent plant to help with the diarrhea. Or if one finds an area where salal grows, one will generally be able to find Oregon grape, and the root of Oregon grape can be used as an anti-viral or anti-bacterial if one has a fever or other infection. These are relatively simple plants to identify, with no common look-alikes. Having knowledge like this can give one peace of mind when one is in the woods."

"Adam. Do you remember how we went camping with Mom and Dad in the Three Sisters Wilderness when we were kids and we were terribly scared of the woods?" I said.

"Yeah. We always thought Big Foot was going to grab us," he said.

"Imagine if Mom or Dad had known any of these skills and had begun to teach us at a young age, that the wilderness was not something to be afraid of, and instead it had all that we needed within it to be safe and comfortable. Do you think we would have been as afraid as we were, or have dreaded these trips as much?" I said.

"Probably not," Adam said.

"Exactly. We learned what Mom and Dad knew, but it wasn't enough to make us comfortable. These classes aim to address these issues, and hopefully after people have studied with us enough, they can teach their children these skills," I said.

"I can see how that would have really influenced our trips into the woods," Adam said.

"Do you want to head out, Roland?" Aaron said.

"Sure. Good seeing you, Adam," I said.

"You too, Bro," Adam said.

"See you later, Adam," Aaron said.

Aaron and I stood up and walked through the doorway that led to the storage room. I turned my head to look back into the kitchen and over my shoulder said, "We are going up to Mickey Finn's. If you want to come up after work and have a pint, I will buy in honor of your successful graduation from school."

"I might just do that," Adam said.

I took another step and then my sandal caught on something on the floor. Time slowed down as I realized I was going to fall. I pushed out with my arms to try to regain my balance, while looking down to see what I had tripped on. In the middle of the hallway was a rolled-up rubber mat. It had been set down so that the rolled up end faced the kitchen and the width of the mat faced the hallway to the deli counter. My right sandal had somehow perfectly caught on the rolled up end, and I began falling to my right. Now, I admit that tallish people are a bit ungainly, and we often have a much higher center of gravity, which makes us more prone to tripping on things. I can own this, as it has happened all my life. On this day though, it so happened that the Deli, just the day before, had bought a stainless steel cooking hood from a business that had closed, and was intending to install it during the weekend. Meanwhile, it was waiting in the storage room. The part of the hood that would hang over the stove was sitting on the ground, and the plate that ran around the top of the hood, where it would be bolted into the ceiling, happened to be sitting at waist level. The edge of this steel plate was square, like the back side of a kitchen knife. As I pushed my arms out to steady myself, then toppled to the right, it was this edge that my right wrist came into contact with. Because I was falling, my wrist had all of my weight behind it. When my wrist hit the edge of the plate, I hit and then slid down the full length of the cooking hood.

"Ow!!" was my first thought when I regained my balance. It was an "ow" like the feeling of bumping your knee into a door, or running into a door jamb with your shoulder, or hitting your funny bone, meaning it was more like the "ow" that hurts a bit and makes you feel a little stupid, but you can walk it off. Therefore, when I lifted my arm to inspect my wrist, I was utterly surprised that I was looking at a gaping slash in my wrist. My hand drooped as it could not support its own weight and I could see my bones.

"I think I am going to pass out," I said as I took four steps forward to the three steps that led up the back door, sat down, and promptly passed out.

I came to, or maybe it might be better said, as I began to come to, I could feel someone holding my chin up, and someone working on my arm. I was awake, and because someone was holding my chin up, I could feel my head looking up.

"I know that I cut my hand, but why am I blind?" I said to no one in particular, and I truly was blind. "I know that there is a light fixture above me, but I can't see anything." The odd thing was that I was completely calm in saying this. It felt about as normal as someone asking, "Can you pass the salt and pepper? Oh, and by the way, I'm blind."

"Give it a minute, Roland, you have lost a lot of blood," Adam said.

"Whoever is holding my head up, is that really necessary?" I asked.

"Adam told me to hold your head up so that you don't swallow your tongue," Aaron said.

"Well, currently, the tongue seems to be working better than my eyes," I said.

I felt the death grip on my chin disappear. "That's better. Thank you," I said. There was a part of me that knew exactly what was happening. I was in shock and I could literally feel my soul standing beside my body. "I think I am beside myself," I said giggling a bit. Yep, I was a little off.

"Hang in there, Bro," Adam said.

Slowly, so very slowly, my vision started to return. First, I saw the light above me as if I were looking through a pin hole. Then, over about what seemed to be five minutes, my field of vision widened. It all felt like when your foot goes numb, and you have to let the blood flow back into it, but it takes a while for the feeling to return. Well, this was how my eyes felt.

When I could see again, I looked down and it literally looked like someone had slaughtered an animal at my feet. The leg of my jeans where my wrist rested was a solid blood-red; there was no blue to be seen. Under my feet was a large pool of blood that easily stretched three feet from me. Blood was spattered all over the walls and everything in the storage room.

"Tell whoever is going to clean this up that I am sorry for being so messy," I said.

There were four rolls of used gauze on the floor. The fifth roll was currently holding my hand together, apparently. My brother's large Conterra first aid kit was on the floor next to him.

"Hey! Is that the kit I bought you last Christmas? Man, that was good planning on my part," I said laughing.

Adam nodded, intent on cutting cardboard into multiple pieces with an X-Acto knife, then putting the pieces one on top of the other, and doing this on three sides, so as to make a makeshift splint for me.

"Aaron, can you gently lift his wrist by both the arm and hand, so that I can slide this under it? Don't help him, Roland. Just let him do it," Adam said.

"OK," both Aaron and I said.

Aaron gently picked up my arm and hand just enough so that Adam could slide the makeshift splint under it. My fingers fell over the cardboard.

"You have severed a bunch of your tendons, Roland, so don't try to move your hand as we drive to the hospital. Who drove here?" Adam said.

"Roland did," Aaron said.

"Roland, where are your keys?" Adam said.

"Right front pocket," I said.

"OK. We are going to stand you up, Roland. Aaron, hold him up in case he passes out again. Roland, I will get your keys out. OK, let's do it," Adam said.

We all stood up, Aaron held me around my shoulders and on my left side, while Adam reached into my pocket to get my keys.

"Hey, Bro, don't fish around too much," I said, giggling.

"You are pretty funny when you are in shock," Adam said with a straight face.

"I told you, I am beside myself," I said chuckling. "I also get to be your first patient as a paramedic. How cool is that?" I laughed.

"Aaron, we are going to walk him out, but first I am going to get the Blazer, back it up to the door, and open the tailgate so that he doesn't have to walk far. Then we will go to the ER. I will be right back, then when I say, we can move him," Adam said.

"OK," Aaron said.

"I guess this means no more beer tonight," I said to Aaron.

"I think this means no more beer for many nights, Roland and probably no class either."

"Yeah, doing a bow drill fire would be a little difficult now," I said.

Adam came back to the door, "OK, let's move him."

They walked on either side of me, then put me in the back of the Blazer, and had me lie down. Then they got in and Adam put the car in drive.

"We will go to Providence. Don't worry, Bro, we will be there soon," Adam said.

Providence (Sisters of Providence is its full name) is the hospital my family had always gone to, partly because it was a straight shot down 39th Avenue right near Interstate 84. Since we were already almost next to 39th Avenue, it was the closest hospital of any consequence.

We started moving. Frankly, from this point on, it all gets a little hazy. We arrived at the hospital, Adam advocated for me, and the next thing I knew I was being prepped for surgery. When I woke up post-surgery, my hand was all wrapped up. I think I was on morphine, but I don't remember. I just knew I didn't have any pain.

When I was aware, after the drugs from surgery wore off, a doctor walked into my room.

"Hi, Roland, I am Dr. Michael. I am your surgeon. How are you doing?"

"I feel good," I said.

"Good. We are going to monitor you for a few hours, and if all goes well, we will discharge you tonight. I will tell your family that they can come in to visit with you," he said.

"OK," I said.

"You will be in this splint for six to nine months. I will want to see you every three weeks or so," he said.

"OK," I said.

Dr. Michael left the room and a few minutes later Adam, Aaron, and my mom walked in.

"Hey, guys," I said.

"Hey, Roland," they said.

"What was the final diagnosis?" I asked.

"The surgeon said that you severed eleven of the thirteen tendons that run through the lateral side of your wrist. You also cut through all the major veins, but didn't cut any arteries. Lastly, you cut halfway through your ulnar styloid," Adam said.

"Go big or go home," I said with a chuckle.

"You went big all right," Aaron said.

"I called Hok Pang and he said to have you come in next week," my mom said.

"Thanks, Mom. I am feeling sleepy and am going to crash for a bit. If the surgeon needs anything else, can you guys document for me? I don't think I will be able to write for a while with my right hand …" I said.

"We are on it," Adam said.

A while later, I woke up and heard Dr. Michael saying, "I have a nurse bringing in a wheelchair. If he starts to bleed, have him elevate his hand. If he bleeds a lot, call me." Dr.

Michael handed my mom his business card. "I will see you for your first appointment in a week, Roland. Your mom can call and make the appointment."

"OK," I said groggily.

A nurse arrived with the wheelchair, Adam and Aaron got me into it, and Adam wheeled me out to my mom's SUV.

"Aaron and I will drive your car home, Roland," Adam said.

"OK. See you soon," I said.

Adam and Aaron put me in the SUV, then mom drove me to my family home with Adam and Aaron following us in the Blazer. When we arrived, Adam and Aaron brought me into the house and put me on the couch while my mom found some blankets and pillows. Once they had made a nice little nest for me, Adam and Aaron said that they would check in on me soon. I could barely keep my eyes open. I promptly fell asleep with my hand elevated, just in case, before Adam and Aaron left.

"Roland," a voice said to me.

I was asleep and standing next to my body, which was lying on the couch. The middle-aged Chinese man was standing there. He had his hands on either side of my right hand, which was propped up and elevated. Gold light streamed out of his hands into my hand. It was so bright, I felt like I was looking into the sun.

"Your injury has come to pass. Do not worry, your hand will heal, and you will be as if you never injured it. Your path is set, and the direction you need to follow will be clear to you when the time comes. I am here for you, and I always will be. When you think all that you have done so far is for naught, this is when I will come, and we will begin your training. Do not fear Brother, your purpose here is important, and you will be ready to do battle for God when God calls upon you. Until then, remember that everything is exactly as it should be. I will see you soon."

"Yes, Master. I will be ready," I said.

Then he disappeared. I walked back into my body and continued my sleep.

Author's Note

Thank you for reading the first volume of Roland Pearce's journey. This is a story that I have been fermenting since I graduated from the University of Puget Sound as a Creative Writing major, more than twenty years ago. It has been fun to look at all of my old notes as to how I thought the story would develop from back then, and how the story has actually developed now. You will notice that in my fiction there is a lot of fact. I have chosen this style because when I read, I also want to learn things. I have enjoyed watching Roland's story as told in his own words. Roland is not trying to impress you with the quality of his words. More importantly he is trying to impress on you the idea that what you believe to be true might not be, and that what you might believe to be fairy tale, myth, legend, et cetera, might be more real than you would want to believe. Roland states this very clearly in Chapter 1: "I think we can agree that that which is deemed impossible is only so, because we have yet to discover that which makes the impossible possible." It is this idea that both I and Roland would like to leave you with. What is truth and what is fiction. How much of Roland's story is fact and how much is fiction? I know, and I think if you read carefully, you will know as well, but you might also be surprised to know what has really happened and what has not.

Wishing you a life full of plenty, joy, and happiness.

Sincerely,

Jonathan Schell L.Ac.
November 29th, 2017
Portland, Oregon